PRAISE FOR
THE BOOK OF KUBERNETES

"Suggested read."

—Chris Short, @ChrisShort,
Senior Developer Advocate at
AWS, Kubernetes Contributor

"A hands-on guidebook to the inner workings of containers. Alan Hohn
peels back the layers to provide a deep explanation of what a container is,
how containerization changes the way programs run, and how Kubernetes
provides computing, networking, and storage."

—iProgrammer

"Looks great."

—Xander Soldaat, @XanderSoldaat,
OpenShift Cloud Success Architect
at Red Hat, Software Engineer

"This book is a deep insight into the containers running in a Kubernetes
cluster. I think it's essential for anyone who is interested in deeper learning
into the containers orchestration. I appreciate the author's hard work and
his depth of knowledge shared in this book."

—RA, Amazon reviewer

THE BOOK OF KUBERNETES

A Complete Guide to Container Orchestration

by Alan Hohn

**no starch
press**

San Francisco

Printed in China

Second printing

27 26 25 24 23   2 3 4 5 6

ISBN-13: 978-1-7185-0264-2 (print)
ISBN-13: 978-1-7185-0265-9 (ebook)

Publisher: William Pollock
Managing Editor: Jill Franklin
Production Manager: Rachel Monaghan
Production Editors: Paula Williamson and Jennifer Kepler
Developmental Editor: Jill Franklin
Cover Illustrator: Gina Redman
Interior Design: Octopod Studios
Technical Reviewer: Xander Soldaat
Production Services: Octal Publishing, Inc.

For information on distribution, bulk sales, corporate sales, or translations, please contact No Starch Press, Inc. directly at info@nostarch.com or:

No Starch Press, Inc.
245 8th Street, San Francisco, CA 94103
phone: 1.415.863.9900
www.nostarch.com

Library of Congress Control Number: 2022020536

For my wife, Sheryl

About the Author

Alan Hohn is the director for software strategy for Lockheed Martin. He has 25 years of experience as a Lockheed Martin Fellow, software developer, architect, lead, and manager. He has delivered real applications to production in Ada, Java, Python, and Go, among others, and has worked with Linux since the early 1990s. He is an Agile and DevSecOps coach and is an experienced trainer for Java, Ansible, containers, software architecture, and Kubernetes. Alan has a degree in computer science from Embry-Riddle Aeronautical University, a master's in business administration from the University of Minnesota, and a master's in industrial engineering from the Georgia Institute of Technology.

About the Technical Reviewer

Xander Soldaat started his Linux journey back in 1994 with a sports bag full of floppy disks, a 486DX2/66, and a spare weekend. He has a deep background in IT infrastructure architecture, as well as embedded systems, compiler, and STEM curriculum development. He is currently an OpenShift Cloud Success Architect at Red Hat. In his spare time, he likes to tinker with robots, electronics, retro computers, and tabletop games.

BRIEF CONTENTS

CONTENTS IN DETAIL

PART I
MAKING AND USING CONTAINERS

2

PROCESS ISOLATION

19

3

RESOURCE LIMITING

33

4

NETWORK NAMESPACES

51

5
CONTAINER IMAGES AND RUNTIME LAYERS   69

PART II
CONTAINERS IN KUBERNETES

6
WHY KUBERNETES MATTERS   87

7
DEPLOYING CONTAINERS TO KUBERNETES   111

8
OVERLAY NETWORKS   129

9
SERVICE AND INGRESS NETWORKS   151

10
WHEN THINGS GO WRONG

11
CONTROL PLANE AND ACCESS CONTROL

12
CONTAINER RUNTIME

13
HEALTH PROBES 219

14
LIMITS AND QUOTAS 233

15
PERSISTENT STORAGE 249

16
CONFIGURATION AND SECRETS 265

17
CUSTOM RESOURCES AND OPERATORS 279

PART III
PERFORMANT KUBERNETES

18
AFFINITY AND DEVICES 295

19
TUNING QUALITY OF SERVICE 309

20
APPLICATION RESILIENCY 323

ACKNOWLEDGMENTS

Thanks to the many people who have been generous with knowledge and help in creating this book. First, thanks to my editor, Jill Franklin, my technical reviewer, Xander Soldaat, and my copyeditor, Bob Russell, for spotting errors I didn't see and filling gaps in my knowledge. The remaining mistakes are mine. They would have been much more numerous without your help.

Thanks to my colleagues at Lockheed Martin, especially our Software Factory team. I have learned a great deal from you, and we have built many cool things together. Thanks to my Application Based Architecture colleagues who explored Kubernetes with me in the early days. Thanks also to the many people who build the open source products and the community around containers and Kubernetes; I am humbled by the chance to contribute.

I am most grateful to my family for helping to make this book possible and for listening patiently as I described each current challenge in writing it.

My thanks goes to all these, but *Soli Deo Gloria*.

INTRODUCTION

 Containers and Kubernetes together are changing the way that applications are architected, developed, and deployed. Containers ensure that software runs reliably no matter where it's deployed, and Kubernetes lets you manage all of your containers from a single control plane.

This book is designed to help you take full advantage of these essential new technologies, using hands-on examples not only to try out the major features but also to explore how each feature works. In this way, beyond simply being ready to deploy an application to Kubernetes, you'll gain the skills to architect applications to be performant and reliable in a Kubernetes cluster, and to quickly diagnose problems when they arise.

The Approach

The biggest advantage of a Kubernetes cluster is that it hides the work of running containers across multiple hosts behind an abstraction layer. A Kubernetes cluster is a "black box" that runs what we tell it to run, with automatic scaling, failover, and upgrades to new versions of our application.

Even though this abstraction makes it easier to deploy and manage applications, it also makes it difficult to understand what a cluster is doing. For this reason, this book presents each feature of container runtimes and Kubernetes clusters from a "debugging" perspective. Every good debugging session starts by treating the application as a black box and observing its behavior, but it doesn't end there. Skilled problem solvers know how to open the black box, diving below the current abstraction layer to see how the program runs, how data is stored, and how traffic flows across the network. Skilled architects use this deep knowledge of a system to avoid performance and reliability issues. This book provides the detailed understanding of containers and Kubernetes that only comes from exploring not only what these technologies do but also how they work.

In Part I, we'll begin by running a container, but then we'll dive into the container runtime to understand what a container is and how we can simulate a container using normal operating system commands. In Part II, we'll install a Kubernetes cluster and deploy containers to it. We'll also see how the cluster works, including how it interacts with the container runtime and how packets flow from container to container across the host network. The purpose is not to duplicate the reference documentation to show every option offered by every feature but to demonstrate how each feature is implemented so that all that documentation will make sense and be useful.

A Kubernetes cluster is complicated, so this book includes extensive hands-on examples, with enough automation to allow you to explore each chapter independently. This automation, which is available at *https://github .com/book-of-kubernetes/examples*, is published under a permissive open source license, so you can explore, experiment, and use it in your own projects.

Running Examples

In many of this book's example exercises, you'll be combining multiple hosts together to make a cluster, or working with low-level features of the Linux kernel. For this reason, and to help you feel more comfortable with experimentation, you'll be running examples entirely on temporary virtual machines. That way, if you make a mistake, you can quickly delete the virtual machine and start over.

The example repository for this book is available at *https://github.com/ book-of-kubernetes/examples*. All of the instructions for setting up to run examples are provided in a *README.md* file within the *setup* folder of the example repository.

What You Will Need

Even though you'll be working in virtual machines, you'll need a control machine to start from that can run Windows, macOS, or Linux. It can even be a Chromebook that supports Linux. If you are running Windows, you'll need to use the Windows Subsystem for Linux (WSL) in order to get Ansible working. See the *README.md* in the *setup* folder for instructions.

Run in the Cloud or Local

To make these examples as accessible as possible, I've provided automation to run them either using Vagrant or Amazon Web Services (AWS). If you have access to a Windows, macOS, or Linux computer with at least eight cores and 8GB of memory, try installing VirtualBox and Vagrant and work with local virtual machines. If not, you can set yourself up to work with AWS.

We use Ansible to perform AWS setup and automate some of the tedious steps. Each chapter includes a separate Ansible playbook that makes use of common roles and collections. This means that you can work examples from chapter to chapter, starting with a fresh installation each time. In some cases, I've also provided an "extra" provisioning playbook that you can optionally use to skip some of the detailed installation steps and get straight to the learning. See the *README.md* in each chapter's directory for more information.

Terminal Windows

After you've used Ansible to provision your virtual machines, you'll need to get at least one terminal window connected to run commands. The *README.md* file in each chapter will tell you how to do that. Before running any examples, you'll first need to become the root user, as follows:

```
sudo su -
```

This will give you a root shell and set up your environment and home directory to match.

> ### RUNNING AS ROOT
>
> If you've worked with Linux before, you probably have a healthy aversion to working as root on a regular basis, so it might surprise you that all of the examples in this book are run as the root user. This is a big advantage of using temporary virtual machines and containers; when we act as the root user, we are doing so in a temporary, confined space that can't reach out and affect anything else.
>
> As you move from learning about containers and Kubernetes to running applications in production, you'll be applying security controls to your cluster that will limit administrative access and will ensure that containers cannot break out of their isolated environment. This often includes configuring your containers so that they run as a non-root user.

In some examples, you'll need to open multiple terminal windows in order to leave one process running while you inspect it from another terminal. How you do that is up to you; most terminal applications support multiple tabs or multiple windows. If you need a way to open multiple terminals within a single tab, try exploring a terminal multiplexer application. All of the temporary virtual machines used in the examples come with both screen and tmux installed and ready to use.

PART I

MAKING AND USING CONTAINERS

Containers are essential to modern application architecture. They simplify packaging, deploying, and scaling application components. They enable building reliable and resilient applications that handle failure gracefully. However, containers can also be confusing. They look like completely different systems, with separate hostnames, networking, and storage, but they do not have many of the features of a separate system, such as a separate console or system services. To understand how containers look like separate systems without really being separate, let's explore containers, container engines, and Linux kernel features.

1

WHY CONTAINERS MATTER

It's a great time to be a software developer. Creating a brand-new application and making it available to millions of people has never been easier. Modern programming languages, open source libraries, and application platforms make it possible to write a small amount of code and end up with lots of functionality. However, although it's easy to get started and create a new application quickly, the best application developers are those who move beyond treating the application platform as a "black box" and really understand how it works. Creating a reliable, resilient, and scalable application requires more than just knowing how to create a Deployment in the browser or on the command line.

In this chapter, we'll look at application architecture in a scalable, cloud native world. We will show why containers are the preferred way to package and deploy application components, and how container orchestration addresses key needs for containerized applications. We'll finish with an example application deployed to Kubernetes to give you an introductory glimpse into the power of these technologies.

Modern Application Architecture

The main theme of modern software applications is *scale*. We live in a world of applications with millions of simultaneous users. What is remarkable is the ability of these applications to achieve not only this scale but also a level of stability such that an outage makes headlines and serves as fodder for weeks or months of technical analysis.

With so many modern applications running at large scale, it can be easy to forget that a lot of hard work goes into architecting, building, deploying, and maintaining applications of this caliber, whether the scale they're designed for is thousands, millions, or billions of users. Our job in this chapter is to identify what we need from our application platform to run a scalable, reliable application, and to see how containerization and Kubernetes meet those requirements. We'll start by looking at three key attributes of modern application architecture. Then we'll move on to looking at three key benefits these attributes bring.

Attribute: Cloud Native

There are lots of ways to define *cloud native* technologies (and a good place to start is the Cloud Native Computing Foundation at *https://cncf.io*). I like to start with an idea of what "the cloud" is and what it enables so that we can understand what kind of architecture can make best use of it.

At its heart, the cloud is an abstraction. We talked about abstractions in the introduction, so you know that abstractions are essential to computing, but we also need a deep understanding of our abstractions to use them properly. In the case of the cloud, the provider is abstracting away the real physical processors, memory, storage, and networking, allowing cloud users to simply declare a need for these resources and have them provisioned on demand. To have a "cloud native" application, then, we need an application that can take advantage of that abstraction. As much as possible, the application shouldn't be tied to a specific host or a specific network layout, because we don't want to constrain our flexibility in how application components are divided among hosts.

Attribute: Modular

Modularity is nothing new to application architecture. The goal has always been *high cohesion*, where everything within a module relates to a single purpose, and *low coupling*, where modules are organized to minimize intermodule communication. However, even though modularity remains a key design goal, the definition of what makes a module is different. Rather than just treat modularity as a way of organizing the code, modern application architecture today prefers to carry modularity into the runtime, providing each module with a separate operating system process and discouraging the use of a shared filesystem or shared memory for communication. Because modules are separate processes, communication between modules is standard network (socket) communication.

This approach seems wasteful of hardware resources. It is more compact and faster to share memory than it is to copy data over a socket. But there are two good reasons to prefer separate processes. First, modern hardware is fast and getting faster, and it would be a form of premature optimization to imagine that sockets are not fast enough for our application. Second, no matter how large a server we have, there is going to be a limit to how many processes we can fit on it, so a shared memory model ultimately limits our ability to grow.

Attribute: Microservice-Based

Modern application architecture is based on modules in the form of separate processes—and these individual modules tend to be very small. In theory, a cloud can provide us with virtual servers that are as powerful as we need; however, in practice, using a few powerful servers is more expensive and less flexible than many small servers. If our modules are small enough, they can be deployed to cheap commodity servers, which means that we can leverage our cloud provider's hardware to best advantage. Although there is no single answer as to how small a module needs to be in order to be a *microservice*, "small enough that we can be flexible regarding where it is deployed" is a good first rule.

A microservice architecture also has practical advantages for organizing teams. Ever since Fred Brooks wrote *The Mythical Man-Month*, architects have understood that organizing people is one of the biggest challenges to developing large, complex systems. Building a system from many small pieces reduces the complexity of testing but also makes it possible to organize a large team of people without everyone getting in everyone else's way.

WHAT ABOUT APPLICATION SERVERS?

The idea of modular services has a long history, and one popular way to implement it was building modules to run in an application server, such as a Java Enterprise environment. Why not then just continue to follow that pattern for applications?

Although application servers were successful for many uses, they don't have the same degree of isolation that a microservice architecture has. As a result, there are more issues with interdependency, leading to more complex testing and reduced team independence. Additionally, the typical model of having a single application server per host, with many applications deployed to it and sharing the same process space, is much less flexible than the containerized approaches you will see in this book.

(continued)

This is not to say that you should immediately throw away your application server architecture to use containers. There are lots of benefits to containerization for any architecture. But as you adopt a containerized architecture, over time it will make sense for you to move your code toward a true microservice architecture to take best advantage of what containers and Kubernetes offer.

We've looked at three key attributes of modern architecture. Now, let's look at three key benefits that result.

Benefit: Scalability

Let's begin by envisioning the simplest application possible. We create a single executable that runs on a single machine and interacts with only a single user at a time. Now, suppose that we want to grow this application so that it can interact with thousands or millions of users at once. Obviously, no matter how powerful a server we use, eventually some computing resource will become a bottleneck. It doesn't matter whether the bottleneck is processing, or memory, or storage, or network bandwidth; the moment we hit that bottleneck, our application cannot handle any additional users without hurting performance for others.

The only possible way to solve this issue is to stop sharing the resource that caused the bottleneck. This means that we need to find a way to distribute our application across multiple servers. But if we're really scaling up, we can't stop there. We need to distribute across multiple networks as well, or we'll hit the limit of what one network switch can do. And eventually, we will even need to distribute geographically, or we'll saturate the broader network.

To build applications with no limit to scalability, we need an architecture that can run additional application instances at will. And because an application is only as slow as its slowest component, we need to find a way to scale *everything*, including our data stores. It's obvious that the only way to do this effectively is to create our application from many independent pieces that are not tied to specific hardware. In other words, cloud native microservices.

Benefit: Reliability

Let's go back to our simplest possible application. In addition to scalability limits, it has another flaw. It runs on one server, and if that server fails, the entire application fails. Our application is lacking reliability. As before, the only possible way to solve this issue is to stop sharing the resource that could potentially fail. Fortunately, when we start distributing our application across many servers, we have the opportunity to avoid a single point of failure in the hardware that would bring down our application. And as an application is only as reliable as its least reliable component, we need to find a way to distribute everything, including storage and networks. Again, we need cloud native microservices that are flexible about where they are run and about how many instances are running at once.

Benefit: Resilience

There is a third, subtler advantage to cloud native microservice architecture. This time, imagine an application that runs on a single server, but it can easily be installed as a single package on as many servers as we like. Each instance can serve a new user. In theory, this application would have good scalability, given that we can always install it on another server. And overall, the application could be said to be reliable because a failure of a single server is going to affect only that one user, whereas the others can keep running as normal.

What is missing from this approach is the concept of resilience, or the ability of an application to respond meaningfully to failure. A truly resilient application can handle a hardware or software failure somewhere in the application without an end user noticing at all. And although separate, unrelated instances of this application keep running when one instance fails, we can't really say that the application exhibits resilience, at least not from the perspective of the unlucky user with the failed system.

On the other hand, if we construct our application out of separate microservices, each of which has the ability to communicate over a network with other microservices on any server, the loss of a single server might cost us several microservice instances, but end users can be moved to other instances on other servers transparently, such that they don't even notice the failure.

Why Containers

I've made modern application architecture with its fancy cloud native microservices sound pretty appealing. Engineering is full of trade-offs, however, so experienced engineers will suspect that there must be some pretty significant trade-offs, and, of course, there are.

It's *very difficult* to build an application from lots of small pieces. Organizing teams around microservices so that they can work independently from one another might be great, but when it comes time to put those together into a working application, the sheer number of pieces means worrying about how to package them up, how to deliver them to the runtime environment, how to configure them, how to provide them with (potentially conflicting) dependencies, how to update them, and how to monitor them to make sure they are working.

This problem only grows worse when we consider the need to run multiple instances of each microservice. Now, we need a microservice to be able to find a working instance of another microservice, balancing the load across all of the working instances. We need that load balancing to reconfigure itself immediately if we have a hardware or software failure. We need to fail over seamlessly and retry failed work in order to hide that failure from the end user. And we need to monitor not just each individual service, but how all of them are working together to get the job done. After all, our users don't care if 99 percent of our microservices are working correctly if the 1 percent failure prevents them from using our application.

We have lots of problems to solve if we want to build an application out of many individual microservices, and we do not want each of our microservice teams working those problems, or they would never have time to write code! We need a common way to manage the packaging, deployment, configuration, and maintenance of our microservices. Let's look at two categories of required attributes: those that apply to a single microservice, and those that apply to multiple microservices working together.

Requirements for Containers

For a single microservice, we need the following:

Packaging   Bundle the application for delivery, which needs to include dependencies so that the package is portable and we avoid conflicts between microservices.

Versioning   Uniquely identify a version. We need to update microservices over time, and we need to know what version is running.

Isolation   Keep microservices from interfering with one another. This allows us to be flexible about what microservices are deployed together.

Fast startup   Start new instances rapidly. We need this to scale and respond to failures.

Low overhead   Minimize required resources to run a microservice in order to avoid limits on how small a microservice can be.

Containers are designed to address exactly these needs. Containers provide isolation together with low overhead and fast startup. And, as we'll see in Chapter 5, a container runs from a container image, which provides a way to package an application with its dependencies and to uniquely identify the version of that package.

Requirements for Orchestration

For multiple microservices working together, we need:

Clustering   Provide processing, memory, and storage for containers across multiple servers.

Discovery   Provide a way for one microservice to find another. Our microservices might run anywhere on the cluster, and they might move around.

Configuration   Separate configuration from runtime, allowing us to reconfigure our application without rebuilding and redeploying our microservices.

Access control   Manage authorization to create containers. This ensures that the right containers run, and the wrong ones don't.

Load balancing   Spread requests among working instances in order to avoid the need for end users or other microservices to track all microservice instances and balance the load themselves.

Monitoring   Identify failed microservice instances. Load balancing won't work well if traffic is going to failed instances.

Resilience   Automatically recover from failures. If we don't have this ability, a chain of failures could kill our application.

These requirements come into play only when we are running containers on multiple servers. It's a different problem from just packaging up and running a single container. To address these needs, we require a *container orchestration* environment. A container orchestration environment such as Kubernetes allows us to treat multiple servers as a single set of resources to run containers, dynamically allocating containers to available servers and providing distributed communication and storage.

Running Containers

By now, hopefully you're excited by the possibilities of building an application using containerized microservices and Kubernetes. Let's walk through the basics so that you can see what these ideas look like in practice, providing a foundation for the deeper dive into container technology that you'll find in the rest of this book.

What Containers Look Like

In Chapter 2, we'll look at the difference between a container platform and a container runtime, and we'll run containers using multiple container runtimes. For now, let's begin with a simple example running in the most popular container platform, *Docker*. Our goal is to learn the basic Docker commands, which align to universal container concepts.

Running a Container

The first command is run, which creates a container and runs a command inside it. We will tell Docker the name of the container image to use. We discuss container images more in Chapter 5; for now, it's enough to know that it provides a unique name and version so that Docker knows exactly what to run. Let's get started using the example for this chapter.

NOTE   *The example repository for this book is at* https://github.com/book-of
-kubernetes/examples. *See "Running Examples" on page xx for details on
getting set up.*

A key idea for this section is that containers look like a completely separate system. To illustrate this, before we run a container, let's look at the host system:

```
root@host01:~# cat /etc/os-release
NAME="Ubuntu"
...
root@host01:~# ps -ef
UID          PID    PPID C STIME TTY         TIME CMD
root           1       0 0 12:59 ?       00:00:07 /sbin/init
...
root@host01:~# uname -v
#...-Ubuntu SMP ...
root@host01:~# ip addr
1: lo: <LOOPBACK,UP,LOWER_UP> mtu 65536 ...
    link/loopback 00:00:00:00:00:00 brd 00:00:00:00:00:00
    inet 127.0.0.1/8 scope host lo
       valid_lft forever preferred_lft forever
    inet6 ::1/128 scope host
       valid_lft forever preferred_lft forever
...
3: enp0s8: <BROADCAST,MULTICAST,UP,LOWER_UP> mtu 1500 qdisc fq_codel ...
    link/ether 08:00:27:bf:63:1f brd ff:ff:ff:ff:ff:ff
    inet 192.168.61.11/24 brd 192.168.61.255 scope global enp0s8
       valid_lft forever preferred_lft forever
    inet6 fe80::a00:27ff:febf:631f/64 scope link
       valid_lft forever preferred_lft forever
...
```

The first command looks at a file called *etc/os-release*, which has information about the installed Linux distribution. In this case, our example virtual machine is running Ubuntu. That matches the output of the next command, in which we see an Ubuntu-based Linux kernel. Finally, we list network interfaces and see an IP address of 192.168.61.11.

The example setup steps automatically installed Docker, so we have it ready to go. First, let's download and start a Rocky Linux container with a single command:

```
root@host01:~# docker run -ti rockylinux:8
Unable to find image 'rockylinux:8' locally
8: Pulling from library/rockylinux
...
Status: Downloaded newer image for rockylinux:8
```

We use -ti in our docker run command to tell Docker that we need an interactive terminal to run commands. The only other parameter to docker run is the container image, rockylinux:8, which specifies the name rockylinux and the version 8. Because we don't provide a command to run, the default bash command for that container image is used.

Now that we have a shell prompt inside the container, we can run a few commands and then use exit to leave the shell and stop the container:

```
❶ [root@18f20e2d7e49 /]# cat /etc/os-release
❷ NAME="Rocky Linux"
   ...
❸ [root@18f20e2d7e49 /]# yum install -y procps iproute
   ...
   [root@18f20e2d7e49 /]# ps -ef
   UID          PID   PPID C STIME TTY          TIME CMD
   root       ❹ 1      0  0 13:30 pts/0     00:00:00 /bin/bash
   root         19      1  0 13:46 pts/0     00:00:00 ps -ef
   [root@18f20e2d7e49 /]# ip addr
   1: lo: <LOOPBACK,UP,LOWER_UP> mtu 65536 ...
   link/loopback 00:00:00:00:00:00 brd 00:00:00:00:00:00
   inet 127.0.0.1/8 scope host lo
      valid_lft forever preferred_lft forever
❺ 18: eth0@if19: <BROADCAST,MULTICAST,UP,LOWER_UP> mtu 1500 ...
   link/ether 02:42:ac:11:00:02 brd ff:ff:ff:ff:ff:ff link-netnsid 0
   inet 172.17.0.2/16 brd 172.17.255.255 scope global eth0
      valid_lft forever preferred_lft forever
   [root@18f20e2d7e49 /]# uname -v
❻ #...-Ubuntu SMP ...
   [root@18f20e2d7e49 /]# exit
```

When we run commands within our container, it looks like we are running in a Rocky Linux system. Compared to the host system, there are multiple differences:

- A different hostname in the shell prompt ❶ (18f20e2d7e49 for mine, though yours will be different)

- Different filesystem contents ❷, including basic files like */etc/os-release*

- The use of yum ❸ to install packages, and the need to install packages even for basic commands

- A limited set of running processes, with no base system services and our bash shell ❹ as process ID (PID) 1

- Different network devices ❺, including a different MAC address and IP address

Strangely, however, when we run uname -v, we see the exact same Ubuntu Linux kernel ❻ as when we were on the host. Clearly, a container is not a wholly separate system as we might otherwise believe.

Images and Volume Mounts

At first glance, a container looks like a mix between a regular process and a virtual machine. And the way we interact with Docker only deepens that impression. Let's illustrate that by running an Alpine Linux container. We'll start by "pulling" the container image, which feels a lot like downloading a virtual machine image:

```
root@host01:~# docker pull alpine:3
3: Pulling from library/alpine
...
docker.io/library/alpine:3
```

Next, we'll run a container from the image. We'll use a *volume mount* to see files from the host, a common task with a virtual machine. However, we'll also tell Docker to specify an environment variable, which is the kind of thing we would do when running a regular process:

```
root@host01:~# docker run -ti -v /:/host -e hello=world alpine:3
/ # hostname
75b51510ab61
```

We can print the contents of */etc/os-release* inside the container, as before with Rocky Linux:

```
/ # cat /etc/os-release
NAME="Alpine Linux"
ID=alpine
...
```

However, this time we can also print the host's */etc/os-release* file because the host filesystem is mounted at */host*:

```
/ # cat /host/etc/os-release
NAME="Ubuntu"
...
```

And finally, within the container we also have access to the environment variable we passed in:

```
/ # echo $hello
world
/ # exit
```

This mix of ideas from virtual machines and regular processes sometimes leads new container users to ask questions like, "Why can't I SSH into my container?" A major goal of the next few chapters is to make clear what containers really are.

What Containers Really Are

Despite what a container looks like, with its own hostname, filesystem, process space, and networking, a container is not a virtual machine. It does not have a separate kernel, so it cannot have separate kernel modules or device drivers. A container can have multiple processes, but they must be started explicitly by the first process (PID 1). So a container will not have an SSH server in it by default, and most containers do not have any system services running.

In the next several chapters, we'll look at how a container manages to look like a separate system while being a group of processes. For now, let's try one more Docker example to see what a container looks like from the host system.

First, we'll download and run NGINX with a single command:

```
root@host01:~# docker run -d -p 8080:80 nginx
Unable to find image 'nginx:latest' locally
latest: Pulling from library/nginx
...
Status: Downloaded newer image for nginx:latest
e9c5e87020372a23ce31ad10bd87011ed29882f65f97f3af8d32438a8340f936
```

This example illustrates a couple of additional useful Docker commands. And again, we are mixing ideas from virtual machines and regular processes. By using the -d flag, we tell Docker to run this container in *daemon mode* (in the background), which is the kind of thing we would do for a regular process. Using -p 8080:80, however, brings in another concept from virtual machines, as it instructs Docker to forward port 8080 on the host to port 80 in the container, letting us connect to NGINX from the host even though the container has its own network interfaces.

NGINX is now running in the background in a Docker container. To see it, run the following:

```
root@host01:~# docker ps
CONTAINER ID IMAGE ... PORTS                 NAMES
e9c5e8702037 nginx ... 0.0.0.0:8080->80/tcp  funny_montalcini
```

Because of the port forwarding, we can connect to it from our host system using curl:

```
root@host01:~# curl http://localhost:8080/
<!DOCTYPE html>
<html>
<head>
<title>Welcome to nginx!</title>
...
```

With this example, we're starting to see how containerization meets some of the needs we identified earlier in this chapter. Because NGINX is packaged into a container image, we can download and run it with a single command, with no concern for any conflict with anything else that might be installed on our host.

Let's run one more command to explore our NGINX server:

```
root@host01:~# ps -fC nginx
UID          PID    PPID C STIME TTY          TIME CMD
root       22812   22777 1 15:01 ?        00:00:00 nginx: master ...
```

If NGINX were running in a virtual machine, we would not see it in a ps listing on the host system. Clearly, NGINX in a container is running as a regular process. At the same time, we didn't need to install NGINX onto our host system to get it working. In other words, we are getting the benefits of a virtual machine approach without the overhead of a virtual machine.

Deploying Containers to Kubernetes

To have load balancing and resilience in our containerized applications, we need a container orchestration framework like Kubernetes. Our example system also has a Kubernetes cluster automatically installed, with a web application and database deployed to it. As a preparation for our deep dive into Kubernetes in Part II, let's look at that application.

There are many different options for installing and configuring a Kubernetes cluster, with distributions available from many companies. We discuss multiple options for Kubernetes distributions in Chapter 6. For this chapter, we'll use a lightweight distribution called "K3s" from a company called Rancher.

To use a container orchestration environment like Kubernetes, we have to give up some control over our containers. Rather than executing commands directly to run containers, we'll tell Kubernetes what containers we want it to run, and it will decide where to run each container. Kubernetes will then monitor our containers for us and handle automatic restart, failover, updates to new versions, and even autoscaling based on load. This style of configuration is called *declarative*.

Talking to the Kubernetes Cluster

A Kubernetes cluster has an API server that we can use to get status and change the cluster configuration. We interact with the API server using the kubectl client application. K3s comes with its own embedded kubectl command that we'll use. Let's begin by getting some basic information about the Kubernetes cluster:

```
root@host01:~# k3s kubectl version
Client Version: version.Info{Major:"1", ...
Server Version: version.Info{Major:"1", ...
root@host01:~# k3s kubectl get nodes
NAME     STATUS   ROLES            AGE   VERSION
host01   Ready    control-plane... 2d    v1...
```

As you can see, we're working with a single-node Kubernetes cluster. Of course, this would not meet our needs for high availability. Most Kubernetes distributions, including K3s, support a multinode, highly available cluster, and we will look at how that works in detail in Part II.

Application Overview

Our example application provides a "to-do" list with a web interface, persistent storage, and tracking of item state. It will take several minutes for this to be running in Kubernetes, even after the automated scripts are finished. After it's running, we can access it in a browser and should see something like Figure 1-1.

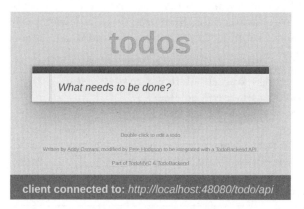

Figure 1-1: An example application in Kubernetes

This application is divided into two types of containers, one for each application component. A Node.js application serves files to the browser and provides a REST API. The Node.js application communicates with a PostgreSQL database. The Node.js component is stateless, so it is easy to scale up to as many instances as we need based on the number of users. In this case, our application's Deployment asked Kubernetes for three Node.js containers:

```
root@host01:~# k3s kubectl get pods
NAME                       READY   STATUS    RESTARTS   AGE
todo-db-7df8b44d65-744mt   1/1     Running   0          2d
todo-655ff549f8-l4dxt      1/1     Running   0          2d
todo-655ff549f8-gc7b6      1/1     Running   1          2d
todo-655ff549f8-qq8ff      1/1     Running   1          2d
```

The command get pods tells Kubernetes to list *Pods*. A Pod is a group of one or more containers that Kubernetes treats as a single unit for scheduling and monitoring. We look at Pods more closely throughout Part II.

Here, we have one Pod whose name starts with todo-db, which is our PostgreSQL database. The other three Pods, with names starting with todo, are the Node.js containers. (We'll explain later why the names have random characters after them; you can ignore that for now.)

According to Kubernetes, our application component containers are running, so we should be able to access our application in a browser. How you do this depends on whether you are running in AWS or Vagrant; the example setup scripts will print out what URL you should use in your browser. If you visit that URL, you should see something like Figure 1-1.

Kubernetes Features

If our only goal were to run four containers, we could have done that just using the Docker commands described earlier. Kubernetes is providing a lot more functionality, though. Let's take a quick tour of the most important features.

In addition to running our containers, Kubernetes is also monitoring them. Because we asked for three instances, Kubernetes will work to keep three instances running. Let's destroy one and watch Kubernetes automatically recover:

```
root@host01:~# k3s kubectl delete pod todo-655ff549f8-qq8ff
pod "todo-655ff549f8-qq8ff" deleted
root@host01:~# k3s kubectl get pods
NAME                        READY   STATUS    RESTARTS   AGE
todo-db-7df8b44d65-744mt    1/1     Running   0          2d
todo-655ff549f8-l4dxt       1/1     Running   0          2d
todo-655ff549f8-gc7b6       1/1     Running   1          2d
todo-655ff549f8-rm8sh       1/1     Running   0          11s
```

To run this command, you will need to copy and paste the full name of one of your three Pods. The name will be a little different from mine. When you delete a Pod, you should see that Kubernetes immediately creates a new one. (You can identify which one is brand new by the AGE field.)

Next let's explore how Kubernetes can automatically scale our application. Later, we'll see how to make Kubernetes do this automatically, but for now, we will do it manually. Suppose that we decide we need five Pods instead of three. We can do this with one command:

```
root@host01:~# k3s kubectl scale --replicas=5 deployment todo
deployment.apps/todo scaled
root@host01:~# k3s kubectl get pods
NAME                        READY   STATUS    RESTARTS   AGE
todo-db-7df8b44d65-744mt    1/1     Running   0          2d
todo-655ff549f8-l4dxt       1/1     Running   0          2d
todo-655ff549f8-gc7b6       1/1     Running   1          2d
todo-655ff549f8-rm8sh       1/1     Running   0          5m13s
todo-655ff549f8-g7lxg       1/1     Running   0          6s
todo-655ff549f8-zsqp6       1/1     Running   0          6s
```

We tell Kubernetes to scale the *Deployment* that manages our Pods. For now, you can think of the Deployment as the "owner" of the Pods; it monitors them and controls how many there are. Here, two extra Pods are immediately created. We just scaled up our application.

Before we close, let's look at one more critically important Kubernetes feature. When you load the application in your web browser, Kubernetes is sending your browser's request to one of the available Pods. Each time you reload, the request might be routed to a different Pod because Kubernetes is automatically balancing the application's load. To make this happen, when we deploy our application to Kubernetes, the application configuration includes a *Service*:

```
root@host01:~# k3s kubectl describe service todo
Name:        todo
...
IPs:         10.43.231.177
Port:        <unset>  80/TCP
TargetPort:  5000/TCP
Endpoints:   10.42.0.10:5000,10.42.0.11:5000,10.42.0.14:5000 + 2 more...
...
```

A Service has its own IP address and routes traffic to one or more endpoints. In this case, because we scaled up to five Pods, the Service is balancing traffic across all five endpoints.

Final Thoughts

Modern applications achieve scalability and reliability through an architecture based on microservices that can be deployed independently and dynamically to available hardware, including cloud resources. By using containers and container orchestration to run our microservices, we achieve a common approach for packaging, scaling, monitoring, and maintaining microservices, enabling our development teams to focus on the hard work of actually building the application.

In this chapter, we saw how containerization can create the appearance of a separate system while really being a regular process run in an isolated way. We also saw how we can use Kubernetes to deploy an entire application as a set of containers, with scalability and self-healing. Of course, Kubernetes has a lot more important features than what we've mentioned here, enough that it will take the whole book for us to cover them all! With this brief overview, I hope you are excited to dive more deeply into containers and Kubernetes in order to understand how to build applications that perform well and are reliable.

We'll come back to Kubernetes in Part II of this book. For now, let's look closely at how containers create the illusion of a separate system. We'll start by looking at process isolation using Linux namespaces.

2

PROCESS ISOLATION

Containers build on a rich history of technologies designed to isolate one computer program from another while allowing many programs to share the same CPU, memory, storage, and network resources. Containers use fundamental capabilities of the Linux kernel, particularly namespaces, which create separate views of process identifiers, users, the filesystem, and network interfaces. Container runtimes use multiple types of namespaces to give each container an isolated view of the system.

In this chapter, we'll consider some of the reasons for process isolation and look at how Linux has historically isolated processes. We'll then examine how containers use namespaces to provide isolation. We'll test this using a couple of different container runtimes. Finally, we will use Linux commands to create namespaces directly.

Understanding Isolation

Before running some containers and inspecting their isolation, let's look at the motivation for process isolation. We'll also consider traditional process isolation in Linux and how that has led to the isolation capabilities that containers use.

Why Processes Need Isolation

The whole idea of a computer is that it is a general-purpose machine that can run many different kinds of programs. Ever since the beginning of computing, there has been a need to share a single computer between multiple programs. It started with people taking turns submitting programs on punch cards, but as computer multitasking became more sophisticated, people could start multiple programs, and the computer would make it seem as if they were all running on the same CPU at once.

Of course, as soon as something needs to be shared, there is a need to make sure it is shared fairly, and computer programs are no different. So although we think of a *process* as an independent program with its own time on the CPU and its own memory space, there are many ways that one process can cause trouble for another, including:

- Using too much CPU, memory, storage, or network
- Overwriting the memory or files of another process
- Extracting secret information from another process
- Sending another process bad data to cause it to misbehave
- Flooding another process with requests so that it stops responding

Bugs can cause processes to do these same things by accident, but a bigger concern is a security vulnerability that allows a bad actor to use one process to cause problems for another. It takes only one vulnerability to create major problems in a system, so we need ways to isolate processes that limit damage from both accidental and intentional behavior.

Physical isolation is best—*air-gapped* systems are regularly used to protect government-classified information and safety-critical systems—but this approach is also too expensive and inconvenient for many uses. Virtual machines can give the appearance of separation while sharing physical hardware, but a virtual machine has the overhead of running its own operating system, services, and virtual devices, making it slower to start and less scalable. The solution is to run regular processes, but use process isolation to reduce the risk of affecting other processes.

File Permissions and Change Root

Most of the effort in process isolation involves preventing one process from seeing things it shouldn't. After all, if a process can't even see another process, it will be far more difficult to cause trouble, either accidentally or on purpose. The traditional ways that Linux has controlled what processes can see and do serve as the foundation for the ideas behind containers.

One of the most basic visibility controls is *filesystem permissions*. Linux associates an owner and group with each file and directory, and manages read, write, and execute permissions. This basic permission scheme works well to ensure that user files are kept private, that a process cannot overwrite the files of another process, and that only a privileged user like root can install new software or modify critical system configuration files.

Of course, this permission scheme relies on us ensuring that each process is run as the authentic user and that users are in the appropriate groups. Typically, each new service install creates a user just for running that service. Even better, this *service user* can be configured without a real login shell, which means that the user cannot be exploited to log in to the system. To make this clear, let's look at an example.

NOTE   *The example repository for this book is at* https://github.com/book-of -kubernetes/examples. *See "Running Examples" on page xx for details on getting set up.*

The Linux rsyslogd service provides logging services, so it needs to write to files in */var/log*, but it should not have permissions to read or write all of the files in that directory. File permissions are used to control this, as shown in this example:

```
root@host01:~# ps -fC rsyslogd
   UID           PID   PPID C STIME TTY          TIME CMD
❶ syslog        711      1 0 15:04 ?        00:00:00 /usr/sbin/rsyslogd -n -iNONE
   root@host01:~# su syslog
❷ This account is currently not available.
   root@host01:~# ls -l /var/log/auth.log
❸ -rw-r----- 1 syslog adm 18396 Mar  6 01:27 /var/log/auth.log
   root@host01:~# ls -ld /var/log/private
❹ drwx------ 2 root root 4096 Mar  5 21:04 /var/log/private
```

The *syslog* user ❶ exists specifically to run rsyslogd, and that user is configured with no login shell for security reasons ❷. Because rsyslogd needs to be able to write to *auth.log*, it's given write permission, as shown in the file mode printout ❸. Members of the admin (*adm*) group have read-only access to this file.

An initial d in the file mode ❹ indicates that this is a directory. The following rwx indicates that the root user has read, write, and execute permissions. The remaining dashes indicate that there are no rights for members of the *root* group or for other system users, so we can conclude that the rsyslogd process cannot see the contents of this directory.

Permission control is important, but it doesn't fully satisfy our goal of process isolation. One reason is that it is not enough to protect us from *privilege escalation*, wherein a vulnerable process and a vulnerable system allow a bad actor to obtain root privileges. To help deal with this, some Linux services go a step beyond by running in an isolated part of the filesystem. This approach is known as chroot for "change root." Running in a chroot environment requires quite a bit of setup, as you can see in this example:

```
root@host01:~# mkdir /tmp/newroot
root@host01:~# ❶ cp --parents /bin/bash /bin/ls /tmp/newroot
root@host01:~# cp --parents /lib64/ld-linux-x86-64.so.2 \
❷ $(ldd /bin/bash /bin/ls | grep '=>' | awk '{print $3}') /tmp/newroot
...
root@host01:~# ❸ chroot /tmp/newroot /bin/bash
bash-5.0# ls -l /bin
total 1296
❹ -rwxr-xr-x 1 0 0 1183448 Mar  6 02:15 bash
-rwxr-xr-x 1 0 0  142144 Mar  6 02:15 ls
bash-5.0# exit
exit
```

First, we need to copy in all of the executables that we intend to run ❶. We also need to copy in all of the shared libraries these executables use, which we specify with the ldd | grep | awk command ❷. When both binaries and libraries are copied in, we can use the chroot command ❸ to move into our isolated environment. Only the files we copied in are visible ❹.

Container Isolation

For experienced Linux system administrators, file permissions and change root are basic-level knowledge. However, those concepts also serve as the foundation for how containers work. Even though a running container appears like a completely separate system, with its own hostname, network, processes, and filesystem (as we saw in Chapter 1), it's really a regular Linux process using isolation rather than a virtual machine.

A container has multiple kinds of isolation, including several essential kinds of isolation that we haven't seen before:

- Mounted filesystems
- Hostname and domain name
- Interprocess communication
- Process identifiers
- Network devices

These separate kinds of isolation work together so that a process or collection of processes looks like a completely separate system. Although these processes still share the kernel and physical hardware, this isolation goes a long way toward ensuring that they cannot cause trouble for other processes, especially when we configure containers correctly to control the CPU, memory, storage, and network resources available to them.

Container Platforms and Container Runtimes

Specifying all the binaries, libraries, and configuration files needed to run a process in an isolated filesystem would be laborious. Fortunately, as we saw in Chapter 1, *container images* come prepackaged with the needed executables and libraries. Using Docker, we were able to easily download and run NGINX in a container. Docker is an example of a *container platform*, providing not only the ability to run containers but also container storage, networking, and security.

Under the covers, modern versions of Docker are using containerd as the *container runtime*, also known as a *container engine*. A container runtime provides low-level functionality to run processes in containers.

To explore isolation further, let's experiment with two different container runtimes to start containers from preexisting images and then inspect how processes in containers are isolated from the rest of the system.

Installing containerd

We'll be using containerd in Part II in support of our Kubernetes clusters, so let's begin by installing and interacting with this runtime directly. Interacting directly with containerd will also benefit our exploration of process isolation.

You can skip install commands by using the *extra* provisioning script provided with this chapter's examples. See the README file for this chapter for instructions.

Even though containerd is available in the standard Ubuntu package repository, we'll install it from the official Docker package registry so that we get the latest stable version. To do that, we need Apt to support HTTP/S, so let's do that first:

```
root@host01:~# apt update
...
root@host01:~# apt -y install apt-transport-https
...
```

Now let's add the package registry and install:

```
root@host01:~# curl -fsSL https://download.docker.com/linux/ubuntu/gpg | \
  gpg --dearmor -o /usr/share/keyrings/docker-archive-keyring.gpg
root@host01:~# echo "deb [arch=amd64" \
  "signed-by=/usr/share/keyrings/docker-archive-keyring.gpg]" \
  "https://download.docker.com/linux/ubuntu focal stable" > \
  /etc/apt/sources.list.d/docker.list
root@host01:~# apt update && apt install -y containerd.io
...
root@host01:~# ctr images ls
REF TYPE DIGEST SIZE PLATFORMS LABELS
```

The final command just ensures that the package installed correctly, that the service is running, and that the ctr command is working. We don't see any images because we haven't installed any yet.

Container runtimes are low-level libraries. They are typically not used directly but are used by a higher-level container platform or orchestration environment such as Docker or Kubernetes. This means that they put a lot of focus into a quality application programming interface (API) but not as much effort into user-facing tools we can use from the command line. Fortunately, command line tools are still needed for testing, and containerd provides the ctr tool that we'll use for experimentation.

Using containerd

Our initial containerd command showed that no images have been downloaded yet. Let's download a small image with which we can run a container. We will use *BusyBox*, a tiny container image that includes a shell and basic Linux utilities. To download the image, we use the pull command:

```
root@host01:~# ctr image pull docker.io/library/busybox:latest
...
root@host01:~# ctr images ls
REF                       ...
docker.io/library/busybox:latest ...
```

Our list of images is no longer empty. Let's run a container from that image:

```
root@host01:~# ctr run -t --rm docker.io/library/busybox:latest v1
/ #
```

This looks similar to using Docker. We use -t to create a TTY for this container, allowing us to interact with it, and we use --rm to tell containerd to delete the container when the main process stops. However, there are some important differences to note. When we used Docker in Chapter 1, we didn't worry about pulling the image before running it, and we were able to use simpler names like nginx or rockylinux:8. The ctr tool requires us to specify *docker.io/library/busybox:latest*, the full path to the image, with registry hostname and tag included. Also, we are required to pull the image first because the runtime won't do this for us automatically.

Now that we're inside this container, we can see that it has an isolated network stack and process space:

```
/ # ip a
1: lo: <LOOPBACK,UP,LOWER_UP> mtu 65536 qdisc noqueue qlen 1000
    link/loopback 00:00:00:00:00:00 brd 00:00:00:00:00:00
    inet 127.0.0.1/8 scope host lo
       valid_lft forever preferred_lft forever
    inet6 ::1/128 scope host
       valid_lft forever preferred_lft forever
```

```
/ # ps
PID   USER      TIME  COMMAND
    1 root      0:00  sh
    8 root      0:00  ps
/ #
```

Inside the container, we see a loopback network interface. We also see our shell process and the ps command that we ran. As far as the processes in our container are concerned, we are running on a separate system with no other processes running or listening on the network.

WHY NO BRIDGE INTERFACE?

If you've worked with Docker, you might be surprised to see that this container has only a loopback interface. Default networking on a container platform also provides an additional interface that is attached to a bridge. This allows containers to see one another and also allows containers to use the host interface to access external networks via Network Address Translation (NAT).

In this case, we are talking directly to a lower-level container runtime. This container runtime handles managing images and running containers only. If we want a bridge interface and a connection to the internet, we'll need to provide it ourselves (and we do exactly that in Chapter 4).

We've illustrated that we can talk to the containerd runtime to run a container, and that inside the container, we're isolated from the rest of the system. How does that isolation work? To find out, let's keep the container running and investigate it from the host system.

Introducing Linux Namespaces

Like other container runtimes, containerd uses a Linux kernel feature called *namespaces* to isolate the processes in the container. As mentioned earlier, most of the effort in process isolation is to ensure that a process can't see things it shouldn't. A process running in a namespace sees a limited view of a particular system resource.

Even though containerization seems like new technology, Linux namespaces have been available for many years. Over time, more types of namespaces were added. We can find out what namespaces are associated with our container using the lsns command, but first we need to know the process ID (PID) on the host for our container's shell process. While leaving the container running, open another terminal tab or window. (See "Running Examples" on page xx for more information.) Then, use ctr to list running containers:

```
root@host01:~# ctr task ls
TASK   PID     STATUS
v1     18088   RUNNING
```

Let's use ps to verify that we have the correct PID. When you run these commands yourself, be sure to use the PID that displays in your listing:

```
root@host01:~# ps -f 18088
UID         PID    PPID C STIME TTY     STAT TIME CMD
root       18088   18067 0 18:46 pts/0  Ss+  0:00 sh
root@host01:~# ps -f 18067
UID         PID    PPID C STIME TTY     STAT TIME CMD
root       18067      1 0 18:46 ?       Sl   0:00
  /usr/bin/containerd-shim-runc-v2 -namespace default -id v1 -address
  /run/containerd/containerd.sock
```

As expected, the parent of this PID is containerd. Next let's use lsns to list the namespaces that containerd has created to isolate this process:

```
root@host01:~# lsns | grep 18088
4026532180 mnt         1 18088 root            sh
4026532181 uts         1 18088 root            sh
4026532182 ipc         1 18088 root            sh
4026532183 pid         1 18088 root            sh
4026532185 net         1 18088 root            sh
```

Here, containerd is using five different types of namespaces in order to fully isolate the processes running in the busybox container:

mnt   Mount points

uts   Unix time sharing (hostname and network domain)

ipc   Interprocess communication (for example, shared memory)

pid   Process identifiers (and list of running processes)

net   Network (including interfaces, routing table, and firewall)

Finally, we'll close out the BusyBox container by running exit from within that container (first terminal window):

```
/ # exit
```

This command returns us to a regular shell prompt so that we can be ready for the next set of examples.

Containers and Namespaces in CRI-O

In addition to containerd, Kubernetes supports other container runtimes. Depending on which Kubernetes distribution you use, you might find that the container runtime is different. For example, Red Hat OpenShift uses *CRI-O*, an alternative container runtime. CRI-O is also used by the Podman, Buildah, and Skopeo suite of tools, which are the standard way to manage containers on Red Hat 8 and related systems.

Let's run the same container image using CRI-O to get a better picture of how container runtimes are different from one another but also to show how they use the same underlying Linux kernel capabilities for process isolation.

You can skip these install commands by using the *extra* provisioning script provided with this chapter's examples. See the README file for this chapter for instructions.

The OpenSUSE Kubic project hosts repositories for CRI-O for various Linux distributions, including Ubuntu, so we will install from there. The exact URL is dependent on the version of CRI-O we want to install, and the URLs are long and challenging to type, so the automation installs a script to configure some useful environment variables. Before proceeding, we need to load that script:

```
root@host01:~# source /opt/crio-ver
```

We can now use the environment variables to set up the CRI-O repositories and install CRI-O:

```
root@host01:~# echo "deb $REPO/$OS/ /" > /etc/apt/sources.list.d/kubic.list
root@host01:~# echo "deb $REPO:/cri-o:/$VERSION/$OS/ /" \
 > /etc/apt/sources.list.d/kubic.cri-o.list
root@host01:~# curl -L $REPO/$OS/Release.key | apt-key add -
...
OK
root@host01:~# apt update && apt install -y cri-o cri-o-runc
...
root@host01:~# systemctl enable crio && systemctl start crio
...
root@host01:~# curl -L -o /tmp/crictl.tar.gz $CRICTL_URL
...
root@host01:~# tar -C /usr/local/bin -xvzf /tmp/crictl.tar.gz
crictl
root@host01:~# rm -f /tmp/crictl.tar.gz
```

We first add to the list of repositories for apt by adding files to */etc/apt/ sources.list.d*. We then use apt to install CRI-O packages. After CRI-O is installed, we use systemd to enable and start its service.

Unlike containerd, CRI-O does not ship with any command line tools that we can use for testing, so the last command installs crictl, which is part of the Kubernetes project and is designed for testing any container runtime compatible with the Container Runtime Interface (CRI) standard. CRI is the programming API that Kubernetes itself uses to communicate with container runtimes.

Because crictl is compatible with any container runtime that supports CRI, it needs configuration to connect to CRI-O. CRI-O has installed a configuration file */etc/crictl.yaml* to configure crictl:

crictl.yaml
```
runtime-endpoint: unix:///var/run/crio/crio.sock
image-endpoint: unix:///var/run/crio/crio.sock
...
```

This configuration tells crictl to connect to CRI-O's socket.

To create and run containers, the crictl command requires us to provide definition files in the JSON or YAML file format. The automated scripts for this chapter added two crictl definition files to */opt*. The first file, shown in Listing 2-1, creates a Pod:

pod.yaml
```
---
metadata:
  name: busybox
  namespace: crio
linux:
  security_context:
    namespace_options:
      network: 2
```

Listing 2-1: CRI-O Pod definition

Similar to the Kubernetes Pod we saw in Chapter 1, the Pod is a group of one or more containers that run in the same isolated space. In our case, we need only one container in the Pod, and the second file, shown in Listing 2-2, defines the container process that CRI-O should start. We provide a name (busybox) and namespace (crio) to distinguish this Pod from any others. Otherwise, we need to provide only network configuration. CRI-O expects to use a Container Network Interface (CNI) plug-in to configure the network namespace. We cover CNI plug-ins in Chapter 8, so for now, we'll use network: 2 to tell CRI-O not to create a separate network namespace and instead use the host network:

container.yaml
```
---
metadata:
  name: busybox
image:
  image: docker.io/library/busybox:latest
args:
  - "/bin/sleep"
  - "36000"
```

Listing 2-2: CRI-O container definition

Again we are using BusyBox because its small size makes it fast and lightweight. However, because crictl will create this container in the background without a terminal, we need to specify */bin/sleep* as the command to be run inside the container; otherwise, the container will immediately terminate when the shell realizes that it doesn't have a TTY.

Before we can run the container, we first need to pull the image:

```
root@host01:~# crictl pull docker.io/library/busybox:latest
Image is up to date for docker.io/library/busybox@sha256:...
```

Then, we provide the *pod.yaml* and *container.yaml* files to crictl to create and start our BusyBox container:

```
root@host01:~# cd /opt
root@host01:~# POD_ID=$(crictl runp pod.yaml)
root@host01:~# crictl pods
POD ID            CREATED                  STATE ...
3bf297ace44b5     Less than a second ago   Ready ...
root@host01:~# CONTAINER_ID=$(crictl create $POD_ID container.yaml pod.yaml)
root@host01:~# crictl start $CONTAINER_ID
91394a7f37e3da3a557782ed6d6eb2cf8c23e5b3dd4e2febd415bba071d10734
root@host01:~# crictl ps
CONTAINER        ... STATE
91394a7f37e3d    ... Running
```

We capture the Pod's unique identifier and the container in POD_ID and CONTAINER_ID variables, so we can use them here and upcoming commands.

Before looking at the Linux namespaces created by CRI-O, let's look inside the busybox container by using the crictl exec command to start a new shell process inside it:

```
root@host01:~# crictl exec -ti $CONTAINER_ID /bin/sh
/ # ip a
1: lo: <LOOPBACK,UP,LOWER_UP> mtu 65536 qdisc noqueue qlen 1000
...
2: enp0s3: <BROADCAST,MULTICAST,UP,LOWER_UP> mtu 1500 qdisc fq_codel qlen 1000
...
3: enp0s8: <BROADCAST,MULTICAST,UP,LOWER_UP> mtu 1500 qdisc fq_codel qlen 1000
...
/ # ps
PID   USER     TIME  COMMAND
    1 root     0:00  /pause
    7 root     0:00  /bin/sleep 36000
   13 root     0:00  /bin/sh
   20 root     0:00  ps
/ # exit
```

This BusyBox container running in CRI-O looks a little different from BusyBox running in containerd. First, because we configured our Pod with network: 2, the container can see the same network devices that a regular process would see. Second, we see a couple of additional processes. We look at the pause process with PID 1 when we discuss container runtimes under

Kubernetes in Chapter 12. The other extra process is sleep, which we created as the entry point for this container.

CRI-O is also using Linux namespaces for process isolation, as we can see from examining the container processes and listing namespaces:

```
root@host01:~# PID=$(crictl inspect $CONTAINER_ID | jq '.info.pid')
root@host01:~# ps -f $PID
UID          PID    PPID C STIME TTY     STAT TIME CMD
root       23906   23894 0 20:15 ?       Ss   0:00 /bin/sleep 36000
root@host01:~# ps -f 23894
UID          PID    PPID C STIME TTY     STAT TIME CMD
root       23894       1 0 20:15 ?       Ssl  0:00 /usr/bin/conmon ...
```

The crictl inspect command provides a wealth of information about the container, but for the moment, we need only the PID. Because crictl returns JSON-formatted output, we can use jq to extract the pid field from the info structure and save it to an environment variable called PID. Try running crictl inspect $CONTAINER_ID to see the full information.

Using the PID we discovered, we can see our sleep command. We then can use its parent PID to verify that it is managed by conmon, a CRI-O utility. Next, let's see the namespaces that CRI-O has created. The allocation of namespaces to processes is more complex in CRI-O, so let's just list all of the namespaces on our Linux system and pick out the ones related to the container:

```
root@host01:~# lsns
        NS TYPE    NPROCS  PID USER          COMMAND
...
4026532183 uts        2 23867 root          /pause
4026532184 ipc        2 23867 root          /pause
4026532185 mnt        1 23867 root          /pause
4026532186 pid        2 23867 root          /pause
4026532187 mnt        1 23906 root          /bin/sleep 36000
...
```

Here, we see only four types of namespaces. Because we told CRI-O to give the container access to the host's network namespace, it didn't need to create a net namespace. Also, with CRI-O, most namespaces are associated with the pause command (although some are shared by multiple processes, as we can see via the NPROCS column). There are two mnt namespaces because each separate container in a Pod gets a different set of mount points for reasons that we cover in Chapter 5.

Running Processes in Namespaces Directly

One of the trickier jobs when running a process in a container is handling the responsibility that comes with being PID 1. To better understand this, we won't have our container runtime create a namespace for us. Instead, we'll talk directly to the Linux kernel to run a process in a namespace manually. We'll use the command line, although container runtimes use the Linux kernel API, but the result will be the same.

Because namespaces are a Linux kernel feature, nothing else needs to be installed or configured. We just use the unshare command when launching the process:

```
root@host01:~# unshare -f -p --mount-proc -- /bin/sh -c /bin/bash
```

The unshare command runs a program with different namespaces from the parent. By adding -p, we specify that a new PID namespace is needed. The option --mount-proc goes along with that, adding a new mount namespace and ensuring */proc* is remounted correctly, so that the process sees the correct process information. Otherwise, the process would still be able to see information about other processes in the system. Finally, the content after -- indicates the command to run.

Because this is an isolated process namespace, it cannot see a list of processes outside this namespace:

```
root@host01:~# ps -ef
UID         PID    PPID  C STIME TTY          TIME CMD
root          1       0  0 22:21 pts/0     00:00:00 /bin/sh -c /bin/bash
root          2       1  0 22:21 pts/0     00:00:00 /bin/bash
root          9       2  0 22:22 pts/0     00:00:00 ps -ef
```

Let's get the ID of this namespace so that we can recognize it in a list:

```
root@host01:~# ls -l /proc/self/ns/pid
lrwxrwxrwx 1 root root 0 Mar  6 22:22 /proc/self/ns/pid -> 'pid:[4026532190]'
```

Now, from another terminal window, list all of the namespaces and look for those related to our isolated shell:

```
root@host01:~# lsns
        NS TYPE NPROCS PID    USER COMMAND
...
4026532189 mnt  3       12110 root unshare -f -p ...
4026532190 pid  2       12111 root /bin/sh -c /bin/bash
...
root@host01:~# exit
```

We see a pid namespace matching what we saw. In addition, we see a mnt namespace. This namespace ensures that our shell sees the proper information in */proc*.

Because the pid namespace is owned by the sh command, that command is PID 1 when we run ps within the namespace. This means that sh has the responsibility to manage its children properly (such as bash). For example, sh is responsible for passing signals to its children to ensure that they terminate correctly. It's important to keep this in mind as it is a common problem when running containers that can result in zombie processes or other issues cleaning up a stopped container.

Fortunately, sh handles its management duties well, as we can see by the fact that when we pass a kill signal to it, it passes that signal on to its children. Run this from the second terminal window, outside the namespace:

```
root@host01:~# kill -9 12111
```

Inside the first window you will see this output:

```
root@host01:~# Killed
```

This indicates that bash received the kill signal and terminated correctly.

Final Thoughts

Although containers create the appearance of a completely separate system, it's done in a way that has nothing in common with virtual machines. Instead, the process is similar to traditional means of process isolation, such as user permissions and separate filesystems. Container runtimes use namespaces, which are built in to the Linux kernel and enable various types of process isolation. In this chapter, we examined how the containerd and CRI-O container runtimes use multiple types of Linux namespaces to give each container an independent view of other processes, network devices, and the filesystem. The use of namespaces prevents processes running in a container from seeing and interfering with other processes.

At the same time, processes in a container are still sharing the same CPU, memory, and network. A process that uses too many of those resources will prevent other processes from running properly. Namespaces can't solve that problem, however. To prevent this issue, we'll need to look at resource limiting—the topic of our next chapter.

3

RESOURCE LIMITING

 The process isolation work we did in Chapter 2 was very important, as a process cannot generally affect what it cannot "see." However, our process can see the host's CPU, memory, and networking, so it is possible for a process to prevent other processes from running correctly by using too much of these resources, not leaving enough room for others. In this chapter, we will see how to guarantee that a process uses only its allocated CPU, memory, and network resources, ensuring that we can divide up our resources accurately. This will help when we move on to container orchestration because it will provide Kubernetes with certainty about the resources available on each host when it schedules a container.

CPU, memory, and network are important, but there's one more really important shared resource: storage. However, in a container orchestration environment like Kubernetes, storage is distributed, and limits need to be applied at the level of the whole cluster. For this reason, our discussion of storage must wait until we introduce distributed storage in Chapter 15.

CPU Priorities

We'll need to look at CPU, memory, and network separately, as the effect of applying limits is different in each case. Let's begin by looking at how to control CPU usage. To understand CPU limits, we first need to look at how the Linux kernel decides which process to run and for how long. In the Linux kernel, the *scheduler* keeps a list of all of the processes. It also tracks which processes are ready to run and how much time each process has received lately. This allows it to create a prioritized list so that it can choose the process that will run next. The scheduler is designed to be as fair as possible (it's even known as the Completely Fair Scheduler); thus, it tries to give all processes a chance to run. However, it does accept outside input on which of these processes are more important than others. This prioritization is made up of two parts: the scheduling policy, and the priority of each process within that policy.

Real-Time and Non-Real-Time Policies

The scheduler supports several different policies, but for our purposes we can group them into real-time policies and non-real-time policies. The term *real-time* means that some real-world event is critical to the process that creates a deadline. The process needs to complete its processing before this deadline expires, or something bad will happen. For example, the process might be collecting data from an embedded hardware device. In that case, the process must read the data before the hardware buffer overflows. A real-time process is typically not extremely CPU intensive, but when it needs the CPU, it cannot wait, so all processes under a real-time policy are higher priority than any process under a non-real-time policy. Let's explore this on an example Linux system.

NOTE *The example repository for this book is at* https://github.com/book-of -kubernetes/examples. *See "Running Examples" on page xx for details on getting set up.*

The Linux ps command tells us the specific policy that applies to each process. Run this command on *host01* from this chapter's examples:

```
root@host01:~# ps -e -o pid,class,rtprio,ni,comm
 PID CLS RTPRIO  NI COMMAND
   1 TS       -   0 systemd
...
   6 TS       - -20 kworker/0:0H-kblockd
...
  11 FF      99   - migration/0
  12 FF      50   - idle_inject/0
...
  85 FF      99   - watchdogd
...
```

```
484 RR       99   - multipathd
...
7967 TS       -   0 ps
```

The -o flag provides ps with a custom list of output fields, including the scheduling policy *class* (CLS) and two numeric priority fields: RTPRIO and NI.

Looking at the CLS field first, lots of processes are listed as TS, which stands for "time-sharing" and is the default non-real-time policy. This includes commands we run ourselves (like the ps command we ran) as well as important Linux system processes like systemd. However, we also see processes with policy FF for first in–first out (FIFO) and policy RR for round-robin. These are real-time processes, and as such, they have priority over all non-real-time policies in the system. Real-time processes in the list include watchdog, which detects system lockups and thus might need to preempt other processes, and multipathd, which watches for device changes and must be able to configure those devices before other processes get a chance to talk to them.

In addition to the class, the two numeric priority fields tell us how processes are prioritized within the policy. Not surprisingly, the RTPRIO field means "real-time priority" and applies only to real-time processes. The NI field is the "nice" level of the process and applies only to non-real-time processes. For historical reasons, the nice level runs from −20 (least nice, or highest priority) to 19 (nicest, lowest priority).

Setting Process Priorities

Linux allows us to set the priority for processes we start. Let's try to use priorities to control CPU usage. We'll run a program called stress that is designed to exercise our system. Let's use a containerized version of stress using CRI-O.

As before, we need to define YAML files for the Pod and container to tell crictl what to run. The Pod YAML shown in Listing 3-1 is almost the same as the BusyBox example in Chapter 2; only the name is different:

po-nolim.yaml
```
---
metadata:
  name: stress
  namespace: crio
linux:
  security_context:
    namespace_options:
      network: 2
```

Listing 3-1: BusyBox Pod

The container YAML has more changes compared to the BusyBox example. In addition to using a different container image, one that already has stress installed, we also need to provide arguments to stress to tell it to exercise a single CPU:

```
co-nolim.yaml  ---
               metadata:
                 name: stress
               image:
                 image: docker.io/bookofkubernetes/stress:stable
               args:
                 - "--cpu"
                 - "1"
                 - "-v"
```

CRI-O is already installed on host01, so it just takes a few commands to start this container. First, we'll pull the image:

```
root@host01:/opt# crictl pull docker.io/bookofkubernetes/stress:stable
Image is up to date for docker.io/bookofkubernetes/stress...
```

Then, we can run a container from the image:

```
root@host01:~# cd /opt
root@host01:/opt# PUL_ID=$(crictl runp po-nolim.yaml)
root@host01:/opt# CUL_ID=$(crictl create $PUL_ID co-nolim.yaml po-nolim.yaml)
root@host01:/opt# crictl start $CUL_ID
...
root@host01:/opt# crictl ps
CONTAINER      IMAGE                                    ...
971e83927329e  docker.io/bookofkubernetes/stress:stable ...
```

The crictl ps command is just to check that our container is running as expected.

The stress program is now running on our system, and we can see the current priority and CPU usage. We want the current CPU usage, so we'll use top:

```
root@host01:/opt# top -b -n 1 -p $(pgrep -d , stress)
top - 18:01:58 up  1:39,  1 user,  load average: 1.01, 0.40, 0.16
Tasks:   2 total,   1 running,   1 sleeping,   0 stopped,   0 zombie
%Cpu(s): 34.8 us,  0.0 sy,  0.0 ni, 65.2 id,  0.0 wa,  0.0 hi,  0.0 si,  0.0 st
MiB Mem :   1987.5 total,   1024.5 free,    195.8 used,    767.3 buff/cache
MiB Swap:      0.0 total,      0.0 free,      0.0 used.   1643.7 avail Mem

  PID   USER  PR  NI  ...  %CPU  %MEM    TIME+ COMMAND
13459 root   20   0  ... 100.0   0.2  0:29.78 stress-ng
13435 root   20   0  ...   0.0   0.2  0:00.01 stress-ng
```

The pgrep command looks up the process IDs (PIDs) for stress; there are two because stress forked a separate process for the CPU exercise we requested. This CPU worker is using up 100 percent of one CPU; fortunately, our VM has two CPUs, so it's not overloaded.

We started this process with default priority, so it has a nice value of 0, as shown in the NI column. What happens if we change that priority? Let's find out using renice:

```
root@host01:/opt# renice -n 19 -p $(pgrep -d ' ' stress)
13435 (process ID) old priority 0, new priority 19
13459 (process ID) old priority 0, new priority 19
```

The ps command used previously expected the PIDs to be separated with a comma, whereas the renice command expects the PIDs to be separated with a space; fortunately, pgrep can handle both.

We have successfully changed the priority of the process:

```
root@host01:/opt# top -b -n 1 -p $(pgrep -d , stress)
top - 18:11:04 up  1:48,  1 user,  load average: 1.07, 0.95, 0.57
Tasks:   2 total,   1 running,   1 sleeping,   0 stopped,   0 zombie
%Cpu(s): 0.0 us, 0.0 sy, 28.6 ni, 71.4 id,  0.0 wa,  0.0 hi,  0.0 si,  0.0 st
MiB Mem :   1987.5 total,   1035.6 free,    182.2 used,    769.7 buff/cache
MiB Swap:      0.0 total,      0.0 free,      0.0 used.   1657.2 avail Mem

  PID   USER   PR  NI  ...  %CPU  %MEM     TIME+ COMMAND
 13459  root   39  19  ... 100.0   0.2   9:35.50 stress-ng
 13435  root   39  19  ...   0.0   0.2   0:00.01 stress-ng
```

The new nice value is 19, meaning that our process is lower priority than before. However, the stress program is still using 100 percent of one CPU! What's going on here? The problem is that priority is only a relative measurement. If nothing else needs the CPU, as is true in this case, even a lower-priority process can use as much as it wants.

This arrangement may seem to be what we want. After all, if the CPU is available, shouldn't we want our application components to be able to use it? Unfortunately, even though that sounds reasonable, it's not suitable for our containerized applications for two main reasons. First, a container orchestration environment like Kubernetes works best when a container can be allocated to any host with enough resources to run it. It's not reasonable for us to know the relative priority of every single container in our Kubernetes cluster, especially when we consider that a single Kubernetes cluster can be *multitenant*, meaning multiple separate applications or teams might be using a single cluster. Second, without some idea of how much CPU a particular container will use, Kubernetes cannot know which hosts are full and which ones have more room available. We don't want to get into a situation in which multiple containers on the same host all become busy at the same time, because they will fight for the available CPU cores, and the whole host will slow down.

Linux Control Groups

As we saw in the last section, process prioritization will not help a container orchestration environment like Kubernetes know what host to use when scheduling a new container, because even low-priority processes can get a lot of CPU time when the CPU is idle. And because our Kubernetes cluster might be multitenant, the cluster can't just trust each container to promise to use only a certain amount of CPU. First, that would allow one process to affect another negatively, either maliciously or accidentally. Second, processes don't really control their own scheduling; they get CPU time when the Linux kernel decides to give them CPU time. We need a different solution for controlling CPU utilization.

To find the answer, we can take an approach used by real-time processing. As we mentioned in the previous section, a real-time process is typically not compute intensive, but when it needs the CPU, it needs it immediately. To ensure that all real-time processes get the CPU they need, it is common to reserve a slice of the CPU time for each process. Even though our container processes are non-real-time, we can use the same strategy. If we can configure our containers so that they can use no more than their allocated slice of the CPU time, Kubernetes will be able to calculate how much space is available on each host and will be able to schedule containers onto hosts with sufficient space.

To manage container use of CPU cores, we will use *control groups*. Control groups (cgroups) are a feature of the Linux kernel that manage process resource utilization. Each resource type, such as CPU, memory, or a block device, can have an entire hierarchy of cgroups associated with it. After a process is in a cgroup, the kernel automatically applies the controls from that group.

The creation and configuration of cgroups is handled through a specific kind of filesystem, similar to the way that Linux reports information on the system through the */proc* filesystem. By default, the filesystem for cgroups is located at */sys/fs/cgroup*:

```
root@host01:~# ls /sys/fs/cgroup
blkio          cpuacct  freezer  net_cls          perf_event  systemd
cpu            cpuset   hugetlb  net_cls,net_prio pids        unified
cpu,cpuacct    devices  memory   net_prio         rdma
```

Each of the entries in */sys/fs/cgroup* is a different resource that can be limited. If we look in one of those directories, we can begin to see what controls can be applied. For example, for *cpu*:

```
root@host01:~# cd /sys/fs/cgroup/cpu
root@host01:/sys/fs/cgroup/cpu# ls -F
cgroup.clone_children  cpuacct.stat           cpuacct.usage_user
cgroup.procs           cpuacct.usage          init.scope/
cgroup.sane_behavior   cpuacct.usage_all      notify_on_release
cpu.cfs_period_us      cpuacct.usage_percpu   release_agent
```

cpu.cfs_quota_us	cpuacct.usage_percpu_sys	system.slice/
cpu.shares	cpuacct.usage_percpu_user	tasks
cpu.stat	cpuacct.usage_sys	user.slice/

The -F flag on ls adds a slash character to directories, which enables us to begin to see the hierarchy. Each of those subdirectories (*init.scope*, *system.slice*, and *user.slice*) is a separate CPU cgroup, and each has its own set of configuration files that apply to processes in that cgroup.

CPU Quotas with cgroups

To understand the contents of this directory, let's see how we can use cgroups to limit the CPU usage of our stress container. We'll begin by checking its CPU usage again:

```
root@host01:/sys/fs/cgroup/cpu# top -b -n 1 -p $(pgrep -d , stress)
top - 22:40:12 up 12 min,  1 user,  load average: 0.81, 0.35, 0.21
Tasks:   2 total,   1 running,   1 sleeping,   0 stopped,   0 zombie
%Cpu(s): 37.0 us,  0.0 sy,  0.0 ni, 63.0 id,  0.0 wa,  0.0 hi,  0.0 si,  0.0 st
MiB Mem :   1987.5 total,   1075.1 free,    179.4 used,    733.0 buff/cache
MiB Swap:      0.0 total,      0.0 free,      0.0 used.   1646.3 avail Mem

   PID USER    PR  NI ...  %CPU  %MEM     TIME+ COMMAND
  5964 root    20  19 ... 100.0   0.2   1:19.72 stress-ng
  5932 root    20  19 ...   0.0   0.2   0:00.02 stress-ng
```

If you don't still see stress running, start it up again using the commands from earlier in this chapter. Next, let's explore what CPU cgroup our stress CPU process is in. We can do this by finding its PID inside a file within the */sys/fs/cgroup/cpu* hierarchy:

```
root@host01:/sys/fs/cgroup/cpu# grep -R $(pgrep stress-ng-cpu)
system.slice/runc-050c.../cgroup.procs:5964
system.slice/runc-050c.../tasks:5964
```

The stress process is part of the *system.slice* hierarchy, and is in a subdirectory created by runc, which is one of the internal components of CRI-O. This is really convenient, as it means we don't need to create our own cgroup and move this process into it. It is also no accident; as we'll see in a moment, CRI-O supports CPU limits on containers, so it naturally needs to create a cgroup for each container it runs. In fact, the cgroup is named after the container ID.

Let's move into the directory for our container's cgroup:

```
root@host01:/sys/fs/cgroup/cpu# cd system.slice/runc-${CUL_ID}.scope
```

We use the container ID variable we saved earlier to change into the appropriate directory. As soon as we're in this directory, we can see that it has the same configuration files as the root of the hierarchy */sys/fs/cgroup/cpu*:

```
root@host01:/sys/fs/...07.scope# ls
cgroup.clone_children  cpu.uclamp.max         cpuacct.usage_percpu_sys
cgroup.procs           cpu.uclamp.min         cpuacct.usage_percpu_user
cpu.cfs_period_us      cpuacct.stat           cpuacct.usage_sys
cpu.cfs_quota_us       cpuacct.usage          cpuacct.usage_user
cpu.shares             cpuacct.usage_all      notify_on_release
cpu.stat               cpuacct.usage_percpu   tasks
```

The *cgroup.procs* file lists the processes in this control group:

```
root@host01:/sys/fs/...07.scope# cat cgroup.procs
5932
5964
```

This directory has many other files, but we are mostly interested in three:

cpu.shares   Slice of the CPU relative to this cgroup's peers

cpu.cfs_period_us   Length of a period, in microseconds

cpu.cfs_quota_us   CPU time during a period, in microseconds

We'll look at how Kubernetes uses *cpu.shares* in Chapter 14. For now, we need a way to get our instance under control so that it doesn't overwhelm our system. To do that, we'll set an absolute quota on this container. First, let's see the value of *cpu.cfs_period_us*:

```
root@host01:/sys/fs/...07.scope# cat cpu.cfs_period_us
100000
```

The period is set to 100,000 µs, or 0.1 seconds. We can use this number to figure out what quota to set in order to limit the amount of CPU the stress container can use. At the moment, there is no quota:

```
root@host01:/sys/fs/...07.scope# cat cpu.cfs_quota_us
-1
```

We can set a quota by just updating the *cpu.cfs_quota_us* file:

```
root@host01:/sys/fs/...07.scope# echo "50000" > cpu.cfs_quota_us
```

This provides the processes in this cgroup with 50,000 µs of CPU time per 100,000 µs, which averages out to 50 percent of a CPU. The processes are immediately affected, as we can confirm:

```
root@host01:/sys/fs/...07.scope# top -b -n 1 -p $(pgrep -d , stress)
top - 23:53:05 up  1:24,  1 user,  load average: 0.71, 0.93, 0.98
```

```
Tasks:   2 total,   1 running,   1 sleeping,   0 stopped,   0 zombie
%Cpu(s):  0.0 us, 3.6 sy, 7.1 ni, 89.3 id,  0.0 wa,  0.0 hi,  0.0 si,  0.0 st
MiB Mem :   1987.5 total,   1064.9 free,    174.6 used,    748.0 buff/cache
MiB Swap:      0.0 total,      0.0 free,      0.0 used.   1663.9 avail Mem

  PID USER    PR  NI  ...  %CPU  %MEM    TIME+ COMMAND
 5964 root    39  19  ...  50.0   0.2 73:45.68 stress-ng-cpu
 5932 root    39  19  ...   0.0   0.2  0:00.02 stress-ng
```

Your listing might not show exactly 50 percent CPU usage, because the period during which the top command measures CPU usage might not align perfectly with the kernel's scheduling period. But on average, our stress container now cannot use more than 50 percent of one CPU.

Before we move on, let's stop the stress container:

```
root@host01:/sys/fs/...07.scope# cd
root@host01:/opt# crictl stop $CUL_ID
...
root@host01:/opt# crictl rm $CUL_ID
...
root@host01:/opt# crictl stopp $PUL_ID
Stopped sandbox ...
root@host01:/opt# crictl rmp $PUL_ID
Removed sandbox ...
```

CPU Quota with CRI-O and crictl

It would be tiresome to have to go through the process of finding the cgroup location in the filesystem and updating the CPU quota for every container in order to control CPU usage. Fortunately, we can specify the quota in our crictl YAML files, and CRI-O will enforce it for us. Let's look at an example that was installed into *opt* when we set up this example virtual machine.

The Pod configuration is only slightly different from Listing 3-1. We add a cgroup_parent setting so that we can control where CRI-O creates the cgroup, which will make it easier to find the cgroup to see the configuration:

po-clim.yaml
```
---
metadata:
  name: stress-clim
  namespace: crio
linux:
  cgroup_parent: pod.slice
  security_context:
    namespace_options:
      network: 2
```

The container configuration is where we include the CPU limits. Our stress1 container will be allotted only 10 percent of a CPU:

co-clim.yaml ---
```
---
metadata:
  name: stress-clim
image:
  image: docker.io/bookofkubernetes/stress:stable
args:
  - "--cpu"
  - "1"
  - "-v"
linux:
  resources:
    cpu_period: 100000
    cpu_quota: 10000
```

The value for cpu_period corresponds with the file *cpu.cfs_period_us* and provides the length of the period during which the quota applies. The value for cpu_quota corresponds with the file *cpu.cfs_quota_us*. Dividing the quota by the period, we can determine that this will set a CPU limit of 10 percent. Let's go ahead and launch this stress container with its CPU limit:

```
root@host01:~# cd /opt
root@host01:/opt# PCL_ID=$(crictl runp po-clim.yaml)
root@host01:/opt# CCL_ID=$(crictl create $PCL_ID co-clim.yaml po-clim.yaml)
root@host01:/opt# crictl start $CCL_ID
...
root@host01:/opt# crictl ps
CONTAINER       IMAGE                                    ...
ea8bccd711b86  docker.io/bookofkubernetes/stress:stable ...
```

Our container is immediately restricted to 10 percent of a CPU:

```
root@host01:/opt# top -b -n 1 -p $(pgrep -d , stress)
top - 17:26:55 up 19 min,  1 user,  load average: 0.27, 0.16, 0.13
Tasks:   4 total,   2 running,   2 sleeping,   0 stopped,   0 zombie
%Cpu(s): 10.3 us, 0.0 sy, 0.0 ni, 89.7 id,  0.0 wa,  0.0 hi,  0.0 si,  0.0 st
MiB Mem :   1987.5 total,   1053.4 free,    189.3 used,    744.9 buff/cache
MiB Swap:      0.0 total,      0.0 free,      0.0 used.   1640.4 avail Mem

  PID USER    PR  NI ... %CPU  %MEM    TIME+ COMMAND
 8349 root    20   0 ... 10.0   0.2  0:22.67 stress-ng
 8202 root    20   0 ...  0.0   0.2  0:00.02 stress-ng
```

As in our earlier example, the CPU usage shown is a snapshot during the time that top was running, so it might not match the limit exactly, but over the long term, this process will use no more than its allocated CPU.

We can inspect the cgroup to confirm that CRI-O put it in the place we specified and automatically configured the CPU quota:

```
root@host01:/opt# cd /sys/fs/cgroup/cpu/pod.slice
root@host01:...pod.slice# cat crio-$CCL_ID.scope/cpu.cfs_quota_us
10000
```

CRI-O created a new cgroup parent *pod.slice* for our container, created a cgroup within it specific to the container, and configured its CPU quota without us having to lift a finger.

We don't need this container any longer, so let's remove it:

```
root@host01:/sys/fs/cgroupcpu/pod.slice# cd
root@host01:~# crictl stop $CCL_ID
...
root@host01:~# crictl rm $CCL_ID
...
root@host01:~# crictl stopp $PCL_ID
Stopped sandbox ...
root@host01:~# crictl rmp $PCL_ID
Removed sandbox ...
```

With these commands we stop and then delete first the container, then the Pod.

Memory Limits

Memory is another important resource for a process. If a system doesn't have sufficient memory to meet a request, the allocation of memory will fail. This usually causes the process to behave badly or to fail entirely. Of course, most Linux systems use *swap space* to write memory contents to disk temporarily, which allows the system memory to appear larger than it is but also reduces system performance. It's a big enough concern that the Kubernetes team discourages having swap enabled in a cluster.

Also, even if we could use swap, we don't want one process grabbing all the resident memory and making other processes very slow. As a result, we need to limit the memory usage of our processes so that they cooperate with one another. We also need to have a clear maximum for memory usage so that Kubernetes can reliably ensure that a host has enough available memory before scheduling a new container onto a host.

Linux systems, like other variants of Unix, have traditionally had to deal with multiple users who are sharing scarce resources. For this reason, the kernel supports limits on system resources, including CPU, memory, number of child processes, and number of open files. We can set these limits from the command line using the `ulimit` command. For example, one type of limit is a limit on "virtual memory." This includes not only the amount of

RAM a process has in resident memory but also any swap space it is using. Here's an example of a `ulimit` command limiting virtual memory:

```
root@host01:~# ulimit -v 262144
```

The `-v` switch specifies a limit on virtual memory. The parameter is in bytes, so 262144 places a virtual memory limit of 256MiB on each additional process we start from this shell session. Setting a virtual memory limit is a total limit; it allows us to ensure that a process can't use swap to get around the limit. We can verify the limit was applied by pulling some data into memory:

```
root@host01:~# cat /dev/zero | head -c 500m | tail
tail: memory exhausted
```

This command reads from */dev/zero* and tries to keep the first 500MiB of zeros it finds in memory. However, at some point, when the `tail` command tries to allocate more space to hold the zeros it is getting from `head`, it fails because of the limit.

Thus, Unix limits give us the ability to control memory usage for our processes, but they won't provide everything we need for containers, for a couple of reasons. First, Unix limits can be applied only to individual processes or to an entire user. Neither of those provide what we need, as a container is really a *group* of processes. A container's initial process might create many child processes, and all processes in a container need to live within the same limit. At the same time, applying limits to an entire user doesn't really help us in a container orchestration environment like Kubernetes, because from the perspective of the operating system, all of the containers belong to the same user. Second, when it comes to CPU limits, the only thing that regular Unix limits can do is limit the maximum CPU time our process gets before it is terminated. That isn't the kind of limit we need for sharing the CPU between long-running processes.

Instead of using traditional Unix limits, we'll use cgroups again, this time to limit the memory available to a process. We'll use the same stress container image, this time with a child process that tries to allocate lots of memory.

If we were to try to apply a memory limit to this stress container after starting it, we would find that the kernel won't let us, because it will have already grabbed too much memory. So instead we'll apply it immediately in the YAML configuration. As before, we need a Pod:

po-mlim.yaml
```
---
metadata:
  name: stress2
  namespace: crio
linux:
  cgroup_parent: pod.slice
  security_context:
    namespace_options:
      network: 2
```

This is identical to the Pod we used for CPU limit, but the name is different to avoid a collision. As we did earlier, we are asking CRI-O to put the cgroup into *pod.slice* so that we can find it easily.

We also need a container definition:

co-mlim.yaml
```
---
---
metadata:
  name: stress2
image:
  image: docker.io/bookofkubernetes/stress:stable
args:
  - "--vm"
  - "1"
  - "--vm-bytes"
❶  - "512M"
  - "-v"
linux:
  resources:
❷   memory_limit_in_bytes: 268435456
    cpu_period: 100000
❸   cpu_quota: 10000
```

The new resource limit is memory_limit_in_bytes, which we set to 256MiB ❷. We keep the CPU quota in there ❸ because continuously trying to allocate memory is going to use a lot of CPU. Finally, in the args section, we tell stress to try to allocate 512MB of memory ❶.

We can run this using similar crictl commands to what we've previously used:

```
root@host01:~# cd /opt
root@host01:/opt# PML_ID=$(crictl runp po-mlim.yaml)
root@host01:/opt# CML_ID=$(crictl create $PML_ID co-mlim.yaml po-mlim.yaml)
root@host01:/opt# crictl start $CML_ID
...
```

If we tell crictl to list containers, everything seems okay:

```
root@host01:/opt# crictl ps
CONTAINER    IMAGE                               ... STATE   ...
31025f098a6c9 docker.io/bookofkubernetes/stress:stable ... Running ...
```

This reports that the container is in a Running state. However, behind the scenes, stress is struggling to allocate memory. We can see this if we print out the log messages coming from the stress container:

```
root@host01:/opt# crictl logs $CML_ID
...
stress-ng: info:  [6] dispatching hogs: 1 vm
...
```

```
stress-ng: debug: [11] stress-ng-vm: started [11] (instance 0)
stress-ng: debug: [11] stress-ng-vm using method 'all'
stress-ng: debug: [11] stress-ng-vm: child died: signal 9 'SIGKILL' (instance 0)
stress-ng: debug: [11] stress-ng-vm: assuming killed by OOM killer, restarting again...
stress-ng: debug: [11] stress-ng-vm: child died: signal 9 'SIGKILL' (instance 0)
stress-ng: debug: [11] stress-ng-vm: assuming killed by OOM killer, restarting again...
```

Stress is reporting that its memory allocation process is being continuously killed by the "out of memory."

And we can see the kernel reporting that the oom_reaper is indeed the reason that the processes are being killed:

```
root@host01:/opt# dmesg | grep -i oom_reaper | tail -n 1
[  696.651056] oom_reaper: reaped process 8756 (stress-ng-vm)...
```

The OOM killer is the same feature Linux uses when the whole system is low on memory and it needs to kill one or more processes to protect the system. In this case, it is sending SIGKILL to the process to keep the cgroup under its memory limit. SIGKILL is a message to the process that it should immediately terminate without any cleanup.

WHY USE THE OOM KILLER?

When we used regular limits to control memory, an attempt to exceed our limits caused the memory allocation to fail, but the kernel didn't use the OOM killer to kill our process. Why the difference? The answer is that this is the nature of containers. As we look at architecting reliable systems using containerized microservices, we'll see that a container is supposed to be quick to start and quick to scale. This means that each individual container in our application is intentionally just not very important. This further means that the idea that one of our containers could be killed unexpectedly is not really a concern. Add to that the fact that not checking for memory allocation errors is one of the most common bugs, so it's considered safer simply to kill the process.

That said, it's worth noting that it is possible to turn off the OOM killer for a cgroup. However, rather than having the memory allocation fail, the effect is to just pause the process until other processes in the group free up memory. That's actually worse, as now we have a process that isn't officially killed but isn't doing anything useful either.

Before we move on, let's put this continuously failing stress container out of its misery:

```
root@host01:/opt# crictl stop $CML_ID
...
root@host01:/opt# crictl rm $CML_ID
...
root@host01:/opt# crictl stopp $PML_ID
Stopped sandbox ...
```

```
root@host01:/opt# crictl rmp $PML_ID
Removed sandbox ...
root@host01:/opt# cd
```

Stopping and removing the container and Pod prevents the stress container from wasting CPU by continually trying to restart the memory allocation process.

Network Bandwidth Limits

In this chapter, we've moved from resources that are easy to limit to resources that are more difficult to limit. We started with CPU, where the kernel is wholly in charge of which process gets CPU time and how much time it gets before being preempted. Then we looked at memory, where the kernel doesn't have the ability to force a process to give up memory, but at least the kernel can control whether a memory allocation is successful, or it can kill a process that requests too much memory.

Now we're moving on to network bandwidth, for which control is even more difficult to exert for two important reasons. First, network devices don't really "sum up" like CPU or memory, so we'll need to limit usage at the level of each individual network device. Second, our system can't really control what is sent to it across the network; we can only completely control *egress* bandwidth, the traffic that is sent on a given network device.

PROPER NETWORK MANAGEMENT

To have a completely reliable cluster, merely controlling egress traffic is clearly insufficient. A process that downloads a large file is going to saturate the available bandwidth just as much as one that uploads lots of data. However, we really can't control what comes into our host via a given network interface, at least not at the host level. If we really want to manage network bandwidth, we need to handle that kind of thing at a switch or a router. For example, it is very common to divide up the physical network into virtual local area networks (VLANs). One VLAN might be an administration network used for auditing, logging, and for administrators to ensure that they can log in. We might also reserve another VLAN for important container traffic, or use traffic shaping to ensure that important packets get through. As long as we perform this kind of configuration at the switch, we can typically allow the remaining bandwidth to be "best effort."

Although Linux does provide some cgroup capability for network interfaces, these would only help us prioritize and classify network traffic. For this reason, rather than using cgroups to control egress traffic, we're going to directly configure the Linux kernel's *traffic control* capabilities. We'll test network performance using iperf3, apply a limit to outgoing traffic, and then test again. In this chapter's examples, *host02* with IP address 192.168.61.12 was set up automatically with an iperf3 server running so that we can send data to it from *host01*.

Let's begin by seeing the egress bandwidth we can get on an unlimited interface:

```
root@host01:~# iperf3 -c 192.168.61.12
Connecting to host 192.168.61.12, port 5201
[  5] local 192.168.61.11 port 49044 connected to 192.168.61.12 port 5201
...
[ ID] Interval           Transfer     Bitrate         Retr
[  5]   0.00-10.00  sec  2.18 GBytes  1.87 Gbits/sec  13184             sender
[  5]   0.00-10.00  sec  2.18 GBytes  1.87 Gbits/sec                    receiver
...
```

This example shows gigabit network speeds. Depending on how you're running the examples, you might see lower or higher figures. Now that we have a baseline, we can use tc to set a quota going out. You'll want to choose a quota that makes sense given your bandwidth; most likely enforcing a 100Mb cap will work:

```
root@host01:~# IFACE=$(ip -o addr | grep 192.168.61.11 | awk '{print $2}')
root@host01:~# tc qdisc add dev $IFACE root tbf rate 100mbit \
  burst 256kbit latency 400ms
```

The name of the network interface may be different on different systems, so we use ip addr to identify which interface we want to control. Then, we use tc to actually apply the limit. The token tbf in the command stands for *token bucket filter*. With a token bucket filter, every packet consumes tokens. The bucket refills with tokens over time, but if at any point the bucket is empty, packets are queued until tokens are available. By controlling the size of the bucket and the rate at which it refills, it is very easy for the kernel to place a bandwidth limit.

Now that we've applied a limit to this interface, let's see it in action by running the exact same iperf3 command again:

```
root@host01:~# iperf3 -c 192.168.61.12
Connecting to host 192.168.61.12, port 5201
[  5] local 192.168.61.11 port 49048 connected to 192.168.61.12 port 5201
...
[ ID] Interval           Transfer     Bitrate         Retr
[  5]   0.00-10.00  sec   114 MBytes  95.7 Mbits/sec    0             sender
[  5]   0.00-10.01  sec   113 MBytes  94.5 Mbits/sec                  receiver
...
```

As expected, we are now limited to 100Mbps on this interface.

Of course, in this case, we limited the bandwidth available on this network interface for everyone on the system. To use this ability properly to control bandwidth usage, we need to target the limits more precisely. However, in order to do that, we need to isolate a process to its own set of network interfaces, which is the subject of the next chapter.

Final Thoughts

Ensuring that a process doesn't cause problems for other processes on the system includes making sure that it fairly shares system resources such as CPU, memory, and network bandwidth. In this chapter, we looked at how Linux provides control groups (cgroups) that manage CPU and memory limits and traffic control capabilities that manage network interfaces. As we create a Kubernetes cluster and deploy containers to it, we'll see how Kubernetes uses these underlying Linux kernel features to ensure that containers are scheduled on hosts with sufficient resources and that containers are well behaved on those hosts.

We've now moved through some of the most important elements of process isolation provided by a container runtime, but there are two types of isolation that we haven't explored yet: network isolation and storage isolation. In the next chapter, we'll look at how Linux network namespaces are used to make each container appear to have its own set of network interfaces, complete with separate IP addresses and ports. We'll also look at how traffic from those separate container interfaces flows through our system so that containers can talk to one another and to the rest of the network.

4

NETWORK NAMESPACES

 Understanding container networking is the biggest challenge in building modern applications based on containerized microservices. First, networking is complicated even without introducing containers. Multiple levels of abstraction are involved just in sending a simple `ping` from one physical server to another. Second, containers introduce additional complexity because each has its own set of virtual network devices to make it look like a separate machine. Not only that, but a container orchestration framework like Kubernetes then adds another layer of complexity by adding an "overlay" network through which containers can communicate even when they are running on different hosts.

In this chapter, we will look in detail at how container networking operates. We will look at a container's virtual network devices, including how each network device is assigned a separate IP address that can reach the host. We'll see how containers on the same host are connected to one another through a bridge device and how container devices are configured to route traffic. Finally, we'll examine how address translation is used to enable containers to connect to other hosts without exposing container networking internals on the host's network.

Network Isolation

In Chapter 2, we discussed how isolation is important to system reliability because processes generally can't affect something they cannot see. This is one important reason for network isolation in containers. Another reason is ease of configuration. To run a process that acts as a server, such as a web server, we need to choose one or more network interfaces on which that server will listen, and we need to choose a port number on which it will listen. We can't have two processes listening on the same port on the same interface.

As a result, it's common for a process that acts as a server to provide a way to configure which port it should use to listen for connections. However, that still requires us to know what other servers are out there and what ports they are using so that we can ensure there are no conflicts. That would be impossible with a container orchestration framework like Kubernetes because new processes can show up at any time, from different users, with a need to listen on any port number.

The way to get around this is to provide separate virtual network interfaces for each container. That way, a process in a container can choose any port it wants—it will be listening on a different network interface from a process in a different container. Let's see a quick example.

NOTE *The example repository for this book is at* https://github.com/book-of
-kubernetes/examples. *See "Running Examples" on page xx for details on getting set up.*

We'll run two instances of an NGINX web server; each instance will listen on port 80. As before, we'll use CRI-O and crictl, but we'll use a script to cut down on the typing:

```
root@host01:~# cd /opt
root@host01:/opt# source nginx.sh
...
```

The source before nginx.sh is important; it ensures that the script is run in a way that makes the environment variables it sets available in our shell for future commands. Inside *nginx.sh* are the usual crictl runp, crictl create, and crictl start commands we've used in previous chapters. The YAML files are also very similar to examples we've seen before; the only difference is that we use a container image that has NGINX installed.

Let's verify that we have two NGINX servers running:

```
root@host01:/opt# crictl ps
CONTAINER      IMAGE        ... NAME      ...
```

```
ae341010886ae  .../nginx:latest ... nginx2  ...
6a95800b16f15  .../nginx:latest ... nginx1  ...
```

We can also verify that both NGINX servers are listening on port 80, the standard port for web servers:

```
root@host01:/opt# crictl exec $N1C_ID cat /proc/net/tcp
  sl  local_address ...
   0: 00000000:0050 ...
root@host01:/opt# crictl exec $N2C_ID cat /proc/net/tcp
  sl  local_address ...
   0: 00000000:0050 ...
```

We look at the open port by printing */proc/net/tcp* because we need to run this command inside the NGINX container, where we don't have standard Linux commands like netstat or ss. As we saw in Chapter 2, in a container we have a separate mnt namespace providing a separate filesystem for each container, so only the executables available in that separate filesystem can be run in that namespace.

The port shown in both cases is 0050 in hexadecimal, which is port 80 in decimal. If these two processes were running together on the same system without network isolation, they wouldn't both be able to listen on port 80, but in this case, the two NGINX instances have separate network interfaces. To explore this further, let's start up a new BusyBox container:

```
root@host01:/opt# source busybox.sh
...
```

BusyBox is now running in addition to our two NGINX containers:

```
root@host01:/opt# crictl ps
CONTAINER      IMAGE                ... NAME     ...
189dd26766d26  .../busybox:latest ... busybox ...
ae341010886ae  .../nginx:latest    ... nginx2  ...
6a95800b16f15  .../nginx:latest    ... nginx1  ...
```

Let's start a shell inside the container:

```
root@host01:/opt# crictl exec -ti $B1C_ID /bin/sh
/ #
```

Listing 4-1 shows the container's network devices and addresses.

```
/ # ip addr
1: lo: <LOOPBACK,UP,LOWER_UP> mtu 65536 qdisc noqueue ...
    link/loopback 00:00:00:00:00:00 brd 00:00:00:00:00:00
    inet 127.0.0.1/8 scope host lo
       valid_lft forever preferred_lft forever
    inet6 ::1/128 scope host
       valid_lft forever preferred_lft forever
```

```
3: eth0@if7: <BROADCAST,MULTICAST,UP,LOWER_UP,M-DOWN> mtu 1500 qdisc noqueue
    link/ether 9a:7c:73:2f:f7:1a brd ff:ff:ff:ff:ff:ff
    inet 10.85.0.4/16 brd 10.85.255.255 scope global eth0
        valid_lft forever preferred_lft forever
    inet6 fe80::987c:73ff:fe2f:f71a/64 scope link
        valid_lft forever preferred_lft forever
```

Listing 4-1: BusyBox network

Ignoring the standard loopback device, we see a network device with
10.85.0.4 for an IP address. This does not correspond at all with the IP address of the host, which is 192.168.61.11; it is on a different network entirely.
Because our container is on a separate network, we might not expect to
be able to ping the underlying host system from inside the container, but it
works, as Listing 4-2 demonstrates.

```
/ # ping -c 1 192.168.61.11
PING 192.168.61.11 (192.168.61.11): 56 data bytes
64 bytes from 192.168.61.11: seq=0 ttl=64 time=7.471 ms

--- 192.168.61.11 ping statistics ---
1 packets transmitted, 1 packets received, 0% packet loss
round-trip min/avg/max = 7.471/7.471/7.471 ms
```

Listing 4-2: BusyBox ping test

For traffic to get from our container to the host network, there must be
an entry in the routing table to make that happen. As Listing 4-3 illustrates,
we can verify this by using the ip command.

```
/ # ip route
default via 10.85.0.1 dev eth0
10.85.0.0/16 dev eth0 scope link  src 10.85.0.4
```

Listing 4-3: BusyBox routes

As expected, there is a default route. When we sent the ping, our Busy-
Box container reached out to 10.85.0.1, which then had the ability to send
the ping onward until it reached 192.168.61.11.

We'll leave all three containers running to explore them further, but
let's exit our BusyBox shell to get back to the host:

```
/ # exit
```

The view of the network from inside the container shows why our two
NGINX servers are both able to listen on port 80. As mentioned earlier, only
one process can listen on a port for a particular interface, but of course, if
each NGINX server has a separate network interface, there is no conflict.

Network Namespaces

CRI-O is using Linux network namespaces to create this isolation. We explored network namespaces briefly in Chapter 2; in this chapter, we'll look at them in more detail.

First, let's use the lsns command to list the network namespaces that CRI-O has created for our containers:

```
root@host01:/opt# lsns -t net
        NS TYPE NPROCS   PID USER    NETNSID NSFS                  COMMAND
4026531992 net     114     1 root   unassigned                     /sbin/init
4026532196 net       4  5801 root          0 /run/netns/ab8be6e6... /pause
4026532272 net       4  5937 root          1 /run/netns/8ffe0394... /pause
4026532334 net       2  6122 root          2 /run/netns/686d71d9... /pause
```

In addition to the root network namespace that is used for all the processes that aren't in a container, we see three network namespaces, one for each Pod we've created.

When we use CRI-O with crictl, the network namespace actually belongs to the Pod. The pause process that is listed here exists so that the namespaces can continue to exist even as containers come and go inside the Pod.

In the previous example, there are four network namespaces. The first one is the root namespace that was created when our host booted. The other three were created for each of the containers we have started so far: two NGINX containers and one BusyBox container.

Inspecting Network Namespaces

To learn about how network namespaces work and manipulate them, we'll use the ip netns command to list network namespaces:

```
root@host01:/opt# ip netns list
7c185da0-04e2-4321-b2eb-da18ceb5fcf6 (id: 2)
d26ca6c6-d524-4ae2-b9b7-5489c3db92ce (id: 1)
38bbb724-3420-46f0-bb50-9a150a9f0889 (id: 0)
```

This command looks in a different configuration location to find network namespaces, so only the three container namespaces are listed.

We want to capture the network namespace for our BusyBox container. It's one of the three listed, and we can guess that it is the one labeled (id: 2) because we created it last, but we can also use crictl and jq to extract the information we need:

```
root@host01:/opt# NETNS_PATH=$(crictl inspectp $B1P_ID |
  jq -r '.info.runtimeSpec.linux.namespaces[]|select(.type=="network").path')
root@host01:/opt# echo $NETNS_PATH
/var/run/netns/7c185da0-04e2-4321-b2eb-da18ceb5fcf6
root@host01:/opt# NETNS=$(basename $NETNS_PATH)
```

```
root@host01:/opt# echo $NETNS
7c185da0-04e2-4321-b2eb-da18ceb5fcf6
```

If you run crictl inspectp $B1P_ID by itself, you'll see a wealth of information about the BusyBox Pod. Out of all that information, we want only the information about the network namespace, so we use jq to extract that information in three steps. First, it reaches down into the JSON data to pull out all of the namespaces associated with this Pod. It then selects only the namespace that has a type field of network. Finally, it extracts the path field for that namespace and stores it in the environment variable NETNS_PATH.

The value that crictl returns is the full path to the network namespace under */var/run*. For our upcoming commands, we want only the value of the namespace, so we use basename to strip off the path. Also, because this information will be a lot more usable if we assign it to an environment variable, we do that, and then we use echo to print the value so that we can confirm it all worked.

Of course, for interactive debugging, you can often just scroll through the entire contents of crictl inspectp (for Pods) and crictl inspect (for containers) and pick out the values you want. But this approach of extracting data with jq is very useful in scripting or in reducing the amount of output to scan through manually.

Now that we've extracted the network namespace for BusyBox from crictl, let's see what processes are assigned to that namespace:

```
root@host01:/opt# ps --pid $(ip netns pids $NETNS)
PID TTY      STAT   TIME COMMAND
5800 ?       Ss     0:00 /pause
5839 ?       Ss     0:00 /bin/sleep 36000
```

If we just ran ip netns pids $NETNS, we would get a list of the process IDs (PIDs), but no extra information. We take that output and send it to ps --pid, which makes it possible for us to see the name of the commands. As expected, we see a pause process and the sleep process that we specified when we ran the BusyBox container.

In the previous section, we used crictl exec to run a shell inside the container, which enabled us to see what network interfaces were available in that network namespace. Now that we know the ID of the network namespace, we can use ip netns exec to run commands individually from within a network namespace. Running ip netns exec is very powerful in that it is not limited to just networking commands, but could be any process such as a web server. However, note that this is not the same as fully running inside the container, because we are not entering any of the container's other namespaces (for example, the pid namespace used for process isolation).

Next, let's try the ip addr command from within the BusyBox network namespace:

```
root@host01:/opt# ip netns exec $NETNS ip addr
1: lo: <LOOPBACK,UP,LOWER_UP> mtu 65536 qdisc noqueue ...
    link/loopback 00:00:00:00:00:00 brd 00:00:00:00:00:00
```

```
    inet 127.0.0.1/8 scope host lo
        valid_lft forever preferred_lft forever
    inet6 ::1/128 scope host
        valid_lft forever preferred_lft forever
3: eth0@if7: <BROADCAST,MULTICAST,UP,LOWER_UP> mtu 1500 qdisc noqueue ...
    link/ether 9a:7c:73:2f:f7:1a brd ff:ff:ff:ff:ff:ff link-netnsid 0
    inet 10.85.0.4/16 brd 10.85.255.255 scope global eth0
        valid_lft forever preferred_lft forever
    inet6 fe80::987c:73ff:fe2f:f71a/64 scope link
        valid_lft forever preferred_lft forever
```

The list of network devices and IP addresses that we see here matches what we saw when we ran commands inside our BusyBox container in Listing 4-1. CRI-O is creating these network devices and placing them in the network namespace. (We will see how CRI-O was configured to perform container networking when we look at Kubernetes networking in Chapter 8.) For now, let's look at how we can create our own devices and namespaces for network isolation. This will also show us how to debug container networking when something isn't working correctly.

Creating Network Namespaces

We can create a network namespace with a single command:

```
root@host01:/opt# ip netns add myns
```

This new namespace immediately shows up in the list:

```
root@host01:/opt# ip netns list
myns
7c185da0-04e2-4321-b2eb-da18ceb5fcf6 (id: 2)
d26ca6c6-d524-4ae2-b9b7-5489c3db92ce (id: 1)
38bbb724-3420-46f0-bb50-9a150a9f0889 (id: 0)
```

This namespace isn't very useful yet; it has a loopback interface but nothing else:

```
root@host01:/opt# ip netns exec myns ip addr
1: lo: <LOOPBACK> mtu 65536 qdisc noop state DOWN group default qlen 1000
    link/loopback 00:00:00:00:00:00 brd 00:00:00:00:00:00
```

In addition, even the loopback interface is down, so it couldn't be used. Let's quickly fix that:

```
root@host01:/opt# ip netns exec myns ip link set dev lo up
root@host01:/opt# ip netns exec myns ip addr
1: lo: <LOOPBACK,UP,LOWER_UP> mtu 65536 qdisc noqueue ...
    link/loopback 00:00:00:00:00:00 brd 00:00:00:00:00:00
    inet 127.0.0.1/8 scope host lo
        valid_lft forever preferred_lft forever
```

```
inet6 ::1/128 scope host
    valid_lft forever preferred_lft forever
```

The loopback interface is now up, and it has the typical IP address of 127.0.0.1. A basic loopback ping will now work in this network namespace:

```
root@host01:/opt# ip netns exec myns ping -c 1 127.0.0.1
PING 127.0.0.1 (127.0.0.1) 56(84) bytes of data.
64 bytes from 127.0.0.1: icmp_seq=1 ttl=64 time=0.035 ms

--- 127.0.0.1 ping statistics ---
1 packets transmitted, 1 received, 0% packet loss, time 0ms
rtt min/avg/max/mdev = 0.035/0.035/0.035/0.000 ms
```

The ability to ping the loopback network interface is a useful first test for any networking stack, as it shows the ability to send and receive packets. So, we now have a basic working network stack in our new network namespace, but it still isn't terribly useful because a loopback interface by itself can't talk to anything else on our system. We need to add another network device in this network namespace in order to establish connectivity to the host and the rest of the network.

To do this, we'll create a *virtual Ethernet* (veth) device. You can think of a veth as a virtual network cable. Like a network cable, it has two ends, and whatever goes in one end comes out the other end. For this reason, the term *veth pair* is often used.

We start with a command that creates the veth pair:

```
root@host01:/opt# ip link add myveth-host type veth \
                  peer myveth-myns netns myns
```

This command does three things:

1. Creates a veth device called myveth-host
2. Creates a veth device called myveth-myns
3. Places the device myveth-myns in the network namespace myns

The host side of the veth pair appears in the regular list of network devices on the host:

```
root@host01:/opt# ip addr
...
8: myveth-host@if2: <BROADCAST,MULTICAST> mtu 1500 ... state DOWN ...
    link/ether fe:7a:5d:86:00:d9 brd ff:ff:ff:ff:ff:ff link-netns myns
```

This output shows myveth-host and also that it is connected to a device in the network namespace myns.

If you run this command for yourself and look at the complete list of host network devices, you will notice additional veth devices connected to each of the container network namespaces. These were created by CRI-O when we deployed NGINX and BusyBox.

Similarly, we can see that our `myns` network namespace has a new network interface:

```
root@host01:/opt# ip netns exec myns ip addr
1: lo: <LOOPBACK,UP,LOWER_UP> mtu 65536 qdisc noqueue ...
    link/loopback 00:00:00:00:00:00 brd 00:00:00:00:00:00
    inet 127.0.0.1/8 scope host lo
       valid_lft forever preferred_lft forever
    inet6 ::1/128 scope host
       valid_lft forever preferred_lft forever
2: myveth-myns@if8: <BROADCAST,MULTICAST> mtu 1500 ... state DOWN ...
    link/ether 26:0f:64:a8:37:1f brd ff:ff:ff:ff:ff:ff link-netnsid 0
```

As before, this interface is currently down. We need to bring up both sides of the veth pair before we can start communicating. We also need to assign an IP address to the `myveth-myns` side to enable it to communicate:

```
root@host01:/opt# ip netns exec myns ip addr add 10.85.0.254/16 \
                    dev myveth-myns
root@host01:/opt# ip netns exec myns ip link set dev myveth-myns up
root@host01:/opt# ip link set dev myveth-host up
```

A quick check confirms that we've successfully configured an IP address and brought up the network:

```
root@host01:/opt# ip netns exec myns ip addr
1: lo: <LOOPBACK,UP,LOWER_UP> mtu 65536 qdisc noqueue ...
    link/loopback 00:00:00:00:00:00 brd 00:00:00:00:00:00
    inet 127.0.0.1/8 scope host lo
       valid_lft forever preferred_lft forever
    inet6 ::1/128 scope host
       valid_lft forever preferred_lft forever
2: myveth-myns@if8: <BROADCAST,MULTICAST,UP,LOWER_UP> ... state UP ...
    link/ether 26:0f:64:a8:37:1f brd ff:ff:ff:ff:ff:ff link-netnsid 0
    inet 10.85.0.254/16 scope global myveth-myns
       valid_lft forever preferred_lft forever
    inet6 fe80::240f:64ff:fea8:371f/64 scope link
       valid_lft forever preferred_lft forever
```

In addition to the loopback interface, we now see an additional interface with the IP address 10.85.0.254. What happens if we try to ping this new IP address? It turns out we can indeed ping it, but only from within the network namespace:

```
root@host01:/opt# ip netns exec myns ping -c 1 10.85.0.254
PING 10.85.0.254 (10.85.0.254) 56(84) bytes of data.
64 bytes from 10.85.0.254: icmp_seq=1 ttl=64 time=0.030 ms

--- 10.85.0.254 ping statistics ---
❶ 1 packets transmitted, 1 received, 0% packet loss, time 0ms
```

```
rtt min/avg/max/mdev = 0.030/0.030/0.030/0.000 ms
root@host01:/opt# ping -c 1 10.85.0.254
PING 10.85.0.254 (10.85.0.254) 56(84) bytes of data.
From 10.85.0.1 icmp_seq=1 Destination Host Unreachable

--- 10.85.0.254 ping statistics ---
❷ 1 packets transmitted, 0 received, +1 errors, 100% packet loss, time 0ms
```

The first ping command, run using ip netns exec so that it runs within
the network namespace, shows a successful response ❶. However, the second ping command, run without ip netns exec, shows that no packets were
received ❷. The problem is that we have successfully created a network interface inside our network namespace, and we have the other end of the veth
pair on our host network, but we haven't connected up a corresponding network device on the host, so there's no host network interface that can talk to
the interface in the network namespace.

At the same time, when we ran a ping test from our BusyBox container
in Listing 4-2, we were able to ping the host with no trouble. Clearly, there
must be more configuration that CRI-O did for us when it created our containers. Let's explore that in the next section.

Bridge Interfaces

The host side of the veth pair currently isn't connected to anything, so it
isn't surprising that our network namespace can't talk to the outside world
yet. To fix that, let's look at one of the veth pairs that CRI-O created:

```
root@host01:/opt# ip addr
...
7: veth062abfa6@if3: <BROADCAST,MULTICAST,UP,LOWER_UP> ... master cni0 ...
    link/ether fe:6b:21:9b:d0:d2 brd ff:ff:ff:ff:ff:ff link-netns ...
    inet6 fe80::fc6b:21ff:fe9b:d0d2/64 scope link
        valid_lft forever preferred_lft forever
...
```

Unlike the interface we created, this interface specifies master cni0, which
shows that it belongs to a *network bridge*. A network bridge exists to connect
multiple interfaces together. You can think of it as an Ethernet switch because it routes traffic from one network interface to another based on the
media access control (MAC) address of the interfaces.

We can see the bridge cni0 in the list of network devices on the host:

```
root@host01:/opt# ip addr
...
4: cni0: <BROADCAST,MULTICAST,UP,LOWER_UP> mtu 1500 qdisc noqueue ...
    link/ether 8e:0c:1c:7d:94:75 brd ff:ff:ff:ff:ff:ff
    inet 10.85.0.1/16 brd 10.85.255.255 scope global cni0
        valid_lft forever preferred_lft forever
    inet6 fe80::8c0c:1cff:fe7d:9475/64 scope link
```

```
            valid_lft forever preferred_lft forever
...
```

The bridge is a little smarter than a typical Ethernet switch in that it provides some firewall and routing capabilities. It also has an IP address of 10.85.0.1. This IP address is the same as we saw with the default route for our BusyBox container in Listing 4-3, so we've started to solve the mystery of how our BusyBox container is able to talk to hosts outside of its own network.

Adding Interfaces to a Bridge

To inspect the bridge and add devices to it, we'll use the brctl command. Let's inspect the bridge first:

```
root@host01:/opt# brctl show
bridge name      bridge id            STP enabled      interfaces
cni0             8000.8e0c1c7d9475    no               veth062abfa6
                                                        veth43ab68cd
                                                        vetha251c619
```

The bridge cni0 has three interfaces on it, corresponding to the host side of the veth pair for each of the three containers we have running (two NGINX and one BusyBox). Let's take advantage of this existing bridge to set up network connectivity to the namespace we created:

```
root@host01:/opt# brctl addif cni0 myveth-host
root@host01:/opt# brctl show
bridge name      bridge id            STP enabled      interfaces
cni0             8000.8e0c1c7d9475    no               myveth-host
                                                        veth062abfa6
                                                        veth43ab68cd
                                                        vetha251c619
```

The host side of our veth pair is now connected to the bridge, which means that we can now ping into the namespace from the host:

```
root@host01:/opt# ping -c 1 10.85.0.254
PING 10.85.0.254 (10.85.0.254) 56(84) bytes of data.
64 bytes from 10.85.0.254: icmp_seq=1 ttl=64 time=0.194 ms

--- 10.85.0.254 ping statistics ---
❶ 1 packets transmitted, 1 received, 0% packet loss, time 0ms
rtt min/avg/max/mdev = 0.194/0.194/0.194/0.000 ms
```

The fact that a packet was received ❶ shows that we set up a working connection. We should be pleased that it worked, but if we want to really understand this, we can't be satisfied with saying that we can ping this interface "from the host." We need to be more specific as to exactly how traffic is flowing.

Tracing Traffic

Let's actually trace this traffic to see what's happening when we run the `ping` command. We will use `tcpdump` to print out the traffic. First, let's start a `ping` command in the background to create some traffic to trace:

```
root@host01:/opt# ping 10.85.0.254 >/dev/null 2>&1 &
...
```

We send the output to */dev/null* so that it doesn't clutter up our session. Now, let's use tcpdump to see the traffic:

```
root@host01:/opt# timeout 1s tcpdump -i any -n icmp
tcpdump: verbose output suppressed, use -v or -vv for full protocol decode
listening on any, link-type LINUX_SLL (Linux cooked v1), ...
17:37:33.204863 IP 10.85.0.1 > 10.85.0.254: ICMP echo request, ...
17:37:33.204894 IP 10.85.0.1 > 10.85.0.254: ICMP echo request, ...
17:37:33.204936 IP 10.85.0.254 > 10.85.0.1: ICMP echo reply, ...
17:37:33.204936 IP 10.85.0.254 > 10.85.0.1: ICMP echo reply, ...

4 packets captured
4 packets received by filter
0 packets dropped by kernel
root@host01:/opt# killall ping
```

We use `timeout` to prevent `tcpdump` from running indefinitely, and we also use `killall` afterward to stop the `ping` command and discontinue it running in the background.

The output shows that the `ping` is originating from the bridge interface, which has IP address `10.85.0.1`. This is because of the host's routing table:

```
root@host01:/opt# ip route
...
10.85.0.0/16 dev cni0 proto kernel scope link src 10.85.0.1
192.168.61.0/24 dev enp0s8 proto kernel scope link src 192.168.61.11
```

When CRI-O created the bridge and configured its IP address, it also set up a route so that all traffic destined for the `10.85.0.0/16` network (that is, all traffic from `10.85.0.0` through `10.85.255.255`) would use `cni0`. This is enough information for the `ping` command to know where to send its packet, and the bridge handles the rest.

The fact that the `ping` is coming from the bridge interface of `10.85.0.1` rather than the host interface of `192.168.61.11` actually makes a big difference, as we can see if we try to run the `ping` the other way around. Let's try to ping from within the namespace to the host network:

```
root@host01:/opt# ip netns exec myns ping -c 1 192.168.61.11
ping: connect: Network is unreachable
```

The issue here is that the interface in our network namespace doesn't know how to reach the host network. The bridge is available and willing to route traffic onto the host network, but we haven't configured the necessary route to use it. Let's do that now:

```
root@host01:/opt# ip netns exec myns ip route add default via 10.85.0.1
```

And now the ping works:

```
root@host01:/opt# ip netns exec myns ping -c 1 192.168.61.11
PING 192.168.61.11 (192.168.61.11) 56(84) bytes of data.
64 bytes from 192.168.61.11: icmp_seq=1 ttl=64 time=0.097 ms

--- 192.168.61.11 ping statistics ---
1 packets transmitted, 1 received, 0% packet loss, time 0ms
rtt min/avg/max/mdev = 0.097/0.097/0.097/0.000 ms
```

This illustrates an important rule to remember when debugging network problems: it's very easy to jump to conclusions about what network traffic is really being sent and received. There is often no substitute for using tracing to see what the traffic really looks like.

IP ADDRESSES ON THE HOST

This approach is not the only one that results in connectivity from the host into the network namespace. We also could have assigned an IP address directly to the host side of the veth pair. However, even though that would have enabled communication from the host into our network namespace, it wouldn't provide a way for multiple network namespaces to communicate with one another. Using a bridge interface, as CRI-O does, enables the interconnection of all of the containers on a host, making them all appear to be on the same network.

This also explains why we didn't assign an IP address to the host side of the veth pair. When working with bridges, only the bridge interface gets an IP address. Interfaces added to the bridge do not.

With that last change, it would seem like we've matched the network configuration of our containers, but we are still missing the ability to communicate with the broader network outside of host01. We can demonstrate this by trying to ping from our network namespace to host02, which is on the same internal network as host01 and has the IP address 192.168.61.12. If we try a ping from our BusyBox container, it works:

```
root@host01:/opt# crictl exec $B1C_ID ping -c 1 192.168.61.12
PING 192.168.61.12 (192.168.61.12): 56 data bytes
64 bytes from 192.168.61.12: seq=0 ttl=63 time=0.816 ms

--- 192.168.61.12 ping statistics ---
1 packets transmitted, 1 packets received, 0% packet loss
round-trip min/avg/max = 0.816/0.816/0.816 ms
```

The `ping` output reports that a packet was received. However, if we try the same command using the network namespace we created, it doesn't work:

```
root@host01:/opt# ip netns exec myns ping -c 1 192.168.61.12
PING 192.168.61.12 (192.168.61.12) 56(84) bytes of data.

--- 192.168.61.12 ping statistics ---
1 packets transmitted, 0 received, 100% packet loss, time 0ms
```

This command reports that no packets were received.

Really, we ought to be surprised that the `ping` from our BusyBox container worked. After all, `host02` doesn't know anything about the BusyBox container, or the `cni0` bridge interface, or the `10.85.0.0/16` network that the containers are in. How is it possible for `host02` to exchange a ping with our BusyBox container? To understand that, we need to look at network masquerade.

Masquerade

Masquerade, also known as Network Address Translation (NAT), is used every day in networking. For example, most home connections to the internet are provided with only a single IP address that is addressable from the internet, but many devices within the home network need an internet connection. It is the job of a router to make it appear that all traffic from that network is originating from a single IP address. It does this by rewriting the *source* IP address of outgoing traffic while tracking all outgoing connections so that it can rewrite the *destination* IP address of any replies.

NOTE *The kind of NAT that we are talking about here is technically known as Source NAT (SNAT). Don't get hung up on the name, though; for it to work correctly, any reply packets must have their destination rewritten. The term Source in this case just means that the source address is what's rewritten when a new connection is initiated.*

Masquerading sounds like just what we need to connect our containers running in the `10.85.0.0/16` network to the host network, `192.168.61.0/24`, and in fact it is exactly how it worked. When we sent a ping from our BusyBox container, the source IP address was rewritten such that the ping appeared to come from the `host01` IP `192.168.61.11`. When `host02` responded, it sent its reply to `192.168.61.11`, but the destination was rewritten so that it was actually sent to the BusyBox container.

Let's trace the `ping` traffic all the way through to demonstrate:

```
root@host01:/opt# crictl exec $B1C_ID ping 192.168.61.12 >/dev/null 2>&1 &
[1] 6335
root@host01:/opt# timeout 1s tcpdump -i any -n icmp
tcpdump: verbose output suppressed, use -v or -vv for full protocol decode
listening on any, link-type LINUX_SLL (Linux cooked v1)...
```

```
18:53:44.310789 IP 10.85.0.4 ❶ > 192.168.61.12: ICMP echo request, id 12, seq 17...
18:53:44.310789 IP 10.85.0.4 > 192.168.61.12: ICMP echo request, id 12, seq 17...
18:53:44.310876 IP 192.168.61.11 ❷ > 192.168.61.12: ICMP echo request, id 12, seq 17...
18:53:44.311619 IP 192.168.61.12 > 192.168.61.11: ICMP echo reply, ❸ id 12, seq 17...
18:53:44.311648 IP 192.168.61.12 > 10.85.0.4: ❹ ICMP echo reply, id 12, seq 17...
18:53:44.311656 IP 192.168.61.12 > 10.85.0.4: ICMP echo reply, id 12, seq 17...

6 packets captured
6 packets received by filter
0 packets dropped by kernel
root@host01:/opt# killall ping
```

When the ping originates from within our BusyBox container, it has a source IP address of 10.85.0.4 ❶. This address is rewritten, making the ping appear to be coming from the host IP 192.168.61.11 ❷. Of course, host02 knows how to respond to a ping coming from that address, so the ping is answered ❸. At this point, the other half of the masquerade takes effect, and the destination is rewritten to 10.85.0.4 ❹. The result is that the BusyBox container is able to send a packet to a separate host and get a reply.

To complete the setup for our network namespace, we need a similar rule to masquerade traffic coming from 10.85.0.254. We can start by using iptables to look at the rules that CRI-O created when it configured the containers:

```
root@host01:/opt# iptables -t nat -n -L
...
Chain POSTROUTING (policy ACCEPT)
target                           prot opt source      destination ...
CNI-f82910b3a7e28baf6aedc0d3     all  --  10.85.0.2   anywhere      ...
CNI-7f8aa3d8a4f621b186149f43     all  --  10.85.0.3   anywhere      ...
CNI-48ad69d30fe932fda9ea71d2     all  --  10.85.0.4   anywhere      ...

Chain CNI-48ad69d30fe932fda9ea71d2 (1 references)
target      prot opt source           destination
ACCEPT      all  --  anywhere         10.85.0.0/16 ...
MASQUERADE  all  --  anywhere         !224.0.0.0/4 ...
...
```

Masquerading starts when the connection is initiated; in this case, when traffic has a source address in the 10.85.0.0/16 network. For this reason, the POSTROUTING chain is used, because it sees all outgoing traffic. There is a rule in the POSTROUTING chain for each container; each rule invokes a CNI chain for that container.

For brevity, only one of the three CNI chains is shown. The other two are identical. The CNI chain first does an ACCEPT for all traffic that is local to the container network, so this traffic won't be masqueraded. It then sets up masquerade for all traffic (except 224.0.0.0/4, which is multicast traffic that cannot be masqueraded because there is no way to properly route replies).

What's missing from this configuration is a matching setup for traffic from 10.85.0.254, the IP address we assigned to the interface in our network namespace. Let's add that. First, create a new chain in the nat table:

```
root@host01:/opt# iptables -t nat -N chain-myns
```

Next, add a rule to accept all traffic for the local network:

```
root@host01:/opt# iptables -t nat -A chain-myns -d 10.85.0.0/16 -j ACCEPT
```

Now all remaining traffic (except multicast) should be masqueraded:

```
root@host01:/opt# iptables -t nat -A chain-myns \
                  ! -d 224.0.0.0/4 -j MASQUERADE
```

And finally, tell iptables to use this chain for any traffic coming from 10.85.0.254:

```
root@host01:/opt# iptables -t nat -A POSTROUTING -s 10.85.0.254 -j chain-myns
```

We can verify that we did all that correctly by listing the rules again:

```
root@host01:/opt# iptables -t nat -n -L
...
Chain POSTROUTING (policy ACCEPT)
target      prot opt source              destination
chain-myns  all  --  10.85.0.254         anywhere
...
Chain chain-myns (1 references)
target      prot opt source              destination
ACCEPT      all  --  anywhere            10.85.0.0/16
MASQUERADE  all  --  anywhere            !224.0.0.0/4
```

It looks like we have the configuration we need, as this configuration matches the way the virtual network devices were configured for the Busy-Box container. To make sure, let's try a ping to host02 again:

```
root@host01:/opt# ip netns exec myns ping -c 1 192.168.61.12
PING 192.168.61.12 (192.168.61.12) 56(84) bytes of data.
64 bytes from 192.168.61.12: icmp_seq=1 ttl=63 time=0.843 ms

--- 192.168.61.12 ping statistics ---
1 packets transmitted, 1 received, 0% packet loss, time 0ms
rtt min/avg/max/mdev = 0.843/0.843/0.843/0.000 ms
```

Success! We've fully replicated the network isolation and connectivity that CRI-O is providing our containers.

Final Thoughts

Container networking looks deceptively simple when running containers. Each container is provided with its own set of network devices, avoiding the need to worry about port conflicts and reducing the effect that one container can have on another. However, as we've seen in this chapter, this "simple" network isolation requires some complex configuration to enable not just isolation, but also connectivity to other containers and other networks. In Part II, after we properly introduce Kubernetes, we'll return to container networking and show how the complexity only increases when we need to connect containers running on different hosts and load balance traffic across multiple container instances.

For now, we have one more key topic to address with containers before we can move on to Kubernetes. We need to understand how container storage works, including the container image that is used as the base filesystem when a new container is started as well as the temporary storage that a running container uses. In the next chapter, we'll investigate how container storage makes application deployment easier and how a layered filesystem is used to save on storage and improve efficiency.

5

CONTAINER IMAGES AND
RUNTIME LAYERS

 To run a process, we need storage. One of the great advantages of containerized software is the ability to bundle an application for delivery together with its dependencies. As a result, we need to store the executable for the program and any shared libraries it uses. We also need to store configuration files, logs, and any data managed by the program. All of this storage must be isolated so that a container can't interfere with the host system or with other containers. Altogether, this represents a large need for storage, and it means container engines must provide some unique features to be efficient in the use of disk space and bandwidth. In this chapter, we'll explore how the use of a layered filesystem makes container images efficient to download and containers efficient to start.

Filesystem Isolation

In Chapter 2, we saw how we could use a *chroot* environment to create a separate, isolated part of the filesystem that contained only the binaries and libraries we needed to run a process. Even to run a simple ls command, we needed the binary and several libraries. A more fully featured container, such as one running the NGINX web server, needs quite a bit more—a complete set of files for a Linux distribution.

In the chroot example, we built the isolated filesystem from the host system when we were ready to use it. That approach would be impractical for containers. Instead, the isolated filesystem is packaged in a *container image*, which is a ready-to-use bundle that includes all files and metadata, such as environment variables and the default executable.

Container Image Contents

Let's take a quick look inside an NGINX container image. For this chapter, we'll be running commands using Docker because it's still the most common tool for building container images.

NOTE *The example repository for this book is at* https://github.com/book-of-kubernetes/examples. *See "Running Examples" on page xx for details on getting set up.*

Run the following command on *host01* from this chapter's examples to download the image:

```
root@host01:~# docker pull nginx
Using default tag: latest
latest: Pulling from library/nginx
...
Status: Downloaded newer image for nginx:latest
docker.io/library/nginx:latest
```

The docker pull command downloads an image from an *image registry*. An image registry is a web server that implements an API for downloading and publishing container images. We can see the image we've downloaded by listing images with docker images:

```
root@host01:~# docker images
REPOSITORY   TAG      IMAGE ID       CREATED      SIZE
nginx        latest   f0b8a9a54136   7 days ago   133MB
```

This image is 133MB and has a unique identifier of f0b8a9a54136. (Your identifier will be different, as new NGINX container images are built every day.) This image includes not only the NGINX executables and required libraries but also a Linux distribution based on Debian. We saw this briefly in Chapter 1 when we demonstrated a Rocky Linux container on an Ubuntu host and kernel, but let's look at it in a little more detail. Start by running an NGINX container:

```
root@host01:~# docker run --name nginx -d nginx
516d13e912a55cfc6f73f0dd473661d6b7d3b868d5a07a2bc7253971015b6799
```

The `--name` flag gives the container a friendly name that we can use for future commands, whereas the `-d` flag sends it to the background.

Now, let's explore the filesystem of our running container:

```
root@host01:~# docker exec -ti nginx /bin/bash
root@516d13e912a5:/#
```

From here, we can see the various libraries needed for NGINX to work:

```
root@516d13e912a5:/# ldd $(which nginx)
        linux-vdso.so.1 (0x00007ffe2a1fa000)
...
        libc.so.6 => /lib/x86_64-linux-gnu/libc.so.6 (0x00007fe0d6531000)
        /lib64/ld-linux-x86-64.so.2 (0x00007fe0d6ed4000)
```

All of these libraries are part of the container image we downloaded, so our NGINX container does not need (and cannot see) any files from the host system.

Not only do we have a healthy number of libraries present, but we have typical configuration files in */etc* that we would expect for a Debian system:

```
root@516d13e912a5:/# ls -1 /etc
...
debian_version
deluser.conf
dpkg
...
systemd/
...
```

This listing shows that the filesystem even includes directories that aren't really needed for a container, like the */etc/systemd* directory. (Remember, a container is just a set of related processes run under isolation, so a container almost never runs a system service manager like systemd.) This full filesystem is included for a couple reasons. First, many processes were written to expect the usual set of files to be present. Second, it's just easier to build container images starting from a typical Linux distribution.

The separate filesystem for our container is writable as well. While we have this shell open, let's send some random data to a file in the container so that we can inspect that storage from the host. We can then exit the shell:

```
root@516d13e912a5:/# dd if=/dev/urandom of=/tmp/data bs=1M count=10
...
```

```
10485760 bytes (10 MB, 10 MiB) copied, 0.0913977 s, 115 MB/s
root@516d13e912a5:/# exit
```

The `dd` command wrote a 10MB file into the */tmp* directory. Even though we exited the shell, the container is still running, so we can use `docker inspect` to see the amount of disk space this container is using:

```
root@host01:~# docker inspect -s nginx | jq '.[0].SizeRw'
10487109
```

The `-s` flag tells `docker inspect` to report the size of the container. Because `docker inspect` produces a huge JSON output, we use the JSON query tool `jq` to choose the field we want.

The reported size is just about 10MB, suggesting that the container is consuming only the amount of read-write storage required for the file we wrote, plus any files written by NGINX. We'll explore this in more detail as we continue in this chapter.

Image Versions and Layers

The ability to quickly download a prepackaged filesystem to run a process is only one of the advantages of container images. Another is the ability to tag different versions of an image to allow for rapid upgrading. Let's explore this by pulling and running two different versions of Redis, the popular in-memory key–value database:

```
root@host01:~# docker pull redis:6.0.13-alpine
6.0.13-alpine: Pulling from library/redis
❶ 540db60ca938: Pull complete
29712d301e8c: Pull complete
8173c12df40f: Pull complete
...
docker.io/library/redis:6.0.13-alpine
root@host01:~# docker pull redis:6.2.3-alpine
6.2.3-alpine: Pulling from library/redis
❷ 540db60ca938: Already exists
29712d301e8c: Already exists
8173c12df40f: Already exists
...
docker.io/library/redis:6.2.3-alpine
```

The data after the colon is the *image tag* and acts as a version identifier. Previously, when we left this off, Docker defaulted to *latest*, which is a tag like any other, but it is used by convention to refer to the latest published image. By specifying the version, we can ensure that even as newer versions of Redis are released, we will continue to run the same version until we are ready to upgrade. The tag can contain any characters, and it is common to add extra information after a hyphen. In this case, the `-alpine` at the end of the tag indicates that this image is based on Alpine Linux, a lightweight

```
```

Linux distribution that is popular for making container images because of its small size.

One other interesting item of note is the fact that when we downloaded the second version of Redis, some of the content ❷ was flagged as Already exists. Looking at the first Redis download, we see the same unique identifiers are present there ❶. This is because a container image is made up of layers, and these identifiers uniquely describe a layer. If a layer we've already downloaded is used by another image, we don't need to download it again, saving download time. Additionally, each layer needs to be stored only once on disk, saving disk space.

We now have two different versions of Redis downloaded:

```
root@host01:~# docker images | grep redis
redis       6.0.13-alpine   a556c77d3dce   2 weeks ago   31.3MB
redis       6.2.3-alpine    efb4fa30f1cf   2 weeks ago   32.3MB
```

Although Docker is reporting that each image has a size of about 30MB, that is the total size of all the layers and doesn't account for the storage savings that come from shared layers. The actual storage on disk is less, as we can see by examining Docker's use of disk space:

```
root@host01:~# docker system df -v
Images space usage:

REPOSITORY TAG            ... SIZE      SHARED SIZE   UNIQUE SIZE ...
redis      6.0.13-alpine ... 31.33MB   6.905MB       24.42MB      ...
redis      6.2.3-alpine  ... 32.31MB   6.905MB       25.4MB       ...
```

The two Redis images are sharing almost 7MB of base layers.
These two versions of Redis can be run separately:

```
root@host01:~# docker run -d --name redis1 redis:6.0.13-alpine
66dbf56ec0e8db24ca78afc07c68b7d0699d68b4749e0c03310857cfce926366
root@host01:~# docker run -d --name redis2 redis:6.2.3-alpine
9dd3f86a1284171e5ca60f7f8a6a13dc517237826a92b3cb256f5ac64a5f5c31
```

Now that both images are running, we can confirm that our containers have exactly the version of Redis we want, independent of what version might be the latest release and independent of the versions available for our host server:

```
root@host01:~# docker logs redis1 | grep version
1:C 21 May 2021 14:18:24.952 # Redis version=6.0.13, ...
root@host01:~# docker logs redis2 | grep version
1:C 21 May 2021 14:18:36.387 # Redis version=6.2.3, ...
```

This is a big advantage for building reliable systems. We can test our application thoroughly with one version of the software and be sure that version will continue to be used until we choose to upgrade. We can also easily test our software against a new version without having to upgrade a host system.

Building Container Images

In the preceding example, we saw how we could reduce the download and disk requirements for container images by sharing layers. This layer sharing can be used with any container image, not just two different versions of the same software.

The layers in a container image come from the way it is built. A container image build starts with a *base image*. For example, both of our two Redis versions started with the same exact Alpine Linux base image, which is why those layers were shared in that image. Starting from the base image, each step in the build process can produce a new layer. This new layer contains only the changes to the filesystem that came from that build step.

A base image must also come from somewhere, and, ultimately, there must be an initial layer, which is typically a minimal Linux filesystem created from some Linux distribution, transferred into an empty container image, and then expanded to become an initial layer.

Using a Dockerfile

There are many different ways to build container images, but the most popular is to create a file known as a *Dockerfile* or *Containerfile* that specifies the commands and configuration for the image. Here's a simple *Dockerfile* that adds web content to an NGINX image:

Dockerfile
```
---
FROM nginx

# Add index.html
RUN echo "<html><body><h1>Hello World!</h1></body></html>" \
    >/usr/share/nginx/html/index.html
```

Each line in a *Dockerfile* starts with a command that is followed by parameters. Blank lines and content after a # are ignored, and a backslash at the end of a line continues that command onto the next line. There are many possible commands; here are the most common:

FROM   Specify the base image for this build.

RUN   Run a command inside the container.

COPY   Copy files into the container.

ENV   Specify an environment variable.

ENTRYPOINT   Configure the initial process for the container.

CMD   Set default parameters for the initial process.

Docker provides the docker build command to build an image from a *Dockerfile*. The docker build command creates a new image by running each command in the *Dockerfile*, one at a time. Listing 5-1 illustrates how to run docker build.

```
root@host01:~# cd /opt/hello
root@host01:/opt/hello# docker build -t hello .
❶ Sending build context to Docker daemon  2.048kB
  Step 1/2 : FROM nginx
❷ ---> f0b8a9a54136
  Step 2/2 : RUN echo "<html><body><h1>Hello World!</h1></body></html>" ...
❸ ---> Running in 77ba9163d0a5
  Removing intermediate container 77ba9163d0a5
   ---> e9ca31d590f9
  Successfully built e9ca31d590f9
❹ Successfully tagged hello:latest
```

Listing 5-1: Docker build

The -t switch tells docker build to store the image from the build process under the name hello.

Examining the steps in this build process will help clarify how container images are made. First, Docker sends the *build context* to the Docker daemon ❶. The build context is a directory and all of its files and subdirectories. In this case, we specified the build context as the current directory when we added . to the end of the docker build command. The actual container image build happens inside the daemon, so the only files that would be available for a COPY command are those that are in the build context.

Second, Docker identifies our base image, in this case nginx. The unique identifier it displays ❷ matches the one displayed earlier for our NGINX image when we ran docker images. Third, Docker executes the command we specified in the RUN step. This command is actually run inside a container based on our NGINX base image ❸, which means that only the commands installed in the container image are available to run. If we need other commands to be available, we might need to create a RUN step that installs them before we can use them.

After all of the build steps are complete, Docker "tags" the new container image with the name we provided using the -t flag. As before, we didn't specify a version, so latest is used as a default. We now can see this image in the list of available images:

```
root@host01:/opt/hello# docker images | grep hello
hello        latest         e9ca31d590f9   9 minutes ago   133MB
```

The unique identifier for this image matches the output from the end of Listing 5-1. This image is shown as 133MB because it has all of the layers from the NGINX image in addition to the new small HTML file we added. As before, the shared layers are stored only once, so the extra storage required to build this image was very small.

When you try this example yourself, the unique identifier displayed for your "hello" image will be different, even though the Dockerfile has the same content for the HTML file. The identifier for each layer is based not only on the layer's file content but also on the identifier for the layer above it. As a result, if two images have the same identifier, we can be confident that the contents are exactly the same, even if they were built separately.

We can run a container based on this new image just as we would any other image:

```
root@host01:/opt/hello# docker run -d -p 8080:80 hello
83a23cf2921bb37474bfcefb0da45f9953940febfefd01ebadf35405d88c4396
root@host01:/opt/hello# curl http://localhost:8080/
<html><body><h1>Hello World!</h1></body></html>
```

As described in Chapter 1, the -p flag forwards a host port into the container, enabling us to access the NGINX server from the host even though it is running in a separate network namespace. We then can use curl to see that our container has the content we provided.

Tagging and Publishing Images

The image is ready to run locally, but we're not ready yet to publish it to a registry. To publish to a registry, we need to give it a name that includes the full host and path for the registry location to ensure that when we refer to an image, we are getting exactly what we expect.

To demonstrate, let's pull multiple BusyBox images from different registries. We'll start with a BusyBox image from *quay.io*, an alternative container image registry:

```
root@host01:/opt/hello# docker pull quay.io/quay/busybox
...
quay.io/quay/busybox:latest
```

This image name specifies both the host quay.io and the location of the image within that host, quay/busybox. As before, because we didn't specify a version, latest is used as a default. We are able to pull a version called latest because someone has explicitly published a latest version of the image to this registry.

The BusyBox image we get using this command is different from the one we get if we just pull busybox:

```
root@host01:/opt/hello# docker pull busybox
...
docker.io/library/busybox:latest
root@host01:/opt/hello# docker images | grep busybox
busybox              latest      d3cd072556c2   3 days ago     1.24MB
quay.io/quay/busybox latest      e3121c769e39   8 months ago   1.22MB
```

When we use the plain name busybox, Docker defaults to pulling the image from docker.io/library. This registry is known as *Docker Hub*, which you can browse at *https://hub.docker.com*.

Similarly, when we used the plain name hello to build our image, Docker sees it as belonging to docker.io/library. That path is for official Docker images, and, of course, we don't have the right to publish images there.

The automated setup for this chapter includes running a local container registry, which means that we can publish this image to that local registry if we name it correctly:

```
root@host01:/opt/hello# docker tag hello registry.local/hello
root@host01:/opt/hello# docker images | grep hello
hello                   latest        e9ca31d590f9    52 minutes ago    133MB
registry.local/hello    latest        e9ca31d590f9    52 minutes ago    133MB
```

The same image now exists under two different names, providing an extra advantage of the way images are stored by layer. It's cheap to add an extra name for an image. Of course, we could also have used the full name in the first place when we ran docker build, but it is convenient to use shorter names when building and using images locally.

Now that we have named the image correctly, we can publish it using docker push:

```
root@host01:/opt/hello# docker push registry.local/hello
Using default tag: latest
The push refers to repository [registry.local/hello]
...
```

Our local registry starts out empty, so this command uploads all of the layers, but if we push any future images that include some of the same layers, they won't be uploaded again. Similarly, if we were to delete an image tag from the registry, that would not remove the layer data.

This ability to publish images is not limited to images that we build ourselves. We can tag and push the BusyBox image we just downloaded from Docker Hub:

```
root@host01:/opt/hello# docker tag busybox registry.local/busybox
root@host01:/opt/hello# docker push registry.local/busybox
Using default tag: latest
The push refers to repository [registry.local/busybox]
...
root@host01:/opt/hello# cd
```

Retagging an image so that we can upload it to a private registry is a common practice that can help an application start faster and avoid being dependent on an internet registry.

The last command (cd) takes us back to our home directory, given that we're finished in */opt/hello*.

Image and Container Storage

As mentioned previously, using individual layers to build up a container image has multiple advantages, including reduced download size, reduced disk space, and the ability to re-tag an image with a new name without using any additional space. The additional disk space needed by a running container is limited to just the files that we write while the container is running. Finally, all of the examples have shown how fast a new container starts up. All of these features together demonstrate why layers must be shared, not only for images but also for new containers. To make the best use of this layered approach in building efficient images, it helps to understand how this layered filesystem works.

Overlay Filesystems

When we run a container, we are presented with what looks like a single filesystem, with all the layers merged together and with the ability to make changes to any file. If we run multiple containers from the same image, we see an independent filesystem in each one, so that changes in one do not affect the other. How does this work without having to copy the entire filesystem every time we start a container? The answer is an *overlay filesystem*.

An overlay filesystem has three main parts. The *lower directory* is where the "base" layer exists. (There may be multiple lower directories.) The *upper* directory has the "overlay" layer, and the *mount* directory is where the unified filesystem is made available for use. A directory listing in the mount directory reflects all of the files from all of the layers, in priority order. Any changes made to the mount directory are really written to the upper directory by copying the changed file to the upper directory from a lower one, and then updating it—a process known as *copy on write*. Deletions are also written to the upper directory as metadata, so the lower directory can remain unmodified. This means that multiple users can share the lower directory without conflict because it is only read from, never written to.

An overlay filesystem is useful for more than just container images and containers. It is also useful for embedded systems, such as a network router, for which a read-only filesystem is written in firmware, making it possible for the device to be safely rebooted to a known state every time. It is also useful for virtual machines, enabling multiple virtual machines to be started from the same image.

Overlay filesystems are provided by a Linux kernel module, enabling very high performance. We can easily create an overlay filesystem. The first step is to create the necessary directories:

```
root@host01:~# mkdir /tmp/{lower,upper,work,mount}
```

The mkdir command creates four separate directories in */tmp*. We've already discussed the *lower* directory, *upper* directory, and *mount* directory. The *work* directory is an extra empty directory that the overlay filesystem uses as temporary space to ensure that changes in the mount directory appear atomic—that is, to ensure that they appear all at once.

Let's put some content into the lower and upper directories:

```
root@host01:~# echo "hello1" > /tmp/lower/hello1
root@host01:~# echo "hello2" > /tmp/upper/hello2
```

Next, we just mount the overlay filesystem:

```
root@host01:~# mount -t overlay \
 -o rw,lowerdir=/tmp/lower,upperdir=/tmp/upper,workdir=/tmp/work \
 overlay /tmp/mount
```

The */tmp/mount* directory now contains the merged content of both the upper and lower directories:

```
root@host01:~# ls -l /tmp/mount
total 8
-rw-r--r-- 1 root root 7 May 24 23:05 hello1
-rw-r--r-- 1 root root 7 May 24 23:05 hello2
root@host01:/opt/hello# cat /tmp/mount/hello1
hello1
root@host01:/opt/hello# cat /tmp/mount/hello2
hello2
```

Any changes that we make are shown in the mount location but are actually made in the upper directory:

```
root@host01:~# echo "hello3" > /tmp/mount/hello3
root@host01:~# ls -l /tmp/mount
total 8
-rw-r--r-- 1 root root 7 May 24 23:05 hello1
-rw-r--r-- 1 root root 7 May 24 23:10 hello2
-rw-r--r-- 1 root root 7 May 24 23:09 hello3
root@host01:~# ls -l /tmp/lower
total 4
-rw-r--r-- 1 root root 7 May 24 23:05 hello1
root@host01:~# ls -l /tmp/upper
total 8
-rw-r--r-- 1 root root 7 May 24 23:10 hello2
-rw-r--r-- 1 root root 7 May 24 23:09 hello3
```

Additionally, even deleting files does not affect the lower directory:

```
root@host01:~# rm /tmp/mount/hello1
root@host01:~# ls -l /tmp/mount
total 8
-rw-r--r-- 1 root root 7 May 24 23:10 hello2
-rw-r--r-- 1 root root 7 May 24 23:09 hello3
root@host01:~# ls -l /tmp/lower
total 4
```

```
-rw-r--r-- 1 root root 7 May 24 23:05 hello1
root@host01:~# ls -l /tmp/upper
total 8
```
❶ `c--------- 1 root root 0, 0 May 24 23:11 hello1`
```
-rw-r--r-- 1 root root    7 May 24 23:10 hello2
-rw-r--r-- 1 root root    7 May 24 23:09 hello3
```

The c next to the listing for hello1 in the upper directory ❶ indicates that this is a *character special file*. Its purpose is to indicate that this file was deleted in the upper directory. As a result, it does not show up in the mounted filesystem, even though it still exists in the lower directory.

Thanks to this approach, we can reuse the lower directory with an independent overlay, similar to how we can run multiple independent containers from the same image:

```
root@host01:~# mkdir /tmp/{upper2,work2,mount2}
root@host01:~# mount -t overlay \
  -o rw,lowerdir=/tmp/lower,upperdir=/tmp/upper2,workdir=/tmp/work2 \
  overlay /tmp/mount2
root@host01:~# ls -l /tmp/mount2
total 4
-rw-r--r-- 1 root root 7 May 24 23:05 hello1
```

Not only does the "deleted" file from the lower directory appear, but none of the content from the first upper directory shows up because it's not part of this new overlay.

Understanding Container Layers

Armed with this information about overlay filesystems, we can explore the filesystem of our running NGINX container:

```
root@host01:~# ROOT=$(docker inspect nginx \
  | jq -r '.[0].GraphDriver.Data.MergedDir')
root@host01:~# echo $ROOT
/var/lib/docker/overlay2/433751e2378f9b11.../merged
```

As before, we use jq to choose just the field we want; in this case, it's the path to the *merged* directory for the container's filesystem. This merged directory is the mount point for an overlay filesystem:

```
root@host01:~# mount | grep $ROOT | tr [:,] '\n'
overlay on /var/lib/docker/overlay2/433751e2378f9b11.../merged ...
lowerdir=/var/lib/docker/overlay2/l/ERVEI5TCULK4PCNO2HSWB4MFDB
/var/lib/docker/overlay2/l/RQDO2PYQ3OKMKDY3DAYPAJTZHF
/var/lib/docker/overlay2/l/LFSBVPYPODQJXDL5WQTI7ISYNC
/var/lib/docker/overlay2/l/TLZUYV2BFQNPFGU3AZFUHOH27V
```

```
/var/lib/docker/overlay2/l/4M66FKSHDBNUWE7UAF2REQHSB2
/var/lib/docker/overlay2/l/LCTKPRHP6LG7KC7JQHETKIL6TZ
/var/lib/docker/overlay2/l/JOECSCSAQ5CPNHGEURVRT4JRQQ
upperdir=/var/lib/docker/overlay2/433751e2378f9b11.../diff
workdir=/var/lib/docker/overlay2/433751e2378f9b11.../work,xino=off)
```

The tr command transforms colons and commas to newlines to make the output more readable.

The mount command shows seven separate entries for lowerdir, one for each of the layers in the NGINX container image. All seven of these directories, plus the upperdir, are merged together in the overlay filesystem.

We can see the 10MB data file we created earlier in both the mount directory and the upper directory:

```
root@host01:~# ls -l $ROOT/tmp/data
-rw-r--r-- 1 root root 10485760 May 25 00:27 /var/lib/.../merged/tmp/data
root@host01:~# ls -l $ROOT/../diff/tmp/data
-rw-r--r-- 1 root root 10485760 May 25 00:27 /var/lib/.../diff/tmp/data
```

The actual file is stored in the upper directory *diff*, whereas the mount directory *merged* is just a view generated by the overlay filesystem.

Usually, we don't need to delve into the container filesystem from the host, because we can just run commands from within the container to explore its files. However, this technique can be useful for pulling files from a container for cases in which the container engine is not behaving correctly.

Practical Image Building Advice

Some important practical implications result from the way that overlay filesystems are used with container images. First, because an overlay filesystem can have multiple lower directories, and merging is performant, breaking our container image into multiple layers causes very little performance penalty. It allows us to be very modular when building container images, enabling reuse of layers. For example, we might start with a base image and then build an image on top that installs some common dependencies, and then another image that adds specialized dependencies for some of our application components, and finally yet another image that adds a specific application. Assembling application container images using a layered approach can result in very efficient image transfer and storage, as the base layers are shared between components where possible.

Second, because a deletion in an upper layer does not actually remove the file from a lower layer, we need to be careful with how we handle large temporary files and also in how we store secrets while building images. In both cases, if we finish a layer while the file is still present, it will be there forever, causing us to waste bandwidth and space, or worse, leak secret information to anyone who downloads the image. In general, you should assume that every line of a *Dockerfile* makes a new layer, and you should also make the assumption that all of the information associated with each command is stored in the image metadata. As a result:

- Perform multiple steps in a single RUN line, and make sure every RUN command cleans up after itself.

- Don't use COPY to transfer large files or secrets into the image, even if you clean them up in a later RUN step.

- Don't use ENV to store secrets, because the resulting values become part of the image metadata.

Open Container Initiative

A container image is more than just the set of layers that make up the overlay filesystem. It also includes important metadata, such as the initial command for the container and any environment variables for that command. The Open Container Initiative (OCI) provides a standard format for storing image information. It ensures that container images built by one tool can be used by any other tool and provides a standard way to transfer images layer by layer or in a complete package.

To demonstrate the OCI format, let's extract a BusyBox container image from Docker and store it in OCI format using Skopeo, a program designed to move container images around between repositories and formats. The first step is to extract the image:

```
root@host01:~# skopeo copy docker-daemon:busybox:latest oci:busybox:latest
...
```

This command tells Skopeo to fetch the image from the Docker engine's storage and write it out in OCI format. We now have a *busybox* directory that contains the image:

```
root@host01:~# ls -l busybox
total 12
drwxr-xr-x 3 root root 4096 May 24 23:59 blobs
-rw-r--r-- 1 root root  247 May 24 23:59 index.json
-rw-r--r-- 1 root root   31 May 24 23:59 oci-layout
```

The *oci-layout* file specifies the OCI version used for this image:

```
root@host01:~# jq . busybox/oci-layout
{
  "imageLayoutVersion": "1.0.0"
}
```

The *index.json* file tells us about the image:

```
root@host01:~# jq . busybox/index.json
{
  "schemaVersion": 2,
```

```
    "manifests": [
      {
        "mediaType": "application/vnd.oci.image.manifest.v1+json",
        "digest": "sha256:9c3c5aeeaa7e1629871808339...",
        "size": 347,
        "annotations": {
          "org.opencontainers.image.ref.name": "latest"
        }
      }
    ]
}
```

The manifests property is an array that allows us to store multiple images in a single OCI directory or package. The actual filesystem content is stored by layer in the *blobs* directory, with each layer as a separate *.tar* file, so any shared layers are stored only once.

This BusyBox image has only a single layer. To look at its contents, we'll need to work through the *index.json* and image manifest to find the path to its *.tar* file:

```
root@host01:~# MANIFEST=$(jq -r \
  .manifests[0].digest busybox/index.json | sed -e 's/sha256://')
root@host01:~# LAYER=$(jq -r \
  .layers[0].digest busybox/blobs/sha256/$MANIFEST | sed -e 's/sha256://')
root@host01:~# echo $LAYER
197dfd3345530fd558a64f2a550e8af75a9cb812df5623daf0392aa39e0ce767
```

The files in the *blobs* directory are named using the SHA-256 digest calculated from the file contents. We start by using jq to get the digest for the BusyBox image's manifest, stripping off the sha256: part at the front to get the name of the manifest file. We then read the manifest to find the first (and only) layer. We now can see the content of this layer:

```
root@host01:~# tar tvf busybox/blobs/sha256/$LAYER
drwxr-xr-x 0/0               0 2021-05-17 19:07 bin/
-rwxr-xr-x 0/0         1149184 2021-05-17 19:07 bin/[
hrwxr-xr-x 0/0               0 2021-05-17 19:07 bin/[[ link to bin/[
...
drwxr-xr-x 0/0               0 2021-05-17 19:07 dev/
drwxr-xr-x 0/0               0 2021-05-17 19:07 etc/
...
```

Passing tvf to the tar command tells it to list a table of contents from the file we specify, which is the BusyBox image layer in this case. This layer contains a complete Linux filesystem, with BusyBox acting as the single executable for most of the standard Linux commands.

Using this *busybox* directory, we can also package up the container image, move it to a separate system, and then pull it into another container engine.

Final Thoughts

When we run a container, we get what appears to be a separate, isolated filesystem that we can modify as desired. Underneath, the container engine is using the overlay filesystem to merge together multiple container image layers and a writeable directory that stores all the changes we make. Not only does the use of an overlay filesystem make a new container fast to start, but it also means that we can run multiple containers from the same image without waiting for file copy to complete, and we can reduce the required disk space by sharing image layers.

Now that we've looked at process isolation, resource limits, network isolation, and container storage, we've covered the main features of containers that make them so valuable for packaging, distributing, updating, and running application components. It's time to move on to the critical features that we can get only from a container orchestration environment like Kubernetes. We'll do that in Part II.

PART II

CONTAINERS IN KUBERNETES

Computers have finite processing, storage, and memory, and are built of parts that fail, especially at the wrong time. To build a scalable, reliable application, we can't be limited by the resources of a single host or dependent on a single point of failure. At the same time, we don't want to give up the modularity and flexibility that containers provide. In Part II, we'll see how Kubernetes meets the essential requirements to run containers across a cluster of machines, with cross-host container networking, scalability, automated failover, and distributed storage.

6

WHY KUBERNETES MATTERS

 Containers enable us to transform the way we package and deploy application components, but orchestration of containers in a cluster enables the real advantage of a containerized microservice architecture. As described in Chapter 1, the main benefits of modern application architecture are scalability, reliability, and resiliency, and all three of those benefits require a container orchestration environment like Kubernetes in order to run many instances of containerized application components across many different servers and networks.

In this chapter, we'll begin by looking at some cross-cutting concerns that exist when running containers across multiple servers in a cluster. We'll then describe the core Kubernetes concepts designed to address those concerns. With that introduction complete, we'll spend the bulk of the chapter actually installing a Kubernetes cluster, including important add-on components like networking and storage.

Running Containers in a Cluster

The need to distribute our application components across multiple servers is not new to modern application architecture. To build a scalable and reliable application, we have always needed to take advantage of multiple servers to handle the application's load and preclude a single point of failure. The fact that we are now running these components in containers does not change the need for multiple servers; we are still ultimately using CPUs and we are still ultimately dependent on hardware.

At the same time, a container orchestration environment brings challenges that may not have existed with other kinds of application infrastructure. When the container is the smallest individual module around which we build our system, we end up with application components that are much more self-contained and "opaque" from the perspective of our infrastructure. This means that instead of having a static application architecture through which we choose in advance what application components are assigned to specific servers, with Kubernetes, we try to make it possible for any container to run anywhere.

Cross-Cutting Concerns

The ability to run any container anywhere maximizes our flexibility, but it adds complexity to Kubernetes itself. Kubernetes does not know in advance what containers it will be asked to run, and the container workload is continuously changing as new applications are deployed or applications experience changes in load. To rise to this challenge, Kubernetes needs to account for the following design parameters that apply to all container orchestration software, no matter what containers are running:

Dynamic scheduling   New containers must be allocated to a server, and allocations can change due to configuration changes or failures.

Distributed state   The entire cluster must keep information about what containers are running and where, even during hardware or network failures.

Multitenancy   It should be possible to run multiple applications in a single cluster, with isolation for security and reliability.

Hardware isolation   Clusters must run in cloud environments and on regular servers of various types, isolating containers from the differences in these environments.

The best term to use to refer to these design parameters is *cross-cutting concern*, because they apply to any kind of containerized software that we might need to deploy, and even to the Kubernetes infrastructure itself. These parameters work together with the container orchestration requirements we saw in Chapter 1 and ultimately drive the Kubernetes architecture and key design decisions.

Kubernetes Concepts

To address these cross-cutting concerns, the Kubernetes architecture allows anything to come and go at any time. This includes not only the containerized applications deployed to Kubernetes, but also the fundamental software components of Kubernetes itself, and even the underlying hardware such as servers, network connections, and storage.

Separate Control Plane

Obviously, for Kubernetes to be a container orchestration environment, it requires the ability to run containers. This ability is provided by a set of worker machines called *nodes*. Each node runs a *kubelet* service that interfaces with the underlying container runtime to start and monitor containers.

Kubernetes also has a set of core software components that manage the worker nodes and their containers, but these software components are deployed separately from the worker nodes. These core Kubernetes software components are together referred to as the *control plane*. Because the control plane is separate from the worker nodes, the worker nodes can run the control plane, gaining the benefits of containerization for the Kubernetes core software components. A separate control plane also means that Kubernetes itself has a microservice architecture, which allows customization of each Kubernetes cluster. For example, one control plane component, the *cloud controller manager*, is used only when deploying Kubernetes to a cloud provider, and it's customized based on the cloud provider used. This design provides hardware isolation for application containers and the rest of the Kubernetes control plane, while still allowing us to take advantage of the specific features of each cloud provider.

Declarative API

One critical component of the Kubernetes control plane is the *API server*. The API server provides an interface for cluster control and monitoring that other cluster users and control plane components use. In defining the API, Kubernetes could have chosen an *imperative* style, in which each API endpoint is a command such as "run a container" or "allocate storage." Instead, the API is *declarative*, providing endpoints such as *create*, *patch*, *get*, and *delete*. The effect of these commands is to create, read, update, and delete *resources* from the cluster configuration—the specific configuration of each resource tells Kubernetes what we want the cluster to do.

This declarative API is essential to meet the cross-cutting concerns of dynamic scheduling and distributed state. Because a declarative API simply reports or updates cluster configuration, reacting to server or network failures that might cause a command to be missed is very easy. Consider an example in which the API server connection is lost just after an apply command is issued to change the cluster configuration. When the connection is restored, the client can simply query the cluster configuration and determine whether the command was received successfully. Or, even easier, the client can just issue the same apply command again, knowing that as long as the cluster configuration ends up as desired, Kubernetes will be trying to do the "right thing" to the actual cluster. This core principle is known as *idempotence*, meaning it is safe to issue the same command multiple times because it will be applied at most once.

Self-Healing

Building on the declarative API, Kubernetes is designed to be *self-healing*. This means that the control plane components continually monitor both the cluster configuration and the actual cluster state and try to bring them into alignment. Every resource in the cluster configuration has an associated status and event log reflecting how the configuration has actually caused a change in the cluster state.

The separation of configuration and state makes Kubernetes very resilient. For example, a resource representing containers may be in a Running state if the containers have been scheduled and are actually running. If the Kubernetes control plane loses connection to the server on which the containers are running, it can immediately set the status to Unknown and then work to either reestablish connection or treat the node as failed and reschedule the containers.

At the same time, using a declarative API and self-healing approach has important implications. Because the Kubernetes API is declarative, a "success" response to a command means only that the cluster configuration was updated. It does not mean that the actual state of the cluster was updated, as it might take time to achieve the requested state, or there might be issues that prevent the cluster from achieving that state. As a result, we cannot assume that just because we created the appropriate resources, the cluster is running the containers we expect. Instead, we must watch the status of the resources and explore the event log to diagnose any issues that the Kubernetes control plane had in making the actual cluster state match the configuration we specified.

Cluster Deployment

With some core Kubernetes concepts under our belts, we'll use the kubeadm Kubernetes administration tool to deploy a highly available Kubernetes cluster across multiple virtual machines.

CHOOSING A KUBERNETES DISTRIBUTION

Rather than using a particular Kubernetes distribution as we did in Chapter 1, we'll deploy a "vanilla" Kubernetes cluster using the generic upstream repository. This approach gives us the best opportunity to follow along with the cluster deployment and will make it easier to explore the cluster in-depth in the next several chapters. However, when you're ready to deploy a Kubernetes cluster of your own, especially for production work, consider using a prebuilt Kubernetes distribution for ease of management and built-in security. The Cloud

---

Native Computing Foundation (CNCF) publishes a set of conformance tests that you can use to ensure that the Kubernetes distribution you choose is conformant to the Kubernetes specification.

Our Kubernetes cluster will be split across four virtual machines, labeled host01 through host04. Three of these, host01 through host03, will run control plane components, whereas the fourth will act solely as a worker node. We'll have three control plane nodes because that is the smallest number required to run a highly available cluster. Kubernetes uses a voting scheme to provide failover, and at least three control plane nodes are required; this allows the cluster to detect which side should keep running in the event of a network failure. Also, to keep the cluster as small as possible for our examples, we'll configure Kubernetes to run regular containers on the control plane nodes even though we would avoid doing that for a production cluster.

NOTE *The example repository for this book is at* https://github.com/book-of -kubernetes/examples. *See "Running Examples" on page xx for details on getting set up.*

Start by following the instructions for this chapter to get all four virtual machines up and running, either in Vagrant or AWS. The automated provisioning will set up all four machines with containerd and crictl, so we don't need to do it manually. The automated provisioning script will also set up either kube-vip or an AWS network load balancer to provide required high-availability functionality, as discussed below.

NOTE *You can install Kubernetes automatically using the extra provisioning script provided with this chapter's examples. See the README file for this chapter for instructions.*

You'll need to run commands on each of the four virtual machines, so you might want to open terminal tabs for each one. However, the first series of commands needs to be run on all of the hosts, so the automation sets up a command called k8s-all to do that from host01. You can explore the content of this script in */usr/local/bin/k8s-all* or by looking at the *k8s* Ansible role in the *setup* directory of the examples.

Prerequisite Packages

The first step is to make sure the br_netfilter kernel module is enabled and set to load on boot. Kubernetes uses advanced features of the Linux firewall to handle networking across the cluster, so we need this module. Run these two commands:

```
root@host01:~# k8s-all modprobe br_netfilter
...
root@host01:~# k8s-all "echo 'br_netfilter' > /etc/modules-load.d/k8s.conf"
```

The first command ensures that the module is installed for the currently running kernel, and the second command adds it to the list of modules to run on boot. The slightly odd quoting in the second command ensures that the shell redirection happens on the remote hosts.

Next, in Listing 6-1, we'll set some Linux kernel parameters to enable advanced network features that are also needed for networking across the cluster by using the sysctl command:

```
root@host01:~# k8s-all sysctl -w net.ipv4.ip_forward=1 \
  net.bridge.bridge-nf-call-ip6tables=1 \
  net.bridge.bridge-nf-call-iptables=1
```

Listing 6-1: Kernel settings

This command enables the following Linux kernel network features:

net.ipv4.ip_forward   Transfer packets from one network interface to another (for example, from an interface inside a container's network namespace to a host network).

net.bridge.bridge-nf-call-ip6tables   Run IPv6 bridge traffic through the iptables firewall.

net.bridge.bridge-nf-call-iptables   Run IPv4 bridge traffic through the iptables firewall.

The need for the last two items will become clear in Chapter 9 when we discuss how Kubernetes provides networking for Services.

These sysctl changes in Listing 6-1 do not persist after a reboot. The automated scripts do handle making the changes persistent, so if you reboot your virtual machines, either run the extra provisioning script, or run these commands again.

We've now finished configuring the Linux kernel to support our Kubernetes deployment and are almost ready for the actual install. First we need to install some prerequisite packages:

```
root@host01:~# k8s-all apt install -y apt-transport-https \
  open-iscsi nfs-common
```

The apt-transport-https package ensures that apt can support connecting to repositories via secure HTTP. The other two packages are needed for one of the cluster add-ons that we'll install after our cluster is up and running.

Kubernetes Packages

We can now add the Kubernetes repository to install the kubeadm tool that will set up our cluster. First, add the GPG key used to check the package signatures:

```
root@host01:~# k8s-all "curl -fsSL \
  https://packages.cloud.google.com/apt/doc/apt-key.gpg | \
  gpg --dearmor -o /usr/share/keyrings/google-cloud-keyring.gpg"
```

This command uses curl to download the GPG key. It then uses gpg to reformat it, and then it writes the result to */usr/share/keyrings*. The command line flags fsSL put curl in a mode that behaves better for chained commands, including avoiding unnecessary output, following server redirects, and terminating with an error if there is a problem.

Next, we add the repository configuration:

```
root@host01:~# k8s-all "echo 'deb [arch=amd64' \
  'signed-by=/usr/share/keyrings/google-cloud-keyring.gpg]' \
  'https://apt.kubernetes.io/ kubernetes-xenial main' > \
  /etc/apt/sources.list.d/kubernetes.list"
```

As before, the quoting is essential to ensure that the command is passed correctly via SSH to all the other hosts in the cluster. The command configures kubernetes-xenial as the distribution; this distribution is used for any version of Ubuntu, starting with the older Ubuntu Xenial.

After we have created this new repository, we then need to run apt update on all hosts to download the list of packages:

```
root@host01:~# k8s-all apt update
...
```

Now we can install the packages we need using apt:

```
root@host01:~# source /opt/k8sver
root@host01:~# k8s-all apt install -y kubelet=$K8SV kubeadm=$K8SV kubectl=$K8SV
```

The source command loads a file with a variable to install a specific Kubernetes version. This file is created by the automated scripts and ensures that we use a consistent Kubernetes version for all chapters. You can update the automated scripts to choose which Kubernetes version to install.

The apt command installs the following three packages along with some dependencies:

kubelet   Service for all worker nodes that interfaces with the container engine to run containers as scheduled by the control plane

kubeadm   Administration tool that we'll use to install Kubernetes and maintain our cluster

kubectl   Command line client that we'll use to inspect our Kubernetes cluster and to create and delete resources

The kubelet package starts its service immediately, but because we haven't installed the control plane yet, the service will be in a failed state at first:

```
root@host01:~# systemctl status kubelet
  kubelet.service - kubelet: The Kubernetes Node Agent
...
  Main PID: 75368 (code=exited, status=1/FAILURE)
```

We need to control the version of the packages we just installed because we want to upgrade all of the components of our cluster together. To protect ourselves from accidentally updating these packages, we'll hold them at their current version:

```
root@host01:~# k8s-all apt-mark hold kubelet kubeadm kubectl
```

This command prevents the standard apt full-upgrade command from updating these packages. Instead, if we upgrade our cluster, we'll need to specify the exact version that we want by using apt install.

Cluster Initialization

The next command, kubeadm init, initializes the control plane and provides the kubelet worker node service configuration for all the nodes. We'll run kubeadm init on one node in our cluster and then use kubeadm join on each of the other nodes so that they join the existing cluster.

To run kubeadm init, we first create a YAML configuration file. This approach has a few advantages. It greatly shortens the number of command line flags that we need to remember, and it lets us keep the cluster configuration in a repository, giving us configuration control over the cluster. We then can update the YAML file and rerun kubeadm to make cluster configuration changes.

The automation scripts for this chapter have populated a YAML configuration file in */etc/kubernetes*, so it's ready to use. The following shows the contents of that file:

kubeadm-init.yaml
```
---
apiVersion: kubeadm.k8s.io/v1beta3
kind: InitConfiguration
bootstrapTokens:
- groups:
  - system:bootstrappers:kubeadm:default-node-token
  token: 1d8fb1.2875d52d62a3282d
  ttl: 2h0m0s
  usages:
  - signing
  - authentication
nodeRegistration:
  kubeletExtraArgs:
    node-ip: 192.168.61.11
```

```
    taints: []
localAPIEndpoint:
  advertiseAddress: 192.168.61.11
certificateKey: "5a7e07816958efb97635e9a66256adb1"
---
apiVersion: kubeadm.k8s.io/v1beta3
kind: ClusterConfiguration
kubernetesVersion: 1.21.4
apiServer:
  extraArgs:
    service-node-port-range: 80-32767
networking:
  podSubnet: "172.31.0.0/16"
controlPlaneEndpoint: "192.168.61.10:6443"
---
apiVersion: kubelet.config.k8s.io/v1beta1
kind: KubeletConfiguration
serverTLSBootstrap: true
```

This YAML file has three documents, separated by dashes (`---`). The
first document is specific to initializing the cluster, the second has more
generic configuration, and the third is used to provide settings for kubelet
across all the nodes. Let's look at the purpose of each of these configuration
items:

apiVersion / kind   Tells Kubernetes about the purpose of each YAML
document, so it can validate the contents.

bootstrapTokens   Configures a secret that other nodes can use to join the
cluster. The token should be kept secret in a production cluster. It is set
to expire automatically after two hours, so if we want to join more nodes
later, we'll need to make another one.

nodeRegistration   Configuration to pass to the kubelet service running
on host01. The node-ip field ensures that kubelet registers the correct IP
address with the API server so that the API server can communicate
with it. The taints field ensures that regular containers can be scheduled onto control plane nodes.

localAPIEndpoint   The local IP address that the API server should use.
Our virtual machine has multiple IP addresses, and we want the API
server listening on the correct network.

certificateKey   Configures a secret that other nodes will use to gain access to the certificates for the API server. It's needed so that all of the
API server instances in our highly available cluster can use the same certificate. Keep it secret in a production cluster.

networking   All containers in the cluster will get an IP address from the
podSubnet, no matter what host they run on. Later, we'll install a network
driver that will ensure that every container on all hosts in the cluster can
communicate.

controlPlaneEndpoint   The API server's external address. For a highly available cluster, this IP address needs to reach any API server instance, not just the first one.

serverTLSBootstrap   Instructs kubelet to use the controller manager's certificate authority to request server certificates.

The apiVersion and kind fields will appear in every Kubernetes YAML file. The apiVersion field defines a group of related Kubernetes resources, including a version number. The kind field then selects the specific resource type within that group. This not only allows the Kubernetes project and other vendors to add new groups of resources over time, but it also allows updates to existing resource specifications while maintaining backward compatibility.

HIGHLY AVAILABLE CLUSTERS

The controlPlaneEndpoint field is used to configure the most important requirement for a highly available cluster: an IP address that reaches all of the API servers. We need to establish this IP address immediately when we initialize the cluster because it is used to generate certificates with which clients will verify the API server's identity. The best way to provide a cluster-wide IP address depends on where the cluster is running; for example, in a cloud environment, using the provider's built-in capability, such as an Elastic Load Balancer (ELB) in Amazon Web Services or an Azure Load Balancer, is best.

Because of the nature of the two different environments, the examples for this book use kube-vip when running with Vagrant, and ELB when running in Amazon Web Services. The top-level *README.md* file in the example documentation has more details. The installation and configuration is done automatically so there's nothing more to configure. We can just use 192.168.61 .10:6443 and expect traffic to get to any of the API server instances running on host01 through host03.

Because we have the cluster configuration ready to go in a YAML file, the kubeadm init command to initialize the cluster is simple. We run this command solely on host01:

```
root@host01:~# /usr/bin/kubeadm init \
  --config /etc/kubernetes/kubeadm-init.yaml --upload-certs
```

The --config option points to the YAML configuration file (*kubeadm-init .yaml*) that we looked at earlier, and the --upload-certs option tells kubeadm that it should upload the API server's certificates to the cluster's distributed storage. The other control plane nodes then can download those certificates when they join the cluster, allowing all API server instances to use the same certificates so that clients will trust them. The certificates are encrypted using the certificateKey we provided, which means that the other nodes will need this key to decrypt them.

The kubeadm init command initializes the control plane's components on host01. These components are run in containers and managed by the kubelet service, which makes them easy to upgrade. Several container images will be downloaded, so the command might take a while, depending on the speed of your virtual machines and your internet connection.

Joining Nodes to the Cluster

The kubeadm init command prints out a kubeadm join command that we can use to join other nodes to the cluster. However, the automation scripts have already prestaged a configuration file to each of the other nodes to ensure that they join as the correct type of node. The servers host02 and host03 will join as additional control plane nodes, whereas host04 will join solely as a worker node.

Here's the YAML configuration file for host02 with its specific settings:

kubeadm
-join.yaml (host02)
```
---
apiVersion: kubeadm.k8s.io/v1beta3
kind: JoinConfiguration
discovery:
  bootstrapToken:
    apiServerEndpoint: 192.168.61.10:6443
    token: 1d8fb1.2875d52d62a3282d
    unsafeSkipCAVerification: true
  timeout: 5m0s
nodeRegistration:
  kubeletExtraArgs:
    cgroup-driver: containerd
    node-ip: 192.168.61.12
  taints: []
  ignorePreflightErrors:
    - DirAvailable--etc-kubernetes-manifests
controlPlane:
  localAPIEndpoint:
    advertiseAddress: 192.168.61.12
  certificateKey: "5a7e07816958efb97635e9a66256adb1"
```

This resource has a type of JoinConfiguration, but most of the fields are the same as the InitConfiguration in the *kubeadm-init.yaml* file. Most important, the token and certificateKey match the secret we set up earlier, so this node will be able to validate itself with the cluster and decrypt the API server certificates.

One difference is the addition of ignorePreflightErrors. This section appears only when we are installing kube-vip, as in that case we need to prestage the configuration file for kube-vip to the */etc/kubernetes/manifests* directory, and we need to tell kubeadm that it is okay for that directory to already exist.

Because we have this YAML configuration file, the kubeadm join command is simple. Run it on host02:

```
root@host02:~# /usr/bin/kubeadm join --config /etc/kubernetes/kubeadm-join.yaml
```

As before, this command runs the control plane components as containers using the `kubelet` service on this node, so it will take some time to download the container images and start the containers.

When it finishes, run the exact same command on host03:

```
root@host03:~# /usr/bin/kubeadm join --config /etc/kubernetes/kubeadm-join.yaml
```

The automation script set up the YAML file with the correct IP address for each host, so the differences in configuration between each of the hosts is already accounted for.

When this command completes, we'll have created a highly available Kubernetes cluster, with the control plane components running on three separate hosts. However, we do not yet have any regular worker nodes. Let's fix that issue.

We'll begin by joining host04 as a regular worker node and running exactly the same `kubeadm join` command on host04, but the YAML configuration file will be a little different. Here's that file:

kubeadm
-join.yaml (host04)
```
---
apiVersion: kubeadm.k8s.io/v1beta3
kind: JoinConfiguration
discovery:
  bootstrapToken:
    apiServerEndpoint: 192.168.61.10:6443
    token: 1d8fb1.2875d52d62a3282d
    unsafeSkipCAVerification: true
  timeout: 5m0s
nodeRegistration:
  kubeletExtraArgs:
    cgroup-driver: containerd
    node-ip: 192.168.61.14
  taints: []
```

This YAML file is missing the `controlPlane` field, so `kubeadm` configures it as a regular worker node rather than a control plane node.

Now let's join host04 to the cluster:

```
root@host04:~# /usr/bin/kubeadm join --config /etc/kubernetes/kubeadm-join.yaml
```

This command completes a little faster because it doesn't need to download the control plane container images and run them. We now have four nodes in the cluster, which we can verify by running `kubectl` back on host01:

```
root@host01:~# export KUBECONFIG=/etc/kubernetes/admin.conf
root@host01:~# kubectl get nodes
NAME     STATUS     ROLES        ...
host01   NotReady   control-plane...
host02   NotReady   control-plane...
```

```
host03   NotReady   control-plane...
host04   NotReady   <none>      ...
```

The first command sets an environment variable to tell kubectl what configuration file to use. The */etc/kubernetes/admin.conf* file was created automatically by kubeadm when it initialized host01 as a control plane node. That file tells kubectl what address to use for the API server, what certificate to use to verify the secure connection, and how to authenticate.

The four nodes currently should be reporting a status of NotReady. Let's run the kubectl describe command to get the node details:

```
root@host01:~# kubectl describe node host04
Name:          host04
...
Conditions:
  Type    Status ... Message
  ----    ------ ... -------
  Ready   False  ... container runtime network not ready...
...
```

We haven't yet installed a network driver for our Kubernetes cluster, and as a result, all of the nodes are reporting a status of NotReady, which means that they won't accept regular application workloads. Kubernetes communicates this by placing a *taint* in the node's configuration. A taint restricts what can be scheduled on a node. We can list the taints on the nodes using kubectl:

```
root@host01:~# kubectl get node -o json | \
  jq '.items[]|.metadata.name,.spec.taints[]'
"host01"
{
  "effect": "NoSchedule",
  "key": "node.kubernetes.io/not-ready"
}
"host02"
{
  "effect": "NoSchedule",
  "key": "node.kubernetes.io/not-ready"
}
"host03"
{
  "effect": "NoSchedule",
  "key": "node.kubernetes.io/not-ready"
}
"host04"
```

```
{
  "effect": "NoSchedule",
  "key": "node.kubernetes.io/not-ready"
}
```

We select an output format of json so that we can use jq to print just the information we need. Because all the nodes have a status of NotReady, they have a not-ready taint set to NoSchedule, which prevents the Kubernetes scheduler from scheduling containers onto them.

By specifying taints as an empty array in the kubeadm configuration, we prevented the three control plane nodes from having an additional control plane taint. In a production cluster, this taint keeps application containers separate from the control plane containers for security reasons, so we would leave it in place. For our example cluster, though, it would mean that we need multiple extra virtual machines to act as worker nodes, which we don't want.

The command kubectl taint would allow us to remove the not-ready taint manually, but the correct approach is to install a network driver as a cluster add-on so that the nodes will properly report Ready, enabling us to run containers on them.

Installing Cluster Add-ons

We've installed kubelet on four separate nodes and installed the control plane on three of those nodes and joined them to our cluster. For the rest, we'll use the control plane to install cluster add-ons. These add-ons are similar to regular applications that we would deploy. They consist of Kubernetes resources and run in containers, but they provide essential services to the cluster that our applications will use.

To get a basic cluster up and running, we need to install three types of add-ons: a *network driver*, a *storage driver*, and an *ingress controller*. We will also install a fourth optional add-on, a *metrics server*.

Network Driver

Kubernetes networking is based on the Container Network Interface (CNI) standard. Anyone can build a new network driver for Kubernetes by implementing this standard, and as a result, several choices are available for Kubernetes network drivers. We'll demonstrate different network plug-ins in Chapter 8, but most of the clusters in this book use the Calico network driver because it is the default choice for many Kubernetes platforms.

First, download the primary YAML configuration file for Calico:

```
root@host01:~# cd /etc/kubernetes/components
root@host01:/etc/kubernetes/components# curl -L -O $calico_url
...
```

The `-L` option tells `curl` to follow any HTTP redirects, whereas the `-O` option tells `curl` to save the content in a file using the same filename as in the URL. The value of the `calico_url` environment variable is set in the `k8s-ver` script that also specified the Kubernetes version. This is essential, as Calico is sensitive to the specific version of Kubernetes we're running, so it's important to choose values that are compatible.

The primary YAML configuration is written to the local file *tigera-operator .yaml*. This refers to the fact that the initial installation is a Kubernetes Operator, which then creates all of the other cluster resources to install Calico. We'll explore operators in Chapter 17.

In addition to this primary YAML configuration, the automated scripts for this chapter have added a file called *custom-resources.yaml* that provides necessary configuration for our example cluster. We now can tell the Kubernetes API server to apply all the resources in these files to the cluster:

```
root@host01:/etc/kubernetes/components# kubectl apply -f tigera-operator.yaml
...
root@host01:/etc/kubernetes/components# kubectl apply -f custom-resources.yaml
```

Kubernetes takes a few minutes to download container images and start containers, and then Calico will be running in our cluster and our nodes should report a status of `Ready`:

```
root@host01:/etc/kubernetes/components# kubectl get nodes
NAME      STATUS   ROLES                     ...
host01    Ready    control-plane,master ...
host02    Ready    control-plane,master ...
host03    Ready    control-plane,master ...
host04    Ready    <none>                    ...
```

Calico works by installing a *DaemonSet*, a Kubernetes resource that tells the cluster to run a specific container or set of containers on every node. The Calico containers then provide network services for any containers running on that node. However, that raises an important question. When we installed Calico in our cluster, all of our nodes had a taint that told Kubernetes not to schedule containers on them. How was Calico able to run its containers on all the nodes? The answer is *tolerations*.

A toleration is a configuration setting applied to a resource that instructs Kubernetes it can be scheduled on a node despite a taint possibly being present. Calico specifies a toleration when it adds its DaemonSet to the cluster, as we can see with kubectl:

```
root@host01:/etc/kubernetes/components# kubectl -n calico-system \
  get daemonsets -o json | \
  jq '.items[].spec.template.spec.tolerations[]'
{
  "key": "CriticalAddonsOnly",
  "operator": "Exists"
}
```

```
{
  "effect": "NoSchedule",
  "operator": "Exists"
}
{
  "effect": "NoExecute",
  "operator": "Exists"
}
```

The -n option selects the calico-system *Namespace*. Namespaces are a way to keep Kubernetes resources separate from one another on a cluster, for security reasons as well as to avoid naming collisions. Also, as before, we request JSON output and use jq to select only the field we're interested in. If you want to see the entire configuration for the resource, use -o=json without jq or use -o=yaml.

This DaemonSet has three tolerations, and the second one provides the behavior we need. It tells the Kubernetes scheduler to go ahead and schedule it even on nodes that have a NoSchedule taint. Calico then can get itself started before the node is ready, and once it's running, the node changes its status to Ready so that normal application containers can be scheduled. The control plane components needed a similar toleration in order to run on nodes before they show Ready.

Installing Storage

The cluster nodes are ready, so if we deployed a regular application, its containers would run. However, applications that require persistent storage would fail to start because the cluster doesn't yet have a storage driver. Like network drivers, several storage drivers are available for Kubernetes. The Container Storage Interface (CSI) provides the standard that storage drivers need to meet to work with Kubernetes. We'll use Longhorn, a storage driver from Rancher; it's easy to install and doesn't require any underlying hardware like extra block devices or access to cloud-based storage.

Longhorn makes use of the iSCSI and NFS software we installed earlier. It expects all of our nodes to have the iscsid service enabled and running, so let's make sure that's true on all our nodes:

```
root@host01:/etc/kubernetes/components# k8s-all systemctl enable --now iscsid
```

We now can install Longhorn on the cluster. The process for installing Longhorn looks a lot like Calico. Start by downloading the Longhorn YAML configuration:

```
root@host01:/etc/kubernetes/components# curl -LO $longhorn_url
```

The longhorn_url environment variable is also set by the k8s-ver script, which allows us to ensure compatibility.

Install Longhorn using `kubectl`:

```
root@host01:/etc/kubernetes/components# kubectl apply -f longhorn.yaml
```

As before, `kubectl apply` ensures that the resources in the YAML file are applied to the cluster, creating or updating them as necessary. The `kubectl apply` command supports URLs as the source of the resource it applies to the cluster, but for these three installs, we run a separate `curl` command because it's convenient to have a local copy of what was applied to the cluster.

Longhorn is now installed on the cluster, which we'll verify as we explore the cluster in the rest of this chapter.

Ingress Controller

We now have networking and storage, but the networking allows access to containers only from within our cluster. We need another service that exposes our containerized applications outside the cluster. The easiest way to do that is to use an ingress controller. As we'll describe in Chapter 9, an ingress controller watches the Kubernetes cluster for *Ingress* resources and routes network traffic.

We begin by downloading the ingress controller YAML configuration:

```
root@host01:/etc/kubernetes/components# curl -Lo ingress-controller.yaml
  $ingress_url
```

As in our earlier example, the `ingress_url` environment variable is set by the k8s-ver script so that we can ensure compatibility. In this case, the URL ends in the generic path of *deploy.yaml*, so we use -o to provide a filename to curl to make clear the purpose of the downloaded YAML file.

Install the ingress controller using `kubectl`:

```
root@host01:/etc/kubernetes/components# kubectl apply -f ingress-controller.yaml
```

This creates a lot of resources, but there are two main parts: an NGINX web server that actually performs routing of HTTP traffic, and a component that watches for changes in Ingress resources in the cluster and configures NGINX accordingly.

There's one more step we need. As installed, the ingress controller tries to request an external IP address to allow traffic to reach it from outside the cluster. Because we're running a sample cluster with no access to external IP addresses, this won't work. Instead, we'll be accessing our ingress controller using port forwarding from our cluster hosts. At the moment, our ingress controller is set up for this port forwarding, but it's using a random port. We would like to select the port to be sure that we know where to find the ingress controller. At the same time, we'll also add an annotation so that this ingress controller will be the default for this cluster.

To apply the port changes, we're going to provide our Kubernetes cluster an with extra YAML configuration with just the changes we need. Here's that YAML:

*ingress
-patch.yaml*

```
---
apiVersion: v1
kind: Service
metadata:
  name: ingress-nginx-controller
  namespace: ingress-nginx
spec:
  ports:
    - port: 80
      nodePort: 80
    - port: 443
      nodePort: 443
```

This file specifies the name and Namespace of the Service to ensure that Kubernetes knows where to apply these changes. It also specifies the port configuration we're updating, along with the nodePort, which is the port on our cluster nodes that will be used for port forwarding. We'll look at Node-Port service types and port forwarding in more detail in Chapter 9.

To patch the service, we use the kubectl patch command:

```
root@host01:/etc/kubernetes/components# kubectl patch -n ingress-nginx \
  service/ingress-nginx-controller --patch-file ingress-patch.yaml
service/ingress-nginx-controller patched
```

To apply the annotation, use the kubectl annotate command:

```
root@host01:/etc/kubernetes/components# kubectl annotate -n ingress-nginx \
  ingressclass/nginx ingressclass.kubernetes.io/is-default-class="true"
ingressclass.networking.k8s.io/nginx annotated
```

Kubernetes reports the change to each resource as we make it, so we know that our changes have been applied.

Metrics Server

Our final add-on is a *metrics server* that collects utilization metrics from our nodes, enabling the use of autoscaling. To do this, it needs to connect to the kubelet instances in our cluster. For security, it needs to verify the HTTP/S certificate when it connects to a kubelet. This is why we configured kubelet to request a certificate signed by the controller manager rather than allowing the kubelet to generate self-signed certificates.

During setup, kubelet created a certificate request on each node, but the requests were not automatically approved. Let's find these requests:

```
root@host01:/etc/kubernetes/components# kubectl get csr
NAME       ... SIGNERNAME                                ... CONDITION
```

```
csr-sgrwz ... kubernetes.io/kubelet-serving              ... Pending
csr-agwb6 ... kubernetes.io/kube-apiserver-client-kubelet ... Approved,Issued
csr-2kwwk ... kubernetes.io/kubelet-serving              ... Pending
csr-5496d ... kubernetes.io/kube-apiserver-client-kubelet ... Approved,Issued
csr-hm61j ... kubernetes.io/kube-apiserver-client-kubelet ... Approved,Issued
csr-jbfmx ... kubernetes.io/kubelet-serving              ... Pending
csr-njjr7 ... kubernetes.io/kube-apiserver-client-kubelet ... Approved,Issued
csr-v7tcs ... kubernetes.io/kubelet-serving              ... Pending
csr-vr27n ... kubernetes.io/kubelet-serving              ... Pending
```

Each kubelet has a client certificate that it uses to authenticate to the API server; these were automatically approved during bootstrap. The requests we need to approve are for kubelet-serving certificates, which are used when clients such as our metrics server connect to kubelet. As soon as the request is approved, the controller manager signs the certificate. The kubelet then collects the certificate and starts using it.

We can approve all of these requests at once by querying for the name of all of the kubelet-serving requests and then passing those names to kubectl certificate approve:

```
root@host01:/etc/kubernetes/components# kubectl certificate approve \$(kubectl
  get csr --field-selector spec.signerName=kubernetes.io/kubelet-serving -o name)
certificatesigningrequest.certificates.k8s.io/csr-sgrwz approved
...
```

We now can install our metrics server by downloading and applying its YAML configuration:

```
root@host01:/etc/kubernetes/components# curl -Lo metrics-server.yaml \$metrics_url
root@host01:/etc/kubernetes/components# kubectl apply -f metrics-server.yaml
...
root@host01:/etc/kubernetes/components# cd
root@host01:~#
```

This component is the last one we need to install, so we can leave this directory. With these cluster add-ons, we now have a complete, highly available Kubernetes cluster.

Exploring a Cluster

Before deploying our first application onto this brand-new Kubernetes cluster, let's explore what's running on it. The commands we use here will come in handy later as we debug our own applications and a cluster that isn't working correctly.

We'll use crictl, the same command we used to explore running containers in Part I, to see what containers are running on host01:

```
root@host01:~# crictl ps
CONTAINER       ... STATE     NAME                          ...
```

```
25c63f29c1442  ... Running  longhorn-csi-plugin           ...
2ffdd044a81d8  ... Running  node-driver-registrar         ...
94468050de89c  ... Running  csi-provisioner               ...
119fbf417f1db  ... Running  csi-attacher                  ...
e74c1a2a0c422  ... Running  kube-scheduler                ...
d1ad93cdbc686  ... Running  kube-controller-manager       ...
76266a522cc3d  ... Running  engine-image-ei-611d1496      ...
fc3cd1679e33e  ... Running  replica-manager               ...
48e792a973105  ... Running  engine-manager                ...
e658baebbc295  ... Running  longhorn-manager              ...
eb51d9ec0f2fc  ... Running  calico-kube-controllers       ...
53e7e3e4a3148  ... Running  calico-node                   ...
772ac45ceb94e  ... Running  calico-typha                  ...
4005370021f5f  ... Running  kube-proxy                    ...
26929cde3a264  ... Running  kube-apiserver                ...
9ea4c2f5af794  ... Running  etcd                          ...
```

The control plane node is very busy, as this list includes Kubernetes control plane components, Calico components, and Longhorn components. Running this command on all the nodes and sorting out what containers are running where and for what purpose would be confusing. Fortunately, kubectl provides a clearer picture, although knowing that we can get down to these lower-level details and see exactly what containers are running on a given node is nice.

To explore the cluster with kubectl, we need to know how the cluster resources are organized into Namespaces. As mentioned previously, Kubernetes Namespaces provide security and avoid name collisions. To ensure idempotence, Kubernetes needs each resource to have a unique name. By dividing resources into Namespaces, we allow multiple resources to have the same name while still enabling the API server to know exactly which resource we mean, which also supports multitenancy, one of our cross-cutting concerns.

Even though we just set up the cluster, it's already populated with several Namespaces:

```
root@host01:~# kubectl get namespaces
NAME              STATUS   AGE
calico-system     Active   50m
default           Active   150m
kube-node-lease   Active   150m
kube-public       Active   150m
kube-system       Active   150m
longhorn-system   Active   16m
tigera-operator   Active   50m
```

As we run kubectl commands, they will apply to the default Namespace unless we use the -n option to specify a different Namespace.

To see what containers are running, we ask kubectl to get the list of Pods. We look at Kubernetes Pods in much more detail in Chapter 7. For now, just know that a Pod is a group of one or more containers, much like the Pods that we created with crictl in Part I.

If we try to list Pods in the default Namespace, we can see that there aren't any yet:

```
root@host01:~# kubectl get pods
No resources found in default namespace.
```

So far, as we installed cluster infrastructure components, they've been created in other Namespaces. That way, when we configure normal user accounts, we can prevent those users from viewing or editing the cluster infrastructure. The Kubernetes infrastructure components were all installed into the kube-system Namespace:

```
root@host01:~# kubectl -n kube-system get pods
NAME                            READY    STATUS   ...
coredns-558bd4d5db-7krwr        1/1      Running  ...
...
kube-apiserver-host01           1/1      Running  ...
...
```

We cover the control plane components in Chapter 11. For now, let's explore just one of the control plane Pods, the API server running on host01. We can get all of the details for this Pod using kubectl describe:

```
root@host01:~# kubectl -n kube-system describe pod kube-apiserver-host01
Name:            kube-apiserver-host01
Namespace:       kube-system
...
Node:            host01/192.168.61.11
...
Status:          Running
Containers:
  kube-apiserver:
    Container ID:  containerd://26929cde3a264e...
...
```

The Namespace and name together uniquely identify this Pod. We also see the node on which the Pod is scheduled, its status, and details about the actual containers, including a container ID that we can use with crictl to find the container in the underlying containerd runtime.

Let's also verify that Calico deployed into our cluster as expected:

```
root@host01:~# kubectl -n calico-system get pods
NAME                                          READY   STATUS    ...
calico-kube-controllers-7f58dbcbbd-ch7zt      1/1     Running   ...
calico-node-cp88k                             1/1     Running   ...
calico-node-dn4rj                             1/1     Running   ...
```

```
calico-node-xnkmg                      1/1        Running    ...
calico-node-zfscp                      1/1        Running    ...
calico-typha-68b99cd4bf-7lwss          1/1        Running    ...
calico-typha-68b99cd4bf-jjdts          1/1        Running    ...
calico-typha-68b99cd4bf-pjr6q          1/1        Running    ...
```

Earlier we saw that Calico installed a DaemonSet resource. Kubernetes has used the configuration in this DaemonSet to automatically create a calico-node Pod for each node. Like Kubernetes itself, Calico also uses a separate control plane to handle overall configuration of the network, and the other Pods provide that control plane.

Finally, we'll see the containers that are running for Longhorn:

```
root@host01:~# kubectl -n longhorn-system get pods
NAME                                     READY    STATUS    RESTARTS    AGE
engine-image-ei-611d1496-8q58f           1/1      Running   0           31m
...
longhorn-csi-plugin-8vkr6                2/2      Running   0           31m
...
longhorn-manager-dl9sb                   1/1      Running   1           32m
...
```

Like Calico, Longhorn uses DaemonSets so that it can run containers on every node. These containers provide storage services to the other containers on the node. Longhorn also includes a number of other containers that serve as a control plane, including providing the CSI implementation that Kubernetes uses to tell Longhorn to create storage when needed.

We put a lot of effort into setting up this cluster, so it would be a shame to end this chapter without running at least one application on it. In the next chapter, we will look at many different ways to run containers, but let's quickly run a simple NGINX web server in our Kubernetes cluster:

```
root@host01:~# kubectl run nginx --image=nginx
pod/nginx created
```

That may look like an imperative command, but under the hood, kubectl is creating a Pod resource using the name and container image we specified, and then it's applying that resource on the cluster. Let's inspect the default Namespace again:

```
root@host01:~# kubectl get pods -o wide
NAME    READY   STATUS    ... IP              NODE   ...
nginx   1/1     Running   ... 172.31.89.203   host02 ...
```

We used -o wide to see extra information about the Pod, including its IP address and where it was scheduled, which can be different each time the Pod is created. In this case, the Pod was scheduled to host02, showing that we were successful in allowing regular application containers to be deployed to our control plane nodes. The IP address comes from the Pod CIDR we configured, and Calico automatically assigns it.

Calico also handles routing traffic so that we can reach the Pod from any container in the cluster as well as from the host network. Let's verify that, starting with a regular `ping`:

```
root@host01:~# ping -c 1 172.31.89.203
PING 172.31.89.203 (172.31.89.203) 56(84) bytes of data.
64 bytes from 172.31.89.203: icmp_seq=1 ttl=63 time=0.848 ms

--- 172.31.89.203 ping statistics ---
1 packets transmitted, 1 received, 0% packet loss, time 0ms
rtt min/avg/max/mdev = 0.848/0.848/0.848/0.000 ms
```

Use your Pod's IP address in the place of the one shown here.

We can also use `curl` to verify that the NGINX web server is working:

```
root@host01:~# curl http://172.31.89.203
...
<title>Welcome to nginx!</title>
...
```

The Kubernetes cluster is working and ready for us to deploy applications. Kubernetes will take advantage of all of the nodes in the cluster to load balance our applications and provide resiliency in the event of any failures.

Final Thoughts

In this chapter, we've explored how Kubernetes is architected with the flexibility to allow cluster components to come and go at any time. This applies not only to containerized applications but also to the cluster components, including control plane microservices and the underlying servers and networks the cluster uses. We were able to bootstrap a cluster and then dynamically add nodes to it, configure those nodes to accept certain types of containers, and then dynamically add networking and storage drivers using the Kubernetes cluster itself to run and monitor them. Finally, we deployed our first container to a Kubernetes cluster, allowing it to automatically schedule the container onto an available node, using our network driver to access the container from the host network.

Now that we have a highly available cluster, we can look at how to deploy an application to Kubernetes. We'll explore some key Kubernetes resources that we need to create a scalable, reliable application. This process will provide a foundation for exploring Kubernetes in detail, including understanding what happens when our applications don't run as expected and how to debug issues with our application or the Kubernetes cluster.

7

DEPLOYING CONTAINERS TO KUBERNETES

We're now ready to begin running containers on our working Kubernetes cluster. Because Kubernetes has a declarative API, we'll create various kinds of resources to run them, and we'll monitor the cluster to see what Kubernetes does for each type of resource.

Different containers have different use cases. Some might require multiple identical instances with autoscaling to perform well under load. Other containers might exist solely to run a one-time command. Still others may require a fixed ordering to enable selecting a single primary instance and providing controlled failover to a secondary instance. Kubernetes provides different *controller* resource types for each of those use cases. We'll look at each in turn, but we'll begin with the most fundamental of them, the *Pod*, which is utilized by all of those use cases.

Pods

A Pod is the most basic resource in Kubernetes and is how we run containers. Each Pod can have one or more containers within it. The Pod is used to provide the process isolation we saw in Chapter 2. Linux kernel namespaces are used at the Pod and the container level:

mnt   Mount points: each container has its own root filesystem; other mounts are available to all containers in the Pod.

uts   Unix time sharing: isolated at the Pod level.

ipc   Interprocess communication: isolated at the Pod level.

pid   Process identifiers: isolated at the container level.

net   Network: isolated at the Pod level.

The biggest advantage of this approach is that multiple containers can act like processes on the same virtual host, using the localhost address to communicate, while still being based on separate container images.

Deploying a Pod

To get started, let's create a Pod directly. Unlike the previous chapter, in which we used kubectl run to have the Pod specification created for us, we'll specify it directly using YAML so that we have complete control over the Pod and to prepare us for using controllers to create Pods, providing scalability and failover.

NOTE *The example repository for this book is at* https://github.com/book-of -kubernetes/examples. *See "Running Examples" on page xx for details on getting set up.*

The automation script for this chapter does a full cluster install with three nodes that run the control plane and regular applications, providing the smallest possible highly available cluster for testing. The automation also creates some YAML files for Kubernetes resources. Here's a basic YAML resource to create a Pod running NGINX:

nginx-pod.yaml
```
---
apiVersion: v1
kind: Pod
metadata:
  name: nginx
spec:
  containers:
  - name: nginx
    image: nginx
```

Pods are part of the *core* Kubernetes API, so we just specify a version number of v1 for the apiVersion. Specifying Pod as the kind tells Kubernetes exactly what resource we're creating in the API group. We will see these fields in all of our Kubernetes resources.

The metadata field has many uses. For the Pod, we just need to provide the one required field of name. We don't specify the namespace in the metadata, so by default this Pod will end up in the default Namespace.

The remaining field, spec, tells Kubernetes everything it needs to know to run this Pod. For now we are providing the minimal information, which is a list of containers to run, but many other options are available. In this case, we have only one container, so we provide just the name and container image Kubernetes should use.

Let's add this Pod to the cluster. The automation added files to */opt*, so we can do it from host01 as follows:

```
root@host01:~# kubectl apply -f /opt/nginx-pod.yaml
pod/nginx created
```

In Listing 7-1, we can check the Pod's status.

```
root@host01:~# kubectl get pods -o wide
NAME    READY   STATUS    RESTARTS   AGE     IP             NODE    ...
nginx   1/1     Running   0          2m26s   172.31.25.202  host03 ...
```

Listing 7-1: Status of NGINX

It can take some time before the Pod shows Running, especially if you just set up your Kubernetes cluster and it's still busy deploying core components. Keep trying this kubectl command to check the status.

Instead of typing the kubectl command multiple times, you can also use watch. The watch command is a great way to observe changes in your cluster over time. Just add watch in front of your command, and it will be run for you every two seconds.

We added -o wide to the command to see the IP address and node assignment for this Pod. Kubernetes manages that for us. In this case, the Pod was scheduled on host03, so we need to go there to see the running container:

```
root@host03:~# crictl pods --name nginx
POD ID          CREATED         STATE   NAME    NAMESPACE ...
9f1d6e0207d7e   19 minutes ago  Ready   nginx   default    ...
```

Run this command on whatever host your NGINX Pod is on.

If we collect the Pod ID, we can see the container as well:

```
root@host03:~# POD_ID=$(crictl pods -q --name nginx)
root@host03:~# crictl ps --pod $POD_ID
CONTAINER       IMAGE           CREATED         STATE     NAME   ...
9da09b3671418   4cdc5dd7eaadf   20 minutes ago  Running   nginx  ...
```

This output looks very similar to the output from kubectl get in Listing 7-1, which is not surprising given that our cluster gets that information from the kubelet service running on this node, which in turn uses the same Container Runtime Interface (CRI) API that crictl is also using to talk to the container engine.

Pod Details and Logging

The ability to use `crictl` with the underlying container engine to explore a container running in the cluster is valuable, but it does require us to connect to the specific host running the container. Much of the time, we can avoid that by using `kubectl` commands to inspect Pods from anywhere by connecting to our cluster's API server. Let's move back to `host01` and explore the NGINX Pod further.

In Chapter 6, we saw how we could use `kubectl describe` to see the status and event log for a cluster node. We can use the same command to see the status and configuration details of other Kubernetes resources. Here's the event log for our NGINX Pod:

```
root@host01:~# kubectl describe pod nginx
Name:          nginx
Namespace: ❶ default
...
Containers:
  nginx:
    Container ID:   containerd://9da09b3671418...
...
❷ Type     Reason     Age   From               Message
   ----     ------     ----  ----               -------
   Normal   Scheduled  22m   default-scheduler  Successfully assigned ...
   Normal   Pulling    22m   kubelet            Pulling image "nginx"
   Normal   Pulled     21m   kubelet            Successfully pulled image ...
   Normal   Created    21m   kubelet            Created container nginx
   Normal · Started    21m   kubelet            Started container nginx
```

We can use `kubectl describe` with many different Kubernetes resources, so we first tell `kubectl` that we are interested in a Pod and provide the name. Because we didn't specify a Namespace, Kubernetes will look for this Pod in the `default` Namespace ❶.

NOTE   *We use the default Namespace for most of the examples in this book to save typing, but it's a good practice to use multiple Namespaces to keep applications separate, both to avoid naming conflicts and to manage access control. We look at Namespaces in more detail in Chapter 11.*

The `kubectl describe` command output provides an event log ❷, which is the first place to look for issues when we have problems starting a container.

Kubernetes takes a few steps when deploying a container. First, it needs to schedule it onto a node, which requires that node to be available with sufficient resources. Then, control passes to `kubelet` on that node, which has to interact with the container engine to pull the image, create a container, and start it.

After the container is started, `kubelet` collects the standard out and standard error. We can view this output by using the `kubectl logs` command:

```
root@host01:~# kubectl logs nginx
...
2021/07/13 22:37:03 [notice] 1#1: start worker processes
2021/07/13 22:37:03 [notice] 1#1: start worker process 33
2021/07/13 22:37:03 [notice] 1#1: start worker process 34
```

The `kubectl logs` command always refers to a Pod because Pods are the basic resource used to run containers, and our Pod has only one container, so we can just specify the name of the Pod as a single parameter to `kubectl logs`. As before, Kubernetes will look in the `default` Namespace because we didn't specify the Namespace.

The container output is available even if the container has exited, so the `kubectl logs` command is the place to look if a container is pulled and started successfully but then crashes. Of course, we have to hope that the container printed a log message explaining why it crashed. In Chapter 10, we look at what to do if we can't get a container going and don't have any log messages.

We're done with the NGINX Pod, so let's clean it up:

```
root@host01:~# kubectl delete -f /opt/nginx-pod.yaml
pod "nginx" deleted
```

We can use the same YAML configuration file to delete the Pod, which is convenient when we have multiple Kubernetes resources defined in a single file, as a single command will delete all of them. The `kubectl` command uses the name of each resource defined in the file to perform the delete.

Deployments

To run a container, we need a Pod, but that doesn't mean we generally want to create the Pod directly. When we create a Pod directly, we don't get all of the scalability and failover that Kubernetes offers, because Kubernetes will run only one instance of the Pod. This Pod will be allocated to a node only on creation, with no re-allocation even if the node fails.

To get scalability and failover, we instead need to create a controller to manage the Pod for us. We'll look at multiple controllers that can run Pods, but let's start with the most common: the *Deployment*.

Creating a Deployment

A Deployment manages one or more *identical* Kubernetes Pods. When we create a Deployment, we provide a Pod template. The Deployment then creates Pods matching that template with the help of a *ReplicaSet*.

DEPLOYMENTS AND REPLICASETS

Kubernetes has evolved its controller resources over time. The first type of controller, the *ReplicationController*, provided only basic functionality. It was replaced by the ReplicaSet, which has improvements in how it identifies which Pods to manage.

Part of the reason to replace ReplicationControllers with ReplicaSets is that ReplicationControllers were becoming more and more complicated, making the code difficult to maintain. The new approach splits up controller responsibility between ReplicaSets and Deployments. ReplicaSets are responsible for basic Pod management, including monitoring Pod status and performing failover. Deployments are responsible for tracking changes to the Pod template caused by configuration changes or container image updates. Deployments and ReplicaSets work together, but the Deployment creates its own ReplicaSet, so we usually need to interact only with Deployments. For this reason, I use the term *Deployment* generically to refer to features provided by the ReplicaSet, such as monitoring Pods to provide the requested number of replicas.

Here's the YAML file we'll use to create an NGINX Deployment:

nginx-deploy.yaml
```
---
kind: Deployment
apiVersion: apps/v1
metadata:
❶ name: nginx
spec:
  replicas: 3
  selector:
    matchLabels:
      app: nginx
  template:
    metadata:
    ❷ labels:
        app: nginx
  ❸ spec:
      containers:
      - name: nginx
        image: nginx
      ❹ resources:
          requests:
            cpu: "100m"
```

Deployments are in the apps API group, so we specify apps/v1 for apiVersion. Like every Kubernetes resource, we need to provide a unique name ❶ to keep this Deployment separate from any others we might create.

The Deployment specification has a few important fields, so let's look at them in detail. The replicas field tells Kubernetes how many identical instances of the Pod we want. Kubernetes will work to keep this many Pods running. The next field, `selector`, is used to enable the Deployment to find its Pods. The content of `matchLabels` must exactly match the content in the `template.metadata.labels` field ❷, or Kubernetes will reject the Deployment.

Finally, the content of `template.spec` ❸ will be used as the `spec` for any Pods created by this Deployment. The fields here can include any configuration we can provide for a Pod. This configuration matches *nginx-pod.yaml* that we looked at earlier except that we add a CPU resource request ❹ so that we can configure autoscaling later on.

Let's create our Deployment from this YAML resource file:

```
root@host01:~# kubectl apply -f /opt/nginx-deploy.yaml
deployment.apps/nginx created
```

We can track the status of the Deployment with `kubectl get`:

```
root@host01:~# kubectl get deployment nginx
NAME    READY   UP-TO-DATE   AVAILABLE   AGE
nginx   3/3     3            3           4s
```

When the Deployment is fully up, it will report that it has three replicas ready and available, which means that we now have three separate NGINX Pods managed by this Deployment:

```
root@host01:~# kubectl get pods
NAME                     READY   STATUS    RESTARTS   AGE
nginx-6799fc88d8-6vn44   1/1     Running   0          18s
nginx-6799fc88d8-dcwx5   1/1     Running   0          18s
nginx-6799fc88d8-sh8qs   1/1     Running   0          18s
```

The name of each Pod begins with the name of the Deployment. Kubernetes adds some random characters to build the name of the ReplicaSet, followed by more random characters so that each Pod has a unique name. We don't need to create or manage the ReplicaSet directly, but we can use `kubectl get` to see it:

```
root@host01:~# kubectl get replicasets
NAME              DESIRED   CURRENT   READY   AGE
nginx-6799fc88d8  3         3         3       30s
```

Although we generally interact only with Deployments, it is important to know about the ReplicaSet, as some specific errors encountered when creating Pods are only reported in the ReplicaSet event log.

The `nginx` prefix on the ReplicaSet and Pod names are purely for convenience. The Deployment does not use names to match itself to Pods. Instead, it uses its selector to match the labels on the Pod. We can see these labels if we run `kubectl describe` on one of the three Pods:

```
root@host01:~# kubectl describe pod nginx-6799fc88d8-6vn44
Name:        nginx-6799fc88d8-6vn44
Namespace:   default
```

```
...
Labels:          app=nginx
...
```

This matches the Deployment's selector:

```
root@host01:~# kubectl describe deployment nginx
Name:                nginx
Namespace:           default
...
Selector:            app=nginx
...
```

The Deployment queries the API server to identify Pods matching its selector. Whereas the Deployment uses the programmatic API, the kubectl get
command in the following example generates a similar API server query,
giving us an opportunity to see how that works:

```
root@host01:~# kubectl get all -l app=nginx
NAME                          READY   STATUS    RESTARTS   AGE
nginx-6799fc88d8-6vn44        1/1     Running   0          69s
nginx-6799fc88d8-dcwx5        1/1     Running   0          69s
nginx-6799fc88d8-sh8qs        1/1     Running   0          69s

NAME                                   DESIRED   CURRENT   READY   AGE
replicaset.apps/nginx-6799fc88d8       3         3         3       69s
```

Using kubectl get all in this case allows us to list multiple different kinds
of resources as long as they match the selector. As a result, we see not only
the three Pods but also the ReplicaSet that was created by the Deployment
to manage those Pods.

It may seem strange that the Deployment uses a selector rather than just
tracking the Pods it created. However, this design makes it easier for Kubernetes to be self-healing. At any time, a Kubernetes node might go offline, or
we might have a network split, during which some control nodes lose their
connection to the cluster. If a node comes back online, or the cluster needs
to recombine after a network split, Kubernetes must be able to look at the
current state of all of the running Pods and figure out what changes are required to achieve the desired state. This might mean that a Deployment that
started an additional Pod as the result of a node disconnection would need
to shut down a Pod when that node reconnects so that the cluster can maintain the appropriate number of replicas. Using a selector avoids the need for
the Deployment to remember all the Pods it has ever created, even Pods on
failed nodes.

Monitoring and Scaling

Because the Deployment is monitoring its Pods to make sure we have the correct number of replicas, we can delete a Pod, and it will be automatically re-created:

```
root@host01:~# kubectl delete pod nginx-6799fc88d8-6vn44
pod "nginx-6799fc88d8-6vn44" deleted
root@host01:~# kubectl get pods
NAME                    READY   STATUS    RESTARTS    AGE
nginx-6799fc88d8-dcwx5  1/1     Running   0           3m52s
nginx-6799fc88d8-dtddk  1/1     Running   0         ❶ 14s
nginx-6799fc88d8-sh8qs  1/1     Running   0           3m52s
```

As soon as the old Pod is deleted, the Deployment created a new Pod ❶. Similarly, if we change the number of replicas for the Deployment, Pods are automatically updated. Let's add another replica:

```
root@host01:~# kubectl scale --replicas=4 deployment nginx
deployment.apps/nginx scaled
root@host01:~# kubectl get pods
NAME                    READY   STATUS    RESTARTS    AGE
nginx-6799fc88d8-dcwx5  1/1     Running   0           8m22s
nginx-6799fc88d8-dtddk  1/1     Running   0           4m44s
nginx-6799fc88d8-kk7r6  1/1     Running   0         ❶ 5s
nginx-6799fc88d8-sh8qs  1/1     Running   0           8m22s
```

The first command sets the number of replicas to four. As a result, Kubernetes needs to start a new identical Pod to meet the number we requested ❶. We can scale the Deployment by updating the YAML file and re-running `kubectl apply`, or we can use the `kubectl scale` command to edit the Deployment directly. Either way, this is a declarative approach; we are updating the Deployment's resource declaration; Kubernetes then updates the actual state of the cluster to match.

Similarly, scaling the Deployment down causes Pods to be automatically deleted:

```
root@host01:~# kubectl scale --replicas=2 deployment nginx
deployment.apps/nginx scaled
root@host01:~# kubectl get pods
NAME                    READY   STATUS    RESTARTS    AGE
nginx-6799fc88d8-dcwx5  1/1     Running   0           10m
nginx-6799fc88d8-sh8qs  1/1     Running   0           10m
```

When we scale down, Kubernetes selects two Pods to terminate. These Pods take a moment to finish shutting down, at which point we have only two NGINX Pods running.

Autoscaling

For an application that is receiving real requests from users, we would choose the number of replicas necessary to provide a quality application, while scaling down when possible to reduce the amount of resources used by our application. Of course, the load on our application is constantly changing, and it would be tedious to monitor each component of our application continually to scale it independently. Instead, we can have the cluster perform the monitoring and scaling for us using a *HorizontalPodAutoscaler*. The term *horizontal* in this case just refers to the fact that the autoscaler can update the number of replicas of the same Pod managed by a controller.

To configure autoscaling, we create a new resource with a reference to our Deployment. The cluster then monitors resources used by the Pods and reconfigures the Deployment as needed. We could add a HorizontalPod-Autoscaler to our Deployment using the kubectl autoscale command, but using a YAML resource file so that we can keep the autoscale configuration under version control is better. Here's the YAML file:

nginx-scaler.yaml
```
---
❶ apiVersion: autoscaling/v2
kind: HorizontalPodAutoscaler
metadata:
  name: nginx
  labels:
    app: nginx
spec:
❷ scaleTargetRef:
    apiVersion: apps/v1
    kind: Deployment
    name: nginx
❸ minReplicas: 1
  maxReplicas: 10
  metrics:
    - type: Resource
      resource:
        name: cpu
        target:
          type: Utilization
          averageUtilization: ❹ 50
```

In the metadata field, we add the label app: nginx. This does not change the behavior of the resource; its only purpose is to ensure that this resource shows up if we use an app=nginx label selector in a kubectl get command. This style of tagging the components of an application with consistent metadata is a good practice to help others understand what resources go together and to make debugging easier.

This YAML configuration uses version 2 of the autoscaler configuration ❶. Providing new versions of API resource groups is how Kubernetes accommodates future capability without losing any of its backward compatibility. Generally, alpha and beta versions are released for new resource groups before the final configuration is released, and there is at least one version of overlap between the beta version and the final release to enable seamless upgrades.

Version 2 of the autoscaler supports multiple resources. Each resource is used to calculate a vote on the desired number of Pods, and the largest number wins. Adding support for multiple resources requires a change in the YAML layout, which is a common reason for the Kubernetes maintainers to create a new resource version.

We specify our NGINX Deployment ❷ as the target for the autoscaler using its API resource group, kind, and name, which is enough to uniquely identify any resource in a Kubernetes cluster. We then tell the autoscaler to monitor the CPU utilization of the Pods that belong to the Deployment ❹. The autoscaler will work to keep average CPU utilization by the Pods close to 50 percent over the long run, scaling up or down as necessary. However, the number of replicas will never go beyond the range we specify ❸.

Let's create our autoscaler using this configuration:

```
root@host01:~# kubectl apply -f /opt/nginx-scaler.yaml
horizontalpodautoscaler.autoscaling/nginx created
```

We can query the cluster to see that it was created:

```
root@host01:~# kubectl get hpa
NAME    REFERENCE         TARGETS   MINPODS   MAXPODS   REPLICAS   AGE
nginx   Deployment/nginx  0%/50%    1         10        3          96s
```

The output shows the autoscaler's target reference, the current and desired resource utilization, and the maximum, minimum, and current number of replicas.

We use hpa as an abbreviation for horizontalpodautoscaler. Kubernetes allows us to use either singular or plural names and provides abbreviations for most of its resources to save typing. For example, we can type deploy for deployment and even po for pods. Every extra keystroke counts!

The autoscaler uses CPU utilization data that the kubelet is already collecting from the container engine. This data is centralized by the metrics server we installed as a cluster add-on. Without that cluster add-on, there would be no utilization data, and the autoscaler would not make any changes to the Deployment. In this case, because we're not really using our NGINX server instances, they aren't consuming any CPU, and the Deployment is scaled down to a single Pod, the minimum we specified:

```
root@host01:~# kubectl get pods
NAME                    READY   STATUS    RESTARTS   AGE
nginx-6799fc88d8-dcwx5  1/1     Running   0          15m
```

The autoscaler has calculated that only one Pod is needed and has scaled the Deployment to match. The Deployment then selected a Pod to terminate to reach the desired scale.

For accuracy, the autoscaler will not use CPU data from the Pod if it recently started running, and it has logic to prevent it from scaling up or down too often, so if you ran through these examples very quickly you might need to wait a few minutes before you see it scale.

We explore Kubernetes resource utilization metrics in more detail when we look at limiting resource usage in Chapter 14.

Other Controllers

Deployments are the most generic and commonly used controller, but Kubernetes has some other useful options. In this section, we explore *Job*s and *CronJob*s, *StatefulSets*, and *DaemonSets*.

Jobs and CronJobs

Deployments are great for application components because we usually want one or more instances to stay running indefinitely. However, for cases for which we need to run a command, either once or on a schedule, we can use a Job. The primary difference is a Deployment ensures that any container that stops running is restarted, whereas a Job can check the exit code of the main process and restart only if the exit code is non-zero, indicating failure.

A Job definition looks very similar to a Deployment:

sleep-job.yaml

```
---
apiVersion: batch/v1
kind: Job
metadata:
  name: sleep
spec:
  template:
    spec:
      containers:
      - name: sleep
        image: busybox
        command:
          - "/bin/sleep"
          - "30"
        restartPolicy: OnFailure
```

The restartPolicy can be set to OnFailure, in which case the container will be restarted for a non-zero exit code, or to Never, in which case the Job will be completed when the container exits regardless of the exit code.

We can create and view the Job and the Pod it has created:

```
root@host01:~# kubectl apply -f /opt/sleep-job.yaml
job.batch/sleep created
root@host01:~# kubectl get job
NAME      COMPLETIONS   DURATION   AGE
sleep     0/1           3s         3s
root@host01:~# kubectl get pods
NAME                      READY   STATUS     RESTARTS   AGE
...
sleep-fgcnz               1/1     Running    0          10s
```

The Job has created a Pod per the specification provided in the YAML file. The Job reflects 0/1 completions because it is waiting for its Pod to exit successfully.

When the Pod has been running for 30 seconds, it exits with a code of zero, indicating success, and the Job and Pod status are updated accordingly:

```
root@host01:~# kubectl get jobs
NAME      COMPLETIONS   DURATION   AGE
sleep     1/1           31s        40s
root@host01:~# kubectl get pods
NAME                      READY   STATUS      RESTARTS   AGE
nginx-65db7cf9c9-2wcng    1/1     Running     0          31m
sleep-fgcnz               0/1     Completed   0          43s
```

The Pod is still available, which means that we could review its logs if desired, but it shows a status of Completed, so Kubernetes will not try to restart the exited container.

A CronJob is a controller that creates Jobs on a schedule. For example, we could set up our sleep Job to run once per day:

sleep-cronjob.yaml
```
---
apiVersion: batch/v1
kind: CronJob
metadata:
  name: sleep
spec:
❶ schedule: "0 3 * * *"
❷ jobTemplate:
  spec:
    template:
      spec:
        containers:
          - name: sleep
            image: busybox
            command:
              - "/bin/sleep"
              - "30"
          restartPolicy: OnFailure
```

The entire contents of the Job specification are embedded inside the jobTemplate field ❷. To this, we add a schedule ❶ that follows the standard format for the Unix cron command. In this case, 0 3 * * * indicates that a Job should be created at 3:00 AM every day.

One of Kubernetes' design principles is that anything could go down at any time. For a CronJob, if the cluster has an issue during the time the Job would be scheduled, the Job might not be scheduled, or it might be scheduled twice, this means that you should take care to write Jobs in an idempotent way so that they can handle missing or duplicated scheduling.

If we create this CronJob

```
root@host01:~# kubectl apply -f /opt/sleep-cronjob.yaml
cronjob.batch/sleep created
```

it now exists in the cluster, but it does not immediately create a Job or a Pod:

```
root@host01:~# kubectl get jobs
NAME    COMPLETIONS   DURATION   AGE
sleep   1/1           31s        2m32s
root@host01:~# kubectl get pods
NAME                      READY   STATUS      RESTARTS   AGE
nginx-65db7cf9c9-2wcng    1/1     Running     0          33m
sleep-fgcnz               0/1     Completed   0          2m23s
```

Instead, the CronJob will create a new Job each time its schedule is triggered.

StatefulSets

So far, we've been looking at controllers that create identical Pods. With both Deployments and Jobs, we don't really care which Pod is which, or where it is deployed, as long as we run enough instances at the right time. However, that doesn't always match the behavior we want. For example, even though a Deployment can create Pods with persistent storage, the storage must either be brand new for each new Pod, or the same storage must be shared across all Pods. That doesn't align well with a "primary and secondary" architecture such as a database. For those cases, we want specific storage to be attached to specific Pods.

At the same time, because Pods can come and go due to hardware failures or upgrades, we need a way to manage the replacement of a Pod so that each Pod is attached to the right storage. This is the purpose of a *StatefulSet*. A StatefulSet identifies each Pod with a number, starting at zero, and each Pod receives matching persistent storage. When a Pod must be replaced, the new Pod is assigned the same numeric identifier and is attached to the same storage. Pods can look at their hostname to determine their identifier, so a StatefulSet is useful both for cases with a fixed primary instance as well as cases for which a primary instance is dynamically chosen.

We'll explore a lot more details related to Kubernetes StatefulSets in the next several chapters, including persistent storage and Services. For this chapter, we'll look at a basic example of a StatefulSet and then build on it as we introduce other important concepts.

For this simple example, let's create two Pods and show how they each get unique storage that stays in place even if the Pod is replaced. We'll use this YAML resource:

sleep-set.yaml

```
---
apiVersion: apps/v1
kind: StatefulSet
metadata:
  name: sleep
spec:
❶ serviceName: sleep
  replicas: 2
  selector:
    matchLabels:
      app: sleep
  template:
    metadata:
      labels:
        app: sleep
    spec:
      containers:
        - name: sleep
          image: busybox
          command:
            - "/bin/sleep"
            - "3600"
❷       volumeMounts:
            - name: sleep-volume
              mountPath: /storagedir
❸ volumeClaimTemplates:
    - metadata:
        name: sleep-volume
      spec:
        storageClassName: longhorn
        accessModes:
          - ReadWriteOnce
        resources:
          requests:
            storage: 10Mi
```

There are a few important differences here compared to a Deployment or a Job. First, we must declare a serviceName to tie this StatefulSet to a Kubernetes Service ❶. This connection is used to create a Domain Name Service (DNS) entry for each Pod. We must also provide a template for the StatefulSet to use to request persistent storage ❸ and then tell Kubernetes where to mount that storage in our container ❷.

The actual *sleep-set.yaml* file that the automation scripts install includes the sleep Service definition. We cover Services in detail in Chapter 9.

Let's create the sleep StatefulSet:

```
root@host01:~# kubectl apply -f /opt/sleep-set.yaml
```

The StatefulSet creates two Pods:

```
root@host01:~# kubectl get statefulsets
NAME    READY   AGE
sleep   2/2     1m14s
root@host01:~# kubectl get pods
NAME      READY   STATUS    RESTARTS   AGE
...
sleep-0   1/1     Running   0          57s
sleep-1   1/1     Running   0          32s
```

The persistent storage for each Pod is brand new, so it starts empty. Let's create some content. The easiest way to do that is from within the container itself, using kubectl exec, which allows us to run commands inside a container, similar to crictl. The kubectl exec command works no matter what host the container is on, even if we're connecting to our Kubernetes API server from outside the cluster.

Let's write each container's hostname to a file and print it out so that we can verify it worked:

```
root@host01:~# kubectl exec sleep-0 -- /bin/sh -c \
  'hostname > /storagedir/myhost'
root@host01:~# kubectl exec sleep-0 -- /bin/cat /storagedir/myhost
sleep-0
root@host01:~# kubectl exec sleep-1 -- /bin/sh -c \
  'hostname > /storagedir/myhost'
root@host01:~# kubectl exec sleep-1 -- /bin/cat /storagedir/myhost
sleep-1
```

Each of our Pods now has unique content in its persistent storage. Let's delete one of the Pods and verify that its replacement inherits its predecessor's storage:

```
root@host01:~# kubectl delete pod sleep-0
pod "sleep-0" deleted
root@host01:~# kubectl get pods
NAME      READY   STATUS    RESTARTS   AGE
...
sleep-0   1/1     Running   0          28s
sleep-1   1/1     Running   0          8m18s
root@host01:~# kubectl exec sleep-0 -- /bin/cat /storagedir/myhost
sleep-0
```

After deleting sleep-0, we see a new Pod created with the same name, which is different from the Deployment for which a random name was generated for every new Pod. Additionally, for this new Pod, the file we created previously is still present because the StatefulSet attached the same persistent storage to the new Pod it created when the old one was deleted.

Daemon Sets

The *DaemonSet* controller is like a StatefulSet in that the DaemonSet also runs a specific number of Pods, each with a unique identity. However, the DaemonSet runs exactly one Pod per node, which is useful primarily for control plane and add-on components for a cluster, such as a network or storage plug-in.

Our cluster already has multiple DaemonSets installed, so let's look at the calico-node DaemonSet that's already running, which runs on each node to provide network configuration for all containers on that node.

The calico-node DaemonSet is in the calico-system Namespace, so we'll specify that Namespace to request information about the DaemonSet:

```
root@host01:~# kubectl -n calico-system get daemonsets
NAME           DESIRED   CURRENT   READY   UP-TO-DATE   AVAILABLE   ...
calico-node    3         3         3       3            3           ...
```

Our cluster has three nodes, so the calico-node DaemonSet has created three instances. Here's the configuration of this DaemonSet in YAML format:

```
root@host01:~# kubectl -n calico-system get daemonset calico-node -o yaml
apiVersion: apps/v1
kind: DaemonSet
metadata:
...
  name: calico-node
  namespace: calico-system
...
spec:
...
  selector:
    matchLabels:
      k8s-app: calico-node
...
```

The -o yaml parameter to kubectl get prints out the configuration and status of one or more resources in YAML format, allowing us to inspect Kubernetes resources in detail.

The selector for this DaemonSet expects a label called k8s-app to be set to calico-node. We can use this to show just the Pods that this DaemonSet creates:

```
root@host01:~# kubectl -n calico-system get pods \
  -l k8s-app=calico-node -o wide
NAME                   READY   STATUS    ... NODE   ...
calico-node-h9kjh      1/1     Running   ... host01 ...
calico-node-rcfk7      1/1     Running   ... host03 ...
calico-node-wj876      1/1     Running   ... host02 ...
```

The DaemonSet has created three Pods, each of which is assigned to one of the nodes in our cluster. If we add additional nodes to our cluster, the DaemonSet will schedule a Pod on the new nodes as well.

Final Thoughts

This chapter explored Kubernetes from the perspective of a regular cluster user, creating controllers that in turn create Pods with containers. Having this core knowledge of controller resource types is essential for building our applications. At the same time, it's important to remember that Kubernetes is using the container technology we explored in Part I.

One key aspect of container technology is the ability to isolate containers in separate network namespaces. Running containers in a Kubernetes cluster adds additional requirements for networking because we now need to connect containers running on different cluster nodes. In the next chapter, we consider multiple approaches to make this work as we look at overlay networks.

8

OVERLAY NETWORKS

Container networking is complex enough when all of the containers are on a single host, as we saw in Chapter 4. When we scale up to a cluster of nodes, all of which run containers, the complexity increases substantially. Not only must we provide each container with its own virtual network devices and manage IP addresses, dynamically creating new network namespaces and devices when containers are created, but we also need to ensure that containers on one node can communicate with containers on all the other nodes.

In this chapter, we'll describe how *overlay networks* are used to provide the appearance of a single container network across all nodes in a Kubernetes cluster. We'll consider two different approaches for routing container traffic across a host network, examining the network configuration and traffic flows for each. Finally, we'll explore how Kubernetes uses the Container Network Interface (CNI) standard to configure networking as a separate plug-in, making it easy to shift to new technology as it becomes available and allowing for custom solutions where needed.

Cluster Networking

The fundamental goal of a Kubernetes cluster is to treat a set of hosts (physical or virtual machines) as a single computing resource that can be allocated as needed to run containers. From a networking standpoint, this means Kubernetes should be able to schedule a Pod onto any node without worrying about connectivity to Pods on other nodes. It also means that Kubernetes should have a way to dynamically allocate IP addresses to Pods in a way that supports that cluster-wide network connectivity.

As we'll see in this chapter, Kubernetes uses a plug-in design to allow any compatible network software to allocate IP addresses and provide cross-node network connectivity. All plug-ins must follow a couple of important rules. First, Pod IP addresses should come from a single pool of IP addresses, although this pool can be subdivided by node. This means that we can treat all Pods as part of a single flat network, no matter where the Pods run. Second, traffic should be routable such that all Pods can see all other Pods and the control plane.

CNI Plug-ins

Plug-ins communicate with the Kubernetes cluster, specifically with kubelet, using the CNI standard. CNI specifies how kubelet finds and invokes CNI plug-ins. When a new Pod is created, kubelet first allocates the network namespace. It then invokes the CNI plug-in, providing it a reference to the network namespace. The CNI plug-in adds network devices to the namespace, assigns an IP address, and passes that IP address back to kubelet.

Let's see that process in action. To do so, our examples for this chapter include two different environments with two different CNI plug-ins: Calico and WeaveNet. Both of these plug-ins provide networking for Pods but with different cross-node networking. We'll begin with the Calico environment.

NOTE *The example repository for this book is at* https://github.com/book-of
*-kubernetes/examples. See "Running Examples" on page xx for details on
getting set up.*

By default, CNI plug-in information is kept in */etc/cni/net.d*. We can see the Calico configuration in that directory:

```
root@host01:~# ls /etc/cni/net.d
10-calico.conflist  calico-kubeconfig
```

The file *10-calico.conflist* contains the actual Calico configuration. The file *calico-kubeconfig* is used by Calico components to authenticate with the control plane; it was created based on a service account created during Calico installation. The configuration filename has the *10-* prefix because kubelet sorts any configuration files it finds and uses the first one.

Listing 8-1 shows the configuration file, which is in JSON format and identifies the network plug-ins to use.

```
root@host01:~# cat /etc/cni/net.d/10-calico.conflist
{
  "name": "k8s-pod-network",
  "cniVersion": "0.3.1",
  "plugins": [
    {
      "type": "calico",
...
    },
    {
      "type": "bandwidth",
      "capabilities": {"bandwidth": true}
    },
    {"type": "portmap", "snat": true, "capabilities": {"portMappings": true}}
  ]
}
```

Listing 8-1: Calico configuration

The most important field is type; it specifies which plug-in to run. In this case, we're running three plug-ins: calico, which handles Pod networking; bandwidth, which we can use to configure network limits; and portmap, which is used to expose container ports to the host network. These two plug-ins inform kubelet of their purposes using the capabilities field; as a result, when kubelet invokes them, it passes in the relevant bandwidth and port mapping configuration so that the plug-in can make the necessary network configuration changes.

To run these plug-ins, kubelet needs to know where they are located. The default location for the actual plug-in executables is *opt/cni/bin*, and the name of the plug-in matches the type field:

```
root@host01:~# ls /opt/cni/bin
bandwidth  calico-ipam  flannel      install    macvlan   sbr      vlan
bridge     dhcp         host-device  ipvlan     portmap   static
calico     firewall     host-local   loopback   ptp       tuning
```

Here, we see a common set of network plug-ins that were installed by kubeadm along with our Kubernetes cluster. We also see calico, which was added to this directory by the Calico DaemonSet we installed after cluster initialization.

Pod Networking

Let's look at an example Pod to get a glimpse of how the CNI plug-ins configure the Pod's network namespace. The behavior is very similar to the work we did in Chapter 4, adding virtual network devices into network namespaces to enable communication between containers and with the host network.

Let's create a basic Pod:

```
---
apiVersion: v1
kind: Pod
metadata:
  name: pod
spec:
  containers:
  - name: pod
    image: busybox
    command:
      - "sleep"
      - "infinity"
    nodeName: host01
```

We've added the extra field nodeName to force this Pod to run on host01, which will make it easier to find and examine how its networking is configured.

We start the Pod via the usual command:

```
root@host01:~# kubectl apply -f /opt/pod.yaml
pod/pod created
```

Next, check to see that it's running:

```
root@host01:~# kubectl get pods
NAME   READY   STATUS    RESTARTS   AGE
pod    1/1     Running   0          2m32s
```

After it's running, we can use crictl to capture its unique ID:

```
root@host01:~# POD_ID=$(crictl pods --name pod -q)
root@host01:~# echo $POD_ID
b7d2391320e07f97add7ccad2ad1a664393348f1dcb6f803f701318999ed0295
```

At this point, using the Pod ID, we can find its network namespace. In Listing 8-2, we use jq to extract only the data we want, just as we did in Chapter 4. We'll then assign it to a variable.

```
root@host01:~# NETNS_PATH=$(crictl inspectp $POD_ID |
  jq -r '.info.runtimeSpec.linux.namespaces[]|select(.type=="network").path')
root@host01:~# echo $NETNS_PATH
/var/run/netns/cni-7cffed61-fb56-9be1-0548-4813d4a8f996
root@host01:~# NETNS=$(basename $NETNS_PATH)
root@host01:~# echo $NETNS
cni-7cffed61-fb56-9be1-0548-4813d4a8f996
```

Listing 8-2: Network namespace

We now can explore the network namespace to see how Calico set up the IP address and network routing for this Pod. First, as expected, this network namespace is being used for our Pod:

```
root@host01:~# ps $(ip netns pids $NETNS)
    PID TTY       STAT   TIME COMMAND
 35574 ?         Ss     0:00 /pause
 35638 ?         Ss     0:00 sleep infinity
```

We see the two processes that we should expect. The first is a pause container that is always created whenever we create a Pod. This is a permanent container to hold the network namespace. The second is our BusyBox container running sleep, as we configured in the Pod YAML file.

Now, let's see the configured network interfaces:

```
root@host03:~# ip netns exec $NETNS ip addr
1: lo: <LOOPBACK,UP,LOWER_UP> mtu 65536 qdisc noqueue state UNKNOWN ...
    link/loopback 00:00:00:00:00:00 brd 00:00:00:00:00:00
    inet 127.0.0.1/8 scope host lo
       valid_lft forever preferred_lft forever
    inet6 ::1/128 scope host
       valid_lft forever preferred_lft forever
3: ❶ eth0@if16: <BROADCAST,MULTICAST,UP,LOWER_UP> mtu 1450 ... state UP ...
    link/ether 7a:9e:6c:e2:30:47 brd ff:ff:ff:ff:ff:ff link-netnsid 0
    inet ❷ 172.31.239.205/32 brd 172.31.25.202 scope global eth0
       valid_lft forever preferred_lft forever
    inet6 fe80::789e:6cff:fee2:3047/64 scope link
       valid_lft forever preferred_lft forever
```

Calico has created the network device eth0@if16 in the network namespace ❶ and given it an IP address of 172.31.239.205 ❷. Note that the network length for that IP address is /32, which indicates that any traffic must go through a configured router. This is different from how our bridged container networking worked in Chapter 4. It is necessary so that Calico can provide firewall capabilities via network policies.

The choice of IP address for this Pod was ultimately up to Calico. Calico is configured with 172.31.0.0/16 for use as the IP address space for Pods. Calico decides how to divide this address space up between nodes and then allocates IP addresses to each Pod from the range allocated to the node. Calico then passes this IP address back to kubelet so that it can update the Pod's status:

```
root@host01:~# kubectl get pods -o wide
NAME   READY   STATUS    RESTARTS   AGE   IP              NODE     ...
pod    1/1     Running   0          16m   172.31.239.205  host01   ...
```

When Calico created the network interface in the Pod, it created it as part of a virtual Ethernet (veth) pair. The veth pair acts as a virtual network wire that creates a connection to a network interface in the root namespace, allowing connections outside the Pod. Listing 8-3 lets us have a look at both halves of the veth pair.

```
root@host01:~# ip netns exec $NETNS ip link
...
3: eth0@if13: <BROADCAST,MULTICAST,UP,LOWER_UP> mtu 1450 qdisc noqueue ...
    link/ether 6e:4c:3a:41:d0:54 brd ff:ff:ff:ff:ff:ff link-netnsid 0
root@host01:~# ip link | grep -B 1 $NETNS
13: cali9381c30abed@if3: <BROADCAST,MULTICAST,UP,LOWER_UP> mtu 1450 ...
    link/ether ee:ee:ee:ee:ee:ee ... link-netns cni-7cffed61-fb56-9be1-0548-4813d4a8f996
```

Listing 8-3: Calico veth pair

The first command prints the network interfaces inside the namespace, whereas the second prints the interfaces on the host. Each contains the field link-netns pointing to the corresponding network namespace of the other interface, showing that these two interfaces create a link between our Pod's namespace and the root namespace.

Cross-Node Networking

So far, the configuration of the virtual network devices in the container looks very similar to the container networking in Chapter 4, where there was no Kubernetes cluster installed. The difference in this case is that the network plug-in is configured not just to connect containers on a single node, but to connect containers running anywhere in the cluster.

WHY NOT NAT?

Regular container networking does, of course, provide connectivity to the host network. However, as we've discussed, it accomplishes this using Network Address Translation (NAT). This is fine for containers running individual client applications, as connection tracking enables Linux to route server responses all the way into the originating container. It does not work for containers that need to act as servers, which is a key use case for a Kubernetes cluster.

For most private networks that use NAT to connect to a broader network, port forwarding is used to expose specific services from within the private network. That isn't a good solution for every container in every Pod, as we would quickly run out of ports to allocate. The network plug-ins do end up using NAT, but only to connect containers acting as clients to make connections to networks outside the cluster. In addition, we will see port forwarding behavior in Chapter 9, where it will be one possible way to expose Services outside the cluster.

The challenge in cross-node networking is that the Pod network has a different range of IP addresses from the host network, so the host network does not know how to route this traffic. There are a couple of different ways that network plug-ins work around this. We'll begin by continuing with our cluster running Calico. Then, we'll show a different cross-node networking technology using WeaveNet.

Calico Networking

Calico performs cross-node networking using Layer 3 routing. This means that it routes based on IP addresses, configuring IP routing tables on each host and in the Pod to ensure that traffic is sent to the correct host and then to the correct Pod. Thus, at the host level, we see the Pod IP addresses as the source and destination. Because Calico relies on the built-in routing capabilities of Linux, we don't need to configure our host network switch to route the traffic, but we do need to configure any security controls on the host network switch to allow Pod IP addresses to travel across the network.

To explore Calico cross-node networking, it helps to have two Pods: one on host01 and the other on host02. We'll use this resource file:

two-pods.yaml
```
---
apiVersion: v1
kind: Pod
metadata:
  name: pod1
spec:
  containers:
  - name: pod1
    image: busybox
    command:
      - "sleep"
      - "infinity"
    nodeName: host01
---
apiVersion: v1
kind: Pod
metadata:
  name: pod2
spec:
  containers:
  - name: pod2
    image: busybox
    command:
      - "sleep"
      - "infinity"
    nodeName: host02
```

As always, these files have been loaded into the */opt* directory by the automated scripts for this chapter.

The --- separator allows us to put two different Kubernetes resources in the same file so that we can manage them together. The only difference in configuration with these two Pods is that they each have a nodeName field to ensure that they are assigned to the correct node.

Let's delete our existing Pod and replace it with the two that we need:

```
root@host01:~# kubectl delete -f /opt/pod.yaml
pod "pod" deleted
root@host01:~# kubectl apply -f /opt/two-pods.yaml
pod/pod1 created
pod/pod2 created
```

After these Pods are running, we'll need to collect their IP addresses:

```
root@host01:~# IP1=$(kubectl get po pod1 -o json | jq -r '.status.podIP')
root@host01:~# IP2=$(kubectl get po pod2 -o json | jq -r '.status.podIP')
root@host01:~# echo $IP1
172.31.239.216
root@host01:~# echo $IP2
172.31.89.197
```

We're able to extract the Pod IP using a simple jq filter because our kubectl get command is guaranteed to return only one item. If we were running kubectl get without a filter, or with a filter that might match multiple Pods, the JSON output would be a list and we would need to change the jq filter accordingly.

Let's quickly verify that we have connectivity between these two Pods:

```
root@host01:~# kubectl exec -ti pod1 -- ping -c 3 $IP2
PING 172.31.89.197 (172.31.89.197): 56 data bytes
64 bytes from 172.31.89.197: seq=0 ttl=62 time=2.867 ms
64 bytes from 172.31.89.197: seq=1 ttl=62 time=0.916 ms
64 bytes from 172.31.89.197: seq=2 ttl=62 time=1.463 ms

--- 172.31.89.197 ping statistics ---
3 packets transmitted, 3 packets received, 0% packet loss
round-trip min/avg/max = 0.916/1.748/2.867 ms
```

The ping command shows that all three packets arrived successfully, so we know the Pods can communicate across nodes.

As in our earlier example, each of these Pods has a network interface with a network length of /32, meaning that all traffic must go through a router. For example, here is the IP configuration and route table for pod1:

```
root@host01:~# kubectl exec -ti pod1 -- ip addr
...
3: eth0@if17: <BROADCAST,MULTICAST,UP,LOWER_UP,M-DOWN> mtu 1450 qdisc noqueue
    link/ether f2:ed:e8:04:00:cc brd ff:ff:ff:ff:ff:ff
    inet 172.31.239.216/32 brd 172.31.239.216 scope global eth0
...
root@host01:~# kubectl exec -ti pod1 -- ip route
default via 169.254.1.1 dev eth0
169.254.1.1 dev eth0 scope link
```

Based on this configuration, when we run our `ping` command, the networking stack recognizes that the destination IP is not local to any interface. It therefore looks up 169.254.1.1 in its Address Resolution Protocol (ARP) table to determine where to send the "next hop." If we try to find an interface either in the container or on the host that has the address 169.254.1.1, we won't be successful. Rather than actually assign that address to an interface, Calico just configures "proxy ARP" so that the packet will be sent through the `eth0` end of the veth pair. As a result, there is an entry for 169.254.1.1 in the ARP table inside the container:

```
root@host01:~# kubectl exec -ti pod1 -- arp -n
? (169.254.1.1) at ee:ee:ee:ee:ee:ee [ether]  on eth0
...
```

As shown in Listing 8-3, the hardware address ee:ee:ee:ee:ee:ee belongs to the host side of the veth pair, so this is sufficient to get the packet out of the container and into the root network namespace. From there, IP routing takes over.

Calico has already configured the routing table to send packets to other cluster nodes based on the destination IP address range for that node and to send packets to local containers based on their individual IP addresses. We can see the result of this in the IP routing table on the host:

```
root@host01:~# ip route
...
172.31.25.192/26 via 192.168.61.13 dev enp0s8 proto 80 onlink
172.31.89.192/26 via 192.168.61.12 dev enp0s8 proto 80 onlink
172.31.239.216 dev calice0906292e2 scope link
...
```

Because the destination address for the ping is within the 172.31.89.192/26 network, the packet now is routed to 192.168.61.12, which is host02.

Let's look at the routing table on host02 so that we can follow along with the next step:

```
root@host02:~# ip route
...
172.31.239.192/26 via 192.168.61.11 dev enp0s8 proto 80 onlink
172.31.25.192/26 via 192.168.61.13 dev enp0s8 proto 80 onlink
172.31.89.197 dev calibd2348b4f67 scope link
...
```

If you want to run this command for yourself, make sure you run it from host02. When our packet arrives at host02, it has a route for the specific IP address that is the destination of the `ping`. This route sends the packet into the veth pair that is attached to the pod2 network namespace.

Now that the ping has arrived, the network stack inside pod2 sends back a reply. The reply goes through the same process to reach the root network namespace of host02. Based on the host02 routing table, it is sent to host01, where a routing table entry for 172.31.239.216 is used to send it to the appropriate container.

Because Calico is using Layer 3 routing, the host network sees the actual container IP addresses. We can confirm that using tcpdump. We'll switch back to host01 for this.

First, let's kick off tcpdump in the background:

```
root@host01:~# tcpdump -n -w pings.pcap -i any icmp &
[1] 70949
tcpdump: listening on any ...
```

The -n flag tells tcpdump to avoid trying to lookup hostnames in DNS for any IP addresses; this saves time. The -w pings.pcap flag tells tcpdump to write its data to the file *pings.pcap*; the -i any flag tells it to listen on all network interfaces; the icmp filter tells it to listen only to ICMP traffic; and finally, & at the end puts it in the background.

The *pcap* filename extension is important because our Ubuntu host system will only allow tcpdump to read files with that extension.

Now, let's run ping again:

```
root@host01:~# kubectl exec -ti pod1 -- ping -c 3 $IP2
...
3 packets transmitted, 3 packets received, 0% packet loss
round-trip min/avg/max = 0.928/0.991/1.115 ms
```

The ICMP requests and replies have been collected, but they are being buffered in memory.

To get them dumped to the file, we'll shut down tcpdump:

```
root@host01:~# killall tcpdump
12 packets captured
12 packets received by filter
0 packets dropped by kernel
```

There were three pings, and each ping consists of a request and a reply. Thus, we might have expected six packets, but in fact we captured 12. To see why, let's print the details of the packets that tcpdump collected:

```
root@host01:~# tcpdump -enr pings.pcap
reading from file pings.pcap, link-type LINUX_SLL (Linux cooked v1)
00:16:23... In f2:ed:e8:04:00:cc ❶ ... 172.31.239.216 > 172.31.89.197: ICMP echo request ...
00:16:23... Out 08:00:27:b7:ef:ef ❷ ... 172.31.239.216 > 172.31.89.197: ICMP echo request ...
00:16:23... In 08:00:27:fc:d2:36 ❸ ... 172.31.89.197 > 172.31.239.216: ICMP echo reply ...
00:16:23... Out ee:ee:ee:ee:ee:ee ❹ ... 172.31.89.197 > 172.31.239.216: ICMP echo reply ...
...
```

The -e flag to tcpdump prints the hardware addresses; otherwise, we wouldn't be able to tell some of the packets apart. The first hardware address ❶ is the hardware address of eth0 inside the Pod. Next is the same packet again, but this time the hardware address is the host interface ❷. We then see the reply, first arriving at the host interface and labeled with the hardware address for host02 ❸. Finally, the packet is routed into the Calico network interface corresponding to our Pod ❹, and our ping has made its round trip.

We're now done with these two Pods, so let's delete them:

```
root@host01:~# kubectl delete -f /opt/two-pods.yaml
pod "pod1" deleted
pod "pod2" deleted
```

Using Layer 3 routing is an elegant solution to cross-node networking for a Kubernetes cluster, as it takes advantage of the routing and traffic forwarding capabilities that are native to Linux. However, it does mean that the host network sees the Pods' IP addresses, which may require security rule changes. For example, the automated scripts that set up virtual machines in Amazon Web Services (AWS) for use with this book not only configure a security group to allow all traffic in the Pod IP address space, but they also turn off the "source/destination check" for the virtual machine instances. Otherwise, the underlying AWS network infrastructure would refuse to pass traffic with unexpected IP addresses to our cluster's nodes.

WeaveNet

Layer 3 routing is not the only solution for cross-node networking. Another option is to "encapsulate" the container packets into a packet that is sent explicitly host to host. This is the approach taken by popular network plugins such as Flannel and WeaveNet. We'll look at a WeaveNet example, but the traffic using Flannel looks very similar.

NOTE   *Larger clusters based on Calico also use encapsulation for some traffic between networks. For example, a cluster that spans multiple regions, or Availability Zones, in AWS would likely need to configure Calico to use encapsulation, given that it may not be possible or practical to configure all of the routers between the regions or Availability Zones with the necessary Pod IP routes for the cluster.*

Because everything you might want to do in networking has some defined standard, it's not surprising that there is a standard for encapsulation: Virtual Extensible LAN (VXLAN). In VXLAN, each packet is wrapped in a UDP datagram and sent to the destination.

We'll use the same *two-pods.yaml* configuration file to create two Pods in our Kubernetes cluster, this time using a cluster built from the *weavenet* directory from this chapter's examples. As before, we end up with one Pod on host01 and the other on host02:

```
root@host01:~# kubectl apply -f /opt/two-pods.yaml
pod/pod1 created
pod/pod2 created
```

Let's check that these Pods are running and allocated correctly to their different hosts:

```
root@host01:~# kubectl get po -o wide
NAME    READY   STATUS     ... IP          NODE      ...
pod1    1/1     Running    ... 10.46.0.8   host01    ...
pod2    1/1     Running    ... 10.40.0.21  host02    ...
```

After these Pods are running, we can collect their IP addresses using the same commands shown earlier:

```
root@host01:~# IP1=$(kubectl get po pod1 -o json | jq -r '.status.podIP')
root@host01:~# IP2=$(kubectl get po pod2 -o json | jq -r '.status.podIP')
root@host01:~# echo $IP1
10.46.0.8
root@host01:~# echo $IP2
10.40.0.21
```

Note that the IP addresses assigned look nothing like the Calico example. Further exploration shows that the address and routing configuration is also different, as demonstrated in Listing 8-4.

```
root@host01:~# kubectl exec -ti pod1 -- ip addr
...
25: eth0@if26: <BROADCAST,MULTICAST,UP,LOWER_UP,M-DOWN> mtu 1376 qdisc noqueue
    link/ether e6:78:69:44:3d:a4 brd ff:ff:ff:ff:ff:ff
    inet 10.46.0.8/12 brd 10.47.255.255 scope global eth0
       valid_lft forever preferred_lft forever
...
root@host01:~# kubectl exec -ti pod1 -- ip route
default via 10.46.0.0 dev eth0
10.32.0.0/12 dev eth0 scope link  src 10.46.0.8
```

Listing 8-4: WeaveNet networking

This time, our Pods are getting IP addresses in a massive /12 network, corresponding to more than one million possible addresses on a single network. In this case, our Pod's networking stack is going to expect to be able to use ARP to directly identify the hardware address of any other Pod on the network rather than routing traffic to a gateway as we saw with Calico.

As before, we do have connectivity between these two Pods:

```
root@host01:~# kubectl exec -ti pod1 -- ping -c 3 $IP2
PING 10.40.0.21 (10.40.0.21): 56 data bytes
64 bytes from 10.40.0.21: seq=0 ttl=64 time=0.981 ms
64 bytes from 10.40.0.21: seq=1 ttl=64 time=0.963 ms
64 bytes from 10.40.0.21: seq=2 ttl=64 time=0.871 ms
```

```
--- 10.40.0.21 ping statistics ---
3 packets transmitted, 3 packets received, 0% packet loss
round-trip min/avg/max = 0.871/0.938/0.981 ms
```

And now that we've run this `ping` command, we should expect that the
ARP table in the `pod1` networking stack is populated with the hardware address of the `pod2` network interface:

```
root@host01:~# kubectl exec -ti pod1 -- arp -n
? (10.40.0.21) at ba:75:e6:db:7c:c6 [ether]  on eth0
? (10.46.0.0) at 1a:72:78:64:36:c6 [ether]  on eth0
```

As expected, `pod1` has an ARP table entry for `pod2`'s IP address, corresponding to the virtual network interface inside `pod2`:

```
root@host01:~# kubectl exec -ti pod2 -- ip addr
...
53: eth0@if54: <BROADCAST,MULTICAST,UP,LOWER_UP,M-DOWN> mtu 1376 qdisc noqueue
    link/ether ❶ ba:75:e6:db:7c:c6 brd ff:ff:ff:ff:ff:ff
    inet 10.40.0.21/12 brd 10.47.255.255 scope global eth0
      valid_lft forever preferred_lft forever
...
```

The hardware address in the `pod1` ARP table matches the hardware address of the virtual network device in `pod2` ❶. To make this happen, Weave-
Net is routing the ARP request over the network so that the network stack in
`pod2` can respond.

Let's look at how the cross-node routing of ARP and ICMP traffic is happening. First, although the IP address management may be different, one
important similarity between Calico and WeaveNet is that both are using
veth pairs to connect containers to the host. If you want to explore that,
use the commands shown in Listing 8-2 and Listing 8-3 to determine the
network namespace for `pod1`, and then use `ip addr` on `host01` to verify that
there is a veth device with a `link-netns` field that corresponds to that network
namespace.

For our purposes, because we've seen that before, we'll take it as a given
that the traffic goes through the virtual network wire created by the veth
pair and gets to the host. Let's start there and trace the ICMP traffic between the two Pods.

If we use the same `tcpdump` capture as we did with Calico, we'll be able to
capture the ICMP traffic, but that will get us only so far. Let's go ahead and
look at that:

```
root@host01:~# tcpdump -w pings.pcap -i any icmp &
[1] 55999
tcpdump: listening on any, link-type LINUX_SLL (Linux cooked v1) ...
root@host01:~# kubectl exec -ti pod1 -- ping -c 3 $IP2
...
```

```
3 packets transmitted, 3 packets received, 0% packet loss
round-trip min/avg/max = 0.824/1.691/3.053 ms
root@host01:~# killall tcpdump
24 packets captured
24 packets received by filter
0 packets dropped by kernel
```

As before, we ran tcpdump in the background to capture ICMP on all net-work interfaces, ran our ping, and then stopped tcpdump so that it would write out the packets it captured. This time we have 24 packets to look at, but they still don't tell the whole story:

```
root@host01:~# tcpdump -enr pings.pcap
reading from file pings.pcap, link-type LINUX_SLL (Linux cooked v1)
16:22:08.211499  P e6:78:69:44:3d:a4 ... 10.46.0.8 > 10.40.0.21: ICMP echo request ...
16:22:08.211551 Out e6:78:69:44:3d:a4 ... 10.46.0.8 > 10.40.0.21: ICMP echo request ...
16:22:08.211553  P e6:78:69:44:3d:a4 ... 10.46.0.8 > 10.40.0.21: ICMP echo request ...
16:22:08.211745 Out e6:78:69:44:3d:a4 ... 10.46.0.8 > 10.40.0.21: ICMP echo request ...
16:22:08.212917  P ba:75:e6:db:7c:c6 ... 10.40.0.21 > 10.46.0.8: ICMP echo reply ...
16:22:08.213704 Out ba:75:e6:db:7c:c6 ... 10.40.0.21 > 10.46.0.8: ICMP echo reply ...
16:22:08.213708  P ba:75:e6:db:7c:c6 ... 10.40.0.21 > 10.46.0.8: ICMP echo reply ...
16:22:08.213724 Out ba:75:e6:db:7c:c6 ... 10.40.0.21 > 10.46.0.8: ICMP echo reply ...
...
```

These lines show four packets for a single ping request and reply, but the hardware addresses aren't changing. What's happening is that these ICMP packets are being handed between network interfaces unmodified. How-ever, we're still not seeing the actual traffic that's going between host01 and host02, because we never see any hardware addresses that correspond to host interfaces.

To see the host-level traffic, we need to tell tcpdump to capture UDP and then treat it as VXLAN, which enables tcpdump to identify the fact that an ICMP packet is inside.

Let's start the capture again, this time looking for UDP traffic:

```
root@host01:~# tcpdump -w vxlan.pcap -i any udp &
...
root@host01:~# kubectl exec -ti pod1 -- ping -c 3 $IP2
...
3 packets transmitted, 3 packets received, 0% packet loss
round-trip min/avg/max = 1.139/1.364/1.545 ms
root@host01:~# killall tcpdump
22 packets captured
24 packets received by filter
0 packets dropped by kernel
```

This time we saved the packet data in *vxlan.pcap*. In this example, tcpdump captured 22 packets. Because there is lots of cross-Pod traffic in our cluster, not just ICMP traffic, you might see a different number.

The packets we captured cover all of the UDP traffic on host01, not just our ICMP, so in printing out the packets shown in Listing 8-5, we'll need to be selective.

```
root@host01:~# tcpdump -enr vxlan.pcap -T vxlan | grep -B 1 ICMP
reading from file vxlan.pcap, link-type LINUX_SLL (Linux cooked v1)
16:45:47.307949 Out 08:00:27:32:a0:28 ...
  length 150: 192.168.61.11.50200 > 192.168.61.12.6784: VXLAN ...
e6:78:69:44:3d:a4 > ba:75:e6:db:7c:c6 ...
  length 98: 10.46.0.8 > 10.40.0.21: ICMP echo request ...
16:45:47.308699  In 08:00:27:67:b9:da ...
  length 150: 192.168.61.12.43489 > 192.168.61.11.6784: VXLAN ...
ba:75:e6:db:7c:c6 > e6:78:69:44:3d:a4 ...
  length 98: 10.40.0.21 > 10.46.0.8: ICMP echo reply ...
16:45:48.308240 Out 08:00:27:32:a0:28 ...
  length 150: 192.168.61.11.50200 > 192.168.61.12.6784: VXLAN ...
...
```

Listing 8-5: VXLAN capture

The -T vxlan flag tells tcpdump to treat the packet data it sees as VXLAN data. This causes tcpdump to look inside and pull out data from the encapsulated packets, enabling it to identify ICMP packets when those are hidden inside. We then use grep with a -B 1 flag to find those ICMP packets and also print the line immediately previous so that we can see the VXLAN wrapper.

This capture shows the host's hardware address, which informs us that we've managed to capture the traffic moving between hosts. Each ICMP packet is wrapped in a UDP datagram and sent across the host network. The IP source and destination for these datagrams are the host network IP addresses 192.168.61.11 and 192.168.61.12, so the host network never sees the Pod IP addresses. However, that information is still there, in the encapsulated ICMP packet, thus when the datagram arrives at its destination, Weave-Net can send the ICMP packet to the correct destination.

The advantage of encapsulation is that all of our cross-node traffic looks like ordinary UDP datagrams between hosts. Typically, we don't need to do any additional network configuration to allow this traffic. However, we do pay a price. As you can see in Listing 8-5, each ICMP packet is 98 bytes, but the encapsulated packet is 150 bytes. The wrapper needed for encapsulation creates network overhead that we have to pay with each packet we send.

Look back at Listing 8-4 for another consequence. The virtual network interface inside the Pod has a maximum transmission unit (MTU) of 1,376. This represents the largest packet that can be sent; anything bigger must to be fragmented into multiple packets and reassembled at the destination. This MTU of 1,376 is considerably smaller than the standard MTU of 1,500 on our host network. The smaller MTU on the Pod interface ensures that the Pod's network stack will do any required fragmenting. This way, we can guarantee that we don't exceed 1,500 at the host layer, even after the wrapper is added. For this reason, if you are using a network plug-in that uses encapsulation, it might be worth exploring how to configure jumbo frames to enable an MTU larger than 1,500 on the host network.

Choosing a Network Plug-in

Network plug-ins can use different approaches to cross-node networking. As is universal in engineering, though, there are trade-offs with each approach. Layer 3 routing uses native capabilities of Linux and is efficient in its use of the network bandwidth, but it may require customization of the underlying host network. Encapsulation with VXLAN works in any network where we can send UDP datagrams between hosts, but it adds overhead with each packet.

Either way, however, our Pods are getting what they need, which is the ability to communicate with other Pods, wherever in the cluster they may be. And in practice, the configuration effort and performance difference tends to be small. For this reason, the best way to choose a network plug-in is to start with the plug-in that is recommended for or installed by default with your particular Kubernetes distribution. If you find specific use cases for which the performance doesn't meet your requirements, you'll then be able to test an alternative plug-in based on real network traffic rather than guesswork.

Network Customization

Some scenarios may require cluster networking that is more complex than a single Pod network connected across all cluster nodes. For example, some regulated industries require certain data, such as security audit logs, to travel across a separated network. Other systems may have specialized hardware so that application components that interface with that hardware must be placed on a specific network or virtual LAN (VLAN).

One of the advantages of a plug-in architecture for networking is that a Kubernetes cluster can accommodate these specialized networking scenarios. As long as Pods have an interface that can reach (and is reachable from) the rest of the cluster, Pods can have additional network interfaces that provide specialized connectivity.

Let's look at an example. We'll configure two Pods on the same node so they have a local host-only network they can use for intercommunication. Being a host-only network, it doesn't provide connectivity to the rest of the cluster, so we'll also use Calico to provide cluster networking for Pods.

Because of the need to configure both Calico and our host-only network, we'll be invoking two separate CNI plug-ins that will create virtual network interfaces in our Pods' network namespaces. As we saw in Listing 8-1, it's possible to configure multiple CNI plug-ins in a single configuration file. However, kubelet expects only one of these CNI plug-ins to actually assign a network interface and IP address. To work around this, we'll use Multus, a CNI plug-in that is designed to invoke multiple plug-ins but will treat one as primary for purposes of reporting IP address information back to kubelet.

Multus also allows us to be selective as to what CNI plug-ins are applied to each Pod.

We'll begin by installing Multus into the `calico` example cluster for this chapter:

```
root@host01:~# kubectl apply -f /opt/multus-daemonset.yaml
customresourcedefinition.../network-attachment-definitions... created
clusterrole.rbac.authorization.k8s.io/multus created
clusterrolebinding.rbac.authorization.k8s.io/multus created
serviceaccount/multus created
configmap/multus-cni-config created
daemonset.apps/kube-multus-ds created
```

As the filename implies, the primary resource in this YAML file is a DaemonSet that runs a Multus container on every host. However, this file installs several other resources, including a *CustomResourceDefinition*. This CustomResourceDefinition will allow us to configure network attachment resources to tell Multus what CNI plug-ins to use for a given Pod.

We'll look at CustomResourceDefinitions in detail in Chapter 17. For now, in Listing 8-6 we'll just see the NetworkAttachmentDefinition that we'll use to configure Multus.

netattach.yaml
```
---
apiVersion: k8s.cni.cncf.io/v1
kind: NetworkAttachmentDefinition
metadata:
  name: macvlan-conf
spec:
  config: '{
      "cniVersion": "0.3.0",
      "type": "macvlan",
      "mode": "bridge",
      "ipam": {
        "type": "host-local",
        "subnet": "10.244.0.0/24",
        "rangeStart": "10.244.0.1",
        "rangeEnd": "10.244.0.254"
      }
    }'
```

Listing 8-6: Network attachment

The `config` field in the `spec` looks a lot like a CNI configuration file, which isn't surprising, as Multus needs to use this information to invoke the `macvlan` CNI plug-in when we ask for it to be added to a Pod.

We need to add this NetworkAttachmentDefinition to the cluster:

```
root@host01:~# kubectl apply -f /opt/netattach.yaml
networkattachmentdefinition.k8s.cni.cncf.io/macvlan-conf created
```

This definition doesn't immediately affect any of our Pods; it just provides a Multus configuration for future use.

Of course, to use this configuration, Multus must be invoked. How does that happen when we've already installed Calico into this cluster? The answer is in the */etc/cni/net.d* directory, which the Multus DaemonSet modified on all of our cluster nodes as part of its initialization:

```
root@host01:~# ls /etc/cni/net.d
00-multus.conf  10-calico.conflist  calico-kubeconfig  multus.d
```

Multus left the existing Calico configuration files in place, but added its own *00-multus.conf* configuration file and a *multus.d* directory. Because the *00-multus.conf* file is ahead of *10-calico.conflist* in an alphabetic sort, kubelet will start to use it the next time it creates a new Pod.

Here's *00-multus.conf*:

00-multus.conf
```
{
    "cniVersion": "0.3.1",
    "name": "multus-cni-network",
    "type": "multus",
    "capabilities": {
      "portMappings": true,
      "bandwidth": true
    },
    "kubeconfig": "/etc/cni/net.d/multus.d/multus.kubeconfig",
    "delegates": [
      {
        "name": "k8s-pod-network",
        "cniVersion": "0.3.1",
        "plugins": [
          {
            "type": "calico",
...
          }
        },
        {
          "type": "bandwidth",
...
        },
        {
          "type": "portmap",
...
        }
      ]
    }
  ]
}
```

The delegates field is pulled from the Calico configuration that Multus found. This field is used to determine the default CNI plug-ins that Multus always uses when it is invoked. The top-level capabilities field is needed to ensure that Multus will get all the correct configuration data from kubelet to be able to invoke the portmap and bandwidth plug-ins.

Now that Multus is fully set up, let's use it to add a host-only network to two Pods. The Pods are defined as follows:

local-pods.yaml

```
---
apiVersion: v1
kind: Pod
metadata:
  name: pod1
  annotations:
    k8s.v1.cni.cncf.io/networks: macvlan-conf
spec:
  containers:
  - name: pod1
    image: busybox
    command:
      - "sleep"
      - "infinity"
    nodeName: host01
---
apiVersion: v1
kind: Pod
metadata:
  name: pod2
  annotations:
    k8s.v1.cni.cncf.io/networks: macvlan-conf
spec:
  containers:
  - name: pod2
    image: busybox
    command:
      - "sleep"
      - "infinity"
    nodeName: host01
```

This time we need both Pods to wind up on host01 so that the host-only networking functions. In addition, we add the k8s.v1.cni.cncf.io/networks annotation to each Pod. Multus uses this annotation to identify what additional CNI plug-ins it should run. The name macvlan-conf matches the name we provided in the NetworkAttachmentDefinition in Listing 8-6.

Let's create these two Pods:

```
root@host01:~# kubectl apply -f /opt/local-pods.yaml
pod/pod1 created
pod/pod2 created
```

After these Pods are running, we can check that they each have an extra network interface:

```
root@host01:~# kubectl exec -ti pod1 -- ip addr
...
3: eth0@if12: <BROADCAST,MULTICAST,UP,LOWER_UP,M-DOWN> mtu 1450 qdisc noqueue
    link/ether 9a:a1:db:ec:c7:91 brd ff:ff:ff:ff:ff:ff
    inet 172.31.239.198/32 brd 172.31.239.198 scope global eth0
        valid_lft forever preferred_lft forever
...
4: net1@if2: <BROADCAST,MULTICAST,UP,LOWER_UP,M-DOWN> mtu 1500 qdisc noqueue
    link/ether 9e:4f:c4:47:40:07 brd ff:ff:ff:ff:ff:ff
    inet 10.244.0.2/24 brd 10.244.0.255 scope global net1
        valid_lft forever preferred_lft forever
root@host01:~# kubectl exec -ti pod2 -- ip addr
...
3: eth0@if13: <BROADCAST,MULTICAST,UP,LOWER_UP,M-DOWN> mtu 1450 qdisc noqueue
    link/ether 52:08:99:a7:d2:bc brd ff:ff:ff:ff:ff:ff
    inet 172.31.239.199/32 brd 172.31.239.199 scope global eth0
        valid_lft forever preferred_lft forever
...
4: net1@if2: <BROADCAST,MULTICAST,UP,LOWER_UP,M-DOWN> mtu 1500 qdisc noqueue
    link/ether a6:e5:01:82:81:82 brd ff:ff:ff:ff:ff:ff
    inet 10.244.0.3/24 brd 10.244.0.255 scope global net1
        valid_lft forever preferred_lft forever
...
```

The macvlan CNI plug-in has added the additional net1 network interface, using the IP address management configuration we provided in the NetworkAttachmentDefinition.

These two Pods are now able to communicate with each other using these interfaces:

```
root@host01:~# kubectl exec -ti pod1 -- ping -c 3 10.244.0.3
PING 10.244.0.3 (10.244.0.3): 56 data bytes
64 bytes from 10.244.0.3: seq=0 ttl=64 time=3.125 ms
64 bytes from 10.244.0.3: seq=1 ttl=64 time=0.192 ms
64 bytes from 10.244.0.3: seq=2 ttl=64 time=0.085 ms

--- 10.244.0.3 ping statistics ---
3 packets transmitted, 3 packets received, 0% packet loss
round-trip min/avg/max = 0.085/1.134/3.125 ms
```

This communication goes over the bridge created by the `macvlan` CNI plug-in, as opposed to travelling via Calico.

Keep in mind that our purpose here is solely to demonstrate custom networking without requiring any particular VLAN or complex setup outside our cluster hosts. For a real cluster, this kind of host-only network is of limited value because it constrains where Pods can be deployed. In this kind of situation, it might be preferable to place the two containers into the same Pod so that they will always be scheduled together and can use `localhost` to communicate.

Final Thoughts

We've looked at a lot of network interfaces and traffic flows in this chapter. Most of the time, it's enough to know that every Pod in the cluster is allocated an IP address from a Pod network, and also that any Pod in the cluster can reach and is reachable from any other Pod. Any of the Kubernetes network plug-ins provide this capability, whether they use Layer 3 routing or VXLAN encapsulation, or possibly both.

At the same time, networking issues do occur in a cluster, and it's essential for cluster administrators and cluster users to understand how the traffic is flowing between hosts and what that traffic looks like to the host network in order to debug issues with switch and host configuration, or simply to build applications that make best use of the cluster.

We're not yet done with the networking layers that are needed to have a fully functioning Kubernetes cluster. In the next chapter, we'll look at how Kubernetes provides a Service layer on top of Pod networking to provide load balancing and automated failover, and then uses the Service networking layer together with Ingress networking to make container services accessible outside the cluster.

9

SERVICE AND INGRESS NETWORKS

A decent amount of complexity was involved in creating a cluster-wide network so that all of our Pods could communicate with one another. At the same time, we still don't have all of the networking functionality we need to build scalable, resilient applications. We need networking that supports load balancing our application components across multiple instances and provides the ability to send traffic to new Pod instances as existing instances fail or need to be upgraded. Additionally, the Pod network is designed to be private, meaning that it is directly reachable only from within the cluster. We need additional traffic routing so that external users can reach our application components running in containers.

In this chapter, we'll look at Service and Ingress networking. Kubernetes Service networking provides an entire additional networking layer on top of Pod networking, including dynamic discovery and load balancing. We'll see how this networking layer works and how we can use it to expose our application components to the rest of the cluster as scalable, resilient services. We'll then look at how Ingress configuration provides traffic routing for these Services to expose them to external users.

Services

Putting together Deployments and overlay networking, we have the ability to create multiple identical container instances with a unique IP address for each. Let's create an NGINX Deployment to illustrate:

nginx-deploy.yaml
```
---
kind: Deployment
apiVersion: apps/v1
metadata:
  name: nginx
spec:
  replicas: 5
  selector:
    matchLabels:
      app: nginx
  template:
    metadata:
      labels:
        app: nginx
    spec:
      containers:
      - name: nginx
        image: nginx
```

This is similar to Deployments we've seen previously. In this case we're asking Kubernetes to maintain five Pods for us, each running an NGINX web server.

NOTE *The example repository for this book is at* https://github.com/book-of -kubernetes/examples. *See "Running Examples" on page xx for details on getting set up.*

The automated scripts have already placed this file in */opt*, so we can apply it to the cluster:

```
root@host01:~# kubectl apply -f /opt/nginx-deploy.yaml
deployment.apps/nginx created
```

After these Pods are running, we can check that they've been distributed across the cluster and each one has an IP address:

```
root@host01:~# kubectl get pods -o wide
NAME                     READY   STATUS    ... IP              NODE     ...
nginx-6799fc88d8-2wqc7   1/1     Running   ... 172.31.239.231  host01   ...
nginx-6799fc88d8-78bwx   1/1     Running   ... 172.31.239.229  host01   ...
nginx-6799fc88d8-dtx7s   1/1     Running   ... 172.31.89.240   host02   ...
nginx-6799fc88d8-wh479   1/1     Running   ... 172.31.239.230  host01   ...
nginx-6799fc88d8-zwx27   1/1     Running   ... 172.31.239.228  host01   ...
```

If these containers were merely clients of some server, that might be all we need to do. For example, if our application architecture was driven by sending and receiving messages, as long as these containers could connect to the messaging server, they'd be able to function as required. However, because these containers act as servers, clients need to be able to find them and connect.

As it is, our separate NGINX instances aren't very practical for clients to use. Sure, it's possible to connect to any one of these NGINX server Pods directly. For example, we can communicate with the first one in the list using its IP address:

```
root@host01:~# curl -v http://172.31.239.231
*    Trying 172.31.239.231:80...
* Connected to 172.31.239.231 (172.31.239.231) port 80 (#0)
> GET / HTTP/1.1
...
< HTTP/1.1 200 OK
< Server: nginx/1.21.3
...
```

Unfortunately, just choosing one instance is not going to provide load balancing or failover. Additionally, we don't have any way of knowing ahead of time what the Pod IP address is going to be, and every time we make any changes to the Deployment, the Pods will be re-created and get new IP addresses.

The solution to this situation needs to have two main features. First, we need to have a well-known name that clients can use to find a server. Second, we need a consistent IP address so that when a client has identified a server, it can continue to use the same address for connections even as Pod instances come and go. This is exactly what Kubernetes provides with a *Service*.

Creating a Service

Let's create a Service for our NGINX Deployment and see what that gets us. Listing 9-1 presents the resource YAML file.

nginx-service.yaml
```
---
kind: Service
apiVersion: v1
```

```
metadata:
  name: nginx
spec:
  selector:
    app: nginx
  ports:
  - protocol: TCP
    port: 80
    targetPort: 80
```

Listing 9-1: NGINX Service

First, a Service has a `selector` much like a Deployment. This selector is used in the same way: to identify the Pods that will be associated with the Service. However, unlike a Deployment, a Service does not manage its Pods in any way; it simply routes traffic to them.

The traffic routing is based on the ports we identify in the `ports` field. Because the NGINX server is listening on port 80, we need to specify that as the `targetPort`. We can use any port we want, but it's simplest to keep it the same, especially as 80 is the default port for HTTP.

Let's apply this Service to the cluster:

```
root@host01:~# kubectl apply -f /opt/nginx-service.yaml
service/nginx created
```

We can now see that the Service was created:

```
root@host01:~# kubectl get services
NAME         TYPE        CLUSTER-IP       EXTERNAL-IP   PORT(S)   AGE
kubernetes   ClusterIP   10.96.0.1        <none>        443/TCP   14d
nginx        ClusterIP   10.100.221.220   <none>        80/TCP    25s
```

This `nginx` Service has the default type of `ClusterIP`. Kubernetes has automatically assigned a cluster IP address for this Service. The IP address is in an entirely different address space from that of our Pods.

Using the selector, this Service will identify our NGINX server Pods and automatically start load balancing traffic to them. As Pods matching the selector come and go, the Service will automatically update its load balancing accordingly. As long as the Service exists, it will keep the same IP address, so clients have a consistent way of finding our NGINX server instances.

Let's verify that we can reach an NGINX server through the Service:

```
root@host01:~# curl -v http://10.100.221.220
*   Trying 10.100.221.220:80...
* Connected to 10.100.221.220 (10.100.221.220) port 80 (#0)
> GET / HTTP/1.1
```

```
...
< HTTP/1.1 200 OK
< Server: nginx/1.21.3
...
```

We can see that the Service has correctly identified all five NGINX Pods:

```
root@host01:~# kubectl describe service nginx
Name:               nginx
Namespace:          default
...
Selector:           app=nginx
...
Endpoints:          172.31.239.228:80,172.31.239.229:80,172.31.239.230:80
+ 2 more...
...
```

The Endpoints field shows that the Service is currently routing traffic to all five NGINX Pods. As a client, we don't need to know which Pod was used to handle our request. We interact solely with the Service IP address and allow the Service to choose an instance for us.

Of course, for this example, we had to look up the IP address of the Service. To make it easier on clients, we still should provide a well-known name.

Service DNS

Kubernetes provides a well-known name for each Service through a DNS (Domain Name System) server that is dynamically updated with the name and IP address of every Service in the cluster. Each Pod is configured with this DNS server such that a Pod can use the name of the Service to connect to an instance.

Let's create a Pod that we can use to try this out:

pod.yaml
```
---
apiVersion: v1
kind: Pod
metadata:
  name: pod
spec:
  containers:
  - name: pod
    image: alpine
    command:
      - "sleep"
      - "infinity"
```

We're using alpine rather than busybox as the image for this Pod because we'll want to use some DNS commands that require us to install a more full-featured DNS client.

NOTE   *BusyBox makes a great debug image for Kubernetes clusters because it's tiny and has many useful commands. However, in the interest of keeping BusyBox tiny, it's typical for the commands to include only the most popular options. Alpine makes a great alternative for debugging. The default Alpine image uses BusyBox to provide many of its initial commands, but it's possible to replace them with a full-featured alternative by just installing the appropriate package.*

Next, create the Pod:

```
root@host01:~# kubectl apply -f /opt/pod.yaml
pod/pod created
```

After it's running, let's use it to connect to our NGINX Service, as demonstrated in Listing 9-2.

```
root@host01:~# kubectl exec -ti pod -- wget -O - http://nginx
Connecting to nginx (10.100.221.220:80)
...
<title>Welcome to nginx!</title>
...
```

Listing 9-2: Connect to NGINX Service

We were able to use the name of the Service, nginx, and that name resolved to the Service IP address. This worked because our Pod is configured to talk to the DNS server that's built in to the cluster:

```
root@host01:~# kubectl exec -ti pod -- cat /etc/resolv.conf
search default.svc.cluster.local svc.cluster.local cluster.local
nameserver 10.96.0.10
options ndots:5
```

We print out the file */etc/resolv.conf* inside the container because this is the file that is used to configure DNS.

The name server 10.96.0.10 referenced is itself a Kubernetes Service, but it's in the kube-system Namespace, so we need to look there for it:

```
root@host01:~# kubectl -n kube-system get services
NAME            TYPE       CLUSTER-IP       ... PORT(S)              AGE
kube-dns        ClusterIP  10.96.0.10       ... 53/UDP,53/TCP,9153/TCP  14d
metrics-server  ClusterIP  10.105.140.176   ... 443/TCP              14d
```

The kube-dns Service connects to a DNS server Deployment called CoreDNS that listens for changes to Services in the Kubernetes cluster. CoreDNS updates the DNS server configuration as required to stay up to date with the current cluster configuration.

Name Resolution and Namespaces

DNS names in a Kubernetes cluster are based on the Namespace as well as the cluster domain. Because our Pod is in the default Namespace, it has been configured with a search path of `default.svc.cluster.local` as the first entry in the list, so it will search the `default` Namespace first when looking for Services. This is why we were able to use the bare Service name `nginx` to find the `nginx` Service—that Service is also in the `default` Namespace.

We could have also found the same Service using the fully qualified name:

```
root@host01:~# kubectl exec -ti pod -- wget -O - http://nginx.default.svc
Connecting to nginx.default.svc (10.100.221.220:80)
...
<title>Welcome to nginx!</title>
...
```

Understanding this interaction between Namespaces and Service lookup is important. One common deployment pattern for a Kubernetes cluster is to deploy the same application multiple times to different Namespaces and use simple hostnames for application components to communicate with one another. This pattern is often used to deploy a "development" and "production" version of an application to the same cluster. If we're planning to use this pattern, we need to be sure that we stick to bare hostnames when our application components try to find one another; otherwise, we could end up communicating with the wrong version of our application.

Another important configuration item in *etc/resolv.conf* is the `ndots` entry. The `ndots` entry tells the hostname resolver that when it sees a hostname with four or fewer dots, it should try appending the various search domains *prior* to performing an absolute search without any domain appended. This is critical to make sure that we try to find services inside the cluster before reaching outside the cluster.

As a result, when we used the name `nginx` in Listing 9-2, the DNS resolver within our container immediately tried `nginx.default.svc.cluster.local` and found the correct Service.

To make sure this is clear, let's try one more example: looking up a Service in another Namespace. The `kube-system` Namespace has a `metrics-server` Service. To find it, let's use the standard host lookup `dig` command in our Pod.

Our Pod is using Alpine Linux, so we need to install the `bind-tools` package to get access to dig:

```
root@host01:~# kubectl exec -ti pod -- apk add bind-tools
...
OK: 13 MiB in 27 packages
```

Now, let's try looking up `metrics-server` using the bare name first:

```
root@host01:~# kubectl exec -ti pod -- dig +search metrics-server
...
;; Got answer:
;; ->>HEADER<<- opcode: QUERY, status: SERVFAIL, id: 38423
...
```

We add the +search flag onto the command to tell dig to use the search path information from */etc/resolv.conf*. However, even with that flag, we don't find the Service, because our Pod is in the default Namespace, so the search path doesn't lead dig to look in the kube-system Namespace.

Let's try again, this time specifying the correct Namespace:

```
root@host01:~# kubectl exec -ti pod -- dig +search metrics-server.kube-system
...
;; ANSWER SECTION:
metrics-server.kube-system.svc.cluster.local. 30 IN A 10.105.140.176
...
```

This lookup works, and we are able to get the IP address for the metrics -server Service. It works because the search path includes svc.cluster.local as its second entry. After initially trying metrics-server.kube-system.default.svc .cluster.local, which doesn't work, dig then tries metrics-server.kube-system .svc.cluster.local, which does.

Traffic Routing

We've seen how to create and use Services, but we haven't yet looked at how the actual traffic routing works. It turns out that Service network traffic works in a way that's completely different from the overlay networks we saw in Chapter 8, which can lead to some confusion.

For example, because we can use wget to reach an NGINX server instance using the nginx Service name, we might expect to be able to use ping, as well, but that doesn't work:

```
root@host01:~# kubectl exec -ti pod -- ping -c 3 nginx
PING nginx (10.100.221.220): 56 data bytes

--- nginx ping statistics ---
3 packets transmitted, 0 packets received, 100% packet loss
command terminated with exit code 1
```

Name resolution worked as expected, so ping knew what destination IP address to use for its ICMP packets. But there was no reply from that IP address. We could look at every host and container network interface in our cluster and never find an interface that carries the Service IP address of 10.100.221.220. So how is our HTTP traffic getting through to an NGINX Service instance?

On every node in our cluster, there is a component called kube-proxy that configures traffic routing for Services. kube-proxy is run as a DaemonSet in the kube-system Namespace. Each kube-proxy instance watches for changes to Services in the cluster and configures the Linux firewall to route traffic.

We can use iptables commands to look at the firewall configuration to see how kube-proxy has configured traffic routing for our nginx Service:

```
root@host01:~# iptables-save | grep 'default/nginx cluster IP'
```
❶ -A KUBE-SERVICES ! -s 172.31.0.0/16 -d 10.100.221.220/32 -p tcp -m comment
   --comment "default/nginx cluster IP" -m tcp --dport 80 -j KUBE-MARK-MASQ
❷ -A KUBE-SERVICES -d 10.100.221.220/32 -p tcp -m comment --comment
   "default/nginx cluster IP" -m tcp --dport 80 -j KUBE-SVC-2CMXP7HKUVJN7L6M

The `iptables-save` command backs up all of the current Linux firewall rules, so it's useful for printing out all rules. The grep command searches for the comment string that kube-proxy applies to the Service rules it creates. In this example, kube-proxy has created two rules for the Service as a whole. The first rule ❶ looks for traffic destined for our Service that is *not* coming from the Pod network. This traffic must be marked for Network Address Translation (NAT) masquerade so that the source of any reply traffic will be rewritten to be the Service IP address rather than the actual Pod that handles the request. The second rule ❷ sends all traffic destined for the Service to a separate rule chain that will send it to a Pod instance. Note that in both cases, the rules only match for TCP traffic that is destined for port 80.

We can examine this separate rule chain to see how the actual routing to individual Pods works. Be sure to replace the name of the rule chain in this command with the one shown in the previous output:

```
root@host01:~# iptables-save | grep KUBE-SVC-2CMXP7HKUVJN7L6M
...
-A KUBE-SVC-2CMXP7HKUVJN7L6M ... -m statistic --mode random
   --probability 0.20000000019 -j KUBE-SEP-PIVU7ZHMCSOWIZ2Z
-A KUBE-SVC-2CMXP7HKUVJN7L6M ... -m statistic --mode random
   --probability 0.25000000000 -j KUBE-SEP-CFQXKE74QEHFB7VJ
-A KUBE-SVC-2CMXP7HKUVJN7L6M ... -m statistic --mode random
   --probability 0.33333333349 -j KUBE-SEP-DHDWEJZ7MGGIR5XF
-A KUBE-SVC-2CMXP7HKUVJN7L6M ... -m statistic --mode random
   --probability 0.50000000000 -j KUBE-SEP-3S3S2VJCXSAISE2Z
-A KUBE-SVC-2CMXP7HKUVJN7L6M ... -j KUBE-SEP-AQWD2Y25T24EHSNI
```

The output shows five rules, corresponding to each of the five NGINX Pod instances the Service's selector matched. The five rules together provide random load balancing across all the instances so that each one has an equal chance of being selected for new connections.

It may seem strange that the `probability` figure increases for each rule. This is necessary because the rules are evaluated sequentially. For the first rule, we want a 20 percent chance of choosing the first instance. However, if we don't select the first instance, only four instances are left, so we want a 25 percent chance of choosing the second one. The same logic applies until we get to the last instance, which we always want to choose if we've skipped all the others.

Let's quickly verify that these rules go to the expected destination (again, be sure to replace the name of the rule chain in this command):

```
root@host01:~# iptables-save | grep KUBE-SEP-PIVU7ZHMCSOWIZ2Z
...
-A KUBE-SEP-PIVU7ZHMC ... -s 172.31.239.235/32 ... --comment "default/nginx" -j KUBE-MARK-MASQ
-A KUBE-SEP-PIVU7ZHMCSOWIZ2Z -p tcp ... -m tcp -j DNAT --to-destination 172.31.239.235:80
```

This output shows two rules. The first is the other half of the NAT masquerade configuration, as we mark all packets that leave our Pod instance so that they can have their source address rewritten to appear to come from the Service. The second rule is the one that actually routes Service traffic to a specific Pod as it performs a rewrite of the destination address so that a packet originally destined for the Service IP is now destined for a Pod. From there, the overlay networking takes over to actually send the packet to the correct container.

With this understanding of how Service traffic is actually routed, it makes sense that our ICMP packets didn't make it through. The firewall rule that kube-proxy created applies only to TCP traffic destined for port 80. As a result, there was no firewall rule to rewrite our ICMP packets and therefore no way for them to make it to a networking stack that could reply to them. Similarly, if we have a container that's listening on multiple ports, we will be able to connect to any of those ports by directly using the Pod IP address, but the Service IP address will route traffic only if we explicitly declare that port in the Service specification. It can be a significant source of confusion when deploying an application where the Pod starts up as expected and listens for traffic, but a misconfiguration of the Service means that the traffic is not being routed to all of the correct destination ports.

External Networking

We now have enough layers of networking to meet all of our internal cluster communication needs. Each Pod has its own IP address and has connectivity to other Pods as well as the control plane, and with Service networking we have automatic load balancing and failover based on running multiple Pod instances with a Service. However, we're still missing the ability for external users to access services running in our cluster.

To provide access for external users, we can no longer rely solely on the cluster-specific IP address ranges that we use for Pods and Services, given that external networks don't recognize those address ranges. Instead, we'll need a way to allocate externally routable IP addresses to our Services, either by explicitly associating an IP address with a Service or by using an *ingress controller* that listens to external traffic and routes it to Services.

External Services

The `nginx` Service we created earlier was a `ClusterIP` Service, the default Service type. Kubernetes supports multiple Service types, including Service types that are made for Services that need to be exposed externally:

None   Also known as a *headless* Service, it's used to enable tracking of selected Pods but without an IP address or any network routing behavior.

ClusterIP   The default Service type that provides tracking of selected Pods, a cluster IP address that is routed internally, and a well-known name in the cluster DNS.

NodePort   Extends `ClusterIP` and also provides a port on all nodes in the cluster that is routed to the Service.

LoadBalancer   Extends `NodePort` and also uses an underlying cloud provider to obtain an IP address that is externally reachable.

ExternalName   Aliases a well-known Service name in the cluster DNS to some external DNS name. Used to make external resources appear to be in-cluster Services.

Of these Service types, the `NodePort` and `LoadBalancer` types are most useful for exposing Services outside the cluster. The `LoadBalancer` type seems the most straightforward, as it simply adds an external IP to the Service. However, it requires integration with an underlying cloud environment to create the external IP address when the Service is created, to route traffic from that IP address to the cluster's nodes, and to create a DNS entry outside the cluster that enables external users to find the Service as a host on some pre-registered domain that we already own, rather than a `cluster.local` domain that works only within the cluster.

For this reason, a `LoadBalancer` Service is most useful for cases in which we know what cloud environment we're using and we're creating Services that will live for a long time. For HTTP traffic, we can get most of the benefit of a `LoadBalancer` Service by using a `NodePort` Service together with an ingress controller, with the added feature of better support for dynamically deploying new applications with new Services.

Before moving on to an ingress controller, let's turn our existing `nginx` Service into a `NodePort` Service so that we can look at the effect. We can do this using a patch file:

nginx-nodeport.yaml
```
---
spec:
  type: NodePort
```

A patch file allows us to update only the specific fields we care about. In this case, we are updating only the type of the Service. For this to work, we just need to specify that one changed field in its correct position in the hierarchy, which allows Kubernetes to know what field to modify. We don't need to change the selector or ports for our Service, only the type, so the patch is very simple.

Let's use the patch:

```
root@host01:~# kubectl patch svc nginx --patch-file /opt/nginx-nodeport.yaml
service/nginx patched
```

For this command, we must specify the resource to be patched and a patch file to be used. The result is identical to if we had edited the YAML resource file for the Service and then used kubectl apply again.

The Service now looks a little different:

```
root@host01:~# kubectl get service nginx
NAME    TYPE      CLUSTER-IP      EXTERNAL-IP   PORT(S)       AGE
nginx   NodePort  10.100.221.220  <none>        80:31326/TCP  2h
```

A NodePort Service provides all the behavior of a ClusterIP Service, so we still have a cluster IP associated with our nginx Service. The Service even kept the same cluster IP. The only change is the PORT field now shows that the Service port 80 is attached to node port 31326.

The kube-proxy Service on every cluster node is listening on this port (be sure to use the correct node port for your Service):

```
root@host01:~# ss -nlp | grep 31326
tcp   LISTEN 0   4096  .0.0.0:31326 ... users:(("kube-proxy",pid=3339,fd=15))
```

As a result, we can still use the nginx Service name inside our Pod, but we can also use the NodePort from the host:

```
root@host01:~# kubectl exec -ti pod -- wget -O - http://nginx
Connecting to nginx (10.100.221.220:80)
...
<title>Welcome to nginx!</title>
...
root@host01:~# wget -O - http://host01:31326
...
Connecting to host01 (host01)|127.0.2.1|:31326... connected.
...
<h1>Welcome to nginx!</h1>
...
```

Because kube-proxy is listening on all network interfaces, we've successfully exposed this Service to external users.

Ingress Services

Although we've successfully exposed our NGINX Service outside the cluster, we still don't provide a great user experience for external users. To use the NodePort Service, external users will need to know the IP address of at least one of our cluster nodes, and they'll need to know the exact port on which each Service is listening. That port could change if the Service is deleted and re-created. We could partially address this by telling Kubernetes which port to use for the `NodePort`, but we don't want to do this with any arbitrary Service because multiple Services may choose the same port.

What we really need is a single external entry point to our cluster that keeps track of multiple services that are available and uses rules to route traffic to them. This way, we can do all of our routing configuration inside the cluster so that Services can come and go dynamically. At the same time, we can have a single well-known entry point for our cluster that all external users can use.

For HTTP traffic, Kubernetes provides exactly this capability, calling it an *Ingress*. To configure our cluster to route external HTTP traffic to Services, we need to define the set of Ingress resources that specify the routing and to deploy the ingress controller that receives and routes the traffic. We already installed our ingress controller when we set up our cluster:

```
root@host01:~# kubectl -n ingress-nginx get deploy
NAME                        READY   UP-TO-DATE   AVAILABLE   AGE
ingress-nginx-controller    1/1     1            1           15d
root@host01:~# kubectl -n ingress-nginx get svc
NAME                        TYPE        ... PORT(S)            ...
ingress-nginx-controller    NodePort    ... 80:80/TCP,443:443/TCP ...
...
```

Our ingress controller includes a Deployment and a Service. As the Service is of type `NodePort`, we know that `kube-proxy` is listening to ports 80 and 443 on all of our cluster's nodes, ready to route traffic to the associated Pod.

As the name implies, our ingress controller is actually an instance of an NGINX web server; however, in this case NGINX is solely acting as an HTTP reverse proxy rather than serving any web content of its own. The ingress controller listens for changes to Ingress resources in the cluster and reconfigures NGINX to connect to backend servers based on the rules that are defined. These rules use host or path information from the HTTP request to select a Service for the request.

Let's create an Ingress resource to route traffic to the `nginx` Service we defined in Listing 9-1. Here's the resource we'll create:

nginx-ingress.yaml
```
---
apiVersion: networking.k8s.io/v1
kind: Ingress
metadata:
  name: web01
spec:
  rules:
    - host: web01
      http:
        paths:
          - path: /
```

```
      pathType: Prefix
      backend:
        service:
          name: nginx
          port:
            number: 80
```

This resource instructs the ingress controller to look at the HTTP Host header. If it sees web01 as the Host header, it then tries to match against a path in the paths we specified. In this case, all paths will match the path / prefix, so all traffic will be routed to the nginx Service.

Before we apply this to the cluster, let's confirm what happens if we try to use a hostname that the ingress controller doesn't recognize. We'll use the high-availability IP address that's associated with our cluster, as the cluster's load balancer will forward that to one of the instances:

```
root@host01:~# curl -vH "Host:web01" http://192.168.61.10
...
> Host:web01
...
<head><title>404 Not Found</title></head>
...
```

The -H "Host:web01" flag in the curl command tells curl to use the value host01 as the Host header in the HTTP request. This is necessary given that we don't have a DNS server in our example cluster that can turn web01 into our cluster's IP address.

As we can see, the NGINX server that's acting as the ingress controller is configured to reply with a 404 Not Found error message whenever it gets a request that doesn't match any configured Ingress resource. In this case, because we haven't created any Ingress resources yet, any request will get this response.

Let's apply the web01 Ingress resource to the cluster:

```
root@host01:~# kubectl apply -f /opt/nginx-ingress.yaml
ingress.networking.k8s.io/web01 created
```

Now that the Ingress resource exists, as Listing 9-3 illustrates, HTTP port 80 requests on both the cluster high-availability IP and individual hosts are routed to the nginx Service:

```
root@host01:~# curl -vH "Host:web01" http://host01
...
> Host:web01
...
<title>Welcome to nginx!</title>
...
root@host01:~# curl -vH "Host:web01" http://192.168.61.10
...
```

```
> Host:web01
...
<title>Welcome to nginx!</title>
...
```

Listing 9-3: NGINX via Ingress

The output in both cases is the same, showing that traffic is being routed to the nginx Service.

In the web01-ingress resource, we were able to use the bare name of the nginx Service. The Service name lookup is based on where the Ingress resource is located. Because we created the Ingress resource in the default Namespace, that is where it looks first for Services.

Putting this all together, we now have a high-availability solution to route traffic from external users to HTTP servers in our cluster. This combines our cluster's high-availability IP address 192.168.61.10 with an ingress controller exposed as a NodePort Service on port 80 of all our cluster's nodes. The ingress controller can be dynamically configured to expose additional Services by creating new Ingress resources.

Ingress in Production

The curl command in Listing 9-3 still looks a little strange, as we're required to override the HTTP Host header manually. We need to perform a few additional steps to use Ingress resources to expose services in a production cluster.

First, we need our cluster to have an externally routable IP address together with a well-known name that is registered in DNS. The best way to do that is with a wildcard DNS scheme so that all hosts in a given domain are all routed to the cluster's external IP. For example, if we own the domain cluster.example.com, we could create a DNS entry so that *.cluster.example.com routes to the cluster's external IP address.

This approach still works with larger clusters that span multiple networks. We just need to have multiple IP addresses associated with the DNS entry, possibly using location-aware DNS servers that route clients to the closest service.

Next, we need to create an SSL certificate for our ingress controller that includes our wildcard DNS as a Subject Alternative Name (SAN). This will allow our ingress controller to provide a secure HTTP connection for external users no matter what specific service hostname they are using.

Finally, when we define our Services, we need to specify the fully qualified domain name for the host field. For the preceding example, we would specify web01.cluster.example.com rather than just web01.

After we've performed these additional steps, any external user would be able to connect via HTTPS to the fully qualified hostname of our Service, such as https://web01.cluster.example.com. This hostname would resolve to our cluster's external IP address, and the load balancer would route it to one of the cluster's nodes. At that point, our ingress controller, listening on the standard port of 443, would offer its wildcard certificate, which would match what the client expects. As soon as the secure connection is established, the ingress controller would inspect the HTTP Host header and proxy a connection to the correct Service, sending back the HTTP response to the client.

The advantage of this approach is that after we have it set up, we can deploy a new Ingress resource at any time to expose a Service externally, and as long as we choose a unique hostname, it won't collide with any other exposed Service. After the initial setup, all of the configuration is maintained within the cluster itself, and we still have a highly available configuration for all of our Services.

Final Thoughts

Routing network traffic in a Kubernetes cluster might involve a great deal of complexity, but the end result is straightforward: we can deploy our application components to a cluster, with automatic scaling and failover, and external users can access our application using a well-known name without having to know how the application is deployed or how many container instances we're using to meet demand. If we build our application to be resilient, our application containers can upgrade to new versions or restart in response to failure without users even being aware of the change.

Of course, if we're going to build application components that are resilient, it's important to know what can go wrong in deploying containers. In the next chapter, we'll look at some common issues with deploying containers to a Kubernetes cluster and how to debug them.

10

WHEN THINGS GO WRONG

So far our installation and configuration of Kubernetes has gone as planned, and our controllers have had no problem creating Pods and starting containers. Of course, in the real world, it's rarely that easy. Although showing everything that might go wrong with a complex application deployment isn't possible, we can look at some of the most common problems. Most important, we can explore debugging tools that will help us diagnose any issue.

In this chapter, we'll look at how to diagnose problems with application containers that we deploy on top of Kubernetes. We'll work our way through the life cycle for scheduling and running containers, examining potential problems at each step as well as how to diagnose and fix them.

Scheduling

Scheduling is the first activity Kubernetes performs on a Pod and its containers. When a Pod is first created, the Kubernetes scheduler assigns it to a node. Normally, this happens quickly and automatically, but some issues can prevent scheduling from happening successfully.

No Available Nodes

One possibility is that the scheduler simply doesn't have any nodes available. This situation might occur because our cluster doesn't have any nodes configured for regular application containers or because all nodes have failed.

To illustrate the case in which no nodes are available for assignment, let's create a Pod with a *node selector*. A node selector specifies one or more node labels that are required for a Pod to be scheduled on that node. Node selectors are useful when some nodes in our cluster are different from others (for example, when some nodes have newer CPUs with support for more advanced instruction sets needed by some of our containers).

NOTE   *The example repository for this book is at* https://github.com/book-of -kubernetes/examples. *See "Running Examples" on page xx for details on getting set up.*

We'll begin with a Pod definition that has a node selector that doesn't match any of our nodes:

nginx-selector.yaml
```
---
apiVersion: v1
kind: Pod
metadata:
  name: nginx
spec:
  containers:
  - name: nginx
    image: nginx
  nodeSelector:
❶ purpose: special
```

The node selector ❶ tells Kubernetes to assign this Pod only to a node with a label called purpose whose value is equal to special. Even though none of our nodes currently match, we can still create this Pod:

```
root@host01:~# kubectl apply -f /opt/nginx-selector.yaml
pod/nginx created
```

However, Kubernetes is stuck trying to schedule the Pod, because it can't find a matching node:

```
root@host01:~# kubectl get pods -o wide
NAME    READY   STATUS    RESTARTS   AGE    IP       NODE     ...
nginx   0/1     Pending   0          113s   <none>   <none>   ...
```

We see a status of Pending and a node assignment of <none>. This is because Kubernetes has not yet scheduled this Pod onto a node.

The kubectl get command is typically the first command we should run to see whether there are issues with a resource we've deployed to our cluster. If we have an issue, as we do in this case, the next step is to view the detailed status and event log using kubectl describe:

```
root@host01:~# kubectl describe pod nginx
Name:           nginx
Namespace:      default
...
Status:         Pending
...
Node-Selectors:                 purpose=special

Events:
  Type     Reason            Age    From               Message
  ----     ------            ----   ----               -------
  Warning  FailedScheduling  4m36s  default-scheduler  0/3 nodes are
    available: 3 node(s) didn't match Pod's node affinity/selector.
  Warning  FailedScheduling  3m16s  default-scheduler  0/3 nodes are
    available: 3 node(s) didn't match Pod's node affinity/selector.
```

The event log informs us as to exactly what the issue is: the Pod can't be scheduled because none of the nodes matched the selector.

Let's add the necessary label to one of our nodes:

```
root@host01:~# kubectl get nodes
NAME    STATUS   ROLES          ...
host01  Ready    control-plane...
host02  Ready    control-plane...
host03  Ready    control-plane...
root@host01:~# kubectl label nodes host02 purpose=special
node/host02 labeled
```

We first list the three nodes we have available and then apply the necessary label to one of them. As soon as we apply this label, Kubernetes can now schedule the Pod:

```
root@host01:~# kubectl get pods -o wide
NAME    READY   STATUS    RESTARTS   AGE   IP             NODE     ...
nginx   1/1     Running   0          10m   172.31.89.196  host02   ...
root@host01:~# kubectl describe pod nginx
Name:           nginx
Namespace:      default
...
Events:
  Type     Reason            Age   From               Message
  ----     ------            ----  ----               -------
  Warning  FailedScheduling  10m   default-scheduler  0/3 nodes are
    available: 3 node(s) didn't match Pod's node affinity/selector.
```

```
Warning  FailedScheduling  9m17s  default-scheduler  0/3 nodes are
    available: 3 node(s) didn't match Pod's node affinity/selector.
Normal   Scheduled          2m22s  default-scheduler  Successfully assigned
    default/nginx to host02
...
```

As expected, the Pod was scheduled onto the node where we applied the label.

This example, like the others we'll see in this chapter, illustrates debugging in Kubernetes. After we've created the resources that we need, we query the cluster state to make sure the actual deployment of those resources was successful. When we find issues, we can correct those issues and our resources will be started as desired without having to reinstall our application components.

Let's clean up this NGINX Pod:

```
root@host01:~# kubectl delete -f /opt/nginx-selector.yaml
pod "nginx" deleted
```

Let's also remove the label from the node. We remove the label by appending a minus sign to it to identify it:

```
root@host01:~# kubectl label nodes host02 purpose-
node/host02 unlabeled
```

We've covered one issue with the scheduler, but there's still another we need to look at.

Insufficient Resources

When choosing a node to host a Pod, the scheduler also considers the resources that are available on each node and the resources the Pod requires. We explore resource limits in detail in Chapter 14; for now it's enough to know that each container in a Pod can request the resources it needs, and the scheduler will ensure that it is scheduled onto a node that has those resources available. Of course, if there aren't any nodes with enough room, the scheduler won't be able to schedule the Pod. Instead the Pod will wait in a Pending state.

Let's look at an example Pod definition to illustrate this:

sleep
-multiple.yaml
```
---
apiVersion: v1
kind: Pod
metadata:
  name: sleep
spec:
  containers:
  - name: sleep
    image: busybox
```

```
      command:
        - "/bin/sleep"
        - "3600"
      resources:
        requests:
          cpu: "2"
    - name: sleep2
      image: busybox
      command:
        - "/bin/sleep"
        - "3600"
      resources:
        requests:
          cpu: "2"
```

In this YAML definition, we create two containers in the same Pod. Each container requests two CPUs. Because all of the containers in a Pod must be on the same host in order to share some Linux namespace types (especially the network namespace so that they can use localhost for communication), the scheduler needs to find a single node with four CPUs available. In our small cluster, that can't happen, as we can see if we try to deploy the Pod:

```
root@host01:~# kubectl apply -f /opt/sleep-multiple.yaml
pod/sleep created
root@host01:~# kubectl get pods -o wide
NAME    READY   STATUS    RESTARTS   AGE   IP        NODE     ...
sleep   0/2     Pending   0          7s    <none>    <none>   ...
```

As before, kubectl describe gives us the event log that reveals the issue:

```
root@host01:~# kubectl describe pod sleep
Name:         sleep
Namespace:    default
...
Events:
  Type      Reason            Age   From               Message
  ----      ------            ----  ----               -------
  Warning   FailedScheduling  71s   default-scheduler  0/3 nodes are
    available: 3 Insufficient cpu.
```

Notice that it doesn't matter how heavily loaded our nodes actually are:

```
root@host01:~# kubectl top node
NAME     CPU(cores)   CPU%   MEMORY(bytes)   MEMORY%
host01   429m         21%    1307Mi          69%
host02   396m         19%    1252Mi          66%
host03   458m         22%    1277Mi          67%
```

Nor does it matter how much CPU our containers will actually use. The scheduler allocates Pods purely based on what it requested; this way, we don't suddenly overwhelm a CPU when load increases.

We can't magically provide our nodes with more CPUs, so to get this Pod scheduled, we're going to need to specify a lower CPU usage for our two containers. Let's use a more sensible figure of 0.1 CPU:

*sleep
-sensible.yaml*

```
---
apiVersion: v1
kind: Pod
metadata:
  name: sleep
spec:
  containers:
  - name: sleep
    image: busybox
    command:
      - "/bin/sleep"
      - "3600"
    resources:
      requests:
    ❶ cpu: "100m"
  - name: sleep2
    image: busybox
    command:
      - "/bin/sleep"
      - "3600"
    resources:
      requests:
        cpu: "100m"
```

The value `100m` ❶ equates to "one hundred millicpu" or one-tenth (0.1) of a CPU.

Even though this is a separate file, it declares the same resource, so Kubernetes will treat it as an update. However, if we try to apply this as a change to the existing Pod, it will fail:

```
root@host01:~# kubectl apply -f /opt/sleep-sensible.yaml
The Pod "sleep" is invalid: spec: Forbidden: pod updates may not change
  fields other than ...
```

We are not allowed to change the resource request of an existing Pod, which makes sense given that a Pod is allocated to a node only once on creation, and a resource usage change might cause the node to be overly full.

If we were using a controller such as a Deployment, the controller could handle replacing the Pods for us. Because we created a Pod directly, we need to manually delete and then re-create it:

```
root@host01:~# kubectl delete pod sleep
pod "sleep" deleted
root@host01:~# kubectl apply -f /opt/sleep-sensible.yaml
pod/sleep created
```

Our new Pod has no trouble with node allocation:

```
root@host01:~# kubectl get pods -o wide
NAME    READY   STATUS    RESTARTS   AGE   IP              NODE   ...
sleep   2/2     Running   0          51s   172.31.89.199   host02 ...
```

And if we run kubectl describe on the node, we can see how our new Pod
has been allocated some of the node's CPU:

```
root@host01:~# kubectl describe node host02
Name:                host02
...
Capacity:
  cpu:               2
...
Non-terminated Pods:              (10 in total)
  Namespace  Name      CPU Requests  CPU Limits   ...
  ---------  ----      ------------  ----------   ...
...
  default    sleep ❶ 200m (10%)    0 (0%)       ...
...
```

Be sure to use the correct node name for the node where your Pod was
deployed. Because our Pod has two containers, each requesting 100m, its total
request is 200m ❶.

Let's finish by cleaning up this Pod:

```
root@host01:~# kubectl delete pod sleep
pod "sleep" deleted
```

Other errors can prevent a Pod from being scheduled, but these are the
most common. Most important, the commands we used here apply in all
cases. First, use kubectl get to determine the Pod's current status, followed
by kubectl describe to view the event log. These two commands are always a
good first step when something doesn't seem to be working properly.

Pulling Images

After a Pod is scheduled onto a node, the local kubelet service interacts with
the underlying container runtime to create an isolated environment and
start containers. However, there's still one application misconfiguration that
can cause our Pod to become stuck in the Pending phase: inability to pull the
container image.

Three main issues can prevent the container runtime from pulling an image:

- Failure to connect to the container image registry
- Authorization issue with the requested image
- Image is missing from the registry

As we described in Chapter 5, an image registry is a web server. Often, the image registry is outside the cluster, and the nodes need to be able to connect to an external network or the internet to reach the registry. Additionally, most registries support publishing private images that require authentication and authorization to access. And, of course, if there is no image published under the name we specify, the container runtime is not going to be able to pull it from the registry.

All of these errors behave the same way in our Kubernetes cluster, with differences only in the message in the event log, so we'll need to explore only one of them. We'll look at what is probably the most common issue: a missing image caused by a typo in the image name.

Let's try to create a Pod using this YAML file:

nginx-typo.yaml
```
---
apiVersion: v1
kind: Pod
metadata:
  name: nginx
spec:
  containers:
  - name: nginx
    image: nginz
```

Because there is no image in Docker Hub called `nginz`, it won't be possible to pull this image. Let's explore what happens when we add this resource to the cluster:

```
root@host01:~# kubectl apply -f /opt/nginx-typo.yaml
pod/nginx created
root@host01:~# kubectl get pods
NAME    READY   STATUS            RESTARTS   AGE
nginx   0/1     ImagePullBackOff  0          20s
```

Our Pod has status `ImagePullBackOff`, which immediately signals two things. First, this Pod is not yet getting to the point at which the containers are running, because it has not yet pulled the container images. Second, as with all errors, Kubernetes will continue attempting the action, but it will use a *back-off* algorithm to avoid overwhelming our cluster's resources.

Pulling an image involves reaching out over the network to communicate with the image registry, and it would be rude and a waste of network bandwidth to flood the registry with many requests in a short amount of time. Moreover, the cause of the failure may be transient, so the cluster will keep trying in hopes that the problem will be resolved.

The fact that Kubernetes uses a back-off algorithm for retrying errors is important for debugging. In this case, we obviously are not going to publish an nginz image to Docker Hub to fix the problem. But for cases in which we do fix the issue by publishing an image, or by changing the permissions for the image, it's important to know that Kubernetes will not pick up that change immediately, because the amount of delay between tries increases with each failure.

Let's explore the event log so that we can see this back-off in action:

```
root@host01:~# kubectl describe pod nginx
Name:        nginx
Namespace:   default
...
Status:      ❶ Pending
...
Events:
  Type     Reason     Age                    From              Message
  ----     ------     ----                   ----              -------
  Normal   Scheduled  114s                   default-scheduler Successfully
    assigned default/nginx to host03
...
  Warning  Failed     25s (x4 over 112s)     kubelet           Failed to pull
    image "nginz": ... ❷ pull access denied, repository does not exist or may
    require authorization  ...
...
  Normal   BackOff    1s ❸ (x7 over 111s)    kubelet              ...
```

As before, our Pod is stuck in a Pending status ❶. In this case, however, the Pod has gotten past the scheduling activity and has moved on to pulling the image. For security reasons, the registry does not distinguish between a private image for which we don't have permission to access and a missing image, so Kubernetes can tell us only that the issue is one or the other ❷. Finally, we can see that Kubernetes has tried to pull the image seven times during the two minutes since we created this Pod ❸, and it last tried to pull the image one second ago.

If we wait a few minutes and then run the same kubectl describe command again, focusing on the back-off behavior, we can see that a long amount of time elapses between tries:

```
root@host01:~# kubectl describe pod nginx
Name:        nginx
Namespace:   default
...
```

```
Events:
  Type     Reason     Age                    From            Message
  ----     ------     ----                   ----            -------
...
  Normal   BackOff    4m38s (x65 over 19m)   kubelet         ...
```

Kubernetes has now tried to pull the image 65 times over the course of 19 minutes. However, the amount of delay has grown over time and has reached the maximum of five minutes between each attempt. This means that as we debug this issue, we will need to wait up to five minutes each time to see whether the problem has been resolved.

Let's go ahead and fix the issue so that we can see this in action. We could fix the YAML file and run kubectl apply again, but we can also fix it using kubectl set:

```
root@host01:~# kubectl set image pod nginx nginx=nginx
pod/nginx image updated
root@host01:~# kubectl get pods
NAME    READY   STATUS              RESTARTS   AGE
nginx   0/1     ImagePullBackOff    0          28m
```

The kubectl set command requires us to specify the resource type and name; in this case pod nginx. We then specify nginx=nginx to provide the name of the container to modify (because a Pod can have multiple containers) along with the new image.

We fixed the image name, but the Pod is still showing ImagePullBackOff because we must wait for the five-minute timer to elapse before Kubernetes tries again. Upon the next try, the pull is successful and the Pod starts running:

```
root@host01:~# kubectl get pods
NAME    READY   STATUS     RESTARTS   AGE
nginx   1/1     Running    0          32m
```

Let's clean up the Pod before moving on:

```
root@host01:~# kubectl delete pod nginx
pod "nginx" deleted
```

Again, we were able to solve this using kubectl get and kubectl describe. However, when we get to the point that the container is running, that won't be sufficient.

Running Containers

After instructing the container runtime to pull any images needed, kubelet then tells the runtime to start the containers. For the rest of the examples in this chapter, we'll assume that the container runtime is working as expected. At this point, then, the main problem we'll run into is the case in which the container does not start as expected. Let's begin with a simpler example of debugging a container that fails to run, and then we'll look at a more complex example.

Debugging Using Logs

For our simple example, we first need a Pod definition with a container that fails on startup. Here's a Pod definition for PostgreSQL that will do what we want:

postgres -misconfig.yaml

```
---
apiVersion: v1
kind: Pod
metadata:
  name: postgres
spec:
  containers:
  - name: postgres
    image: postgres
```

It might not seem like there are any issues with this definition, but PostgreSQL has some required configuration when running in a container.

We can create the Pod using `kubectl apply`:

```
root@host01:~# kubectl apply -f /opt/postgres-misconfig.yaml
pod/postgres created
```

After a minute or so to allow time to pull the image, we can check the status with `kubectl get`, and we'll notice a status we haven't seen before:

```
root@host01:~# kubectl get pods
NAME       READY   STATUS             RESTARTS      AGE
postgres   0/1     CrashLoopBackOff   1 (8s ago)    25s
```

The `CrashLoopBackOff` status indicates that a container in the Pod has exited. As this is not a Kubernetes Job, it doesn't expect the container to exit, so it's considered a crash.

If you catch the Pod at the right time, you might see an `Error` status rather than `CrashLoopBackOff`. This is temporary: the Pod transitions through that status immediately after crashing.

Like the `ImagePullBackOff` status, a `CrashLoopBackOff` uses an algorithm to retry the failure, increasing the time between retries with every failure, to avoid overwhelming the cluster. We can see this back-off if we wait a few minutes and then print the status again:

```
root@host01:~# kubectl get pods
NAME       READY   STATUS             RESTARTS       AGE
postgres   0/1     CrashLoopBackOff   5 (117s ago)   5m3s
```

After five restarts, we're already up to more than a minute of wait time between retries. The wait time will continue to increase until we reach five minutes, and then Kubernetes will continue to retry every five minutes thereafter indefinitely.

Let's use kubectl describe, as usual, to try to get more information about this failure:

```
root@host01:~# kubectl describe pod postgres
Name:         postgres
Namespace:    default
...
Containers:
  postgres:
...
    State:          Waiting
      Reason:       CrashLoopBackOff
    Last State:     Terminated
      Reason:       Error
      Exit Code:    1
...
Events:
  Type      Reason    Age                 From        Message
  ----      ------    ----                ----        -------
...
  Warning   BackOff   3m13s (x24 over 8m1s)  kubelet     Back-off
    restarting failed container
```

The kubectl describe command does give us one piece of useful information: the exit code for the container. However, that really just tells us there was an error of some kind; it isn't enough to fully debug the failure. To establish why the container is failing, we'll look at the container logs using the kubectl logs command:

```
root@host01:~# kubectl logs postgres
Error: Database is uninitialized and superuser password is not specified.
  You must specify POSTGRES_PASSWORD to a non-empty value for the
  superuser. For example, "-e POSTGRES_PASSWORD=password" on "docker run".
...
```

We can see the logs even though the container has already stopped, because the container runtime has captured them.

This message comes directly from PostgreSQL itself. Fortunately, it tells us exactly what the issue is: we are missing a required environment variable. We can quickly fix this with an update to the YAML resource file:

postgres
-fixed.yaml
```
---
apiVersion: v1
kind: Pod
metadata:
```

```
    name: postgres
spec:
  containers:
  - name: postgres
    image: postgres
❶ env:
    - name: POSTGRES_PASSWORD
      value: "supersecret"
```

The env field ❶ adds a configuration to pass in the required environment variable. Of course, in a real system we would not put this directly in a YAML file in plaintext. We look at how to secure this kind of information in Chapter 16.

To apply this change, we first need to delete the Pod definition and then apply the new resource configuration to the cluster:

```
root@host01:~# kubectl delete pod postgres
pod "postgres" deleted
root@host01:~# kubectl apply -f /opt/postgres-fixed.yaml
pod/postgres created
```

As before, if we were using a controller such as a Deployment, we could just update the Deployment, and it would handle deleting the old Pod and creating a new one for us.

Now that we've fixed the configuration, our PostgreSQL container starts as expected:

```
root@host01:~# kubectl get pods
NAME       READY   STATUS    RESTARTS   AGE
postgres   1/1     Running   0          77s
```

Let's clean up this Pod before we continue to our next example:

```
root@host01:~# kubectl delete pod postgres
pod "postgres" deleted
```

Most well-written applications will print log messages before terminating, but we need to be prepared for more difficult cases. Let's look at one more example that includes two new debugging approaches.

Debugging Using Exec

For this example, we'll need an application that behaves badly. We'll use a C program that does some very naughty memory access. This program is packaged into an Alpine Linux container so that we can run it as a container in Kubernetes. Here's the C source code:

crasher.c
```
int main() {
    char *s = "12";
    s[2] = '3';
```

```
    return 0;
}
```

The first line of code creates a pointer to a string that is two characters long; the second line then tries to write to the non-existent third character, causing the program to terminate immediately.

This C program can be compiled on any system by using gcc to create a crasher executable. If you build it on a host Linux system, use this gcc command:

```
$ gcc -g -static -o crasher crasher.c
```

The -g argument ensures that debugging symbols are available. We'll use those in a moment. The -static argument is the most important; we want to package this as a standalone application inside an Alpine container image. If we are building on a different Linux distribution, such as Ubuntu, the standard libraries are based on a different toolchain, and dynamic linking will fail. For this reason, we want our executable to have all of its dependencies statically linked. Finally, we use -o to specify the output executable name and then provide the name of our C source file.

Alternatively, you can just use the container image that's already been built and published to Docker Hub under the name bookofkubernetes/crasher:stable. This image is built and published automatically using GitHub Actions based on the code in the repository *https://github.com/book-of-kubernetes/crasher*. Here's the *Dockerfile* from that repository:

Dockerfile
```
FROM alpine AS builder
COPY ./crasher.c /
RUN apk --update add gcc musl-dev && \
    gcc -g -o crasher crasher.c

FROM alpine
COPY --from=builder /crasher /crasher
CMD [ "/crasher" ]
```

This *Dockerfile* takes advantage of Docker's multistage builds capability to reduce the final image size. To compile inside an Alpine container, we need gcc and the core C include files and libraries. However, these have the effect of making the container image significantly larger. We only need them at compile time, so we want to avoid having that extra content in the final image.

When we run this build using the docker build command that we saw in Chapter 5, Docker will create one container based on Alpine Linux, copy our source code into it, install the developer tools, and compile the application. Docker will then start over with a fresh Alpine Linux container and will copy the resulting executable from the first container. The final container image is captured from this second container, so we avoid adding the developer tools to the final image.

Let's run this image in our Kubernetes cluster. We'll use a Deployment resource this time so that we can illustrate editing it to work around the crashing container:

*crasher
-deploy.yaml*
```
---
kind: Deployment
apiVersion: apps/v1
metadata:
  name: crasher
spec:
  replicas: 1
  selector:
    matchLabels:
      app: crasher
  template:
    metadata:
      labels:
        app: crasher
    spec:
      containers:
      - name: crasher
        image: bookofkubernetes/crasher:stable
```

This basic Deployment is very similar to what we saw when we introduced Deployments in Chapter 7. We specify the image field to match the location where the image is published.

We can add this Deployment to the cluster in the usual way:

```
root@host01:~# kubectl apply -f /opt/crasher-deploy.yaml
deployment.apps/crasher created
```

As soon as Kubernetes has had a chance to schedule the Pod and pull the image, it starts crashing, as expected:

```
root@host01:~# kubectl get pods
NAME                      READY   STATUS            RESTARTS      AGE
crasher-76cdd9f769-5blbn  0/1     CrashLoopBackOff  3 (24s ago)   73s
```

As before, using kubectl describe tells us only the exit code of the container. There's another way to get this exit code; we can use the JSON output format of kubectl get and the jq tool to capture just the exit code:

```
root@host01:~# kubectl get pod crasher-7978d9bcfb-wvx6q -o json | \
  jq '.status.containerStatuses[].lastState.terminated.exitCode'
139
```

Be sure to use the correct name for your Pod based on the output of kubectl get pods. The path to the specific field we need is based on how Kubernetes tracks this resource internally; with some practice it becomes easier to craft a path to jq to capture a specific field, which is a very handy trick in scripting.

The exit code of 139 tells us that the container terminated with a segmentation fault. However, the logs are unhelpful in diagnosing the problem, because our program didn't print anything before it crashed:

```
root@host01:~# kubectl logs crasher-76cdd9f769-5blbn
[ no output ]
```

We have quite a problem. The logs aren't helpful, so the next step would be to use kubectl exec to get inside the container. However, the container stops immediately when our application crashes and is not around long enough for us to do any debugging work.

To fix this, we need a way to start this container without running the crashing program. We can do that by overriding the default command to have our container remain running. Because we built on an Alpine Linux image, the sleep command is available to us for this purpose.

We could edit our YAML file and update the Deployment that way, but we can also edit the Deployment directly using kubectl edit, which will bring up the current definition in an editor, and any changes we make will be saved to the cluster:

```
root@host01:~# kubectl edit deployment crasher
```

This will bring up vi in an editor window with the Deployment resource in YAML format. The resource will include a lot more fields than we provided when we created it because Kubernetes will show us the status of the resource as well as some fields with default values.

If you don't like vi, you can preface the kubectl edit command with KUBE_EDITOR=nano to use the Nano editor, instead.

Within the file, find these lines:

```
spec:
  containers:
  - image: bookofkubernetes/crasher:stable
    imagePullPolicy: IfNotPresent
```

You will see the imagePullPolicy line even though it wasn't in the YAML resource, as Kubernetes has added the default policy to the resource automatically. Add a new line between image and imagePullPolicy so that the result looks like this:

```
spec:
  containers:
  - image: bookofkubernetes/crasher:stable
    args: ["/bin/sleep", "infinity"]
    imagePullPolicy: IfNotPresent
```

This added line overrides the default command for the container so that it runs sleep instead of running our crashing program. Save and exit the editor, and kubectl will pick up the new definition:

```
deployment.apps/crasher edited
```

After kubectl applies this change to the cluster, the Deployment must delete the old Pod and create a new one. This is done automatically, so the only difference we'll notice is the automatically generated part of the Pod name. Of course, we'll also see the Pod running:

```
root@host01:~# kubectl get pods
NAME                     READY  STATUS   RESTARTS  AGE
crasher-58d56fc5df-vghbt  1/1    Running  0         3m29s
```

Our Pod is now running, but it's only running sleep. We still need to debug our actual application. To do that, we can now get a shell prompt inside our container:

```
root@host01:~# kubectl exec -ti crasher-58d56fc5df-vghbt -- /bin/sh
/ #
```

The Deployment replaced the Pod when we changed the definition, so the name has changed. As before, use the correct name for your Pod. At this point we can try out our crashing program manually:

```
/ # /crasher
Segmentation fault (core dumped)
```

In many cases, the ability to run a program this way, playing with different environment variables and command line options, may be enough to find and fix the problem. Alternatively, we could try running the program with strace, which would tell us what system calls the program is trying to make and what files it is trying to open prior to crashing. In this case, we know that the program is crashing with a segmentation fault, meaning that the problem is likely a programming error, so our best approach is to connect a debugging tool to the application using port forwarding.

Debugging Using Port Forwarding

We'll illustrate port forwarding using the text-based debugger gdb, but any debugger that can connect via a network port will work. First, we need to get our application created inside the container using a debugger that will listen on a network port and wait before it runs the code. To do that, we'll need to install gdb inside our container. Because this is an Alpine container, we'll use apk:

```
/ # apk add gdb
...
(13/13) Installing gdb (10.1-r0)
```

```
Executing busybox-1.32.1-r3.trigger
OK: 63 MiB in 27 packages
```

The version of gdb we installed includes gdbserver, which enables us to start a networked debug session.

Because gdb is a text-based debugger, we could obviously just start it directly to debug our application, but it is often nicer to use a debugger with a GUI, making it easier for us to step through source, set breakpoints, and watch variables. For this reason, I'm showing the process for connecting a debugger over the network.

Let's start gdbserver and set it up to listen on port 2345:

```
/ # gdbserver localhost:2345 /crasher
Process /crasher created; pid = 25
Listening on port 2345
```

Note that we told gdbserver to listen to the localhost interface. We'll still be able to connect to the debugger because we'll have Kubernetes provide us with port forwarding with the kubectl port-forward command. This command causes kubectl to connect to the API server and request it to forward traffic to a specific port on a specific Pod. The advantage is that we can use this port forwarding capability from anywhere we can connect to the API server, even outside the cluster.

Using port forwarding specifically to run a remote debugger may not be an everyday occurrence for either a Kubernetes cluster administrator or the developer of a containerized application, but it's a valuable skill to have when there's no other way to find the bug. It's also a great way to illustrate the power of port forwarding to reach a Pod.

Because we have our debugger running in our first terminal, we'll need another terminal tab or window for the port forwarding, which can be done from any of the hosts in our cluster. Let's use host01:

```
root@host01:~# kubectl port-forward pods/crasher-58d56fc5df-vghbt 2345:2345
Forwarding from 127.0.0.1:2345 -> 2345
Forwarding from [::1]:2345 -> 2345
```

This kubectl command starts listening on port 2345 and forwards all traffic through the API server to the Pod we specified. Because this command keeps running, we need yet another terminal window or tab for our final step, which is to run the debugger we'll use to connect to our debug server running in the container. This must be done from the same host as our kubectl port-forward command because that program is listening only on local interfaces.

At this point, we could run any debugger that knows how to talk to the debug server. For simplicity, we'll use gdb again. We'll begin by changing to the /opt directory because our C source file is there:

```
root@host01:~# cd /opt
```

Now we can kick off gdb and use it to connect to the debug server:

```
root@host01:/opt# gdb -q
(gdb) target remote localhost:2345
Remote debugging using localhost:2345
...
Reading /crasher from remote target...
Reading symbols from target:/crasher...
0x0000000000401bc0 in _start ()
```

Our debug session connects successfully and is waiting for us to start the program, which we'll do by using the continue command:

```
(gdb) continue
Continuing.

Program received signal SIGSEGV, Segmentation fault.
main () at crasher.c:3
3           s[2] = '3';
```

With the debugger, we're able to see exactly which line of our source code is causing the segmentation fault, and now we can figure out how to fix it.

Final Thoughts

When we move our application components into container images and run them in a Kubernetes cluster, we gain substantial benefits in scalability and automated failover, but we introduce a number of new possibilities that can go wrong when getting our application running, and we introduce new challenges in debugging those problems. In this chapter, we've looked at how to use Kubernetes commands to systematically track our application startup and operation to determine what is preventing it from working correctly. With these commands, we can debug any kind of issue happening at the application level, even if an application component won't start correctly in its containerized environment.

Now that we have a clear picture of running containers using Kubernetes, we can begin to look in depth into the capabilities of the cluster itself. As we do this, we'll be sure to explore how each component works so as to have the tools needed to diagnose problems. We'll start in the next chapter by looking in detail at the Kubernetes control plane.

11

CONTROL PLANE AND ACCESS CONTROL

The control plane manages the Kubernetes cluster, storing the desired state of applications, monitoring the current state to detect and recover from any issues, scheduling new containers, and configuring network routing. In this chapter, we'll look closely at the API server, the primary interface for the control plane and the entry point for any status retrieval and changes made to the entire cluster.

Although we will focus on the API server, the control plane includes multiple other services, each with a role to play. The other control plane services act as clients to the API server, watching cluster changes and taking appropriate action to update the state of the cluster. The following list describes the other control plane components:

Scheduler   Assigns each new Pod to a node.

Controller manager   Has multiple responsibilities, including creating Pods for Deployments, monitoring nodes, and reacting to outages.

Cloud controller manager   This optional component interfaces with an underlying cloud provider to check on nodes and configure network traffic routing.

As we demonstrate the workings of the API server, we'll also see how Kubernetes manages security to ensure that only authorized users and services can query the cluster and make changes. The purpose of a container orchestration environment like Kubernetes is to provide a platform for any kind of containerized application we might need to run, so this security is critically important to ensure that the cluster is used only as intended.

API Server

Despite its centrality to the Kubernetes architecture, the API server's purpose is simple. It exposes an interface using HTTP and representational state transfer (REST) to perform basic creation, retrieval, update, and deletion of resources in the cluster. It performs authentication to identify clients, authorization to ensure that clients have permission for the specific request, and validation to ensure that any created or updated resources match the corresponding specification. It also reads from and writes to a data store based on the commands it receives from clients.

However, the API server is not responsible for actually updating the current state of the cluster to match the desired state. That is the responsibility of other control plane and node components. For example, if a client creates a new Kubernetes Deployment, the API server's job is solely to update the data store with the resource information. It is then the job of the scheduler to decide where the Pods will run, and the job of the kubelet service on the assigned nodes to create and monitor the containers and to configure networking to route traffic to the containers.

For this chapter, we have a three-node Kubernetes cluster configured by our automation scripts. Each of the three nodes acts as a control plane node, so three copies of the API server are running. We can communicate with any of these three because they all share the same backend database. The API server is listening for secure HTTP connections on port 6443, the default port.

NOTE   *The example repository for this book is at* https://github.com/book-of -kubernetes/examples. *See "Running Examples" on page xx for details on getting set up.*

We've been using kubectl to communicate with the API server to create and delete resources and retrieve status, and kubectl has been using secure HTTP on port 6443 to talk to the cluster. It knows to do this because of a Kubernetes configuration file that was installed into */etc/kubernetes* by kubeadm when the cluster was initialized. This configuration file also contains authentication information that gives us permission to read cluster status and make changes.

Because the API server is expecting secure HTTP, we can use `curl` to communicate directly with the Kubernetes API. This will give us a better feel for how the communication actually works. Let's begin with a simple `curl` command:

```
root@host01:~# curl https://192.168.61.11:6443/
curl: (60) SSL certificate problem: unable to get local issuer certificate
More details here: https://curl.se/docs/sslcerts.html
...
```

This error message shows that `curl` does not trust the certificate that the API server is offering. We can use `curl` to see this certificate:

```
root@host01:~# curl -kv https://192.168.61.11:6443/
...
* Server certificate:
*  subject: CN=kube-apiserver
...
*  issuer: CN=kubernetes
...
```

The `-k` option tells `curl` to ignore any certificate issues, whereas `-v` tells `curl` to provide us with extra logging information about the connection.

For `curl` to trust this certificate, it will need to trust the `issuer`, as the issuer is the signer of the certificate. Let's fetch the certificate from our Kubernetes installation so that we can point `curl` to it:

```
root@host01:~# cp /etc/kubernetes/pki/ca.crt .
```

Be sure to add the . at the end to copy this file to the current directory. We're doing this solely to make the following commands easier to type.

Let's examine this certificate before we use it:

```
root@host01:~# openssl x509 -in ca.crt -text
Certificate:
...
        Issuer: CN = kubernetes
...
        Subject: CN = kubernetes
```

The `Issuer` and the `Subject` are the same, so this is a *self-signed* certificate. It was created by `kubeadm` when we initialized this cluster. Using a generated certificate allows `kubeadm` to adapt to our particular cluster networking configuration and allows our cluster to have a unique certificate and key without requiring an external certificate authority (CA). However, it does mean that we need to configure `kubectl` to trust this certificate on any system for which we need to communicate with this API server.

We can now tell `curl` to use this certificate to verify the API server:

```
root@host01:~# curl --cacert ca.crt https://192.168.61.11:6443/
{
...
  "status": "Failure",
  "message": "forbidden: User \"system:anonymous\" cannot get path \"/\"",
...
  "code": 403
}
```

Now that we're providing curl with the correct root certificate, curl can validate the API server certificate and we can successfully connect to the API server. However, the API server responds with a 403 error, indicating that we are not authorized. This is because at the moment we are not providing any authentication information for curl to pass to the API server, so the API server sees us as an anonymous user.

One final note: for this curl command to work, we need to be selective in the hostname or IP address we use. The API server is listening on all network interfaces, so we could connect to it using localhost or 127.0.0.1. However, those are not listed in the kube-apiserver certificate and cannot be used for secure HTTP because curl will not trust the connection.

API Server Authentication

We need to provide authentication information before the API server will accept our requests, so let's understand the API server's process for authentication. Authentication is handled through a set of plug-ins, each of which looks at the request to determine whether it can identify the client. The first plug-in that successfully identifies the client provides identity information to the API server. This identity is then used with authorization to determine what the client is allowed to do.

Because authentication is based on plug-ins, it's possible to have as many different ways of authenticating clients as needed. It's even possible to add a proxy in front of the API server that performs custom authentication logic and passes the user's identity to the API server in an HTTP header.

For our purposes, we'll focus on three authentication primary plug-ins that are used within the cluster itself or as part of the cluster setup process: *client certificates*, *bootstrap tokens*, and *service accounts*.

Client Certificates

As mentioned previously, an HTTP client like curl validates the server's identity by comparing the server's hostname to its certificate and also by checking the certificate's signature against a list of trusted CAs. In addition to checking the server identity, secure HTTP also allows a client to submit a certificate to the server. The server checks the signature against its list of trusted authorities and then uses the subject of the certificate as the client's identity.

Kubernetes uses HTTP client certificate authentication extensively to enable cluster services to authenticate with the API server. This includes control plane components as well as the kubelet service running on each node. We can use kubeadm to list the certificates used by the control plane:

```
root@host01:~# kubeadm certs check-expiration
...
CERTIFICATE                ... RESIDUAL TIME   CERTIFICATE AUTHORITY ...
admin.conf                 ... 363d                                  ...
apiserver                  ... 363d            ca                    ...
apiserver-etcd-client      ... 363d            etcd-ca               ...
apiserver-kubelet-client   ... 363d            ca                    ...
controller-manager.conf    ... 363d                                  ...
etcd-healthcheck-client    ... 363d            etcd-ca               ...
etcd-peer                  ... 363d            etcd-ca               ...
etcd-server                ... 363d            etcd-ca               ...
front-proxy-client         ... 363d            front-proxy-ca        ...
scheduler.conf             ... 363d                                  ...
...
```

The RESIDUAL TIME column shows how much time is left before these certificates expire; by default, they expire after one year. Use kubeadm certs renew to renew them, passing the name of the certificate as a parameter.

The first item in the list, admin.conf, is how we've been authenticating ourselves to the cluster in the past few chapters. During initialization, kubeadm created this certificate and stored its information in the */etc/kubernetes/admin.conf* file. Every kubectl command we've run has been using this file because our automation scripts are setting the KUBECONFIG environment variable:

```
root@host01:~# echo $KUBECONFIG
/etc/kubernetes/admin.conf
```

If we had not set KUBECONFIG, kubectl would be using the default, which is a file called *.kube/config* in the user's home directory.

The *admin.conf* credentials are designed to provide emergency access to the cluster, bypassing authorization. In a production cluster, we would avoid using these credentials directly for everyday operations. Instead, the best practice for a production cluster is to integrate a separate identity manager for administrators and normal users. For our example, because we don't have a separate identity manager, we'll instead create an additional certificate for a regular user. This kind of certificate may be useful for an automated process that runs outside the cluster, but it can't integrate with the identity manager.

We can create a new client certificate using kubeadm:

```
root@host01:~# kubeadm kubeconfig user --client-name=me \
  --config /etc/kubernetes/kubeadm-init.yaml > kubeconfig
```

The kubeadm kubeconfig user command asks the API server to generate a new client certificate. Because this certificate is signed by the cluster's CA, it is valid for authentication. The certificate is saved into the *kubeconfig* file along with the necessary configuration to connect to the API server:

```
root@host01:~# cat kubeconfig
apiVersion: v1
clusters:
- cluster:
    certificate-authority-data: ...
    server: https://192.168.61.10:6443
  name: kubernetes
contexts:
- context:
    cluster: kubernetes
    user: me
  name: me@kubernetes
current-context: me@kubernetes
kind: Config
preferences: {}
users:
- name: me
  user:
    client-certificate-data: ...
    client-key-data: ...
```

The clusters section defines the information needed to connect to the API server, including the load-balanced address shared by all three API servers in our highly available configuration. The users section defines the new user we created along with its client certificate.

Thus far, we've successfully created a new user, but we haven't given that user any permissions yet, so we won't be very successful using these credentials:

```
root@host01:~# KUBECONFIG=kubeconfig kubectl get pods
Error from server (Forbidden): pods is forbidden: User "me" cannot list
  resource "pods" in API group "" in the namespace "default"
```

Later in the chapter, we'll see how to give permissions to this user.

Bootstrap Tokens

Initializing a distributed system like a Kubernetes cluster is challenging. The kubelet service running on each node must be added to the cluster. To do this, kubelet must connect to the API server and obtain a client certificate signed by the cluster's CA. The kubelet service then uses this client certificate to authenticate to the cluster.

This certificate generation must be done securely so that we eliminate the possibility of adding rogue nodes to the cluster and eliminate the possibility of a rogue process being able to impersonate a real node. For this reason, the API server cannot provide a certificate for just any node that asks to be added to the cluster. Instead, the node must generate its own private key, submit a certificate signing request (CSR) to the API server, and receive a signed certificate.

To keep this process secure, we need to ensure that a node is authorized to submit a certificate signing request. But this submission must happen before the node has the client certificate that it uses for more permanent authentication—we have a chicken-or-egg problem! Kubernetes solves this via time-limited tokens, known as *Bootstrap Tokens*. The bootstrap token becomes a preshared secret that is known to the API server and the new nodes. Making this token time limited reduces the risk to the cluster if it is exposed. The Kubernetes controller manager has the task of automatically cleaning up bootstrap tokens when they expire.

When we initialized our cluster, kubeadm created a bootstrap token, but it was configured to expire after two hours. If we need to join additional nodes to the cluster after that, we can use kubeadm to generate a new bootstrap token:

```
root@host01:~# TOKEN=$(kubeadm token create)
root@host01:~# echo $TOKEN
pqcnd6.4wawyqgkfaet06zm
```

This token is added as a Kubernetes *Secret* in the kube-system Namespace. We look at secrets in more detail in Chapter 16. For now, let's just verify that it exists:

```
root@host01:~# kubectl -n kube-system get secret
NAME                       TYPE                            DATA    AGE
...
bootstrap-token-pqcnd6    bootstrap.kubernetes.io/token  6       64s
...
```

We can use this token to make requests of the API server by using HTTP Bearer authentication. This means that we provide the token in an HTTP header called Authorization, prefaced with the word Bearer. When the bootstrap token authentication plug-in sees that header and matches the provided token against the corresponding secret, it authenticates us to the API server and allows us access to the API.

For security reasons, bootstrap tokens have access only to the certificate signing request functionality of the API server, so that's all our token will be allowed to do.

Let's use our bootstrap token to list all of the certificate signing requests:

```
root@host01:~# curl --cacert ca.crt \
  -H "Authorization: Bearer $TOKEN" \
  https://192.168.61.11:6443/apis/certificates.k8s.io/v1/certificatesigningrequests
{
  "kind": "CertificateSigningRequestList",
```

```
  "apiVersion": "certificates.k8s.io/v1",
  "metadata": {
    "resourceVersion": "21241"
  },
  "items": [
...
  ]
}
```

It's important to know how bootstrap tokens work, given that they're essential to adding nodes to the cluster. However, as the name implies, that's really the only purpose for a bootstrap token; it's not typical to use them for normal API server access. For normal API server access, especially from inside the cluster, we need a *ServiceAccount*.

Service Accounts

Containers running in the Kubernetes cluster often need to communicate with the API server. For example, all of the various components we deployed on top of our cluster in Chapter 6, including the Calico network plug-in, the Longhorn storage driver, and the metrics server, communicate with the API server to watch and modify the cluster state. To support this, Kubernetes automatically injects credentials into every running container.

Of course, for security reasons, giving each container only the API server permissions it requires is important, so we should create a separate ServiceAccount for each application or cluster component to do that. The information for these ServiceAccounts is then added to the Deployment or other controller so that Kubernetes will inject the correct credentials. In some cases, we may use multiple ServiceAccount with a single application, restricting each application component to only the access it needs.

In addition to using a separate ServiceAccount per application or component, it's also good practice to use a separate Namespace per application. As we'll see in a moment, permissions can be limited to a single Namespace. Let's start by creating the Namespace:

```
root@host01:~# kubectl create namespace sample
namespace/sample created
```

A ServiceAccount uses a bearer token, which is stored in a secret automatically generated by Kubernetes when the ServiceAccount is created. Let's make a ServiceAccount for a Deployment that we'll create in this chapter:

read-pods
-sa.yaml
```
---
apiVersion: v1
kind: ServiceAccount
metadata:
  name: read-pods
  namespace: sample
```

Note that we use the metadata to place this ServiceAccount in the `sample` Namespace we just created. We could also use the `-n` flag with `kubectl` to specify the Namespace. We'll use the usual `kubectl apply` to create this ServiceAccount:

```
root@host01:~# kubectl apply -f /opt/read-pods-sa.yaml
serviceaccount/read-pods created
```

When the ServiceAccount is created, the controller manager detects this and automatically creates a Secret with the credentials:

```
root@host01:~# kubectl -n sample get serviceaccounts
NAME          SECRETS   AGE
default       1         27s
read-pods     1         8s
root@host01:~# kubectl -n sample get secrets
NAME                  TYPE                                   DATA   AGE
default-token-mzwpt   kubernetes.io/service-account-token    3      43s
read-pods-token-m4scq kubernetes.io/service-account-token    3      25s
```

Note that in addition to the `read-pods` ServiceAccount we just created, there is already a `default` ServiceAccount. This account was created automatically when the Namespace was created; it will be used if we don't specify to Kubernetes which ServiceAccount to use for a Pod.

The newly created ServiceAccount does not have any permissions yet. To start adding permissions, we need to take a look at *role-based access control* (RBAC).

Role-Based Access Controls

After the API server has found an authentication plug-in that can identify the client, it uses the identity to determine whether the client has permissions to perform the desired action, which is done by assembling a list of roles that belong to the user. Roles can be associated directly with a user or with a group in which the user is a member. Group membership is part of the identity. For example, client certificates can specify a user's groups by including organization fields as part of the certificate's subject.

Roles and Cluster Roles

Each role has a set of permissions. A permission allows a client to perform one or more actions on one or more types of resources.

As an example, let's define a role that will give a client permission to read Pod status. We have two choices: we can create a *Role* or a *ClusterRole*. A Role is visible and usable within a single Namespace, whereas a Cluster-Role is visible and usable across all Namespaces. This difference allows administrators to define common roles across the cluster that are immediately available when new Namespaces are created, while also allowing the delegation of access control for a specific Namespace.

Here's an example definition of a ClusterRole. This role only has the ability to read data about Pods; it cannot change Pods or access any other cluster information:

pod-reader.yaml
```
---
apiVersion: rbac.authorization.k8s.io/v1
kind: ClusterRole
metadata:
  name: pod-reader
rules:
- apiGroups: [""]
  resources: ["pods"]
  verbs: ["get", "watch", "list"]
```

Because this is a cluster-wide role, it doesn't make sense to assign it to a Namespace, so we don't specify one.

The critical part of this definition is the list of rules. Each ClusterRole or Role can have as many rules as necessary. Each rule has a list of verbs that define what actions are allowed. In this case, we identified get, watch, and list as the verbs, with the effect that the role allows reading Pods but not any actions that would modify them.

Each rule applies to one or more resource types, based on the combination of apiGroups and resources identified. Each rule gives permissions for the actions listed as verbs. In this case, the empty string "" is used to refer to the default API group, which is where Pods are located. If we wanted to also include Deployments and StatefulSets, we would need to define our rule as follows:

```
- apiGroups: ["", "apps"]
  resources: ["pods", "deployments", "statefulsets"]
  verbs: ["get", "watch", "list"]
```

We need to add "apps" to the apiGroups field because Deployment and StatefulSet are part of that group (as identified in the apiVersion when we declare the resource). When we declare a Role or ClusterRole, the API server will accept any strings in the apiGroups and resources fields, regardless of whether the combination actually identifies any resource types, so it's important to pay attention to which group a resource is in.

Let's define our pod-reader ClusterRole:

```
root@host01:~# kubectl apply -f /opt/pod-reader.yaml
clusterrole.rbac.authorization.k8s.io/pod-reader created
```

Now that the ClusterRole exists, we can apply it. To do that, we need to create a role binding.

Role Bindings and Cluster Role Bindings

Let's apply this pod-reader ClusterRole to the read-pods ServiceAccount we created earlier. We have two options: we can create a *RoleBinding*, which will assign the permissions in a specific Namespace, or a *ClusterRoleBinding*, which will assign the permissions across all Namespaces. This feature is beneficial because it means we can create a ClusterRole such as pod-reader once and have it visible across the cluster, but create the binding in an individual Namespace so that users and ServiceAccount are restricted to only the Namespaces they should be allowed to access. This helps us apply the pattern we saw earlier of having a Namespace per application, while at the same time it keeps non-administrators away from key infrastructure components such as the components running in the kube-system Namespace.

In keeping with this practice, we'll create a RoleBinding so that our ServiceAccount has permissions to read Pods only in the sample Namespace:

read-pods
-bind.yaml
```
---
apiVersion: rbac.authorization.k8s.io/v1
kind: RoleBinding
metadata:
  name: read-pods
  namespace: sample
subjects:
- kind: ServiceAccount
  name: read-pods
  namespace: sample
roleRef:
  kind: ClusterRole
  name: pod-reader
  apiGroup: rbac.authorization.k8s.io
```

Not surprisingly, a RoleBinding ties together a Role or a ClusterRole and a subject. The RoleBinding can contain multiple subjects, so we can bind the same role to multiple users or groups with a single binding.

We define a Namespace in both the metadata and where we identify the subject. In this case, these are both sample, as we want to grant the ServiceAccount the ability to read Pod status in its own Namespace. However, these could be different to allow a ServiceAccount in one Namespace to have specific permissions in another Namespace. And of course we could also use a ClusterRoleBinding to give out permissions across all Namespaces.

We can now create the RoleBinding:

```
root@host01:~# kubectl apply -f /opt/read-pods-bind.yaml
rolebinding.rbac.authorization.k8s.io/read-pods created
```

We've now given permission for the read-pods ServiceAccount to read Pods in the sample Namespace. To demonstrate how it works, we need to create a Pod that is assigned to the read-pods ServiceAccount.

Assigning a Service Account to Pods

To assign a ServiceAccount to a Pod, just add the `serviceAccountName` field to the Pod spec:

*read-pods
-deploy.yaml*

```
---
kind: Deployment
apiVersion: apps/v1
metadata:
  name: read-pods
  namespace: sample
spec:
  replicas: 1
  selector:
    matchLabels:
      app: read-pods
  template:
    metadata:
      labels:
        app: read-pods
    spec:
      containers:
      - name: read-pods
        image: alpine
        command: ["/bin/sleep", "infinity"]
        serviceAccountName: read-pods
```

The ServiceAccount identified must exist in the Namespace that the Pod is created in. Kubernetes will inject the Pod's containers with the Service-Account token so that the containers can authenticate to the API server.

Let's walk through an example to show how this works and how the authorization is applied. Start by creating this Deployment:

```
root@host01:~# kubectl apply -f /opt/read-pods-deploy.yaml
deployment.apps/read-pods created
```

This creates an Alpine container running `sleep` that we can use as a base for shell commands.

To get to a shell prompt, we'll first get the generated name of the Pod and then use `kubectl exec` to create the shell:

```
root@host01:~# kubectl -n sample get pods
NAME                        READY   STATUS    RESTARTS   AGE
read-pods-9d5565548-fbwjb   1/1     Running   0          6s
root@host01:~# kubectl -n sample exec -ti read-pods-9d5565548-fbwjb -- /bin/sh
/ #
```

The ServiceAccount token is mounted in the directory */run/secrets/ kubernetes.io/serviceaccount*, so change to that directory and list its contents:

```
/ # cd /run/secrets/kubernetes.io/serviceaccount
/run/secrets/kubernetes.io/serviceaccount # ls -l
total 0
lrwxrwxrwx    1 root     root   ...  ca.crt -> ..data/ca.crt
lrwxrwxrwx    1 root     root   ...  namespace -> ..data/namespace
lrwxrwxrwx    1 root     root   ...  token -> ..data/token
```

These files show up as odd looking symbolic links, but the contents are there as expected. The *ca.crt* file is the root certificate for the cluster, which is needed to trust the connection to the API server.

Let's save the token in a variable so that we can use it:

```
/run/secrets/kubernetes.io/serviceaccount # TOKEN=$(cat token)
```

We can now use this token with curl to connect to the API server. First, though, we need to install curl into our Alpine container:

```
default/run/secrets/kubernetes.io/serviceaccount # apk add curl
...
OK: 8 MiB in 19 packages
```

Our ServiceAccount is allowed to perform get, list, and watch operations on Pods. Let's list all Pods in the sample Namespace:

```
/run/secrets/kubernetes.io/serviceaccount # curl --cacert ca.crt \
  -H "Authorization: Bearer $TOKEN" \
  https://kubernetes.default.svc/api/v1/namespaces/sample/pods
"kind": "PodList",
"apiVersion": "v1",
"metadata": {
  "resourceVersion": "566610"
},
"items": [
  {
    "metadata": {
      "name": "read-pods-9d5565548-fbwjb",
...
  ]
}
```

As with the bootstrap token, we use HTTP Bearer authentication to pass the ServiceAccount token to the API server. Because we're operating from inside a container, we can use the standard address kubernetes.default.svc to find the API server. This works because a Kubernetes cluster always has a service in the default Namespace that routes traffic to API server instances using the Service networking we saw in Chapter 9.

The curl command is successful because our ServiceAccount is bound to the pod-reader Role we created. However, the RoleBinding is limited to the sample Namespace, and as a result, we aren't allowed to list Pods in a different Namespace:

```
/run/secrets/kubernetes.io/serviceaccount # curl --cacert ca.crt \
  -H "Authorization: Bearer $TOKEN" \
  https://kubernetes.default.svc/api/v1/namespaces/kube-system/pods
{
  "kind": "Status",
  "apiVersion": "v1",
  "metadata": {
  },
  "status": "Failure",
  "message": "pods is forbidden: User
    \"system:serviceaccount:default:read-pods\" cannot list resource
    \"pods\" in API group \"\" in the namespace \"kube-system\"",
  "reason": "Forbidden",
  "details": {
    "kind": "pods"
  },
  "code": 403
}
```

We can use the error message to be certain that our ServiceAccount assignment and authentication worked as expected because the API server recognizes us as the read-pods ServiceAccount. However, we don't have a RoleBinding with the right permissions to read Pods in the kube-system Namespace, so the request is rejected.

Similarly, because we have permission only for Pods, we can't list our Deployment, even though it is also in the sample Namespace:

```
/run/secrets/kubernetes.io/serviceaccount # curl --cacert ca.crt \
  -H "Authorization: Bearer $TOKEN" \
  https://kubernetes.default.svc/apis/apps/v1/namespaces/sample/deploy
ments
{
  "kind": "Status",
  "apiVersion": "v1",
  "metadata": {
  },
  "status": "Failure",
  "message": "deploy.apps is forbidden: User
    \"system:serviceaccount:default:read-pods\" cannot list resource
    \"deploy\" in API group \"apps\" in the namespace \"sample\"",
  "reason": "Forbidden",
  "details": {
    "group": "apps",
    "kind": "deploy"
  },
```

```
  "code": 403
}
```

The slightly different path scheme for the URL, starting with */apis/apps/v1* instead of */api/v1*, is needed because Deployments are in the apps API group rather than the default group. This command fails in a similar way because we don't have the necessary permissions to list Deployments.

We're finished with this shell session, so let's exit it:

```
/run/secrets/kubernetes.io/serviceaccount # exit
```

Before we leave the RBAC topic, though, let's illustrate an easy way to grant normal user permissions for a Namespace without allowing any administrator functions.

Binding Roles to Users

To grant normal user permissions, we'll leverage an existing ClusterRole called edit that's already set up to grant view and edit permissions for most of the resource types users need.

Let's take a quick look at the edit ClusterRole to see what permissions it has:

```
root@host01:~# kubectl get clusterrole edit -o yaml
...
apiVersion: rbac.authorization.k8s.io/v1
kind: ClusterRole
...
rules:
...
- apiGroups:
  - ""
  resources:
  - pods
  - pods/attach
  - pods/exec
  - pods/portforward
  - pods/proxy
  verbs:
  - create
  - delete
  - deletecollection
  - patch
  - update
...
```

The full list has a large number of different rules, each with its own set of permissions. The subset in this example shows just one rule, used to provide edit permission for Pods.

Some commands related to Pods, such as exec, are listed separately to allow for more granular control. For example, for a production system, it can be useful to allow some individuals the ability to create and delete Pods and see logs, but not provide the ability to use exec, because that might be used to access sensitive production data.

Previously, we created a user called *me* and saved the client certificate to a file called *kubeconfig*. However, we didn't bind any roles to that user yet, so the user has only the very limited permissions that come with automatic membership in the *system:authenticated* group.

As a result, as we saw earlier, our normal user can't even list Pods in the default Namespace. Let's bind this user to the edit role. As before, we'll use a regular RoleBinding, scoped to the sample Namespace, so this user won't be able to access our cluster infrastructure components in the kube-system Namespace.

Listing 11-1 presents the RoleBinding we need.

edit-bind.yaml
```
---
apiVersion: rbac.authorization.k8s.io/v1
kind: RoleBinding
metadata:
  name: editor
  namespace: sample
subjects:
- kind: User
  name: me
  apiGroup: rbac.authorization.k8s.io
roleRef:
  kind: ClusterRole
  name: edit
  apiGroup: rbac.authorization.k8s.io
```

Listing 11-1: Bind the edit role to a user

Now we apply this RoleBinding to add permissions to our user:

```
root@host01:~# kubectl apply -f /opt/edit-bind.yaml
rolebinding.rbac.authorization.k8s.io/editor created
```

We're now able to use this user to view and modify Pods, Deployments, and many other resources:

```
root@host01:~# KUBECONFIG=kubeconfig kubectl -n sample get pods
NAME                       READY   STATUS    RESTARTS   AGE
read-pods-9d5565548-fbwjb  1/1     Running   0          54m
root@host01:~# KUBECONFIG=kubeconfig kubectl delete -f /opt/read-pods-deploy.yaml
deployment.apps "read-pods" deleted
```

However, because we used a RoleBinding and not a ClusterRoleBinding, this user has no visibility into other Namespaces:

```
root@host01:~# KUBECONFIG=kubeconfig kubectl get -n kube-system pods
Error from server (Forbidden): pods is forbidden: User "me" cannot list
  resource "pods" in API group "" in the namespace "kube-system"
```

The error message displayed by kubectl is identical in form to the message field that is part of the API server's JSON response. This is not a coincidence; kubectl is a friendly command line interface in front of the API server's REST API.

Final Thoughts

The API server is an essential component in the Kubernetes control plane. Every other service in the cluster is continuously connected to the API server, watching the cluster for changes, so it can take appropriate action. Users also use the API server to deploy and configure applications and to monitor state. In this chapter, we saw the underlying REST API that the API server provides to create, retrieve, update, and delete resources. We also saw the extensive authentication and authorization capabilities built in to the API server to ensure that only authorized users and services can access and modify the cluster state.

In the next chapter, we'll examine the other side of our cluster's infrastructure: the node components. We'll see how the kubelet Service hides any differences between container engines and how it uses the container capabilities we saw in Part I to create, start, and configure containers in the cluster.

12

CONTAINER RUNTIME

In the previous chapter, we saw how the control plane manages and monitors the state of the cluster. However, it is the container runtime, especially the kubelet service, that creates, starts, stops, and deletes containers to actually bring the cluster to the desired state. In this chapter, we'll explore how kubelet is configured in our cluster and how it operates.

As part of this exploration, we'll address how kubelet manages to host the control plane while also being dependent on it. Finally, we'll look at node maintenance in a Kubernetes cluster, including how to shut down a node for maintenance, issues that can prevent a node from working correctly, how the cluster behaves if a node suddenly becomes unavailable, and how the node behaves when it loses its cluster connection.

Node Service

The primary service that turns a regular host into a Kubernetes node is kubelet. Because of its criticality to a Kubernetes cluster, we'll look in detail at how it is configured and how it behaves.

CONTAINERD AND CRI-O

The examples for this chapter provide automated scripts to launch a cluster using either of two container runtimes: containerd and CRI-O. We'll primarily use the containerd installation, though we'll briefly look at the configuration difference. The CRI-O cluster is there to allow you to experiment with a separate container runtime. It also illustrates the fact that kubelet hides this difference from the rest of the cluster, as the rest of the cluster configuration is unaffected by a container runtime change.

We installed kubelet as a package on all of our nodes when we set up our cluster in Chapter 6, and the automation has been setting it up similarly for each chapter thereafter.

NOTE *The example repository for this book is at* https://github.com/book-of
-kubernetes/examples. *See "Running Examples" on page xx for details on getting set up.*

The kubelet package also includes a system service. Our operating system is using systemd to run services, so we can get service information using systemctl:

```
root@host01:~# systemctl status kubelet
   kubelet.service - kubelet: The Kubernetes Node Agent
     Loaded: loaded (/lib/systemd/system/kubelet.service; enabled; ...
     Drop-In: /etc/systemd/system/kubelet.service.d
              10-kubeadm.conf
     Active: active (running) since ...
```

The first time kubelet started, it didn't have the configuration needed to join the cluster. When we ran kubeadm, it created the file *10-kubeadm.conf* shown in the preceding output. This file configures the kubelet service for the cluster by setting command line parameters.

Listing 12-1 gives us a look at the command line parameters that are passed to the kubelet service.

```
root@host01:~# strings /proc/$(pgrep kubelet)/cmdline
/usr/bin/kubelet
--bootstrap-kubeconfig=/etc/kubernetes/bootstrap-kubelet.conf
--kubeconfig=/etc/kubernetes/kubelet.conf
--config=/var/lib/kubelet/config.yaml
--container-runtime=remote
--container-runtime-endpoint=/run/containerd/containerd.sock
--node-ip=192.168.61.11
--pod-infra-container-image=k8s.gcr.io/pause:3.4.1
```

Listing 12-1: Kubelet command line

The `pgrep kubelet` embedded command outputs the process ID of the kubelet service. We then use this to print the command line of the process using the */proc* Linux virtual filesystem. We use `strings` to print this file rather than cat because each separate command line parameter is null-terminated and `strings` turns this into a nice multiline display.

The kubelet service needs three main groups of configuration options: *cluster configuration, container runtime configuration*, and *network configuration*.

Kubelet Cluster Configuration

The cluster configuration options tell `kubelet` how to communicate with the cluster and how to authenticate. When `kubelet` starts for the first time, it uses the `bootstrap-kubeconfig` shown in Listing 12-1 to find the cluster, verify the server certificate, and authenticate using the bootstrap token we discussed in Chapter 11. This bootstrap token is used to submit a Certificate Signing Request (CSR) for this new node. The kubelet then downloads the signed client certificate from the API server and stores it in */etc/kubernetes/kubelet.conf*, the location specified by the `kubeconfig` option. This *kubelet.conf* file follows the same format that is used to configure kubectl to talk to the API server, as we saw in Chapter 11. After *kubelet.conf* has been written, the bootstrap file is deleted.

The */var/lib/kubelet/config.yaml* file specified in Listing 12-1 also contains important configuration information. To pull metrics from `kubelet`, we need to set it up with its own server certificate, not just a client certificate, and we need to configure how it authenticates its own clients. Here is the relevant content from the configuration file, created by `kubeadm`:

```
root@host01:~# cat /var/lib/kubelet/config.yaml
...
authentication:
  anonymous:
    enabled: false
  webhook:
    cacheTTL: 0s
    enabled: true
  x509:
    clientCAFile: /etc/kubernetes/pki/ca.crt
...
```

The authentication section tells `kubelet` not to allow anonymous requests, but to allow both webhook bearer tokens as well as any client certificates signed by the cluster certificate authority. The YAML resource file we installed for the metrics server includes a ServiceAccount that is used in its Deployment, so it is automatically injected with credentials that it can use to authenticate to `kubelet` instances, as we saw in Chapter 11.

Kubelet Container Runtime Configuration

The container runtime configuration options tell kubelet how to connect to the container runtime so that kubelet can manage containers on the local machine. Because kubelet expects the runtime to support the Container Runtime Interface (CRI) standard, only a couple of settings are needed, as shown in Listing 12-1.

The first key setting is container-runtime, which can be set to either remote or docker. Kubernetes predates the separation of the Docker engine from the containerd runtime, so it had legacy support for Docker that used a *shim* to emulate the standard CRI interface. Because we are using containerd directly and not via the Docker shim or Docker engine, we set this to remote.

Next, we specify the path to the container runtime using the container -runtime-endpoint setting. The value in this case is */run/containerd/containerd .sock*. The kubelet connects to this Unix socket to send CRI requests and receive status.

The container-runtime-endpoint command line setting is the only difference needed to switch the cluster between containerd and CRI-O. Additionally, it is automatically detected by kubeadm when the node is initialized, so the only difference in the automated scripts is to install CRI-O rather than containerd prior to installing Kubernetes. If we look at the command line for kubelet in our CRI-O cluster, we see only one change in the command line options:

```
root@host01:~# strings /proc/$(pgrep kubelet)/cmdline
...
--container-runtime-endpoint=/var/run/crio/crio.sock
...
```

The rest of the command line options are identical to our containerd cluster.

Finally, we have one more setting that is relevant to the container runtime: pod-infra-container-image. This specifies the Pod infrastructure image. We saw this image in Chapter 2 in the form of a pause process that was the owner of Linux namespaces created for our containers. In this case, this pause process will come from the container image k8s.gcr.io/pause:3.4.1.

It's highly convenient to have a separate container to own the namespaces that are shared between the containers in a Pod. Because the pause process doesn't really do anything, it is very reliable and isn't likely to crash, so it can continue to own these shared namespaces even if the other containers in the Pod terminate unexpectedly.

The pause image clocks in at around 300kb, as we can see by running crictl on one of our nodes:

```
root@host01:~# crictl images
IMAGE               TAG          IMAGE ID        SIZE
,,,
k8s.gcr.io/pause   3.4.1         0f8457a4c2eca   301kB
...
```

Additionally, the pause process uses practically no CPU, so the effect on our nodes of having an extra process for every Pod is minimal.

Kubelet Network Configuration

Network configuration helps kubelet integrate itself into the cluster and to integrate Pods into the overall cluster network. As we saw in Chapter 8, the actual Pod network setup is performed by a network plug-in, but the kubelet has a couple of important roles as well.

Our kubelet command line includes one option relevant to the network configuration: node-ip. It's an optional flag, and if it is not present, kubelet will try to determine the IP address it should use to communicate with the API server. However, specifying the flag directly is useful because it guarantees that our cluster works in cases for which nodes have multiple network interfaces (such as the Vagrant configuration in this book's examples, where a separate internal network is used for cluster communication).

In addition to this one command line option, kubeadm places two important network settings in */var/lib/kubelet/config.yaml*:

```
root@host01:~# cat /var/lib/kubelet/config.yaml
...
clusterDNS:
- 10.96.0.10
clusterDomain: cluster.local
...
```

These settings are used to provide the */etc/resolv.conf* file to all containers. The clusterDNS entry provides the IP address of this DNS server, whereas the clusterDomain entry provides a default domain for searches so that we can distinguish between hostnames inside the cluster and hostnames on external networks.

Let's take a quick look at how these values are provided to the Pod. We'll begin by creating a Pod:

```
root@host01:~# kubectl apply -f /opt/pod.yaml
pod/debug created
```

After a few seconds, when the Pod is running, we can get a shell:

```
root@host01:~# kubectl exec -ti debug -- /bin/sh
/ #
```

Notice that */etc/resolv.conf* is a separately mounted file in our container:

```
/ # mount | grep resolv
/dev/sda1 on /etc/resolv.conf type ext4 ...
```

Its contents reflect the kubelet configuration:

```
/ # cat /etc/resolv.conf
search default.svc.cluster.local svc.cluster.local cluster.local
nameserver 10.96.0.10
options ndots:5
```

This DNS configuration points to the DNS server that is part of the Kubernetes cluster core components, enabling the Service lookup we saw in Chapter 9. Depending on the DNS configuration in your network, you might see other items in the search list beyond what is shown here.

While we're here, note also that */run/secrets/kubernetes.io/serviceaccount* is also a separately mounted directory in our container. This directory contains the ServiceAccount information we saw in Chapter 11 to enable authentication with the API server from within a container:

```
/ # mount | grep run
tmpfs on /run/secrets/kubernetes.io/serviceaccount type tmpfs (ro,relatime)
```

In this case, the mounted directory is of type `tmpfs` because kubelet has created an in-memory filesystem to hold the authentication information.

Let's finish by exiting the shell session and deleting the Pod (we no longer need it):

```
/ # exit
root@host01:~# kubectl delete pod debug
```

This cleanup will make upcoming Pod listings clearer as we look at how the cluster reacts when a node stops working. Before we do that, we have one more key mystery to solve: how kubelet can host the control plane and also depend on it.

Static Pods

We have something of a chicken-or-egg problem with creating our cluster. We want kubelet to manage the control plane components as Pods because that makes it easier to monitor, maintain, and update the control plane components. However, kubelet is dependent on the control plane to determine what containers to run. The solution is for kubelet to support static Pod definitions that it pulls from the filesystem and runs automatically prior to having its control plane connection.

This static Pod configuration is handled in */var/lib/kubelet/config.yaml*:

```
root@host01:~# cat /var/lib/kubelet/config.yaml
...
staticPodPath: /etc/kubernetes/manifests
...
```

If we look in */etc/kubernetes/manifests*, we see a number of YAML files. These files were placed by kubeadm and define the Pods necessary to run the control plane components for this node:

```
root@host01:~# ls -1 /etc/kubernetes/manifests
etcd.yaml
kube-apiserver.yaml
kube-controller-manager.yaml
kube-scheduler.yaml
```

As expected, we see a YAML file for each of the three essential control plane services we discussed in Chapter 11. We also see a Pod definition for etcd, the component that stores the cluster's state and helps elect a leader for our highly available cluster. We'll look at etcd in more detail in Chapter 16.

Each of these files contains a Pod definition just like the ones we've already seen:

```
root@host01:~# cat /etc/kubernetes/manifests/kube-apiserver.yaml
apiVersion: v1
kind: Pod
metadata:
...
  name: kube-apiserver
  namespace: kube-system
spec:
  containers:
  - command:
    - kube-apiserver
...
```

The kubelet service continually monitors this directory for any changes, and updates the corresponding static Pod accordingly, which makes it possible for kubeadm to upgrade the cluster's control plane on a rolling basis without any downtime.

Cluster add-ons like Calico and Longhorn could also be run using this directory, but they instead use a DaemonSet to have the cluster run a Pod on each node. This makes sense, as a DaemonSet can be managed once for the whole cluster, guaranteeing a consistent configuration across all nodes.

This static Pod directory is different on our three control plane nodes, *host01* through *host03*, compared to our "normal" node, *host04*. To make *host04* a normal node, kubeadm omits the control plane static Pod files from */etc/kubernetes/manifests*:

```
root@host04:~# ls -1 /etc/kubernetes/manifests
root@host04:~#
```

Note that this command is run from *host04*, our sole normal node in this cluster.

Node Maintenance

The controller manager component of the control plane continuously monitors nodes to ensure that they are still connected and healthy. The kubelet service has the responsibility of reporting node information, including node memory consumption, disk consumption, and connection to the underlying container runtime. If a node becomes unhealthy, the control plane will shift Pods to other nodes to maintain the requested scale for Deployments, and will not schedule any new Pods to the node until it is healthy again.

Node Draining and Cordoning

If we know that we need to perform maintenance on a node, such as a reboot, we can tell the cluster to transfer Pods off of the node and mark the node as unscheduleable. We do this using the kubectl drain command.

To see an example, let's create a Deployment with eight Pods, making it likely that each of our nodes will get a Pod:

```
root@host01:~# kubectl apply -f /opt/deploy.yaml
deployment.apps/debug created
```

If we allow enough time for startup, we can see that the Pods are distributed across the nodes:

```
root@host01:~# kubectl get pods -o wide
NAME                      READY   STATUS      ... NODE   ...
debug-8677494fdd-7znxn    1/1     Running     ... host02 ...
debug-8677494fdd-9dgvd    1/1     Running     ... host03 ...
debug-8677494fdd-hv6mt    1/1     Running     ... host04 ...
debug-8677494fdd-ntqjp    1/1     Running     ... host02 ...
debug-8677494fdd-pfw5n    1/1     Running     ... host03 ...
debug-8677494fdd-qbhmn    1/1     Running     ... host02 ...
debug-8677494fdd-qp9zv    1/1     Running     ... host03 ...
debug-8677494fdd-xt8dm    1/1     Running     ... host03 ...
```

To minimize the size of our test cluster, our normal node host04 is small in terms of resources, so in this example it gets only one of the Pods. But that's sufficient to see what happens when we shut down the node. This process is somewhat random, so if you don't see any Pods allocated to host04, you can delete the Deployment and try again or scale it down and then back up, as we do in the next example.

To shut down the node, we use the kubectl drain command:

```
root@host01:~# kubectl drain --ignore-daemonsets host04
node/host04 cordoned
WARNING: ignoring DaemonSet-managed Pods: ...
...
pod/debug-8677494fdd-hv6mt evicted
node/host04 evicted
```

We need to provide the `--ignore-daemonsets` option because all of our nodes have Calico and Longhorn DaemonSets, and of course, those Pods cannot be transferred to another node.

The eviction will take a little time. When it's complete, we can see that the Deployment has created a Pod on another node, which keeps our Pod count at eight:

```
root@host01:~# kubectl get pods -o wide
NAME                      READY   STATUS    ... NODE    ...
debug-8677494fdd-7znxn    1/1     Running   ... host02  ...
debug-8677494fdd-9dgvd    1/1     Running   ... host03  ...
debug-8677494fdd-ntqjp    1/1     Running   ... host02  ...
debug-8677494fdd-pfw5n    1/1     Running   ... host03  ...
debug-8677494fdd-qbhmn    1/1     Running   ... host02  ...
debug-8677494fdd-qfnml    1/1     Running   ... host01  ...
debug-8677494fdd-qp9zv    1/1     Running   ... host03  ...
debug-8677494fdd-xt8dm    1/1     Running   ... host03  ...
```

Additionally, the node has been *cordoned*, thus no more Pods will be scheduled on it:

```
root@host01:~# kubectl get nodes
NAME     STATUS                   ROLES           ...
host01   Ready                    control-plane...
host02   Ready                    control-plane...
host03   Ready                    control-plane...
host04   Ready,SchedulingDisabled <none>          ...
```

At this point, it is safe to stop kubelet or the container runtime, to reboot the node, or even to delete it from Kubernetes entirely:

```
root@host01:~# kubectl delete node host04
node "host04" deleted
```

This deletion removes the node information from the cluster's storage, but because the node still has a valid client certificate and all its configuration, a simple restart of the kubelet service on host04 will add it back to the cluster. First let's restart kubelet:

```
root@host04:~# systemctl restart kubelet
```

Be sure to do this on host04. Next, back on host01, if we wait for kubelet on host04 to finish cleaning up from its previous run and to reinitialize, we can see it return in the list of nodes:

```
root@host01:~# kubectl get nodes
NAME     STATUS   ROLES          ...
host01   Ready    control-plane...
host02   Ready    control-plane...
```

```
host03    Ready    control-plane...
host04    Ready    <none>        ...
```

Note that the cordon has been removed and host04 no longer shows a status that includes SchedulingDisabled. This is one way to remove the cordon. The other is to do it directly using kubectl uncordon.

Unhealthy Nodes

Kubernetes will also shift Pods on a node automatically if the node becomes unhealthy as a result of resource constraints such as insufficient memory or disk space. Let's simulate a low-memory condition on host04 so that we can see this in action.

First, we'll need to reset the scale of our debug Deployment to ensure that new Pods are allocated onto host04:

```
root@host01:~# kubectl scale deployment debug --replicas=1
deployment.apps/debug scaled
root@host01:~# kubectl scale deployment debug --replicas=12
deployment.apps/debug scaled
```

We first scale the Deployment all the way down, and then we scale it back up. This way, we get more chances to schedule at least one Pod on host04. As soon as the Pods have had a chance to settle, we see Pods on host04 again:

```
root@host01:~# kubectl get pods -o wide
NAME                      READY   STATUS      ... NODE      ...
...
debug-8677494fdd-j7cth    1/1     Running     ... host04    ...
debug-8677494fdd-jlj4v    1/1     Running     ... host04    ...
...
```

We can check the current statistics for our nodes using kubectl top:

```
root@host01:~# kubectl top nodes
NAME      CPU(cores)    CPU%    MEMORY(bytes)    MEMORY%
host01    503m          25%     1239Mi           65%
host02    518m          25%     1346Mi           71%
host03    534m          26%     1382Mi           73%
host04    288m          14%     542Mi            29%
```

We have 2GB total on host04, and currently we're using more than 500MiB. By default, kubelet will evict Pods when there is less than 100MiB of memory remaining. We could try to use up memory on the node to get below that default threshold, but it's chancy because using up so much memory could make our node behave badly. Instead, let's update the eviction limit. To do this, we'll add lines to *var/lib/kubelet/config.yaml* and then re-start kubelet.

Here's the additional configuration we'll add to our kubelet config file:

node-evict.yaml
```
evictionHard:
    memory.available: "1900Mi"
```

This tells kubelet to start evicting Pods if it has less than 1,900MiB available. For nodes in our example cluster, that will happen right away. Let's apply this change:

```
root@host04:~# cat /opt/node-evict.yaml >> /var/lib/kubelet/config.yaml
root@host04:~# systemctl restart kubelet
```

Be sure to run these commands on host04. The first command adds additional lines to the kubelet config file. The second command restarts kubelet so that it picks up the change.

If we check on the node status for host04, it will appear to still be ready:

```
root@host01:~# kubectl get nodes
NAME     STATUS   ROLES          ...
host01   Ready    control-plane...
host02   Ready    control-plane...
host03   Ready    control-plane...
host04   Ready    <none>         ...
```

However, the node's event log makes clear what is happening:

```
root@host01:~# kubectl describe node host04
Name:            host04
...
  Normal   NodeHasInsufficientMemory  6m31s                 ...
  Warning  EvictionThresholdMet       7s (x14 over 6m39s)  ...
```

The node starts evicting Pods, and the cluster automatically creates new Pods on other nodes as needed to stay at the desired scale:

```
root@host01:~# kubectl get pods -o wide
NAME                    READY   STATUS       ... NODE    ...
debug-8677494fdd-4274k  1/1     Running      ... host01  ...
debug-8677494fdd-4pnzb  1/1     Running      ... host01  ...
debug-8677494fdd-5nw6n  1/1     Running      ... host01  ...
debug-8677494fdd-7kbp8  1/1     Running      ... host03  ...
debug-8677494fdd-dsnp5  1/1     Running      ... host03  ...
debug-8677494fdd-hgdbc  1/1     Running      ... host01  ...
debug-8677494fdd-j7cth  1/1     Running      ... host04  ...
debug-8677494fdd-jlj4v  0/1     OutOfmemory  ... host04  ...
debug-8677494fdd-lft7h  1/1     Running      ... host01  ...
debug-8677494fdd-mnk6r  1/1     Running      ... host01  ...
debug-8677494fdd-pc8q8  1/1     Running      ... host01  ...
```

```
debug-8677494fdd-sr2kw   0/1   OutOfmemory   ... host04   ...
debug-8677494fdd-tgpb2   1/1   Running       ... host03   ...
debug-8677494fdd-vnjks   0/1   OutOfmemory   ... host04   ...
debug-8677494fdd-xn8t8   1/1   Running       ... host02   ...
```

Pods allocated to host04 show OutOfMemory, and they have been replaced with Pods on other nodes. The Pods are stopped on the node, but unlike the previous case for which we drained the node, the Pods are not automatically terminated. Even if the node recovers from its low-memory situation, the Pods will continue to show up in the list of Pods, stuck in the OutOfMemory state, until kubelet is restarted.

Node Unreachable

We have one more case to look at. In our previous two examples, kubelet could communicate with the control plane to update its status, allowing the control plane to act accordingly. But what happens if there is a network issue or sudden power failure and the node loses its connection to the cluster without being able to report that it is shutting down? In that case, the cluster will record the node status as unknown, and after a timeout, it will start shifting Pods onto other nodes.

Let's simulate this. We'll begin by restoring host04 to its proper working order:

```
root@host04:~# sed -i '/^evictionHard/,+2d' /var/lib/kubelet/config.yaml
root@host04:~# systemctl restart kubelet
```

Be sure to run these commands on host04. The first command removes the two lines we added to the kubelet config, whereas the second restarts kubelet to pick up the change. We now can rescale our Deployment again so that it is redistributed:

```
root@host01:~# kubectl scale deployment debug --replicas=1
root@host01:~# kubectl scale deployment debug --replicas=12
```

As before, after you've run these commands, allow a few minutes for the Pods to settle. Then, use **kubectl get pods -o wide** to verify that at least one Pod was allocated to host04.

We're now ready to forcibly disconnect host04 from the cluster. We'll do this by adding a firewall rule:

```
root@host04:~# iptables -I INPUT -s 192.168.61.10 -j DROP
root@host04:~# iptables -I OUTPUT -d 192.168.61.10 -j DROP
```

Be sure to run this on host04. The first command tells the firewall to drop all traffic coming from the IP address 192.168.61.10, which is the highly available IP that is shared by all three control plane nodes. The second command tells the firewall to drop all traffic going to that same IP address.

After a minute or so, host04 will show a state of NotReady:

```
root@host01:~# kubectl get nodes
NAME      STATUS     ROLES          ...
host01    Ready      control-plane...
host02    Ready      control-plane...
host03    Ready      control-plane...
host04    NotReady   <none>         ...
```

And if we wait a few minutes, the Pods on host04 will be shown as Terminating because the cluster gives up on those Pods and shifts them to other nodes:

```
root@host01:~# kubectl get pods -o wide
NAME                       READY   STATUS        ... NODE     ...
debug-8677494fdd-2wrn2     1/1     Running       ... host01   ...
debug-8677494fdd-4lz48     1/1     Running       ... host02   ...
debug-8677494fdd-78874     1/1     Running       ... host01   ...
debug-8677494fdd-7f8fw     1/1     Running       ... host01   ...
debug-8677494fdd-9vb5m     1/1     Running       ... host03   ...
debug-8677494fdd-b7vj6     1/1     Running       ... host03   ...
debug-8677494fdd-c2c4v     1/1     Terminating   ... host04   ...
debug-8677494fdd-c8tzv     1/1     Running       ... host03   ...
debug-8677494fdd-d2r6b     1/1     Terminating   ... host04   ...
debug-8677494fdd-d5t6b     1/1     Running       ... host01   ...
debug-8677494fdd-j7cth     1/1     Terminating   ... host04   ...
debug-8677494fdd-jjfsl     1/1     Terminating   ... host04   ...
debug-8677494fdd-nqb8z     1/1     Running       ... host03   ...
debug-8677494fdd-sskd5     1/1     Running       ... host02   ...
debug-8677494fdd-wz6c6     1/1     Terminating   ... host04   ...
debug-8677494fdd-x5b4w     1/1     Running       ... host02   ...
debug-8677494fdd-zfbml     1/1     Running       ... host01   ...
```

However, because kubelet on host04 can't connect to the control plane, it is unaware that it should be shutting down its Pods. If we check to see what containers are running on host04, we still see multiple containers:

```
root@host04:~# crictl ps
CONTAINER         IMAGE            ...  STATE      NAME  ...
2129a1cb00607     16ea53ea7c652    ...  Running    debug ...
cfd7fd6142321     16ea53ea7c652    ...  Running    debug ...
0289ffa5c816d     16ea53ea7c652    ...  Running    debug ...
fb2d297d11efb     16ea53ea7c652    ...  Running    debug ...
...
```

Not only are the Pods still running, but because of the way we cut off the connection, they are still able to communicate with the rest of the cluster. This is very important. Kubernetes will do its best to run the number of instances requested and to respond to errors, but it can only do that based on the information it has available. In this case, because `kubelet` on `host04` can't talk to the control plane, Kubernetes has no way of knowing that the Pods are still running. When building applications for a distributed system like a Kubernetes cluster, you should recognize that some types of errors can have surprising results, like partial network connectivity or a different number of instances compared to what is specified. In more advanced application architectures that include rolling updates, this can even lead to cases in which old versions of application components are still running unexpectedly. Be sure to build applications that are resilient in the face of these kinds of surprising behaviors.

Final Thoughts

Ultimately, to have a Kubernetes cluster, we need nodes that can run containers, and that means instances of `kubelet` connected to the control plane and a container runtime. In this chapter, we've inspected how to configure `kubelet` and how the cluster behaves when nodes leave or enter the cluster, either intentionally or through an outage.

One of the key themes of this chapter is the way that Kubernetes acts to keep the specified number of Pods running, even in the face of node issues. In the next chapter, we'll see how that monitoring extends inside the container to its processes, ensuring that the processes run as expected. We'll see how to specify probes that allow Kubernetes to monitor containers, and how the cluster responds when a container is unhealthy.

13

HEALTH PROBES

 Having a reliable application is about more than just keeping application components running. Application components also need to be able to respond to requests in a timely way and get data from and make requests of dependencies. This means that the definition of a "healthy" application component is different for each individual component.

At the same time, Kubernetes needs to know when a Pod and its containers are healthy so that it can route traffic to only healthy containers and replace failed ones. For this reason, Kubernetes allows configuration of custom health checks for containers and integrates those health checks into management of workload resources such as Deployment.

In this chapter, we'll look at how to define health probes for our applications. We'll look at both network-based health probes and probes that are internal to a container. We'll see how Kubernetes runs these health probes and how it responds when a container becomes unhealthy.

About Probes

Kubernetes supports three different types of probes:

Exec   Run a command or script to check on a container.

TCP   Determine whether a socket is open.

HTTP   Verify that an HTTP GET succeeds.

In addition, we can use any of these three types of probes for any of three different purposes:

Liveness   Detect and restart failed containers.

Startup   Give extra time before starting liveness probes.

Readiness   Avoid sending traffic to containers when they are not prepared for it.

Of these three purposes, the most important is the liveness probe because it runs during the primary life cycle of the container and can result in container restarts. We'll look closely at liveness probes and use that knowledge to understand how to use startup and readiness probes.

Liveness Probes

A *liveness* probe runs continuously as soon as the container has started running. Liveness probes are created as part of the container definition, and a container that fails its liveness probe will be restarted automatically.

Exec Probes

Let's begin with a simple liveness probe that runs a command inside the container. Kubernetes expects the command to finish before a timeout and return zero to indicate success, or a non-zero code to indicate a problem.

NOTE   *The example repository for this book is at* https://github.com/book-of-kubernetes/examples. *See "Running Examples" on page xx for details on getting set up.*

Let's illustrate this with an NGINX web server container. We'll use this Deployment definition:

nginx-exec.yaml   ------
```
kind: Deployment
apiVersion: apps/v1
metadata:
  name: nginx
spec:
  replicas: 1
  selector:
    matchLabels:
```

```
      app: nginx
template:
  metadata:
    labels:
      app: nginx
  spec:
    containers:
    - name: nginx
      image: nginx
      livenessProbe:
        exec:
          command: ["/usr/bin/curl", "-fq", "http://localhost"]
        initialDelaySeconds: 10
        periodSeconds: 5
```

The exec section of the livenessProbe tells Kubernetes to run a command inside the container. In this case, curl is used with a -q flag so that it doesn't print the page contents but just returns a zero exit code on success. Additionally, the -f flag causes curl to return a non-zero exit code for any HTTP error response (that is, any response code of 300 or above).

The curl command runs every 5 seconds based on the periodSeconds; it starts 10 seconds after the container is started, based on initialDelaySeconds.

The automated scripts for this chapter add the *nginx-exec.yaml* file to */opt*. Create this Deployment as usual:

```
root@host01:~# kubectl apply -f /opt/nginx-exec.yaml
deployment.apps/nginx created
```

The resulting Pod status doesn't look any different from a Pod without a liveness probe:

```
root@host01:~# kubectl get pods
NAME                   READY   STATUS    RESTARTS   AGE
nginx-68dc5f984f-jq5xl 1/1     Running   0          25s
```

However, in addition to the regular NGINX server process, curl is being run inside the container every 5 seconds, verifying that it is possible to connect to the server. The detailed output from kubectl describe shows this configuration:

```
root@host01:~# kubectl describe deployment nginx
Name:                   nginx
Namespace:              default
...
Pod Template:
  Labels:  app=nginx
  Containers:
   nginx:
...
```

```
        Liveness:      exec [/usr/bin/curl -q http://localhost] delay=10s
        timeout=1s period=5s #success=1 #failure=3
...
```

Because a liveness probe is defined, the fact that the Pod continues to show a Running status and no restarts indicates that the check is successful. The #success field shows that one successful run is sufficient for the container to be considered live, whereas the #failure value shows that three consecutive failures will cause the Pod to be restarted.

We used -q to discard the logs from curl, but even without that flag, any logs from a successful liveness probe are discarded. If we want to save the ongoing log information from a probe, we need to send it to a file or use a logging library to ship it across the network.

Before moving on to another type of probe, let's see what happens if a liveness probe fails. We'll patch the curl command to try to retrieve a nonexistent path on the server, which will cause curl to return a non-zero exit code, so our probe will fail.

We used a patch file in Chapter 9 when we edited a Service type. Let's do that again here to make the change:

nginx-404.yaml
```
---
spec:
  template:
    spec:
      containers:
      ❶ - name: nginx
          livenessProbe:
            exec:
              command: ["/usr/bin/curl", "-fq", "http://localhost/missing"]
```

Although a patch file allows us to update only the specific fields we care about, in this case the patch file has several lines because we need to specify the full hierarchy, and we also must specify the name of the container we want to modify ❶, so Kubernetes will merge this content into the existing definition for that container.

To patch the Deployment, use the kubectl patch command:

```
root@host01:~# kubectl patch deploy nginx --patch-file /opt/nginx-404.yaml
deployment.apps/nginx patched
```

Because we changed the Pod specification within the Deployment, Kubernetes needs to terminate the old Pod and create a new one:

```
root@host01:~# kubectl get pods
NAME                      READY   STATUS        RESTARTS   AGE
nginx-679f866f5b-7lzsb    1/1     Terminating   0          2m28s
nginx-6cb4b995cd-6jpd7    1/1     Running       0          3s
```

Initially, the new Pod shows a Running status. However, if we check back again in about 30 seconds, we get an indication that the Pod has an issue:

```
root@host01:~# kubectl get pods
NAME                      READY   STATUS    RESTARTS   AGE
nginx-6cb4b995cd-6jpd7    1/1     Running   1          28s
```

We didn't change the initial delay or the period for our liveness probe, so the first probe started after 10 seconds and the probe runs every 5 seconds. It takes three failures to trigger a restart, so it's not surprising that we see one restart after 25 seconds have elapsed.

The Pod's event log indicates the reason for the restart:

```
root@host01:~# kubectl describe pod
Name:          nginx-6cb4b995cd-6jpd7
...
Containers:
  nginx:
...
    Last State:      Terminated
...
Events:
  Type      Reason       Age               From      Message
  ----      ------       ----              ----      -------
...
  Warning   Unhealthy    20s (x9 over 80s)  kubelet   Liveness probe failed: ...
curl: (22) The requested URL returned error: 404 Not Found
...
```

The event log helpfully provides the output from curl telling us the reason for the failed liveness probe. Kubernetes will continue to restart the container every 25 seconds as each new container starts running and then fails three consecutive liveness probes.

HTTP Probes

The ability to run a command within a container to check health allows us to perform custom probes. However, for a web server like this one, we can take advantage of the HTTP probe capability within Kubernetes, avoiding the need for curl inside our container image and also verifying connectivity from outside the Pod.

Let's replace our NGINX Deployment with a new configuration that uses an HTTP probe:

nginx-http.yaml
```
---
kind: Deployment
apiVersion: apps/v1
metadata:
  name: nginx
spec:
  replicas: 1
```

```
selector:
  matchLabels:
    app: nginx
template:
  metadata:
    labels:
      app: nginx
  spec:
    containers:
    - name: nginx
      image: nginx
      livenessProbe:
        httpGet:
          path: /
          port: 80
```

With this configuration, we tell Kubernetes to connect to port 80 of our Pod and do an HTTP GET at the root path of /. Because our NGINX server is listening on port 80 and will serve a welcome file for the root path, we can expect this to work.

We've specified the entire Deployment rather than using a patch, so we'll use kubectl apply to update the Deployment:

```
root@host01:~# kubectl apply -f /opt/nginx-http.yaml
deployment.apps/nginx configured
```

We could use a patch to make this change as well, but it would be more complex this time, because a patch file is merged into the existing configuration. As a result, we would require two commands: one to remove the existing liveness probe and one to add the new HTTP liveness probe. Better to just replace the resource entirely.

NOTE *The kubectl patch command is a valuable command for debugging, but production applications should have YAML resource files under version control to allow for change tracking and peer review, and the entire file should always be applied every time to ensure that the cluster reflects the current content of the repository.*

Now that we've applied the new Deployment configuration, Kubernetes will make a new Pod:

```
root@host01:~# kubectl get pods
NAME                    READY   STATUS    RESTARTS   AGE
nginx-d75d4d675-wvhxl   1/1     Running   0          2m38s
```

For an HTTP probe, kubelet has the responsibility of running an HTTP GET request on the appropriate schedule and confirming the result. By default, any HTTP return code in the 200 or 300 series is considered a successful response.

The NGINX server is logging all of its requests, so we can use the container logs to see the probes taking place:

```
root@host01:~# kubectl logs nginx-d75d4d675-wvhxl
...
... 22:23:31 ... "GET / HTTP/1.1" 200 615 "-" "kube-probe/1.21" "-"
... 22:23:41 ... "GET / HTTP/1.1" 200 615 "-" "kube-probe/1.21" "-"
... 22:23:51 ... "GET / HTTP/1.1" 200 615 "-" "kube-probe/1.21" "-"
```

We didn't specify `periodSeconds` this time, so `kubelet` is probing the server at the default rate of once every 10 seconds.

Let's clean up the NGINX Deployment before moving on:

```
root@host01:~# kubectl delete deployment nginx
deployment.apps "nginx" deleted
```

We've looked at two of the three types of probes; let's finish by looking at TCP.

TCP Probes

A database server such as PostgreSQL listens for network connections, but it does not use HTTP for communication. We can still create a probe for these kinds of containers using a TCP probe. It won't provide the configuration flexibility of an HTTP or exec probe, but it will verify that a container in the Pod is listening for connections on the specified port.

Here's a PostgreSQL Deployment with a TCP probe:

*postgres
-tcp.yaml*
```
---
kind: Deployment
apiVersion: apps/v1
metadata:
  name: postgres
spec:
  replicas: 1
  selector:
    matchLabels:
      app: postgres
  template:
    metadata:
      labels:
        app: postgres
    spec:
      containers:
      - name: postgres
        image: postgres
        env:
        - name: POSTGRES_PASSWORD
          value: "supersecret"
        livenessProbe:
```

```
        tcpSocket:
            port: 5432
```

We saw the requirement for the POSTGRES_PASSWORD environment variable in Chapter 10. The only configuration that's changed for this example is the livenessProbe. We specify a TCP socket of 5432, as this is the standard port for PostgreSQL.

As usual, we can create this Deployment and, after a while, observe that it's running:

```
root@host01:~# kubectl apply -f /opt/postgres-tcp.yaml
deployment.apps/postgres created
...
root@host01:~# kubectl get pods
NAME                     READY   STATUS    RESTARTS   AGE
postgres-5566ff748-jqp5d 1/1     Running   0          29s
```

Again, it is the job of kubelet to perform the probe. It does this solely by making a TCP connection to the port and then disconnecting. PostgreSQL doesn't emit any logging when this happens, so the only way we know that the probe is working is to check that the container continues to run and doesn't show any restarts:

```
root@host01:~# kubectl get pods
NAME                     READY   STATUS    RESTARTS   AGE
postgres-5566ff748-jqp5d 1/1     Running   0          2m7s
```

Before we move on, let's clean up the Deployment:

```
root@host01:~# kubectl delete deploy postgres
deployment.apps "postgres" deleted
```

We've now looked at all three types of probes. And although we used these three types to create liveness probes, the same three types will work with both startup and readiness probes as well. The only difference is the change in the behavior of our cluster when a probe fails.

Startup Probes

Unhealthy containers can create all kinds of difficulties for an application, including lack of responsiveness, errors responding to requests, or bad data, so we want Kubernetes to respond quickly when a container becomes unhealthy. However, when a container is first started, it can take time before it is fully initialized. During that time, it might not be able to respond to liveness probes.

Because of that delay, we're left with a need to have a long timeout before a container fails a probe, so we can give our container enough time for initialization. However, at the same time, we need to have a short timeout in order to detect a failed container quickly and restart it. The solution is to configure a separate *startup probe*. Kubernetes will use the startup probe configuration until the probe is successful; then it will switch over to the liveness probe.

For example, we might configure our NGINX server Deployment as follows:

```
...
spec:
...
  template:
...
    spec:
      containers:
      - name: nginx
        image: nginx
        livenessProbe:
          httpGet:
            path: /
            port: 80
        startupProbe:
          httpGet:
            path: /
            port: 80
          periodSeconds:
          initialDelaySeconds: 30
          periodSeconds: 10
          failureThreshold: 60
```

Given this configuration, Kubernetes would start checking the container 30 seconds after startup. It would continue checking every 10 seconds until the probe is successful or until there are 60 failed attempts. The effect is that the container has 10 minutes to finish initialization and respond to a probe successfully. If the container does not have a successful probe in that time, it will be restarted.

As soon as the container has one successful probe, Kubernetes will switch to the configuration for livenessProbe. Because we didn't override any timing parameters, this will transition to a probe every 10 seconds, with three consecutive failed probes leading to a restart. We give the container 10 minutes to be live initially, but after that we will allow no more than 30 seconds before restarting it.

The fact that the startupProbe is defined completely separately means that it is possible to create a different check for startup from the one used for liveness. Of course, it's important to choose wisely so that the container doesn't pass its startup probe before the liveness probe would also pass, because that would result in inappropriate restarts.

Readiness Probes

The third probe purpose is to check the *readiness* of the Pod. The term *readiness* might seem redundant with the startup probe. However, even though completing initialization is an important part of readiness for a piece of software, an application component might not be ready to do work for many reasons, especially in a highly available microservice architecture where components can come and go at any time.

Rather than being used for initialization, readiness probes should be used for any case in which the container cannot perform any work because of a failure outside its control. It may be a temporary situation, as retry logic somewhere else could fix the failure. For example, an API that relies on an external database might fail its readiness probe if the database is unreachable, but that database might return to service at any time.

This also creates a valuable contrast with startup and liveness probes. As we examined earlier, Kubernetes will restart a container if it fails the configured number of startup or liveness probes. But it makes no sense to do that if the issue is a failed or missing external dependency, given that restarting the container won't fix whatever is wrong externally.

At the same time, if a container is missing a required external dependency, it can't do work, so we don't want to send any work to it. In that situation, the best thing to do is to leave the container running and give it an opportunity to reestablish the connections it needs, but avoid sending any requests to it. In the meantime, we can hope that somewhere in the cluster another Pod for the same Deployment is working as expected, making our application as a whole resilient to a localized failure.

This is exactly how readiness probes work in Kubernetes. As we saw in Chapter 9, a Kubernetes Service continually watches for Pods that match its selector and configures load balancing for its cluster IP that routes traffic to those Pods. If a Pod reports itself as not ready, the Service will stop routing traffic to it, but kubelet will not trigger any other action such as a container restart.

Let's illustrate this situation. We want to have individual control over Pod readiness, so we'll use a somewhat contrived example rather than a real external dependency to determine readiness. We'll deploy a set of NGINX Pods, this time with a corresponding Service:

nginx-ready.yaml
```
---
kind: Deployment
apiVersion: apps/v1
metadata:
  name: nginx
spec:
  replicas: 3
  selector:
    matchLabels:
      app: nginx
  template:
```

```
    metadata:
      labels:
        app: nginx
    spec:
      containers:
      - name: nginx
        image: nginx
        livenessProbe:
          httpGet:
            path: /
            port: 80
        readinessProbe:
          httpGet:
            path: /ready
            port: 80
---
kind: Service
apiVersion: v1
metadata:
  name: nginx
spec:
  selector:
    app: nginx
  ports:
  - protocol: TCP
    port: 80
    targetPort: 80
```

This Deployment keeps its livenessProbe as an indicator that NGINX is working correctly and adds a readinessProbe. The Service definition is identical to what we saw in Chapter 9 and will route traffic to our NGINX Pods.

This file has already been written to */opt*, so we can apply it to the cluster:

```
root@host01:~# kubectl apply -f /opt/nginx-ready.yaml
deployment.apps/nginx created
service/nginx created
```

After these Pods are up and running, they stay running because the liveness probe is successful:

```
root@host01:~# kubectl get pods
NAME                     READY   STATUS    RESTARTS   AGE
nginx-67fb6485f5-2k2nz   0/1     Running   0          38s
nginx-67fb6485f5-vph44   0/1     Running   0          38s
nginx-67fb6485f5-xzmj5   0/1     Running   0          38s
```

In addition, the Service we created has been allocated a cluster IP:

```
root@host01:~# kubectl get services
NAME            TYPE        CLUSTER-IP      EXTERNAL-IP    PORT(S)   AGE
...
nginx           ClusterIP   10.101.98.80    <none>         80/TCP    3m1s
```

However, we aren't able to use that IP address to reach any Pods:

```
root@host01:~# curl http://10.101.98.80
curl: (7) Failed to connect to 10.101.98.80 port 80: Connection refused
```

This is because, at the moment, there is nothing for NGINX to serve on the */ready* path, so it's returning 404, and the readiness probe is failing. A detailed inspection of the Pod shows that it is not ready:

```
root@host01:~# kubectl describe pod
Name:           nginx-67fb6485f5-2k2nz
...
Containers:
  nginx:
...
    Ready:        False
...
```

As a result, the Service does not have any Endpoints to which to route traffic:

```
root@host01:~# kubectl describe service nginx
Name:           nginx
...
Endpoints:
...
```

Because the Service has no Endpoints, it has configured iptables to reject all traffic:

```
root@host01:~# iptables-save | grep default/nginx
-A KUBE-SERVICES -d 10.101.98.80/32 -p tcp -m comment --comment "default/nginx has no endpoints"
  -m tcp --dport 80 -j REJECT --reject-with icmp-port-unreachable
```

To fix this, we'll need at least one Pod to become ready to ensure that NGINX has something to serve on the */ready* path. We'll use the container's hostname to keep track of which Pod is serving our request.

To make one of our Pods ready, let's first get the list of Pods again, just to have the Pod names handy:

```
root@host01:~# kubectl get pods
NAME                     READY   STATUS    RESTARTS   AGE
nginx-67fb6485f5-2k2nz   0/1     Running   0          10m
```

```
nginx-67fb6485f5-vph44    0/1     Running    0              10m
nginx-67fb6485f5-xzmj5    0/1     Running    0              10m
```

Now, we'll choose one and make it report that it is ready:

```
root@host01:~# kubectl exec -ti nginx-67fb6485f5-2k2nz -- \
  cp -v /etc/hostname /usr/share/nginx/html/ready
'/etc/hostname' -> '/usr/share/nginx/html/ready'
```

Our Service will start to show a valid Endpoint:

```
root@host01:~# kubectl describe svc nginx
Name:           nginx
...
Endpoints:      172.31.239.199:80
...
```

Even better, we can now reach an NGINX instance via the cluster IP, and the content corresponds to the hostname:

```
root@host01:~# curl http://10.101.98.80/ready
nginx-67fb6485f5-2k2nz
```

Note the /ready at the end of the URL so the response is the hostname. If we run this command many times, we'll see that the hostname is the same every time. This is because the one Pod that is passing its readiness probe is handling all of the Service traffic.

Let's make the other two Pods ready as well:

```
root@host01:~# kubectl exec -ti nginx-67fb6485f5-vph44 -- \
  cp -v /etc/hostname /usr/share/nginx/html/ready
'/etc/hostname' -> '/usr/share/nginx/html/ready'
root@host01:~# kubectl exec -ti nginx-67fb6485f5-xzmj5 -- \
  cp -v /etc/hostname /usr/share/nginx/html/ready
'/etc/hostname' -> '/usr/share/nginx/html/ready'
```

Our Service now shows all three Endpoints:

```
root@host01:~# kubectl describe service nginx
Name:           nginx
...
Endpoints:      172.31.239.199:80,172.31.239.200:80,172.31.89.210:80
...
```

Running the curl command multiple times shows that the traffic is now being distributed across multiple Pods:

```
root@host01:~# for i in $(seq 1 5); do curl http://10.101.98.80/ready; done
nginx-67fb6485f5-xzmj5
nginx-67fb6485f5-2k2nz
nginx-67fb6485f5-xzmj5
```

```
nginx-67fb6485f5-vph44
nginx-67fb6485f5-vph44
```

The embedded command $(seq 1 5) returns the numbers one through five, causing the for loop to run curl five times. If you run this same for loop several times, you will see a different distribution of hostnames. As described in Chapter 9, load balancing is based on a random uniform distribution wherein each endpoint has an equal chance of being selected for each new connection.

A good practice is to offer an HTTP readiness endpoint for each application that checks the current state of the application and its dependencies and returns an HTTP success code (such as 200) if the component is healthy, and an HTTP error code (such as 500) if not. Some application frameworks such as Spring Boot provide application state management that automatically exposes liveness and readiness endpoints.

Final Thoughts

Kubernetes offers the ability to check on our containers and make sure they are working as expected, not just that the process is running. These probes can include any arbitrary command run inside the container, verifying that a port is open for TCP connections, or that the container responds correctly to an HTTP request. To build resilient applications, we should define both a liveness probe and a readiness probe for each application component. The liveness probe is used to restart an unhealthy container; the readiness probe determines whether the Pod can handle Service traffic. Additionally, if a component needs extra time for initialization, we should also define a startup probe to make sure that give it the required initialization time while responding quickly to failure as soon as initialization is complete.

Of course, for our containers to run as expected, other containers in the cluster must also be well behaved, not using too many of the cluster's resources. In the next chapter, we'll look at how we can limit our containers in their use of CPU, memory, disk space, and network bandwidth, as well as how we can control the maximum amount of total resources available to a user. This ability to specify limits and quotas is important to ensure that our cluster can support multiple applications with reliable performance.

14

LIMITS AND QUOTAS

For our cluster to provide a predictable environment for applications, we need some control over what resources each individual application component uses. If an application component can use all of the CPU or memory on a given node, the Kubernetes scheduler will not be able to allocate a new Pod to a node confidently, as it won't know how much available space each node has.

In this chapter, we'll explore how to specify requested resources and limits to ensure that containers get the resources they need without impacting other containers. We'll inspect individual containers at the runtime level so that we can see how Kubernetes configures the container technology we saw in Part I to adequately meet the resource requirements of a container without allowing the container to exceed its limits.

Finally, we'll look at how role-based access control is used to manage quotas, limiting the amount of resources a given user or application can demand, which will help us understand how to administer a cluster in a manner that allows it to reliably support multiple separate applications or development teams.

Requests and Limits

Kubernetes supports many different types of resources, including processing, memory, storage, network bandwidth, and use of special devices such as graphics processing units (GPUs). We'll look at network limits later in this chapter, but let's start with the most commonly specified resource types: processing and memory.

Processing and Memory Limits

The specifications for processing and memory resources serve two purposes: scheduling and preventing conflicts. Kubernetes provides a different kind of resource specification for each purpose. The Pod's containers consume processing and memory resources in Kubernetes, so that's where resource specifications are applied.

When scheduling Pods, Kubernetes uses the requests field in the container specification, summing this field across all containers in the Pod and finding a node with sufficient margin in both processing and memory. Generally, the requests field is set to the expected average resource requirements for each container in the Pod.

The second purpose of resource specification is preventing denial-of-service issues in which one container takes all of a node's resources, negatively affecting other containers. This requires runtime enforcement of container resources. Kubernetes uses the limits field of the container specification for this purpose, thus we need to be sure to set the limits field high enough that a container is able to run correctly without reaching the limit.

TUNING FOR PERFORMANCE

The idea that requests should match the expected average resource requirements is based on an assumption that any load spikes in the various containers in the cluster are unpredictable and uncorrelated, and load spikes can therefore be assumed to happen at different times. Even with that assumption, there is a risk that simultaneous load spikes in multiple containers on a node will result in that node being overloaded. And if the load spikes between different Pods are correlated, this risk of overload increases. At the same time, if we configure requests for the worst case scenario, we can end up with a very large cluster that is idle most of the time. In Chapter 19, we explore the different Quality of Service (QoS) classes that Kubernetes offers for Pods and discuss how to find a balance between performance guarantees and cluster efficiency.

Listing 14-1 kicks off our examination with an example of using requests and limits with a Deployment.

nginx-limit.yaml
```
---
kind: Deployment
apiVersion: apps/v1
metadata:
  name: nginx
```

```
spec:
  replicas: 1
  selector:
    matchLabels:
      app: nginx
  template:
    metadata:
      labels:
        app: nginx
    spec:
      containers:
      - name: nginx
        image: nginx
        resources:
          requests:
            memory: "64Mi"
            cpu: "250m"
          limits:
            memory: "128Mi"
            cpu: "500m"
      nodeName: host01
```

Listing 14-1: Deployment with limits

We'll use this Deployment to explore how limits are configured at the level of the container runtime, so we use the `nodeName` field to make sure the container ends up on *host01*. This constrains where the scheduler can place the Pod, but the scheduler still uses the `requests` field to ensure that there are sufficient resources. If *host01* becomes too busy, the scheduler will just refuse to schedule the Pod, similar to what we saw in Chapter 10.

The `resources` field is defined at the level of the individual container, allowing us to specify separate resource requirements for each container in a Pod. For this container, we specify a memory request of `64Mi` and a memory limit of `128Mi`. The suffix `Mi` means that we are using the power-of-2 unit *mebibytes*, which is 2 to the 20th power, rather than the power-of-10 unit *megabytes*, which would be the slightly smaller value of 10 to the 6th power.

Meanwhile, the processing request and limit specified using the `cpu` fields is not based on any absolute unit of processing. Rather, it is based on a synthetic *cpu unit* for our cluster. Each cpu unit roughly corresponds to one virtual CPU or core. The `m` suffix specifies a *millicpu* so that our `requests` value of `250m` equates to one quarter of a core, whereas the `limit` of `500m` equates to half of a core.

NOTE   *The example repository for this book is at* https://github.com/book-of
-kubernetes/examples. *See "Running Examples" on page xx for details on
getting set up.*

Let's create this Deployment:

```
root@host01:~# kubectl apply -f /opt/nginx-limit.yaml
deployment.apps/nginx created
```

The Pod will be allocated to host01 and started:

```
root@host01:~# kubectl get pods
NAME                      READY   STATUS    RESTARTS   AGE
nginx-56dbd744d9-vg5rj    1/1     Running   0          22m
```

And host01 will show that resources have been allocated for the Pod:

```
root@host01:~# kubectl describe node host01
Name:              host01
...
Non-terminated Pods:          (15 in total)
  Namespace Name                      CPU Requests CPU Limits Memory Requests Memory Limits Age
  --------- ----                      ------------ ---------- --------------- ------------- ---
...
  default   nginx-56dbd744d9-vg5rj 250m (12%)   500m (25%) 64M (3%)        128M (6%)     61s
...
```

This is true even though our NGINX web server is idle and is not using a lot of processing or memory resources:

```
root@host01:~# kubectl top pods
...
NAME                      CPU(cores)   MEMORY(bytes)
nginx-56dbd744d9-vg5rj    0m           5Mi
```

Similar to what we saw in Chapter 12, this command queries the metrics add-on that is collecting data from kubelet running on each cluster node.

Cgroup Enforcement

The processing and memory limits we specified are enforced using the Linux control group (cgroup) functionality we described in Chapter 3. Kubernetes manages its own space within each hierarchy inside the */sys/fs/cgroup* filesystem. For example, memory limits are configured in the memory cgroup:

```
root@host01:~# ls -1F /sys/fs/cgroup/memory
...
kubepods.slice/
...
```

Each Pod on a given host has a directory within the *kubepods.slice* tree. However, finding the specific directory for a given Pod takes some work because Kubernetes divides Pods into different classes of service, and because the name of the cgroup directory does not match the ID of the Pod or its containers.

To save us from searching around inside */sys/fs/cgroup*, we'll use a script installed by this chapter's automated scripts: */opt/cgroup-info*. This script uses crictl to query the container runtime for the cgroup path and then collects CPU and memory limit data from that path. The most important part of the script is this section that collects the path:

```
#!/bin/bash
...
POD_ID=$(crictl pods --name ${POD} -q)
...
cgp_field='.info.config.linux.cgroup_parent'
CGP=$(crictl inspectp $POD_ID | jq -r "$cgp_field")

CPU=/sys/fs/cgroup/cpu/$CGP
MEM=/sys/fs/cgroup/memory/$CGP
...
```

The crictl pods command collects the Pod's ID, which is then used with crictl inspectp and jq to collect one specific field, called cgroup_parent. This field is the cgroup subdirectory created for that pod within each resource type.

Let's run this script with our NGINX web server to see how the CPU and memory limits have been configured:

```
root@host01:~# kubectl get pods
NAME                      READY   STATUS    RESTARTS   AGE
nginx-56dbd744d9-vg5rj    1/1     Running   0          59m
root@host01:~# /opt/cgroup-info nginx-56dbd744d9-vg5rj

Container Runtime
-----------------
Pod ID: 54602befbd141a74316323b010fb38dae0c2b433cdbe12b5c4d626e6465c7315
Cgroup path: /kubepods.slice/...9f8f3dcf_6cca_49b8_a3df_d696ece01f59.slice

CPU Settings
------------
CPU Shares: 256
CPU Quota (us): 50000 per 100000

Memory Settings
---------------
Limit (bytes): 134217728
```

We first collect the name of the Pod and then use it to collect cgroup information. Note that this works only because the Pod is running on host01; the script will work for any Pod, but it must be run from the host on which that Pod is running.

There are two key pieces of data for the CPU configuration. The quota is the hard limit; it means that in any given 100,000 microsecond period, this Pod can use only 50,000 microseconds of processor time. This value corresponds to the 500m CPU limit specified in Listing 14-1 (recall that the 500m limit equates to half a core).

In addition to this hard limit, the CPU request field we specified in Listing 14-1 has been used to configure the CPU shares. As we saw in Chapter 3, this field configures the CPU usage on a relative basis. Because it is relative to the values in neighboring directories, it is unitless, so Kubernetes computes the CPU share on the basis of one core equaling 1,024. We specified a CPU request of 250m, so this equates to 256.

The CPU share does not set any kind of limit on CPU usage, so if the system is idle, a Pod can use processing up to its hard limit. However, as the system becomes busy, the CPU share determines how much processing each Pod is allotted relative to others in the same class of service. This helps to ensure that if the system becomes overloaded, all Pods will be degraded fairly based on their CPU request.

Finally, for memory, there is a single relevant value. We specified a memory limit of 128Mi, which equates to 128MiB. As we saw in Chapter 3, if our container tries to exceed this limit, it will be terminated. For this reason, it is critical to either configure the application such that it does not exceed this value, or to understand how the application acts under load to choose the optimum limit.

The amount of memory actually used by a process is ultimately up to that process, meaning that the memory request value has no purpose beyond its initial use in ensuring sufficient memory to schedule the Pod. For this reason, we don't see the memory request value of 64Mi being used anywhere in the cgroup configuration.

The way that resource allocations are reflected in cgroups shows us something important about cluster performance. Because requests is used for scheduling and limits is used for runtime enforcement, it is possible for a node to overcommit processing and memory. For the case in which containers have higher limit than requests, and containers consistently operate above their requests, this can cause performance issues with the containers on a node. We'll discuss this in more detail in Chapter 19.

We're finished with our NGINX Deployment, so let's delete it:

```
root@host01:~# kubectl delete -f /opt/nginx-limit.yaml
deployment.apps "nginx" deleted
```

So far, the container runtime can enforce the limits we've seen. However, the cluster must enforce other types of limits, such as networking.

Network Limits

Ideally, our application will be architected so that required bandwidth for intercommunication is moderate, and our cluster will have sufficient bandwidth to meet the demand of all the containers. However, if we do have a container that tries to take more than its share of the network bandwidth, we need a way to limit it.

Because the network devices are configured by plug-ins, we need a plug-in to manage bandwidth. Fortunately, the bandwidth plug-in is part of the standard set of CNI plug-ins installed with our Kubernetes cluster. Additionally, as we saw in Chapter 8, the default CNI configuration enables the bandwidth plug-in:

```
root@host01:~# cat /etc/cni/net.d/10-calico.conflist
{
  "name": "k8s-pod-network",
  "cniVersion": "0.3.1",
  "plugins": [
...
    {
      "type": "bandwidth",
      "capabilities": {"bandwidth": true}
    },
...
  ]
```

As a result, kubelet is already calling the bandwidth plug-in every time a new Pod is created. If a Pod is configured with bandwidth limits, the plug-in uses the Linux kernel's traffic control capabilities that we saw in Chapter 3 to ensure the Pod's virtual network devices don't exceed the specified limit.

Let's look at an example. First, let's deploy an iperf3 server that will listen for client connections:

iperf-server.yaml
```
---
kind: Deployment
apiVersion: apps/v1
metadata:
  name: iperf-server
spec:
  replicas: 1
  selector:
    matchLabels:
      app: iperf-server
  template:
    metadata:
      labels:
        app: iperf-server
    spec:
      containers:
      - name: iperf
        image: bookofkubernetes/iperf3:stable
        env:
        - name: IPERF_SERVER
          value: "1"
        resources: ...
```

```
---
kind: Service
apiVersion: v1
metadata:
  name: iperf-server
spec:
  selector:
    app: iperf-server
  ports:
  - protocol: TCP
    port: 5201
    targetPort: 5201
```

In addition to a Deployment, we also create a Service. This way, our
iperf3 clients can find the server under its well-known name of iperf-server.
We specify port 5201, which is the default port for iperf3.

Let's deploy this server:

```
root@host01:~# kubectl apply -f /opt/iperf-server.yaml
deployment.apps/iperf-server created
service/iperf-server created
```

Let's run an iperf3 client without applying any bandwidth limits. This
will give us a picture of how fast our cluster's network is without any traffic
control. Here's the client definition:

iperf.yaml
```
---
kind: Pod
apiVersion: v1
metadata:
  name: iperf
spec:
  containers:
  - name: iperf
    image: bookofkubernetes/iperf3:stable
    resources: ...
```

Normally, iperf3 in client mode would run once and then terminate.
This image has a script that runs iperf3 repeatedly, sleeping for one minute
between each run. Let's start a client Pod:

```
root@host01:~# kubectl apply -f /opt/iperf.yaml
pod/iperf created
```

It will take a few seconds for the Pod to start running, after which it will take 10 seconds for the initial run. After 30 seconds or so, the Pod log will show the results:

```
root@host01:~# kubectl logs iperf
Connecting to host iperf-server, port 5201
[  5] local 172.31.89.200 port 54346 connected to 10.96.0.192 port 5201
[ ID] Interval           Transfer     Bitrate         Retr  Cwnd
[  5]   0.00-1.00   sec   152 MBytes  1.28 Gbits/sec  225   281 KBytes
[  5]   1.00-2.00   sec   154 MBytes  1.29 Gbits/sec  153   268 KBytes
[  5]   2.00-3.00   sec   163 MBytes  1.37 Gbits/sec  230   325 KBytes
[  5]   3.00-4.00   sec   171 MBytes  1.44 Gbits/sec  254   243 KBytes
[  5]   4.00-5.00   sec   171 MBytes  1.44 Gbits/sec  191   319 KBytes
[  5]   5.00-6.00   sec   174 MBytes  1.46 Gbits/sec  230   302 KBytes
[  5]   6.00-7.00   sec   180 MBytes  1.51 Gbits/sec  199   221 KBytes
[  5]   7.00-8.01   sec   151 MBytes  1.26 Gbits/sec  159   270 KBytes
[  5]   8.01-9.00   sec   160 MBytes  1.36 Gbits/sec  145   298 KBytes
[  5]   9.00-10.00  sec   147 MBytes  1.23 Gbits/sec  230   276 KBytes
- - - - - - - - - - - - - - - - - - - - - - - - -
[ ID] Interval           Transfer     Bitrate         Retr
[  5]   0.00-10.00  sec   1.59 GBytes 1.36 Gbits/sec  2016            sender
[  5]   0.00-10.00  sec   1.59 GBytes 1.36 Gbits/sec                  receiver

iperf Done.
```

In this case, we see a transfer rate of 1.36 GBits/sec between our client and server. Your results will be different depending on how your cluster is deployed and whether the client and server end up on the same host.

Before moving on, we'll shut down the existing client to prevent it from interfering with our next test:

```
root@host01:~# kubectl delete pod iperf
pod "iperf" deleted
```

Obviously, while it's running, iperf3 is trying to use as much network bandwidth as possible. That's fine for a test application, but it isn't polite behavior for an application component in a Kubernetes cluster. To limit its bandwidth, we'll add an annotation to the Pod definition:

iperf-limit.yaml
```
---
kind: Pod
apiVersion: v1
metadata:
  name: iperf-limit
❶ annotations:
    kubernetes.io/ingress-bandwidth: 1M
    kubernetes.io/egress-bandwidth: 1M
spec:
  containers:
```

```
  - name: iperf
    image: bookofkubernetes/iperf3:stable
    resources: ...
  nodeName: host01
```

We'll want to inspect how the limits are being applied to the network devices, which will be easier if this Pod ends up on host01, so we set nodeName accordingly. Otherwise, the only change in this Pod definition is the annotations
section in the Pod metadata ❶. We set a value of 1M for ingress and egress,
corresponding to a 1Mb bandwidth limit on the Pod. When this Pod is
scheduled, kubelet will pick up these annotations and send the specified
bandwidth limits to the bandwidth plug-in so that it can configure Linux
traffic shaping accordingly.

Let's create this Pod and get a look at this in action:

```
root@host01:~# kubectl apply -f /opt/iperf-limit.yaml
pod/iperf-limit created
```

As before, we wait long enough for the client to complete one test with
the server and then print the logs:

```
root@host01:~# kubectl logs iperf-limit
Connecting to host iperf-server, port 5201
[  5] local 172.31.239.224 port 45680 connected to 10.96.0.192 port 5201
[ ID] Interval           Transfer     Bitrate         Retr  Cwnd
[  5]   0.00-1.01   sec  22.7 MBytes  190 Mbits/sec    0   1.37 KBytes
[  5]   1.01-2.01   sec  0.00 Bytes   0.00 bits/sec    0    633 KBytes
[  5]   2.01-3.00   sec  0.00 Bytes   0.00 bits/sec    0    639 KBytes
[  5]   3.00-4.00   sec  0.00 Bytes   0.00 bits/sec    0    646 KBytes
[  5]   4.00-5.00   sec  0.00 Bytes   0.00 bits/sec    0    653 KBytes
[  5]   5.00-6.00   sec  1.25 MBytes  10.5 Mbits/sec   0    658 KBytes
[  5]   6.00-7.00   sec  0.00 Bytes   0.00 bits/sec    0    658 KBytes
[  5]   7.00-8.00   sec  0.00 Bytes   0.00 bits/sec    0    658 KBytes
[  5]   8.00-9.00   sec  0.00 Bytes   0.00 bits/sec    0    658 KBytes
[  5]   9.00-10.00  sec  0.00 Bytes   0.00 bits/sec    0    658 KBytes
- - - - - - - - - - - - - - - - - - - - - - - - -
[ ID] Interval           Transfer     Bitrate         Retr
[  5]   0.00-10.00  sec  24.0 MBytes  20.1 Mbits/sec    0             sender
[  5]   0.00-10.10  sec  20.7 MBytes  17.2 Mbits/sec                  receiver

iperf Done.
```

The change is significant, as the Pod is limited to a fraction of the speed
we saw with an unlimited client. However, because the traffic shaping is
based on a token bucket filter, the traffic control is inexact over shorter in-
tervals, so we see a bitrate of around 20Mb rather than 1Mb. To see why,
let's look at the actual traffic shaping configuration.

The `bandwidth` plug-in is applying this token bucket filter to the host side of the virtual Ethernet (veth) pair that was created for the Pod, so we can see it by showing traffic control configuration for the host interfaces:

```
root@host01:~# tc qdisc show
...
qdisc tbf 1: dev calid43b03f2e06 ... rate 1Mbit burst 21474835b lat 4123.2s
...
```

The combination of rate and burst shows why our Pod was able to achieve 20Mb over the 10-second test run. Because of the burst value, the Pod was able to send a large quantity of data immediately, at the cost of spending several seconds without any ability to send or receive. Over a much longer interval, we would see an average of 1Mbps, but we would still see this bursting behavior.

Before moving on, let's clean up our client and server:

```
root@host01:~# kubectl delete -f /opt/iperf-server.yaml
deployment.apps "iperf-server" deleted
service "iperf-server" deleted
root@host01:~# kubectl delete -f /opt/iperf-limit.yaml
pod "iperf-limit" deleted
```

Managing the bandwidth of a Pod can be useful, but as we've seen, the bandwidth limit can behave like an intermittent connection from the Pod's perspective. For that reason, this kind of traffic shaping should be considered a last resort for containers that cannot be configured to moderate their own bandwidth usage.

Quotas

Limits allow our Kubernetes cluster to ensure that each node has sufficient resources for its assigned Pods. However, if we want our cluster to host multiple applications reliably, we need a way to control the amount of resources that any one application can request.

To do this, we'll use quotas. Quotas are allocated based on Namespaces; they specify the maximum amount of resources that can be allocated within that Namespace. This includes not only the primary resources of CPU and memory but also specialized cluster resources such as GPUs. We can even use quotas to specify the maximum number of a specific object type, such as a Deployment, Service, or CronJob, that can be created within a given Namespace.

Because quotas are allocated based on Namespaces, they need to be used in conjunction with the access controls we described in Chapter 11 to ensure that a given user is bound by the quotas we create. This means that creating Namespaces and applying quotas is typically handled by the cluster administrator.

Let's create a sample Namespace for our Deployment:

```
root@host01:~# kubectl create namespace sample
namespace/sample created
```

Now, let's create a *ResourceQuota* resource type to apply a quota to the Namespace:

quota.yaml
```
---
apiVersion: v1
kind: ResourceQuota
metadata:
  name: sample-quota
  namespace: sample
spec:
  hard:
    requests.cpu: "1"
    requests.memory: 256Mi
    limits.cpu: "2"
    limits.memory: 512Mi
```

This resource defines a quota for CPU and memory for both requests and limits. The units are the same as those used for limits in the Deployment specification in Listing 14-1.

Let's apply this quota to the sample Namespace:

```
root@host01:~# kubectl apply -f /opt/quota.yaml
resourcequota/sample-quota created
```

We can see that this quota has been applied successfully:

```
root@host01:~# kubectl describe namespace sample
Name:         sample
Labels:       kubernetes.io/metadata.name=sample
Annotations:  <none>
Status:       Active

Resource Quotas
  Name:              sample-quota
  Resource           Used  Hard
  --------           ---   ---
  limits.cpu         0     2
  limits.memory      0     512Mi
  requests.cpu       0     1
  requests.memory    0     256Mi
...
```

Even though this quota will apply to all users that try to create Pods in the Namespace, even cluster administrators, it's more realistic to use a normal user, given that an administrator can always create new Namespaces to get around a quota. Thus, we'll also create a user:

```
root@host01:~# kubeadm kubeconfig user --client-name=me \
  --config /etc/kubernetes/kubeadm-init.yaml > kubeconfig
```

As we did in Chapter 11, we'll bind the edit role to this user to provide the right to create and edit resources in the sample Namespace. We'll use the same RoleBinding that we saw in Listing 11-1:

```
root@host01:~# kubectl apply -f /opt/edit-bind.yaml
rolebinding.rbac.authorization.k8s.io/editor created
```

Now that our user is set up, let's set the KUBECONFIG environment variable so that future kubectl commands will operate as our normal user:

```
root@host01:~# export KUBECONFIG=kubeconfig
```

First, we can verify that the edit role possessed by our normal user does not enable making changes to quotas in a Namespace, which makes sense—quotas are an administrator function:

```
root@host01:~# kubectl delete -n sample resourcequota sample-quota
Error from server (Forbidden): resourcequotas "sample-quota" is forbidden:
User "me" cannot delete resource "resourcequotas" in API group "" in the
namespace "sample"
```

We can now create some Pods in the sample Namespace to test the quota. First, let's try to create a Pod with no limits:

```
root@host01:~# kubectl run -n sample nginx --image=nginx
Error from server (Forbidden): pods "nginx" is forbidden: failed quota:
sample-quota: must specify limits.cpu,limits.memory...
```

Because our Namespace has a quota, we are no longer allowed to create Pods without specifying limits.

In Listing 14-2, we try it again, this time using a Deployment that specifies resource limits for the Pods it creates.

sleep.yaml
```
---
kind: Deployment
apiVersion: apps/v1
metadata:
  name: sleep
  namespace: sample
spec:
  replicas: 1
  selector:
    matchLabels:
      app: sleep
  template:
```

```
metadata:
  labels:
    app: sleep
spec:
  containers:
  - name: sleep
    image: busybox
    command:
      - "/bin/sleep"
      - "3600"
    resources:
      requests:
        memory: "64Mi"
        cpu: "250m"
      limits:
        memory: "128Mi"
        cpu: "512m"
```

Listing 14-2: Deployment with Limit

Now we can apply this to the cluster:

```
root@host01:~# kubectl apply -n sample -f /opt/sleep.yaml
deployment.apps/sleep created
```

This is successful because we specified the necessary request and limit fields and we didn't exceed our quota. Additionally, a Pod is started with the limits we specified:

```
root@host01:~# kubectl get -n sample pods
NAME                    READY   STATUS    RESTARTS   AGE
sleep-688dc46d95-wtppg  1/1     Running   0          72s
```

However, we can see that we're now using resources out of our quota:

```
root@host01:~# kubectl describe namespace sample
Name:          sample
Labels:        kubernetes.io/metadata.name=sample
Annotations:   <none>
Status:        Active

Resource Quotas
  Name:            sample-quota
  Resource         Used   Hard
  --------         ---    ---
  limits.cpu       512m   2
  limits.memory    128Mi  512Mi
  requests.cpu     250m   1
  requests.memory  64Mi   256Mi
...
```

This will limit our ability to scale this Deployment. Let's illustrate:

```
root@host01:~# kubectl scale -n sample deployment sleep --replicas=12
deployment.apps/sleep scaled
root@host01:~# kubectl get -n sample pods
NAME                     READY   STATUS    RESTARTS   AGE
sleep-688dc46d95-trnbl   1/1     Running   0          6s
sleep-688dc46d95-vzfsx   1/1     Running   0          6s
sleep-688dc46d95-wtppg   1/1     Running   0          3m13s
```

We've asked for 12 replicas, but we see only three running. If we describe the Deployment we can see an issue:

```
root@host01:~# kubectl describe -n sample deployment sleep
Name:      sleep
Namespace: sample
...
Replicas:   12 desired | 3 updated | 3 total | 3 available | 9 unavailable
...
Conditions:
  Type            Status   Reason
  ----            ------   ------
  Progressing     True     NewReplicaSetAvailable
  Available       False    MinimumReplicasUnavailable
  ReplicaFailure  True     FailedCreate
OldReplicaSets:   <none>
NewReplicaSet:    sleep-688dc46d95 (3/12 replicas created)
...
```

And the Namespace now reports that we have used up enough of our quota that there is no room to allocate the resources needed for another Pod:

```
root@host01:~# kubectl describe namespace sample
Name:           sample
...
Resource Quotas
  Name:            sample-quota
  Resource         Used    Hard
  --------         ---     ---
  limits.cpu       1536m   2
  limits.memory    384Mi   512Mi
  requests.cpu     750m    1
  requests.memory  192Mi   256Mi
...
```

Our Pods are running sleep, so we know they're barely using any CPU or memory. However, Kubernetes bases the quota utilization on what we specified, not what the Pod is actually using. This is critical because processes may use more CPU or allocate more memory as they get busy, and Kubernetes needs to make sure it leaves enough resources for the rest of the cluster to operate correctly.

Final Thoughts

For our containerized applications to be reliable, we need to know that one application component can't take too many resources and effectively starve the other containers running in a cluster. Kubernetes is able to use the resource limit functionality of the underlying container runtime and the Linux kernel to limit each container to only the resources it has been allocated. This practice ensures more reliable scheduling of containers onto nodes in the cluster and ensures that the available cluster resources are shared in a fair way even as the cluster becomes heavily loaded.

In this chapter, we've seen how to specify resource requirements for our Deployments and how to apply quotas to Namespaces, effectively enabling us to treat all of the nodes in our cluster as one large pool of available resources. In the next chapter, we'll examine how that same principle extends to storage as we look at dynamically allocating storage to Pods, no matter where they are scheduled.

15

PERSISTENT STORAGE

 Scalability and rapid failover are big advantages of containerized applications, and it's a lot easier to scale, update, and replace stateless containers that don't have any persistent storage. As a result, we've mostly used Deployments to create one or more instances of Pods with only temporary storage.

However, even if we have an application architecture in which most of the components are stateless, we still need some amount of persistent storage for our application. At the same time, we don't want to lose the ability to deploy a Pod to any node in the cluster, and we don't want to lose the contents of our persistent storage if a container or a node fails.

In this chapter, we'll see how Kubernetes offers persistent storage on demand to Pods by using a plug-in architecture that allows any supported distributed storage engine to act as the backing store.

Storage Classes

The Kubernetes storage plug-in architecture is highly flexible; it recognizes that some clusters may not need storage at all, whereas others need multiple storage plug-ins to handle large amounts of data or low-latency storage.

For this reason, `kubeadm` doesn't set up storage immediately during cluster installation; it's configured afterward by adding *StorageClass* resources to the cluster.

Each StorageClass identifies a particular storage plug-in that will provide the actual storage along with any additional required parameters. We can use multiple storage classes to define different plug-ins or parameters, or even multiple storage classes with the same plug-in but different parameters, allowing for separate classes of service for different purposes. For example, a cluster may provide in-memory, solid-state, and traditional spinning-disk media to give applications the opportunity to select the storage type that is most applicable for a given purpose. The cluster may offer smaller quotas for more expensive and lower-latency storage, while offering large quotas for slower storage that is more suitable for infrequently accessed data.

Kubernetes has a set of internal storage provisioners built in. This includes storage drivers for popular cloud providers such as Amazon Web Services, Microsoft Azure, and Google Container Engine. However, using any storage plug-in is easy as long as it has support for the Container Storage Interface (CSI), a published standard for interfacing with a storage provider.

Of course, to be compatible with CSI, the storage provider must include a minimum set of features that are essential for storage in a Kubernetes cluster. The most important of these are dynamic storage management (provisioning and deprovisioning) and dynamic storage attachment (mounting storage on any node in the cluster). Together, these two key features allow the cluster to allocate storage for any Pod that requests it, schedule that Pod on any node, and start a new Pod with the same storage on any node if the existing node fails or the Pod is replaced.

Storage Class Definition

Our Kubernetes cluster deployment in Chapter 6 included the Longhorn storage plug-in (see "Installing Storage" on page 102). The automation scripts have installed it in the cluster for each following chapter. Part of this installation created a DaemonSet so that Longhorn components exist on every node. That DaemonSet kicked off a number of Longhorn components and then created a StorageClass resource to tell Kubernetes how to use Longhorn to provision storage for a Pod.

NOTE *The example repository for this book is at* https://github.com/book-of-kubernetes/examples. *See "Running Examples" on page xx for details on getting set up.*

Listing 15-1 shows the StorageClass that Longhorn created.

```
root@host01:~# kubectl get storageclass
NAME       PROVISIONER       RECLAIMPOLICY   VOLUMEBINDINGMODE   ALLOWVOLUMEEXPANSION ...
longhorn   driver.longhorn.io Delete         Immediate          true                 ...
```

Listing 15-1: Longhorn StorageClass

The two most important fields show the name of the StorageClass and the provisioner. The name is used in resource specifications to identify that the Longhorn StorageClass should be used to provision the requested volume, whereas the provisioner is used internally by kubelet to communicate with the Longhorn CSI plug-in.

CSI Plug-in Internals

Let's look quickly at how kubelet finds and communicates with the Longhorn CSI plug-in before moving on to provisioning volumes and attaching them to Pods. Note that kubelet runs as a service directly on the cluster nodes; on the other hand, all of the Longhorn components are containerized. This means that the two need a little help to communicate in the form of a Unix socket that is created on the host filesystem and then mounted into the filesystem of the Longhorn containers. A Unix socket allows two processes to communicate by streaming data, similar to a network connection but without the network overhead.

To explore how this communication works, first we'll list the Longhorn containers that are running on host01:

```
root@host01:~# crictl ps --name 'longhorn.*|csi.*'
CONTAINER      ... STATE     NAME ...
c8347a513f71e ... Running   csi-provisioner ...
47f950a3e8dbf ... Running   csi-provisioner ...
3aad0fef7454e ... Running   longhorn-csi-plugin ...
9bfb61f786afa ... Running   csi-snapshotter ...
24a2994a264a1 ... Running   csi-snapshotter ...
7ee4c748b4c02 ... Running   csi-snapshotter ...
8d92886fdacda ... Running   csi-resizer ...
9868014407fe0 ... Running   csi-resizer ...
408d16181af51 ... Running   csi-attacher ...
0c6c341debb0c ... Running   longhorn-driver-deployer ...
ba328a9d0aaf2 ... Running   longhorn-manager ...
c39e5c4fee3bb ... Running   longhorn-ui ...
```

Longhorn creates containers with names that start with either longhorn or csi, so we use a regular expression with crictl to show only those containers.

Let's capture the container ID of the csi-attacher container and then inspect it to see what volume mounts it has:

```
root@host01:~# CID=$(crictl ps -q --name csi-attacher)
root@host01:~# crictl inspect $CID
{
...
    "mounts": [
      {
        "containerPath": "/csi/",
```

```
❶ "hostPath": "/var/lib/kubelet/plugins/driver.longhorn.io",
  "propagation": "PROPAGATION_PRIVATE",
  "readonly": false,
  "selinuxRelabel": false
}
...
"envs": [
  {
    "key": "ADDRESS",
❷  "value": "/csi/csi.sock"
  },
...
}
```

The `crictl inspect` command returns a lot of data from the container, but we show only the relevant data in this example. We can see that this Longhorn component is instructed to connect to */csi/csi.sock* ❷, which is the mount point inside the container for the Unix socket that kubelet uses to communicate with the storage driver. We can also see that */csi* inside the container is */var/lib/kubelet/plugins/driver.longhorn.io* ❶. The location */var/lib/kubelet/plugins* is a standard location for kubelet to look for storage plug-ins, and of course, *driver.longhorn.io* is the value of the provisioner field, as defined in the Longhorn StorageClass in Listing 15-1.

If we look on the host, we can confirm that this Unix socket exists:

```
root@host01:~# ls -l /var/lib/kubelet/plugins/driver.longhorn.io
total 0
srwxr-xr-x 1 root root 0 Feb 18 20:17 csi.sock
```

The s as the first character indicates that this is a Unix socket.

Persistent Volumes

Now that we've seen how kubelet communicates with an external storage driver, let's look at how to request allocation of storage and then attach that storage to a Pod.

Stateful Sets

The easiest way to get storage in a Pod is to use a StatefulSet (a resource described in Chapter 7). Like a Deployment, a StatefulSet creates multiple Pods, which can be allocated to any node. However, a StatefulSet also creates persistent storage as well as a mapping between each Pod and its storage. If a Pod needs to be replaced, it is replaced with a new Pod with the same identifier and the same persistent storage.

Listing 15-2 presents an example StatefulSet that creates two PostgreSQL Pods with persistent storage.

```
---
apiVersion: apps/v1
kind: StatefulSet
metadata:
  name: postgres
spec:
  serviceName: postgres
  replicas: 2
  selector:
    matchLabels:
      app: postgres
  template:
    metadata:
      labels:
        app: postgres
    spec:
      containers:
      - name: postgres
        image: postgres
        env:
        - name: POSTGRES_PASSWORD
❶        value: "supersecret"
        - name: PGDATA
❷        value: /data/pgdata
        volumeMounts:
        - name: postgres-volume
❸        mountPath: /data
  volumeClaimTemplates:
  - metadata:
      name: postgres-volume
    spec:
      storageClassName: longhorn
      accessModes:
        - ReadWriteOnce
      resources:
        requests:
          storage: 1Gi
```

Listing 15-2: PostgreSQL StatefulSet

In addition to setting the password using an environment variable ❶, we also set PGDATA to */data/pgdata* ❷, which tells PostgreSQL where to store the files for the database. It aligns with the volume mount we also declare as part of the StatefulSet, as that persistent volume will be mounted at */data* ❸. The PostgreSQL container image documentation recommends configuring the database files to reside in a subdirectory beneath the mount point to avoid a potential issue with ownership of the data directory.

Separate from the configuration for the PostgreSQL Pods, we supply the StatefulSet with the `volumeClaimTemplates` field. This field tells the StatefulSet how we want the persistent storage to be configured. It includes the name of the StorageClass and the requested size, and it also includes an `accessMode` of `ReadWriteOnce`, which we'll explore later. The StatefulSet will use this specification to allocate independent storage for each Pod.

As mentioned in Chapter 7, this StatefulSet references a Service using the `serviceName` field, and this Service is used to create the domain name for the Pods. The Service is defined in the same file as follows:

pgsql-set.yaml
```
---
apiVersion: v1
kind: Service
metadata:
  name: postgres
spec:
  clusterIP: None
  selector:
    app: postgres
```

Setting the `clusterIP` field to `None` makes this a *Headless Service*, which means that no IP address is allocated from the service IP range and none of the load balancing described in Chapter 9 is configured for this Service. This approach is typical for a StatefulSet. With a StatefulSet, each Pod has its own unique identity and unique storage. Because service load balancing just randomly chooses a destination, it is typically not useful with a StatefulSet. Instead, clients explicitly select a Pod instance as a destination.

Let's create the Service and StatefulSet:

```
root@host01:~# kubectl apply -f /opt/pgsql-set.yaml
service/postgres created
statefulset.apps/postgres created
```

It will take some time to get the Pods up and running because they are created sequentially, one at a time. After they are running, we can see how they've been named:

```
root@host01:~# kubectl get pods
NAME         READY   STATUS    RESTARTS   AGE
postgres-0   1/1     Running   0          97s
postgres-1   1/1     Running   0          51s
```

Let's examine the persistent storage from within the container:

```
root@host01:~# kubectl exec -ti postgres-0 -- /bin/sh
# findmnt /data
TARGET SOURCE                       FSTYPE OPTIONS
/data  /dev/longhorn/pvc-83becdac-... ext4   rw,relatime
# exit
```

As requested, we see a Longhorn device that has been mounted at */data*. Kubernetes will keep this persistent storage even if the node fails or the Pod is upgraded.

This StatefulSet has two more important resources to explore. First is the headless Service that we created:

```
root@host01:~# kubectl get svc
NAME         TYPE        CLUSTER-IP    EXTERNAL-IP   PORT(S)   AGE
kubernetes   ClusterIP   10.96.0.1     <none>        443/TCP   54m
postgres     ClusterIP   None          <none>        <none>    19m
```

The postgres Service exists, but no cluster IP address is shown because we created it as a headless Service. However, it has created DNS entries for the associated Pods, so we can use it to connect to specific PostgreSQL Pods without knowing the Pod IP address.

We need to use the cluster DNS to do the lookup. The easiest way to do that is from within a container:

```
root@host01:~# kubectl run -ti --image=alpine --restart=Never alpine
If you don't see a command prompt, try pressing enter.
/ #
```

This form of the run command stays in the foreground and gives us an interactive terminal. It also tells Kubernetes not to try to restart the container when we exit the shell.

From inside this container, we can refer to either of our PostgreSQL Pods by a well-known name:

```
/ # ping -c 1 postgres-0.postgres.default.svc
PING postgres-0.postgres.default.svc (172.31.239.198): 56 data bytes
64 bytes from 172.31.239.198: seq=0 ttl=63 time=0.093 ms
...

/# ping -c 1 postgres-1.postgres.default.svc
PING postgres-1.postgres.default.svc (172.31.239.199): 56 data bytes
64 bytes from 172.31.239.199: seq=0 ttl=63 time=0.300 ms
...

# exit
```

The naming convention is identical to what we saw for Services in Chapter 9, but with an extra hostname prefix for the name of the Pod; in this case, either postgres-0 or postgres-1.

The other important resource is the *PersistentVolumeClaim* that the StatefulSet created automatically. The PersistentVolumeClaim is what actually allocates storage using the Longhorn StorageClass:

```
root@host01:~# kubectl get pvc
NAME                       STATUS   VOLUME        ...   CAPACITY   ...
postgres-volume-postgres-0 Bound    pvc-83becdac...     1Gi        ...
postgres-volume-postgres-1 Bound    pvc-0d850889...     1Gi        ...
```

We use the abbreviation pvc in lieu of its full name, persistentvolumeclaim.

The StatefulSet used the data in the volumeClaimTemplates field in Listing 15-2 to create these two PersistentVolumeClaims. However, if we delete the StatefulSet, the PersistentVolumeClaims continue to exist:

```
root@host01:~# kubectl delete -f /opt/pgsql-set.yaml
service "postgres" deleted
statefulset.apps "postgres" deleted
root@host01:~# kubectl get pvc
NAME                        STATUS   VOLUME        ...   CAPACITY   ...
postgres-volume-postgres-0  Bound    pvc-83becdac...      1Gi       ...
postgres-volume-postgres-1  Bound    pvc-0d850889...      1Gi       ...
```

This protects us from accidentally deleting our persistent storage. If we create the StatefulSet again and keep the same name in the volume claim template, our new Pods will get the same storage back.

HIGHLY AVAILABLE POSTGRESQL

We've deployed two separate instances of PostgreSQL, each with its own independent persistent storage. However, that's only the first step in deploying a highly available database. We would also need to configure one instance as primary and the other as backup, configure replication from the primary to the backup, and configure failover. We would also need to configure clients to talk to the primary and switch to a new primary when there's a failure. Fortunately, we don't need to do this configuration ourselves. In Chapter 17, we'll see how to take advantage of the power of custom resources to deploy a Kubernetes Operator for PostgreSQL that automatically will handle all of this.

The StatefulSet is the best way to handle the case in which we need multiple instances of a container, each with its own independent storage. However, we can also use persistent volumes more directly, which gives us more control over how they're mounted into our Pods.

Volumes and Claims

Kubernetes has both a *PersistentVolume* and a PersistentVolumeClaim resource type. The PersistentVolumeClaim represents a request for allocated storage, whereas the PersistentVolume holds information on the allocated storage. For the most part, this distinction doesn't matter, and we can just focus on the PersistentVolumeClaim. However, the difference is important in two cases:

- Administrators can create a PersistentVolume manually, and this PersistentVolume can be directly mounted into a Pod.

- If there is an issue allocating storage as specified in the PersistentVolumeClaim, the PersistentVolume will not be created.

To illustrate, first we'll start with a PersistentVolumeClaim that automatically allocates storage:

pvc.yaml
```
---
apiVersion: v1
kind: PersistentVolumeClaim
metadata:
  name: nginx-storage
spec:
  storageClassName: longhorn
  accessModes:
    - ReadWriteOnce
  resources:
    requests:
      storage: 100Mi
```

We named this PersistentVolumeClaim `nginx-storage` because that's how we'll use it in a moment. The PersistentVolumeClaim requests 100MiB of storage from the `longhorn` StorageClass. When we apply this PersistentVolumeClaim to the cluster, Kubernetes invokes the Longhorn storage driver and allocates the storage, creating a PersistentVolume in the process:

```
root@host01:~# kubectl apply -f /opt/pvc.yaml
persistentvolumeclaim/nginx-storage created
root@host01:~# kubectl get pv
NAME            ... CAPACITY ... STATUS  CLAIM                               STORAGECLASS ...
pvc-0b50e5b4-... 1Gi      ... Bound   default/postgres-volume-postgres-1  longhorn     ...
pvc-ad092ba9-... 1Gi      ... Bound   default/postgres-volume-postgres-0  longhorn     ...
pvc-cb671684-... 100Mi    ... Bound   default/nginx-storage               longhorn     ...
```

The abbreviation `pv` is short for `persistentvolumes`.

Even though no Pod is using the storage, it still shows a status of `Bound` because there is an active PersistentVolumeClaim for the storage.

If we try to create a PersistentVolumeClaim without a matching storage class, the cluster won't be able to create the corresponding PersistentVolume:

pvc-man.yaml
```
---
apiVersion: v1
kind: PersistentVolumeClaim
metadata:
  name: manual
spec:
  storageClassName: manual
  accessModes:
    - ReadWriteOnce
  resources:
    requests:
      storage: 100Mi
```

Because there is no StorageClass called manual, Kubernetes can't create this storage automatically:

```
root@host01:~# kubectl apply -f /opt/pvc-man.yaml
persistentvolumeclaim/manual created
root@host01:~# kubectl get pvc
NAME                      STATUS    ... STORAGECLASS   AGE
manual                    Pending   ... manual         6s
...
root@host01:~# kubectl get pv
NAME                                          ...
pvc-0b50e5b4-9889-4c8d-a651-df78fa2bc764      ...
pvc-ad092ba9-cf30-4b7d-af01-ff02a5924db7      ...
pvc-cb671684-1719-4c33-9dd8-bcbbf24523b4      ...
```

Our PersistentVolumeClaim has a status of Pending and there is no corresponding PersistentVolume. However, as a cluster administrator, we can create this PersistentVolume manually:

pv.yaml
```
---
apiVersion: v1
kind: PersistentVolume
metadata:
  name: manual
spec:
  claimRef:
    name: manual
    namespace: default
  accessModes:
    - ReadWriteOnce
  capacity:
    storage: 100Mi
  csi:
    driver: driver.longhorn.io
    volumeHandle: manual
```

When creating a PersistentVolume in this way, we need to specify the type of volume we want. In this case, by including the csi field, we identify this as a volume created by a CSI plug-in. We then specify the driver to use and provide a unique value for volumeHandle. After the PersistentVolume is created, Kubernetes directly invokes the Longhorn storage driver to allocate storage.

We create the PersistentVolume with the following:

```
root@host01:~# kubectl apply -f /opt/pv.yaml
persistentvolume/manual created
```

Because we specified a claimRef for this PersistentVolume, it will automatically move into the Bound state:

```
root@host01:~# kubectl get pv manual
NAME      CAPACITY   ACCESS MODES   RECLAIM POLICY   STATUS   ...
manual    100Mi      RWO            Retain           Bound    ...
```

It will take a few seconds, so the PersistentVolume may show up as
Available briefly.

The PersistentVolumeClaim also moves into the Bound state:

```
root@host01:~# kubectl get pvc manual
NAME      STATUS   VOLUME   CAPACITY   ACCESS MODES   STORAGECLASS   AGE
manual    Bound    manual   100Mi      RWO            manual         2m20s
```

It is useful for an administrator to create a PersistentVolume manually
for those rare cases when specialized storage is needed for an application.
However, for most persistent storage, it is much better to automate storage
allocation through a StorageClass and either a PersistentVolumeClaim or a
StatefulSet.

Deployments

Now that we've directly created a PersistentVolumeClaim and we have the
associated volume, we can use it in a Deployment. To demonstrate this, we'll
show how we can use persistent storage to hold HTML files served by an
NGINX web server:

nginx.yaml

```
---
apiVersion: apps/v1
kind: Deployment
metadata:
  name: nginx
spec:
  replicas: 1
  selector:
    matchLabels:
      app: nginx
  template:
    metadata:
      labels:
        app: nginx
    spec:
      containers:
      - name: nginx
        image: nginx
        volumeMounts:
❶      - name: html
          mountPath: /usr/share/nginx/html
      volumes:
❷      - name: html
```

```
    persistentVolumeClaim:
        claimName: nginx-storage
```

It takes two steps to get the persistent storage mounted into our container. First, we declare a `volume` named `html` ❷ that references the PersistentVolumeClaim we created. This makes the storage available in the Pod. Next, we declare a `volumeMount` ❶ to specify where in the container's filesystem this particular volume should appear. The advantage of having these two separate steps is that we can mount the same volume in multiple containers within the same Pod, which enables us to share data between processes using files even for cases in which the processes come from separate container images.

This capability allows for some interesting use cases. For example, suppose that we're building a web application that includes some static content. We might deploy an NGINX web server to serve that content, as we're doing here. At the same time, we also need a way to update the content. We might do that by having an additional container in the Pod that periodically checks for new content and updates a persistent volume that is shared with the NGINX container.

Let's create the NGINX Deployment so that we can demonstrate that HTML files can be served from the persistent storage. The persistent storage will start empty, so at first there won't be any web content to serve. Let's see how NGINX behaves in that case:

```
root@host01:~# kubectl apply -f /opt/nginx.yaml
deployment.apps/nginx created
```

As soon as the NGINX server is up and running, we need to grab its IP address so that we can make an HTTP request using `curl`:

```
root@host01:~# IP=$(kubectl get po -l app=nginx -o jsonpath='{..podIP}')
root@host01:~# curl -v http://$IP
...
* Connected to 172.31.25.200 (172.31.25.200) port 80 (#0)
> GET / HTTP/1.1
...
< HTTP/1.1 403 Forbidden
```

To grab the IP address in this case, we use the `jsonpath` output format for `kubectl` rather than use `jq` to filter JSON output; `jsonpath` has a very useful syntax for searching into a JSON object and pulling out a single uniquely named field (in this example, `podIP`). We could use a `jq` filter similar to what we did in Chapter 8, but the `jq` syntax for recursion is more complex.

After we have the IP, we use `curl` to contact NGINX. As expected, we don't see an HTML response, because our persistent storage is empty. However, we know that our volume mounted correctly because in this case we don't even see the default NGINX welcome page.

Let's copy in an *index.html* file to give our NGINX server something to serve:

```
root@host01:~# POD=$(kubectl get po -l app=nginx -o jsonpath='{..metadata.name}')
root@host01:~# kubectl cp /opt/index.html $POD:/usr/share/nginx/html
```

First, we capture the name of the Pod as randomly generated by the Deployment and then we use kubectl cp to copy in an HTML file. If we try running curl again, we'll see a much better response:

```
root@host01:~# curl -v http://$IP
...
* Connected to 172.31.239.210 (172.31.239.210) port 80 (#0)
> GET / HTTP/1.1
...
< HTTP/1.1 200 OK
...
<html>
  <head>
    <title>Hello, World</title>
  </head>
  <body>
    <h1>Hello, World!</h1>
  </body>
</html>
...
```

Because this is persistent storage, this HTML content will remain available even if we delete the Deployment and create it again.

However, we still have one significant problem to overcome. One of the primary reasons to have a Deployment is to be able to scale to multiple Pod instances. Scaling this Deployment makes a lot of sense, as we could have multiple Pod instances serving the same HTML content. Unfortunately, scaling won't currently work:

```
root@host01:~# kubectl scale --replicas=3 deployment/nginx
deployment.apps/nginx scaled
```

The Deployment appears to scale, but if we look at the Pods, we will see that we don't really have multiple running instances:

```
root@host01:~# kubectl get pods
NAME                   READY   STATUS             RESTARTS   AGE
...
nginx-db4f4d5d9-7q7rd  0/1     ContainerCreating  0          46s
nginx-db4f4d5d9-gbqxm  0/1     ContainerCreating  0          46s
nginx-db4f4d5d9-vrzr4  1/1     Running            0          10m
```

The two new instances are stuck in `ContainerCreating`. Let's examine one of those two Pods to see why:

```
root@host01:~# kubectl describe pod/nginx-db4f4d5d9-7q7rd
Name:           nginx-db4f4d5d9-7q7rd
...
Status:         Pending
Events:
  Type     Reason             Age    From                    Message
  ----     ------             ----   ----                    -------
...
  Warning  FailedAttachVolume  110s   attachdetach-controller  Multi-Attach
    error for volume "pvc-cb671684-1719-4c33-9dd8-bcbbf24523b4" Volume is
    already used by pod(s) nginx-db4f4d5d9-vrzr4
```

The first Pod we created has claimed the volume, and no other Pods can attach to it, so they are stuck in a `Pending` state. Even worse, this doesn't just prevent scaling, it also prevents upgrading or making other configuration changes to the Deployment. If we update the Deployment configuration, Kubernetes will try to start a Pod using the new configuration before shutting down any old Pods. The new Pods can't attach to the volume and therefore can't start, so the old Pod will never be cleaned up and the configuration change will never take place.

We could force a Pod update in a couple ways. First, we could manually delete and re-create the Deployment anytime we made changes. Second, we could configure Kubernetes to delete the old Pod first by using a `Recreate` update strategy. We explore update strategy options in greater detail in Chapter 20. For now, it's worth noting that this still would not allow us to scale the Deployment.

If we want to fix this so that we can scale the Deployment, we'll need to allow multiple Pods to attach to the volume at the same time. We can do this by changing the access mode for the persistent volume.

Access Modes

Kubernetes is refusing to attach multiple Pods to the same persistent volume because we configured the PersistentVolumeClaim with an access mode of `ReadWriteOnce`. An alternate access mode, `ReadWriteMany`, will allow all of the NGINX server Pods to mount the storage simultaneously. Only some storage drivers support the `ReadWriteMany` access mode, because it requires the ability to manage simultaneous changes to files, including communicating changes dynamically to all of the nodes in the cluster.

Longhorn does support `ReadWriteMany`, so creating a PersistentVolume-Claim with `ReadWriteMany` access mode is an easy change:

pvc-rwx.yaml
```
---
apiVersion: v1
kind: PersistentVolumeClaim
```

```
metadata:
  name: storage
spec:
  storageClassName: longhorn
  accessModes:
    - ReadWriteMany
  resources:
    requests:
      storage: 100Mi
```

Unfortunately, we can't modify our existing PersistentVolumeClaim to change the access mode. And we can't delete the PersistentVolumeClaim while the storage is in use by our Deployment. So we need to clean up everything and then deploy again:

```
root@host01:~# kubectl delete deploy/nginx pvc/storage
deployment.apps "nginx" deleted
persistentvolumeclaim "storage" deleted
root@host01:~# kubectl apply -f /opt/pvc-rwx.yaml
persistentvolumeclaim/storage created
root@host01:~# kubectl apply -f /opt/nginx.yaml
deployment.apps/nginx created
```

We specify `deploy/nginx` and `pvc/storage` as the resources to delete. This style of identifying the resources allows us to operate on two resources in the same command.

After a minute or so, the new NGINX Pod will be running:

```
root@host01:~# kubectl get pods
NAME                   READY   STATUS    RESTARTS   AGE
...
nginx-db4f4d5d9-6thzs  1/1     Running   0          44s
```

At this point, we need to copy our HTML content over again because deleting the PersistentVolumeClaim deleted the previous storage:

```
root@host01:~# POD=$(kubectl get po -l app=nginx -o jsonpath='{..metadata.name}')
root@host01:~# kubectl cp /opt/index.html $POD:/usr/share/nginx/html
... no output ...
```

This time, when we scale our NGINX Deployment, the additional two Pods are able to mount the storage and start running:

```
root@host01:~# kubectl scale --replicas=3 deploy nginx
deployment.apps/nginx scaled
root@host01:~# kubectl get po
NAME                   READY   STATUS    RESTARTS   AGE
...
nginx-db4f4d5d9-2j629  1/1     Running   0          23s
```

```
nginx-db4f4d5d9-6thzs    1/1    Running    0    5m19s
nginx-db4f4d5d9-7r5qj    1/1    Running    0    23s
```

All three NGINX Pods are serving the same content, as we can see if we fetch the IP address for one of the new Pods and connect to it:

```
root@host01:~# IP=$(kubectl get po nginx-db4f4d5d9-2j629 -o jsonpath='{..podIP}')
root@host01:~# curl http://$IP
<html>
  <head>
    <title>Hello, World</title>
  </head>
  <body>
    <h1>Hello, World!</h1>
  </body>
</html>
```

At this point, we could use any NGINX Pod to update the HTML content and all Pods would serve the new content. We could even use a separate CronJob with an application component that updates the content dynamically, and NGINX would happily serve whatever files are in place.

Final Thoughts

Persistent storage is an essential requirement for building a fully functioning application. After a cluster administrator has configured one or more storage classes, it's easy for application developers to dynamically request persistent storage as part of their application deployment. In most cases, the best way to do this is with a StatefulSet, as Kubernetes will automatically handle allocating independent storage for each Pod and will maintain a one-to-one relationship between Pod and storage during failover and upgrades.

At the same time, there are other storage use cases, such as having multiple Pods access the same storage. We can easily handle those use cases by directly creating a PersistentVolumeClaim resource and then declaring it as a volume in a controller such as a Deployment or Job.

Although persistent storage is an effective way to make file content available to containers, Kubernetes has other powerful resource types that can store configuration data and pass it to containers as either environment variables or file content. In the next chapter, we'll explore how to manage application configuration and secrets.

16

CONFIGURATION AND SECRETS

 Any high-quality application is designed so that key configuration items can be injected at runtime rather than being embedded in the source code. When we move our application components to containers, we need a way to tell the container runtime what configuration information to inject to ensure that our application components behave the way they should.

Kubernetes provides two primary resource types for injecting this configuration information: ConfigMap and Secret. These two resources are very similar in capability but have slightly different use cases.

Injecting Configuration

When we looked at container runtimes in Part I, we saw that we could pass environment variables to our containers. Of course, as Kubernetes manages the container runtime for us, we'll first need to pass that information to Kubernetes, which will then pass it to the container runtime for us.

The example repository for this book is at https://github.com/book-of
-kubernetes/examples. *See "Running Examples" on page xx for details on
getting set up.*

For simple configuration injection, we can provide environment variables directly from the Pod specification. We saw an example of this in Pod
form when we created a PostgreSQL server in Chapter 10. Here's a Postgre-
SQL Deployment with a similar configuration in its embedded Pod
specification:

pgsql.yaml
```
---
kind: Deployment
apiVersion: apps/v1
metadata:
  name: postgres
spec:
  replicas: 1
  selector:
    matchLabels:
      app: postgres
  template:
    metadata:
      labels:
        app: postgres
    spec:
      containers:
      - name: postgres
        image: postgres
        env:
        - name: POSTGRES_PASSWORD
          value: "supersecret"
```

When we provide environment variables directly in the Deployment,
those environment variables are stored directly in the YAML file and in the
cluster's configuration for that Deployment. There are two important problems with embedding environment variables in this manner. First, we're reducing flexibility because we can't specify a new value for the environment
variable without changing the Deployment YAML file. Second, the password
is visible in plaintext directly in the Deployment YAML file. YAML files are
often checked in to source control, so we're going to have a hard time adequately protecting the password.

Let's first look at moving the configuration out of the Deployment; then we'll consider how best to protect the password.

Externalizing Configuration

Embedding configuration in the Deployment makes the resource definition less reusable. If, for example, we wanted to deploy a PostgreSQL server for both test and production versions of our application, it would be useful to reuse the same Deployment to avoid duplication and to avoid configuration drift between the two versions. However, for security, we would not want to use the same password in both environments.

It's better if we externalize the configuration by storing it in a separate resource and referring to it from the Deployment. To enable this, Kubernetes offers the *ConfigMap* resource. A ConfigMap specifies a set of key–value pairs that can be referenced when specifying a Pod. For example, we can define our PostgreSQL configuration this way:

pgsql-cm.yaml
```
---
kind: ConfigMap
apiVersion: v1
metadata:
  name: pgsql
data:
  POSTGRES_PASSWORD: "supersecret"
```

By storing this configuration information in a ConfigMap, it is no longer directly part of the Deployment YAML file or the cluster configuration for the Deployment.

After we've defined our ConfigMap, we can reference it in our Deployment, as demonstrated in Listing 16-1.

```
---
kind: Deployment
apiVersion: apps/v1
metadata:
  name: postgres
spec:
  replicas: 1
  selector:
    matchLabels:
      app: postgres
  template:
    metadata:
      labels:
        app: postgres
    spec:
      containers:
      - name: postgres
        image: postgres
        envFrom:
        - configMapRef:
            name: pgsql
```

Listing 16-1: PostgreSQL with ConfigMap

In place of the env field, we have an envFrom field that specifies one or more ConfigMaps to serve as environment variables for the container. All of the key–value pairs in the ConfigMap will become environment variables.

This has the same effect as specifying one or more environment variables directly in the Deployment, but our Deployment specification is now reusable. The Deployment will look for the identified ConfigMap in its own Namespace, so we can have multiple Deployments from the same specification in separate Namespaces, and each can be configured differently.

This use of Namespace isolation to prevent naming conflicts, together with the Namespace-scoped security controls we saw in Chapter 11 and the Namespace-scoped quotas we saw in Chapter 14, allows a single cluster to be used for many different purposes, by many different groups, a concept known as *multitenancy*.

Let's create this Deployment and see how Kubernetes injects the configuration. First, let's create the actual Deployment:

```
root@host01:~# kubectl apply -f /opt/pgsql-ext-cfg.yaml
deployment.apps/postgres created
```

This command completes successfully because the Deployment has been created in the cluster, but Kubernetes will not be able to start any Pods because the ConfigMap is missing:

```
root@host01:~# kubectl get pods
NAME                         READY   STATUS                      RESTARTS   AGE
postgres-6bf595fcbc-s8dqz    0/1     CreateContainerConfigError  0          53s
```

If we now create the ConfigMap, we see that the Pod is then created:

```
root@host01:~# kubectl apply -f /opt/pgsql-cm.yaml
configmap/pgsql created
root@host01:~# kubectl get pods
NAME                         READY   STATUS    RESTARTS   AGE
postgres-6bf595fcbc-s8dqz    1/1     Running   0          2m41s
```

It can take a minute or so for Kubernetes to determine that the Config-Map is available and start the Pod. As soon as the Pod is running, we can verify that the environment variables were injected based on the data in the ConfigMap:

```
root@host01:~# kubectl exec -ti postgres-6bf595fcbc-s8dqz -- /bin/sh -c env
...
POSTGRES_PASSWORD=supersecret
...
```

The command env prints out all of the environment variables associated with a process. Because Kubernetes provides the same environment variables to our /bin/sh process as it provided to our main PostgreSQL process, we know that the environment variable was set as expected. It's important to note, however, that even though we can change the ConfigMap at any time, doing so will not cause the Deployment to update its Pods; the application will not automatically pick up any environment variable changes. Instead, we need to apply some configuration change to the Deployment to cause it to create new Pods.

Although the configuration has been externalized, we still are not protecting it. Let's do that next.

Protecting Secrets

When protecting secrets, thinking through the nature of the protection that makes sense is important. For example, we might need to protect authentication information that our application uses to connect to a database. However, given that the application itself needs that information to make the connection, anyone who can inspect the inner details of the application is going to be able to extract those credentials.

As we saw in Chapter 11, Kubernetes provides fine-grained access control over each individual resource type in a given Namespace. To enable protection of secrets, Kubernetes provides a separate resource type, *Secret*. This way, access to secrets can be limited to only those users who require access, a principle known as *least privilege*.

One more advantage to the Secret resource type is that it uses base64 encoding for all of its data, with automatic decoding when the data is provided to the Pod, which simplifies the storage of binary data.

ENCRYPTING SECRET DATA

By default, data stored in a Secret is base64 encoded but is not encrypted. It is possible to encrypt secret data, and doing so is good practice for a production cluster, but remember that the data must be decrypted so that it can be provided to the Pod. For this reason, anyone who can control what Pods exist in a namespace can access secret data, as can any cluster administrators who can access the underlying container runtime. This is true even if the secret data is encrypted when stored. Proper access controls are essential to keep a cluster secure.

A Secret definition looks almost identical to a ConfigMap definition:

pgsql-secret.yaml
```
---
kind: Secret
apiVersion: v1
metadata:
  name: pgsql
stringData:
  POSTGRES_PASSWORD: "supersecret"
```

The one obvious difference is the resource type of Secret rather than ConfigMap. However, there is a subtle difference as well. When we define this Secret, we place the key–value pairs in a field called stringData rather than just data. This tells Kubernetes that we are providing unencoded strings. When it creates the Secret, Kubernetes will encode the strings for us:

```
root@host01:~# kubectl apply -f /opt/pgsql-secret.yaml
secret/pgsql created
root@host01:~# kubectl get secret pgsql -o json | jq .data
{
  "POSTGRES_PASSWORD": "c3VwZXJzZWNyZXQ="
}
```

Even though we specified the data using the field stringData and an unencoded string, the actual Secret uses the field data and stores the value using base64 encoding. We can also do the base64 encoding ourselves. In that case, we place the value directly into the data field:

pgsql -secret-2.yaml
```
---
kind: Secret
apiVersion: v1
metadata:
  name: pgsql
```

```
data:
  POSTGRES_PASSWORD: c3VwZXJzZWNyZXQ=
```

This approach is necessary to define binary content for the Secret in order for us to be able to supply that binary content as part of a YAML resource definition.

We use a Secret in a Deployment definition in exactly the same way we use a ConfigMap:

pgsql-ext-sec.yaml
```
---
kind: Deployment
apiVersion: apps/v1
metadata:
  name: postgres
spec:
  replicas: 1
  selector:
    matchLabels:
      app: postgres
  template:
    metadata:
      labels:
        app: postgres
    spec:
      containers:
      - name: postgres
        image: postgres
        envFrom:
        - secretRef:
            name: pgsql
```

The only change is the use of `secretRef` in place of `configMapRef`.
To test this, let's apply this new Deployment configuration:

```
root@host01:~# kubectl apply -f /opt/pgsql-ext-sec.yaml
deployment.apps/postgres configured
```

From the perspective of our Pod, the behavior is exactly the same. Kubernetes handles the base64 decoding, making the decoded value visible to our Pod:

```
root@host01:~# kubectl get pods
NAME                         READY   STATUS        RESTARTS   AGE
postgres-6bf595fcbc-s8dqz    1/1     Terminating   0          12m
postgres-794ff85bbf-xzz49    1/1     Running       0          26s
root@host01:~# kubectl exec -ti postgres-794ff85bbf-xzz49 -- /bin/sh -c env
...
POSTGRES_PASSWORD=supersecret
...
```

As before, we use the env command to show that the POSTGRES_PASSWORD environment variable was set as expected. The Pod sees the same behavior whether we specify the environment variable directly or use a ConfigMap or Secret.

Before we move on, let's delete this Deployment:

```
root@host01:~# kubectl delete deploy postgres
deployment.apps "postgres" deleted
```

Using ConfigMaps and Secrets, we have the ability to externalize environment variable configuration for our application so that our Deployment specification can be reusable and to facilitate fine-grained access control over secret data.

Injecting Files

Of course, environment variables are not the only way we commonly configure applications. We also need a way to provide configuration files. We can do that using the same ConfigMap and Secret resources we've seen already.

Any files we inject in this way override files that exist in the container image, which means that we can supply the container image with a sensible default configuration and then override that configuration with each container we run. This makes it much easier to reuse container images.

The ability to specify file content in a ConfigMap and then mount it in a container is immediately useful for configuration files, but we can also use it to update the NGINX web server example we showed in Chapter 15. As we'll see, with this version we can declare our HTML content solely using Kubernetes resource YAML files, with no need for console commands to copy content into a PersistentVolume.

The first step is to define a ConfigMap with the HTML content we want to serve:

nginx-cm.yaml
```
---
kind: ConfigMap
apiVersion: v1
metadata:
  name: nginx
data:
  index.html: |
    <html>
      <head>
        <title>Hello, World</title>
      </head>
      <body>
        <h1>Hello, World from a ConfigMap!</h1>
      </body>
    </html>
```

The key part of the key–value pair is used to specify the desired file-name, in this case *index.html*. For ease of reading, we use a pipe character (|) to start a YAML multiline string. This string continues as long as the following lines are indented, or until the end of the YAML file. We can define multiple files in this way by just adding more keys to the ConfigMap.

In the Deployment we saw in Listing 16-1, we specified the ConfigMap as the source of environment variables. Here, we specify it as the source of a volume mount:

```
---
kind: Deployment
apiVersion: apps/v1
metadata:
  name: nginx
spec:
  replicas: 1
  selector:
    matchLabels:
      app: nginx
  template:
    metadata:
      labels:
        app: nginx
    spec:
      containers:
      - name: nginx
        image: nginx
        volumeMounts:
        - name: nginx-files
          mountPath: /usr/share/nginx/html
      volumes:
      - name: nginx-files
        configMap:
          name: nginx
```

This volume definition looks similar to the one we saw in Chapter 15. As before, the volume specification comes in two parts. The `volume` field specifies where the volume comes from, in this case the ConfigMap. The `volumeMounts` allows us to specify the path in the container where the files should be made available. In addition to making it possible to use the same volume in multiple containers in a Pod, this also means that we can share the same syntax when mounting persistent volumes and when mounting the configuration as files in the container filesystem.

Let's create the ConfigMap and then get this Deployment started:

```
root@host01:~# kubectl apply -f /opt/nginx-cm.yaml
configmap/nginx created
```

```
root@host01:~# kubectl apply -f /opt/nginx-deploy.yaml
deployment.apps/nginx created
```

After the Pod is running, we can see that the file content is as expected, and NGINX is serving our HTML file:

```
root@host01:~# IP=$(kubectl get po -l app=nginx -o jsonpath='{..podIP}')
root@host01:~# curl http://$IP
<html>
  <head>
    <title>Hello, World</title>
  </head>
  <body>
    <h1>Hello, World from a ConfigMap!</h1>
  </body>
</html>
```

The output looks similar to what we saw in Chapter 15 when we provided the HTML content as a PersistentVolume, but we were able to avoid the effort of attaching the PersistentVolume and then copying content into it. In practice, both approaches have value, as maintaining a ConfigMap with a large amount of data would be unwieldy.

To make the contents of the ConfigMap appear as files in a directory, Kubernetes is writing out the contents of the ConfigMap to the host filesystem and then mounting the directory from the host into the container. This means that the specific directory shows up as part of the output for the mount command inside the container:

```
root@host01:~# kubectl exec -ti nginx-58bc54b5cd-4lbkq -- /bin/mount
...
/dev/sda1 on /usr/share/nginx/html type ext4 (ro,relatime)
...
```

The mount command reports that the directory */usr/share/nginx/html* is a separately mounted path coming from the host's primary disk */dev/sda1*.

We're finished with the NGINX Deployment, so go ahead and delete it:

```
root@host01:~# kubectl delete deploy nginx
deployment.apps "nginx" deleted
```

Next, let's look at how ConfigMap and Secret information is stored in a typical Kubernetes cluster so that we can see where kubelet is getting this content.

Cluster Configuration Repository

Although it's possible to run a Kubernetes cluster with different choices of configuration repository, most Kubernetes clusters use etcd as the backing store for all cluster configuration data. This includes not only the ConfigMap and Secret storage but also all of the other cluster resources and the current cluster state. Kubernetes also uses etcd to elect a leader when running in a highly available configuration with multiple API servers.

Although etcd is generally stable and reliable, node failures can lead to cases in which the etcd cluster can't reestablish itself and elect a leader. Our purpose in demonstrating etcd is not just to see how configuration data is stored, but also to provide some valuable background into an essential cluster component that an administrator might need to debug.

For all of our example clusters, etcd is installed on the same nodes as the API server, which is common in smaller clusters. In large clusters, running etcd on separate nodes to allow it to scale separately from the Kubernetes control plane is common.

To explore the contents of the etcd backing store, we'll use etcdctl, a command line client designed for controlling and troubleshooting etcd.

Using etcdctl

We need to tell etcdctl where our etcd server instance is located and how to authenticate to it. For authentication, we'll use the same client certificate that the API server uses.

For convenience, we can set environment variables that etcdctl will read, so we don't need to pass in those values via the command line with every command.

Here are the environment variables we need:

etcd-env
```
export ETCDCTL_API=3
export ETCDCTL_CACERT=/etc/kubernetes/pki/etcd/ca.crt
export ETCDCTL_CERT=/etc/kubernetes/pki/apiserver-etcd-client.crt
export ETCDCTL_KEY=/etc/kubernetes/pki/apiserver-etcd-client.key
export ETCDCTL_ENDPOINTS=https://192.168.61.11:2379
```

These variables configure etcdctl as follows:

ETCDCTL_API   Use version 3 of the etcd API. With recent versions of etcd, only version 3 is supported.

ETCDCTL_CACERT   Verify the etcd host using the provided certificate authority.

ETCDCTL_CERT   Authenticate to etcd using this certificate.

ETCDCTL_KEY   Authenticate to etcd using this private key.

ETCDCTL_ENDPOINTS   Connect to etcd at this URL. While etcd is running on all three nodes, we only need one node to talk to it.

In our example, these environment variables are conveniently stored in a script in */opt* so that we can load them for use with upcoming commands:

```
root@host01:~# source /opt/etcd-env
```

We can now use etcdctl commands to inspect the cluster and the config-uration data it's storing. Let's begin by listing only the cluster members:

```
root@host01:~# etcdctl member list
45a2b6125030fdde, started, host02, https://192.168.61.12:2380, https://192.168.61.12:2379
91007aab9448ce27, started, host03, https://192.168.61.13:2380, https://192.168.61.13:2379
bf7b9991d532ba78, started, host01, https://192.168.61.11:2380, https://192.168.61.11:2379
```

As expected, each of the control plane nodes has an instance of etcd. For a highly available configuration, we need to run at least three instances, and we need a majority of those instances to be running for the cluster to be healthy. This etcdctl command is a good first step to determine whether the cluster has any failed nodes.

As long as the cluster is healthy, we can store and retrieve data. Within etcd, information is stored in key–value pairs. Keys are specified as paths in a hierarchy. We can list the paths that have content:

```
root@host01:~# etcdctl get / --prefix --keys-only
...
/registry/configmaps/default/nginx
/registry/configmaps/default/pgsql
...
/registry/secrets/default/pgsql
...
```

The --prefix flag tells etcdctl to get all keys that start with /, whereas --keys-only ensures that we print only the keys to prevent being overwhelmed with data. Still, a lot of information is returned, including all of the various Kubernetes resource types that we've described in this book. Also included are the ConfigMaps and Secrets we just created.

Deciphering Data in etcd

We can generally rely on Kubernetes to store the correct configuration data in etcd, and we can rely on kubectl to see the current cluster configuration. However, it is useful to know how the underlying data store works in case we need to inspect the configuration when the cluster is down or in an anoma-lous state.

To save storage space and bandwidth, both etcd and Kubernetes use the protobuf library, a language-neutral binary data format. Because we're us-ing etcdctl to retrieve data from etcd, we can ask it to return data in JSON format, instead; however, that JSON data will include an embedded protobuf structure with the data from Kubernetes, so we'll need to decode that as well.

Let's begin by examining the JSON format for a Kubernetes Secret in etcd. We'll send the output through jq for formatting:

```
root@host01:~# etcdctl -w json get /registry/secrets/default/pgsql | jq
{
```

```
    "header": {
...
    },
    "kvs": [
      {
        "key": "L3J1Z21zdHJ5L3N1Y3J1dHMvZGVmYXVsdC9wZ3NxbA==",
        "create_revision": 14585,
        "mod_revision": 14585,
        "version": 1,
        "value": "azhzAAoMCgJ2MRIGU2..."
      }
    ],
    "count": 1
}
```

The kvs field has the key–value pair that Kubernetes stored for this Secret. The value for the key is a simple base64-encoded string:

```
root@host01:~# echo $(etcdctl -w json get /registry/secrets/default/pgsql \
| jq -r '.kvs[0].key' | base64 -d)
/registry/secrets/default/pgsql
```

We use jq to extract just the key's value and return it in raw format (without quotes), and then we use base64 to decode the string.

Of course, the interesting part of this key–value pair is the value because it contains the actual Kubernetes Secret. Although the value is also base64 encoded, we need to do a bit more detangling to access its information.

After we decode the base 64 value, we'll have a protobuf message. However, it has a magic prefix that Kubernetes uses to allow for future changes in the storage format. We can see that prefix if we look at the first few bytes of the decoded value:

```
root@host01:~# etcdctl -w json get /registry/secrets/default/pgsql \
| jq -r '.kvs[0].value' | base64 -d | head --bytes=10 | xxd
00000000: 6b38 7300 0a0c 0a02 7631           k8s.....v1
```

We use head to retrieve the first 10 bytes of the decoded value and then use xxd to see a hex dump. The first few bytes are k8s followed by an ASCII null character. The rest of the data, starting with byte 5, is the actual protobuf message.

Let's run one more command to actually decode the protobuf message using the protoc tool:

```
root@host01:~# etcdctl -w json get /registry/secrets/default/pgsql \
| jq -r '.kvs[0].value' | base64 -d | tail --bytes=+5 | protoc --decode_raw
1 {
  1: "v1"
  2: "Secret"
}
```

```
2 {
  1 {
    1: "pgsql"
    2: ""
    3: "default"
    4: ""
  ...
  }
  2 {
    1: "POSTGRES_PASSWORD"
    2: "supersecret"
  }
  3: "Opaque"
}
...
```

The protoc tool is mostly used for generating source code to read and write protobuf messages, but it's also handy for message decoding. As we can see, within the protobuf message is all of the data Kubernetes stores for this Secret, including the resource version and type, the resource name and namespace, and the data. This illustrates, as mentioned earlier, that access to the hosts on which Kubernetes runs provides access to all of the secret data in the cluster. Even if we configured Kubernetes to encrypt data before storing it in etcd, the encryption keys themselves need to be stored unencrypted in etcd so that the API server can use them.

Final Thoughts

With the ability to provide either environment variables or files to Pods, ConfigMaps and Secrets allow us to externalize the configuration of our containers, which makes it possible to reuse both Kubernetes resource definitions such as Deployments and container images in a variety of applications.

At the same time, we need to be aware of how Kubernetes stores this configuration data and how it provides it to containers. Anyone with the right role can access configuration data using kubectl; anyone with access to the host running the container can access it from the container runtime; and anyone with the right authentication information can access it directly from etcd. For a production cluster, it's critical that all of these mechanisms are correctly secured.

So far, we've seen how Kubernetes stores built-in cluster resource data in etcd, but Kubernetes can also store any kind of custom resource data we might choose to declare. In the next chapter, we'll explore how custom resource definitions enable us to add new behavior to a Kubernetes cluster in the form of operators.

17

CUSTOM RESOURCES AND OPERATORS

 We've seen many different resource types used in a Kubernetes cluster to run container workloads, scale them, configure them, route network traffic to them, and provide storage for them. One of the most powerful features of a Kubernetes cluster, however, is the ability to define custom resource types and integrate these into the cluster alongside all of the built-in resource types we've already seen.

Custom resource definitions enable us to define any new resource type and have the cluster track corresponding resources. We can use this capability to add complex new behavior to our cluster, such as automating the deployment of a highly available database engine, while taking advantage of all of the existing capabilities of the built-in resource types and the resource and status management of the cluster's control plane.

In this chapter, we'll see how custom resource definitions work and how we can use them to deploy Kubernetes operators, extending our cluster to take on any additional behavior we desire.

Custom Resources

In Chapter 6, we discussed how the Kubernetes API server provides a declarative API, where the primary actions are to create, read, update, and delete resources in the cluster. A declarative API has advantages for resiliency, as the cluster can track the desired state of resources and work to ensure that the cluster stays in that desired state. However, a declarative API also has a significant advantage in extensibility. The actions provided by the API server are generic enough that extending them to any kind of resource is easy.

We've already seen how Kubernetes takes advantage of this extensibility to update its API over time. Not only can Kubernetes support new versions of a resource over time, but brand-new resources with new capabilities can be added to the cluster while backward compatibility is maintained through the old resources. We saw this in Chapter 7 in our discussion on the new capabilities of version 2 of the HorizontalPodAutoscaler as well as the way that the Deployment replaced the ReplicationController.

We really see the power of this extensibility in the use of *CustomResource-Definitions*. A CustomResourceDefinition, or CRD, allows us to add any new resource type to a cluster dynamically. We simply provide the API server with the name of the new resource type and a specification that's used for validation, and immediately the API server will allow us to create, read, update, and delete resources of that new type.

CRDs are extremely useful and in widespread use. For example, the infrastructure components that are already deployed to our cluster include CRDs.

NOTE *The example repository for this book is at* https://github.com/book-of-kubernetes/examples. *See "Running Examples" on page xx for details on/line-break getting set up.*

Let's see the CRDs that are already registered with our cluster:

```
root@host01:~# kubectl get crds
NAME                                          CREATED AT
...
clusterinformations.crd.projectcalico.org        ...
...
installations.operator.tigera.io                 ...
...
volumes.longhorn.io                              ...
```

To avoid naming conflicts, the CRD name must include a group, which is commonly based on a domain name to ensure uniqueness. This group is also used to establish the path to that resource for the REST API provided by the API server. In this example, we see CRDs in the crd.projectcalico.org group and the operator.tigera.io group, both of which are used by Calico. We also see a CRD in the longhorn.io group, used by Longhorn.

These CRDs allow Calico and Longhorn to use the Kubernetes API to record configuration and status information in etcd. CRDs also simplify custom configuration. For example, as part of deploying Calico to the cluster, the automation created an Installation resource that corresponds to the `installations.operator.tigera.io` CRD:

custom
-resources.yaml
```
---
apiVersion: operator.tigera.io/v1
kind: Installation
metadata:
  name: default
spec:
  calicoNetwork:
    ipPools:
    - blockSize: 26
      cidr: 172.31.0.0/16
...
```

This configuration is the reason why we see Pods getting IP addresses in the 172.31.0.0/16 network block. This YAML file was automatically placed in */etc/kubernetes/components* and automatically applied to the cluster as part of Calico installation. On deployment, Calico queries the API server for instances of this Installation resource and configures networking accordingly.

Creating CRDs

Let's explore CRDs further by creating our own. We'll use the definition provided in Listing 17-1.

crd.yaml
```
---
apiVersion: apiextensions.k8s.io/v1
kind: CustomResourceDefinition
metadata:
❶ name: samples.bookofkubernetes.com
spec:
❷ group: bookofkubernetes.com
  versions:
❸ - name: v1
    served: true
    storage: true
    schema:
      openAPIV3Schema:
        type: object
        properties:
          spec:
            type: object
            properties:
              value:
                type: integer
❹ scope: Namespaced
```

```
      names:
❺ plural: samples
❻ singular: sample
❼ kind: Sample
      shortNames:
      ❽ - sam
```

Listing 17-1: Sample CRD

There are multiple important parts to this definition. First, several types of names are defined. The metadata name field ❶ must combine the plural name of the resource ❺ and the group ❷. These naming components will also be critical for access via the API.

Naming also includes the kind ❼, which is used in YAML files. This means that when we create specific resources based on this CRD, we will identify them with kind: Sample. Finally, we need to define how to refer to instances of this CRD on the command line. This includes the full name of the resource, specified in the singular ❻ field, as well as any shortNames ❽ that we want the command line to recognize.

Now that we've provided Kubernetes with all of the necessary names for instances based on this CRD, we can move on to how the CRD is tracked and what data it contains. The scope ❹ field tells Kubernetes whether this resource should be tracked at the Namespace level or whether resources are cluster wide. Namespaced resources receive an API path that includes the Namespace they're in, and authorization to access and modify Namespaced resources can be controlled on a Namespace-by-Namespace basis using Roles and RoleBindings, as we saw in Chapter 11.

Third, the versions section allows us to define the actual content that is valid when we create resources based on this CRD. To enable updates over time, there can be multiple versions. Each version has a schema that declares what fields are valid. In this case, we define a spec field that contains one field called value, and we declare this one field to be an integer.

There was a lot of required configuration here, so let's review the result. This CRD enables us to tell the Kubernetes cluster to track a brand new kind of resource for us, a *Sample*. Each instance of this resource (each Sample) will belong to a Namespace and will contain an integer in a value field.

Let's create this CRD in our cluster:

```
root@host01:~# kubectl apply -f /opt/crd.yaml
customresourcedefinition...k8s.io/samples.bookofkubernetes.com created
```

We can now create objects of this type and retrieve them from our cluster. Here's an example YAML definition to create a new Sample using the CRD we defined:

```
sample.yaml   ---
              apiVersion: bookofkubernetes.com/v1
              kind: Sample
              metadata:
```

```
  namespace: default
  name: somedata
spec:
  value: 123
```

We match the apiVersion and kind to our CRD and ensure that the spec is in alignment with the schema. This means that we're required to supply a field called value with an integer value.

We can now create this resource in the cluster just like any other resource:

```
root@host01:~# kubectl apply -f /opt/somedata.yaml
sample.bookofkubernetes.com/somedata created
```

There is now a Sample called somedata that is part of the default Namespace.

When we defined the CRD in Listing 17-1, we specified a plural, singular, and short name for Sample resources. We can use any of these names to retrieve the new resource:

```
root@host01:~# kubectl get samples
NAME        AGE
somedata    56s
root@host01:~# kubectl get sample
NAME        AGE
somedata    59s
root@host01:~# kubectl get sam
NAME        AGE
somedata    62s
```

Just by declaring our CRD, we've extended the behavior of our Kubernetes cluster so that it understands what samples are, and we can use that not only in the API but also in the command line tools.

This means that kubectl describe also works for Samples. We can see that Kubernetes tracks other data related to our new resource, beyond just the data we specified:

```
root@host01:~# kubectl describe sample somedata
Name:         somedata
Namespace:    default
...
API Version:  bookofkubernetes.com/v1
Kind:         Sample
Metadata:
  Creation Timestamp:  ...
...
  Resource Version:  9386
  UID:               37cc58db-179f-40e6-a9bf-fbf6540aa689
```

```
Spec:
  Value:  123
Events:   <none>
```

This additional data, including timestamps and resource versioning, is essential if we want to use the data from our CRD. To use our new resource effectively, we're going to need a software component that continually monitors for new or updated instances of our resource and takes action accordingly. We'll run this component using a regular Kubernetes Deployment that interacts with the Kubernetes API server.

Watching CRDs

With core Kubernetes resources, the control plane components communicate with the API server to take the correct action when a resource is created, updated, or deleted. For example, the controller manager includes a component that watches for changes to Services and Pods, enabling it to update the list of endpoints for each Service. The kube-proxy instance on each node then makes the necessary network routing changes to send traffic to Pods based on those endpoints.

With CRDs, the API server merely tracks the resources as they are created, updated, and deleted. It is the responsibility of some other software to monitor instances of the resource and take the correct action. To make it easy to monitor resources, the API server offers a watch action, using *long polling* to keep a connection open and continually feed events as they occur. Because a long-polling connection could be cut off at any time, the timestamp and resource version data that Kubernetes tracks for us will enable us to detect what cluster changes we've already processed when we reconnect.

We could use the API server's watch capability directly from a curl command or directly in an HTTP client, but it's much easier to use a Kubernetes client library. For this example, we'll use the Python client library to illustrate how to watch our custom resource. Here's the Python script we'll use:

watch.py
```python
#!/usr/bin/env python3
from kubernetes import client, config, watch
import json, os, sys

try:
❶ config.load_incluster_config()
except:
    print("In cluster config failed, falling back to file", file=sys.stderr)
❷ config.load_kube_config()

❸ group = os.environ.get('WATCH_GROUP', 'bookofkubernetes.com')
version = os.environ.get('WATCH_VERSION', 'v1')
namespace = os.environ.get('WATCH_NAMESPACE', 'default')
resource = os.environ.get('WATCH_RESOURCE', 'samples')
```

```
api = client.CustomObjectsApi()

w = watch.Watch()
❹ for event in w.stream(api.list_namespaced_custom_object,
        group=group, version=version, namespace=namespace, plural=resource):
❺ json.dump(event, sys.stdout, indent=2)
    sys.stdout.flush()
```

To connect to the API server, we need to load cluster configuration. This includes the location of the API server as well as the authentication information we saw in Chapter 11. If we're running in a container within a Kubernetes Pod, we'll automatically have that information available to us, so we first try to load an in-cluster config ❶. However, if we're outside a Kubernetes cluster, the convention is to use a Kubernetes config file, so we try that as a secondary option ❷.

After we've established how to talk to the API server, we use the custom objects API and a watch object to stream events related to our custom resource ❹. The stream() method takes the name of a function and the associated parameters, which we've loaded from the environment or from default values ❸. We use the list_namespaced_custom_object function because we're interested in our custom resource. All of the various list_* methods in the Python library are designed to work with watch to return a stream of add, update, and remove events rather than simply retrieving the current list of objects. As events occur, we then print them to the console in an easy-to-read format ❺.

We'll use this Python script within a Kubernetes Deployment. I've built and published a container image to run it, so this is an easy task. Here's the Deployment definition:

watch.yaml
```
---
kind: Deployment
apiVersion: apps/v1
metadata:
  name: watch
spec:
  replicas: 1
  selector:
    matchLabels:
      app: watch
  template:
    metadata:
      labels:
        app: watch
    spec:
      containers:
      - name: watch
        image: bookofkubernetes/crdwatcher:stable
      serviceAccountName: watcher
```

This Deployment will run the Python script that watches for events on instances of the Sample CRD. However, before we can create this Deployment, we need to ensure that our watcher script will have permissions to read our custom resource. The default ServiceAccount has minimal permissions, so we need to create a ServiceAccount for this Deployment and ensure that it has the rights to see our Sample custom resources.

We could bind a custom Role to our ServiceAccount to do this, but it's more convenient to take advantage of role aggregation to add our Sample custom resource to the view ClusterRole that already exists. This way, any user in the cluster with the view ClusterRole will acquire rights to our Sample custom resource.

We start by defining a new ClusterRole for our custom resource:

sample-reader.yaml
```
---
apiVersion: rbac.authorization.k8s.io/v1
kind: ClusterRole
metadata:
  name: sample-reader
  labels:
  ❶ rbac.authorization.k8s.io/aggregate-to-view: "true"
rules:
❷ - apiGroups: ["bookofkubernetes.com"]
    resources: ["samples"]
    verbs: ["get", "watch", "list"]
```

This ClusterRole gives permission to get, watch, and list our Sample custom resources ❷. We also add a label to the metadata ❶ to signal the cluster that we want these permissions to be aggregated into the view ClusterRole. Thus, rather than bind our ServiceAccount into the sample-reader ClusterRole we're defining here, we can bind our ServiceAccount into the generic view ClusterRole, giving it read-only access to all kinds of resources.

We also need to declare the ServiceAccount and bind it to the view ClusterRole:

sa.yaml
```
---
apiVersion: v1
kind: ServiceAccount
metadata:
  name: watcher
  namespace: default
---
kind: RoleBinding
apiVersion: rbac.authorization.k8s.io/v1
metadata:
  name: viewer
  namespace: default
subjects:
- kind: ServiceAccount
```

```
    name: watcher
    namespace: default
roleRef:
  kind: ClusterRole
  name: view
  apiGroup: rbac.authorization.k8s.io
```

We use a RoleBinding to limit this ServiceAccount to read-only access solely within the default Namespace. The RoleBinding binds the watcher ServiceAccount to the generic view ClusterRole. This ClusterRole will have access to our Sample custom resources thanks to the role aggregation we specified.

We're now ready to apply all of these resources, including our Deployment:

```
root@host01:~# kubectl apply -f /opt/sample-reader.yaml
clusterrole.rbac.authorization.k8s.io/sample-reader created
root@host01:~# kubectl apply -f /opt/sa.yaml
serviceaccount/watcher created
rolebinding.rbac.authorization.k8s.io/viewer created
root@host01:~# kubectl apply -f /opt/watch.yaml
deployment.apps/watch created
```

After a little while, our watcher Pod will be running:

```
root@host01:~# kubectl get pods
NAME                      READY   STATUS    RESTARTS   AGE
watch-69876b586b-jp25m    1/1     Running   0          47s
```

We can print the watcher's logs to see the events it has received from the API server:

```
root@host01:~# kubectl logs watch-69876b586b-jp25m
{
  "type": "ADDED",
  "object": {
    "apiVersion": "bookofkubernetes.com/v1",
    "kind": "Sample",
    "metadata": {
...
      "creationTimestamp": "...",
...
      "name": "somedata",
      "namespace": "default",
      "resourceVersion": "9386",
      "uid": "37cc58db-179f-40e6-a9bf-fbf6540aa689"
```

```
      },
      "spec": {
        "value": 123
      }
    },
    ...
```

Note that the watcher Pod receives an ADDED event for the somedata Sample we created, even though we created that Sample before we deployed our watcher. The API server is able to determine that our watcher has not yet retrieved this object, so it sends us an event immediately on connection as if the object were newly created, which avoids a race condition that we would otherwise be forced to handle. However, note that if the client is restarted, it will appear as a new client to the API server and will see the same ADDED event again for the same Sample. For this reason, when we implement the logic to handle our custom resources, it's essential to make the logic idempotent so that we can handle processing the same event multiple times.

Operators

What kinds of actions would we take in response to the creation, update, or deletion of custom resources, other than just logging the events to the console? As we saw when we examined the way that custom resources are used to configure Calico networking in our cluster, one use for custom resources is to configure for cluster infrastructure components such as networking and storage. But another pattern that really makes the best use of custom resources is the Kubernetes *Operator*.

The Kubernetes Operator pattern extends the behavior of the cluster to make it easier to deploy and manage specific application components. Rather than using the standard set of Kubernetes resources such as Deployments and Services directly, we simply create custom resources that are specific to the application component, and the operator manages the underlying Kubernetes resources for us.

Let's look at an example to illustrate the power of the Kubernetes Operator pattern. We'll add a Postgres Operator to our cluster that will enable us to deploy a highly available PostgreSQL database to our cluster by just adding a single custom resource.

Our automation has staged the files that we need into */etc/kubernetes/ components* and has performed some initial setup, so the only step remaining is to add the operator. The operator is a normal Deployment that will run in whatever Namespace we choose. It then will watch for custom postgresql resources and will create PostgreSQL instances accordingly.

Let's deploy the operator:

```
root@host01:~# kubectl apply -f /etc/kubernetes/components/postgres-operator.yaml
deployment.apps/postgres-operator created
```

This creates a Deployment for the operator itself, which creates a single Pod:

```
root@host01:~# kubectl get pods
NAME                                 READY   STATUS    RESTARTS   AGE
postgres-operator-5cdbff85d6-cclxf   1/1     Running   0          27s
...
```

The Pod communicates with the API server to create the CRD needed to define a PostgreSQL database:

```
root@host01:~# kubectl get crd postgresqls.acid.zalan.do
NAME                        CREATED AT
postgresqls.acid.zalan.do   ...
```

No instances of PostgreSQL are running in the cluster yet, but we can easily deploy PostgreSQL by creating a custom resource based on that CRD:

pgsql.yaml
```
---
apiVersion: "acid.zalan.do/v1"
kind: postgresql
metadata:
  name: pgsql-cluster
  namespace: default
spec:
  teamId: "pgsql"
  volume:
    size: 1Gi
    storageClass: longhorn
  numberOfInstances: 3
  users:
    dbuser:
    - superuser
    - createdb
  databases:
    defaultdb: dbuser
  postgresql:
    version: "14"
```

This custom resource tells the Postgres Operator to spawn a PostgreSQL database using server version 14, with three instances (a primary and two backups). Each instance will have persistent storage. The primary instance will be configured with the specified user and database.

The real value of the Kubernetes Operator pattern is that the YAML resource file we declare is short, simple, and clearly relates to the PostgreSQL configuration we want to see. The operator's job is to convert this information into a StatefulSet, Services, and other cluster resources as needed to operate this database.

We apply this custom resource to the cluster like any other resource:

```
root@host01:~# kubectl apply -f /opt/pgsql.yaml
postgresql.acid.zalan.do/pgsql-cluster created
```

After we apply it, the Postgres Operator will receive the add event and will create the necessary cluster resources for PostgreSQL:

```
root@host01:~# kubectl logs postgres-operator-5cdbff85d6-cclxf
... level=info msg="Spilo operator..."
...
... level=info msg="ADD event has been queued"
  cluster-name=default/pgsql-cluster pkg=controller worker=0
... level=info msg="creating a new Postgres cluster"
  cluster-name=default/pgsql-cluster pkg=controller worker=0
...
... level=info msg="statefulset
  \"default/pgsql-cluster\" has been successfully created"
  cluster-name=default/pgsql-cluster pkg=cluster worker=0
...
```

Ultimately, there will be a StatefulSet and three Pods running (in addition to the Pod for the operator itself, which is still running):

```
root@host01:~# kubectl get sts
NAME            READY   AGE
pgsql-cluster   3/3     2m39s
root@host01:~# kubectl get po
NAME                                READY   STATUS    RESTARTS   AGE
pgsql-cluster-0                     1/1     Running   0          2m40s
pgsql-cluster-1                     1/1     Running   0          2m18s
pgsql-cluster-2                     1/1     Running   0          111s
postgres-operator-5cdbff85d6-cclxf  1/1     Running   0          4m6s
...
```

It can take several minutes for all of these resources to be fully running on the cluster.

Unlike the PostgreSQL StatefulSet we created in Chapter 15, all instances in this StatefulSet are configured for high availability, as we can demonstrate by inspecting the logs for each Pod:

```
root@host01:~# kubectl logs pgsql-cluster-0
...
... INFO: Lock owner: None; I am pgsql-cluster-0
... INFO: trying to bootstrap a new cluster
...
... INFO: initialized a new cluster
...
... INFO: no action. I am (pgsql-cluster-0) the leader with the lock
root@host01:~# kubectl logs pgsql-cluster-1
```

```
...
... INFO: Lock owner: None; I am pgsql-cluster-1
... INFO: waiting for leader to bootstrap
... INFO: Lock owner: pgsql-cluster-0; I am pgsql-cluster-1
...
... INFO: no action. I am a secondary (pgsql-cluster-1) and following
    a leader (pgsql-cluster-0)
```

As we can see, the first instance, pgsql-cluster-0, has identified itself as the leader, whereas pgsql-cluster-1 has configured itself as a follower that will replicate any updates to the leader's databases.

To manage the PostgreSQL leaders and followers and enable database clients to reach the leader, the operator has created multiple Services:

```
root@host01:~# kubectl get svc
NAME                   TYPE        CLUSTER-IP     ... PORT(S)    AGE
...
pgsql-cluster          ClusterIP   10.101.80.163  ... 5432/TCP   6m52s
pgsql-cluster-config   ClusterIP   None           ... <none>     6m21s
pgsql-cluster-repl     ClusterIP   10.96.13.186   ... 5432/TCP   6m52s
```

The pgsql-cluster Service routes traffic to the primary only; the other Services are used to manage replication to the backup instances. The operator handles the task of updating the Service if the primary instance changes due to failover.

To remove the PostgreSQL database, we need to remove only the custom resource, and the Postgres Operator handles the rest:

```
root@host01:~# kubectl delete -f /opt/pgsql.yaml
postgresql.acid.zalan.do "pgsql-cluster" deleted
```

The operator detects the removal and cleans up the associated Kubernetes cluster resources:

```
root@host01:~# kubectl logs postgres-operator-5cdbff85d6-cclxf
...
... level=info msg="deletion of the cluster started"
  cluster-name=default/pgsql-cluster pkg=controller worker=0
... level=info msg="DELETE event has been queued"
  cluster-name=default/pgsql-cluster pkg=controller worker=0
...
... level=info msg="cluster has been deleted"
  cluster-name=default/pgsql-cluster pkg=controller worker=0
```

The Postgres Operator has now removed the StatefulSet, persistent storage, and other resources associated with this database cluster.

The ease with which we were able to deploy and remove a PostgreSQL database server, including multiple instances automatically configured in a highly available configuration, demonstrates the power of the Kubernetes

Operator pattern. By defining a CRD, a regular Deployment can act to extend the behavior of our Kubernetes cluster. The result is a seamless addition of new cluster capability that is fully integrated with the built-in features of the Kubernetes cluster.

Final Thoughts

CustomResourceDefinitions and Kubernetes Operators bring advanced features to a cluster, but they do so by building on the basic Kubernetes cluster functionality we've seen throughout this book. The Kubernetes API server has the extensibility to handle storage and retrieval of any type of cluster resource. As a result, we're able to define new resource types dynamically and have the cluster manage them for us.

We've seen this pattern across many of the features we've examined in Part II of this book. Kubernetes itself is built on the fundamental features of containers that we saw in Part I, and it is built so that its more advanced features are implemented by bringing together its more basic features. By understanding how those basic features work, we're better able to understand the more advanced features, even if the behavior looks a bit magical at first.

We've now worked our way through the key capabilities of Kubernetes that we need to understand to build high-quality, performant applications. Next, we'll turn our attention to ways to improve the performance and resiliency of our applications when running them in a Kubernetes cluster.

PART III

PERFORMANT KUBERNETES

Even though containers are designed to hide some of the complexity of the individual hosts in a cluster and their underlying hardware, real-world applications need tuning to get the most out of the available computing power. This tuning must be done in a way that works with the scalability and resiliency of our Kubernetes cluster so that we don't lose the advantages of dynamic scheduling and horizontal scaling. In other words, we need to provide hints to a cluster to help it schedule containers in the most efficient way.

18

AFFINITY AND DEVICES

 The ideal application exhibits complete simplicity. It is simple to design. It is simple to develop. It is simple to deploy. Its individual components are stateless, so it's easy to scale to serve as many users as needed. The individual service endpoints act as pure functions where the output is determined solely by the input. The application operates on a reasonable amount of data, with modest CPU and memory requirements, and requests and responses easily fit into a JSON structure that is at most a couple of kilobytes.

Of course, outside of tutorials, ideal applications don't exist. Real-world applications store state, both in long-term persistent storage and in caches that can be accessed quickly. Real-world applications have data security and authorization concerns, so they need to authenticate users, remember who those users are, and limit access accordingly. And many real-world applications need to access specialized hardware rather than just using idealized CPU, memory, storage, and network resources.

We want to deploy real-world applications on our Kubernetes cluster, not just idealized applications. This means that we need to make smart decisions about how to deploy the application components that move us away from an ideal world in which the cluster decides how many container instances to run and where to schedule them. However, we don't want to create an application architecture that is so rigid that we lose our cluster's scalability and resiliency. Instead, we want to work within the cluster to give it hints about how to deploy our application components while still maintaining as much flexibility as possible. In this chapter, we'll explore how our application components can enforce a little bit of coupling to other components or to specialized hardware without losing the benefits of Kubernetes.

Affinity and Anti-affinity

We'll begin by looking at the case in which we want to manage the scheduling of Pods so that we can prefer or avoid co-locating multiple containers on the same node. For example, if we have two containers that consume significant network bandwidth communicating with each other, we might want those two containers to run together on a node to reduce latency and avoid slowing down the rest of the cluster. Or, if we want to ensure that a highly available component can survive the loss of a node in the cluster, we may want to split Pod instances so they run on as many different cluster nodes as possible.

One way to co-locate containers is to combine multiple separate containers into a single Pod specification. That is a great solution for cases in which two processes are completely dependent on each other. However, it removes the ability to scale the instances separately. For example, in a web application backed by distributed storage, we might need many more instances of the web server process than we would need of the storage process. We need to place those application components in different Pods to be able to scale them separately.

In Chapter 8, when we wanted to guarantee that a Pod ran on a specified node, we added the `nodeName` field to the Pod specification to override the scheduler. That was fine for an example, but for a real application it would eliminate the scaling and failover that are essential for performance and reliability. Instead, we'll use the Kubernetes concept of *affinity* to give the scheduler hints about how to allocate Pods without forcing any Pod to run on a specific node.

Affinity allows us to restrict where a Pod should be scheduled based on the presence of other Pods. Let's look at an example using the `iperf3` network testing application.

> **CLUSTER ZONES**
>
> Pod affinity is most valuable for large clusters that span multiple networks. For example, we might deploy a Kubernetes cluster to multiple different data centers to eliminate single points of failure. In those cases, we would configure affinity based on a zone, which might contain many nodes. Here, we have only a small example cluster, so we'll treat each node in our cluster as a separate zone.

Anti-affinity

Let's start with the opposite of affinity: *anti-affinity*. Anti-affinity causes the Kubernetes scheduler to avoid co-locating Pods. In this case, we'll create a Deployment with three separate iperf3 server Pods, but we'll use anti-affinity to distribute those three Pods across our nodes so that each node gets a Pod.

NOTE *The example repository for this book is at* https://github.com/book-of -kubernetes/examples. *See "Running Examples" on page xx for details on getting set up.*

Here's the YAML definition we need:

ipf-server.yaml
```
---
kind: Deployment
apiVersion: apps/v1
metadata:
  name: iperf-server
spec:
  replicas: 3
  selector:
    matchLabels:
      app: iperf-server
  template:
    metadata:
      labels:
        app: iperf-server
    spec:
❶     affinity:
        podAntiAffinity:
❷       requiredDuringSchedulingIgnoredDuringExecution:
          - labelSelector:
              matchExpressions:
              - key: app
                operator: In
                values:
                - iperf-server
❸           topologyKey: "kubernetes.io/hostname"
```

```
      containers:
      - name: iperf
        image: bookofkubernetes/iperf3:stable
        env:
        - name: IPERF_SERVER
          value: "1"
```

This Deployment resource is typical except for the new affinity section ❶. We specify an anti-affinity rule that is based on the same label that the Deployment uses to manage its Pods. With this rule, we specify that we don't want a Pod to be scheduled into a zone that already has a Pod with the app=iperf-server label.

The topologyKey ❸ specifies the size of the zone. In this case, each node in the cluster has a different hostname label, so each node is considered to be a different zone. The anti-affinity rule therefore prevents kube-scheduler from placing a second Pod onto a node after the first Pod has already been scheduled there.

Finally, because we specified the rule using requiredDuringScheduling ❷, it's a *hard* anti-affinity rule, which means that the scheduler won't schedule the Pod unless it can satisfy the rule. It is also possible to use preferredDuring Scheduling and assign a weight to give the scheduler a hint without preventing Pod scheduling if the rule can't be satisfied.

NOTE   *The topologyKey can be based on any label that's applied on the node. Cloud-based Kubernetes distributions typically automatically apply labels to each node based on the availability zone for that node, making it easy to use anti-affinity to spread Pods across availability zones for redundancy.*

Let's apply this Deployment and see the result:

```
root@host01:~# kubectl apply -f /opt/ipf-server.yaml
deployment.apps/iperf-server created
```

As soon as our Pods are running, we see that a Pod has been allocated to each node in the cluster:

```
root@host01:~# kubectl get po -o wide
NAME                           READY   STATUS    ... NODE      ...
iperf-server-7666fb76d8-7rz8j  1/1     Running   ... host01    ...
iperf-server-7666fb76d8-cljkh  1/1     Running   ... host02    ...
iperf-server-7666fb76d8-ktk92  1/1     Running   ... host03    ...
```

Because we have three nodes and three instances, it's essentially identical to using a DaemonSet, but this approach is more flexible because it doesn't require an instance on every node. In a large cluster, we still might need only a few Pod instances to meet demand for this service. Using anti-affinity with zones based on hostnames allows us to specify the correct scale for our Deployment while still distributing each Pod to a distinct node for higher availability. And anti-affinity can be used to distribute Pods across other types of zones as well.

Before we continue, let's create a Service with which our `iperf3` clients will be able to find a server instance. Here's the YAML:

ipf-svc.yaml

```
---
kind: Service
apiVersion: v1
metadata:
  name: iperf-server
spec:
  selector:
    app: iperf-server
  ports:
  - protocol: TCP
    port: 5201
    targetPort: 5201
```

Let's apply this to the cluster:

```
root@host01:~# kubectl apply -f /opt/ipf-svc.yaml
service/iperf-server created
```

The Service picks up all three Pods:

```
root@host01:~# kubectl get ep iperf-server
NAME            ENDPOINTS                                                      ...
iperf-server    172.31.239.207:5201,172.31.25.214:5201,172.31.89.206:5201 ...
```

The `ep` is short for `endpoints`. Each Service has an associated Endpoint object that records the current Pods that are receiving traffic for the Service.

Affinity

We're now ready to deploy our `iperf3` client to use these server instances. We would like to distribute the clients to each node in the same way, but we want to make sure that each client is deployed to a node that has a server instance. To do this, we'll use both an affinity and an anti-affinity rule:

ipf-client.yaml

```
---
kind: Deployment
apiVersion: apps/v1
metadata:
  name: iperf
spec:
  replicas: 3
  selector:
    matchLabels:
      app: iperf
  template:
    metadata:
      labels:
```

```
        app: iperf
  spec:
    affinity:
      podAntiAffinity:
        requiredDuringSchedulingIgnoredDuringExecution:
        - labelSelector:
            matchExpressions:
            - key: app
              operator: In
              values:
              - iperf
          topologyKey: "kubernetes.io/hostname"
❶ podAffinity:
        requiredDuringSchedulingIgnoredDuringExecution:
        - labelSelector:
            matchExpressions:
            - key: app
              operator: In
              values:
              - iperf-server
          topologyKey: "kubernetes.io/hostname"
    containers:
    - name: iperf
      image: bookofkubernetes/iperf3:stable
```

The additional podAffinity rule ❶ ensures that each client instance is deployed to a node only if a server instance is already present. The fields in an affinity rule work the same way as an anti-affinity rule.

Let's deploy the client instances:

```
root@host01:~# kubectl apply -f /opt/ipf-client.yaml
deployment.apps/iperf created
```

After these Pods are running, we can see that they have also been distributed across all three nodes in the cluster:

```
root@host01:~# kubectl get po -o wide
NAME                        READY   STATUS    ... NODE     ...
iperf-c8d4566f-btppf        1/1     Running   ... host02   ...
iperf-c8d4566f-s6rpn        1/1     Running   ... host03   ...
iperf-c8d4566f-v9v8m        1/1     Running   ... host01   ...
...
```

It may seem like we've deployed our iperf3 client and server in a way that enables each client to talk to its local server instance, maximizing the bandwidth between client and server. However, that's not actually the case. Because the iperf-server Service is configured with all three Pods, each client Pod is connecting to a random server. As a result, our clients may not behave correctly. You might see logs indicating that a client is able to connect to a server, but you might also see client Pods in the `Error` or `CrashLoopBackOff` state, with log output like this:

```
root@host01:~# kubectl logs iperf-c8d4566f-v9v8m
iperf3: error - the server is busy running a test. try again later
iperf3 error - exiting
```

This indicates that a client is connecting to a server that already has a client connected, which means that we must have at least two clients using the same server.

Service Traffic Routing

We would like to configure our client Pods with the ability to access the local server Pod we deployed rather than a server Pod on a different node. Let's start by confirming that traffic is being routed randomly across all three server Pods. We can examine the `iptables` rules created by `kube-proxy` for this Service:

```
root@host01:~# iptables-save | grep iperf-server
...
-A KUBE-SVC-KN2SIRYEH2IFQNHK -m comment --comment "default/iperf-server"
  -m statistic --mode random --probability 0.33333333349 -j KUBE-SEP-IGBNNG5F5VCPRRWI
-A KUBE-SVC-KN2SIRYEH2IFQNHK -m comment --comment "default/iperf-server"
  -m statistic --mode random --probability 0.50000000000 -j KUBE-SEP-FDPADR4LUNHDJSPL
-A KUBE-SVC-KN2SIRYEH2IFQNHK -m comment --comment "default/iperf-server"
  -j KUBE-SEP-TZDPKVKUEZYBFM3V
```

We're running this command on *host01*, and we see that there are three separate `iptables` rules, with a random selection of the destination. This means that the `iperf3` client on *host01* could potentially be routed to any server Pod.

To fix that, we need to change the internal traffic policy configuration of our Service. By default, the policy is `Cluster`, indicating that all Pods in the cluster are valid destinations. We can change the policy to `Local`, which restricts the Service to route only to Pods on the same node.

Let's patch the Service to change this policy:

```
root@host01:~# kubectl patch svc iperf-server -p '{"spec":{"internalTrafficPolicy":"Local"}}'
service/iperf-server patched
```

The change takes effect immediately, as we can see by looking at the `iptables` rules again:

```
root@host01:~# iptables-save | grep iperf-server
...
-A KUBE-SVC-KN2SIRYEH2IFQNHK -m comment --comment "default/iperf-server" \
  -j KUBE-SEP-IGBNNG5F5VCPRRWI
```

This time, only one possible destination is configured on *host01*, as there is only one local Pod instance for this Service.

After a few minutes, the `iperf3` clients now show the kind of output we expect to see:

```
root@host01:~# kubectl logs iperf-c8d4566f-btppf
Connecting to host iperf-server, port 5201
...
[ ID] Interval           Transfer     Bitrate         Retr
[  5]   0.00-10.00  sec  8.67 GBytes  7.45 Gbits/sec  1250             sender
[  5]   0.00-10.00  sec  8.67 GBytes  7.45 Gbits/sec                   receiver
...
```

Not only are all of the clients able to connect to a unique server, but the performance is consistently high as the network connection is local to each node.

Before we go further, let's clean up these resources:

```
root@host01:~# kubectl delete svc/iperf-server deploy/iperf deploy/iperf-server
service "iperf-server" deleted
deployment.apps "iperf" deleted
deployment.apps "iperf-server" deleted
```

Although the Local internal traffic policy is useful for maximizing bandwidth between client and server, it has a major limitation. If a node does not contain a healthy Pod instance, clients on that node will not be able to access the Service at all, even if there are healthy instances on other nodes. It is critical when using this design pattern to also configure a readiness probe, as described in Chapter 13, that checks not only the Pod itself but also its Service dependencies. This way, if a Service is inaccessible on a particular node, the client on that node will also report itself to be unhealthy so that no traffic will be routed to it.

The affinity and anti-affinity capabilities we've seen allows us to give hints to the scheduler without losing the scalability and resilience we want for our application components. However, even though it might be tempting to use these features whenever we have closely connected components in our application architecture, it's probably best to allow the scheduler to work unhindered and add affinity only for cases in which real performance testing shows that it makes a significant difference.

Service routing for improved performance is an active area of development in Kubernetes. For clusters running across multiple zones, a new feature called Topology Aware Hints can enable Kubernetes to route connections to Services to the closest instances wherever possible, improving network performance while still allowing cross-zone traffic where necessary.

Hardware Resources

Affinity and anti-affinity allow us to control where Pods are scheduled but should be used only if necessary. But what about cases for which a Pod needs access to some specialized hardware that is available only on some nodes? For example, we might have processing that would benefit from a graphics processing unit (GPU), but we might limit the number of GPU nodes in the cluster to reduce cost. In that case, it is absolutely necessary to ensure that the Pod is scheduled in the right place.

As before, we could tie our Pod directly to a node using nodeName. But we might have many nodes in our cluster with the right hardware, so what we really want is to be able to tell Kubernetes about the requirement and then let the scheduler decide how to satisfy it.

Kubernetes provides two related methods to address this need: device plug-ins and extended resources. A device plug-in provides the most complete functionality, but the plug-in itself must exist for the hardware device. Meanwhile, extended resources can be used for any hardware device, but the Kubernetes cluster only tracks allocation of the resource; it doesn't actually manage its availability in the container.

Implementing a device plug-in requires close collaboration with kubelet. Similar to the storage plug-in architecture we saw in Chapter 15, a device plug-in registers itself with the kubelet instance running on a node, identifying any devices it manages. Pods identify any devices they require, and the device manager tells kubelet how to make the device available inside the container (typically by mounting the device from the host into the container's filesystem).

Because we're operating in a virtualized example cluster, we don't have any specialized hardware to demonstrate a device plug-in, but an extended resource works identically from an allocation standpoint, so we can still get a feel for the overall approach.

Let's begin by updating the cluster to indicate that one of the nodes has an example extended resource. We do this by patching the status for the node. Ideally, we could do this with kubectl patch, but unfortunately it's not possible to update the status of a resource with that command, so we're reduced to using curl to call the Kubernetes API directly. The */opt* directory has a script to make this easy. Listing 18-1 presents the relevant part.

---

add-hw.sh
```bash
#!/bin/bash
...
patch='
[
  {
    "op": "add",
    "path": "/status/capacity/bookofkubernetes.com~1special-hw",
    "value": "3"
  }
]
'
```

```
curl --cacert $ca --cert $cert --key $key \
  -H "Content-Type: application/json-patch+json" \
  -X PATCH -d "$patch" \
  https://192.168.61.10:6443/api/v1/nodes/host02/status
...
```

Listing 18-1: Special hardware script

This curl command sends a JSON patch object to update the status field for the node, adding an entry called bookofkubernetes.com/special-hw under capacity. The ~1 acts as a slash character.

Run the script to update the node:

```
root@host01:~# /opt/add-hw.sh
...
```

The response from the API server includes the entire Node resource. Let's double-check just the field we care about to make sure it applied:

```
root@host01:~# kubectl get node host02 -o json | jq .status.capacity
{
  "bookofkubernetes.com/special-hw": "3",
  "cpu": "2",
  "ephemeral-storage": "40593612Ki",
  "hugepages-2Mi": "0",
  "memory": "2035228Ki",
  "pods": "110"
}
```

The extended resource shows up alongside the standard resources for the node. We can now request this resource similar to how we request standard resources, as we saw in Chapter 14.

Here's a Pod that requests the special hardware:

```
hw.yaml  ---
         apiVersion: v1
         kind: Pod
         metadata:
           name: sleep
         spec:
           containers:
           - name: sleep
             image: busybox
             command: ["/bin/sleep", "infinity"]
             resources:
               limits:
                 bookofkubernetes.com/special-hw: 1
```

We specify the requirement for the special hardware using the resources field. The resource is either allocated or not allocated; thus, there's no distinction between requests and limits, so Kubernetes expects us to specify it using limits. When we apply this to the cluster, the Kubernetes scheduler will ensure that this Pod runs on a node that can meet this requirement:

```
root@host01:~# kubectl apply -f /opt/hw.yaml
pod/sleep created
```

As a result, the Pod ends up on host02:

```
root@host01:~# kubectl get po -o wide
NAME    READY   STATUS      ... NODE     ...
sleep   1/1     Running     ... host02   ...
```

Additionally, the node status now reflects an allocation for this extended resource:

```
root@host01:~# kubectl describe node host02
Name:                   host02
...
Allocated resources:
...
  Resource                         Requests    Limits
  --------                         --------    ------
...
  bookofkubernetes.com/special-hw  1           1
...
```

Both the available quantity of three special-hw that we specified when we added the extended resource in Listing 18-1 and the allocation of that resource to our Pod are arbitrary. The extended resource acts like a semaphore in preventing too many users from using the same resource, but we would need to add additional processing to deconflict multiple users if we really had three separate special hardware devices on the same node.

If we do try to over-allocate based on what we specified is available, the Pod won't be scheduled. We can confirm this if we try to add another Pod that needs all three of our special hardware devices:

hw3.yaml
```
---
apiVersion: v1
kind: Pod
metadata:
  name: sleep3
spec:
  containers:
  - name: sleep
    image: busybox
    command: ["/bin/sleep", "infinity"]
    resources:
```

```
        limits:
            bookofkubernetes.com/special-hw: 3
```

Let's try to add this Pod to the cluster:

```
root@host01:~# kubectl apply -f /opt/hw3.yaml
pod/sleep created
```

Because there aren't enough special hardware devices available, this Pod stays in the Pending state:

```
root@host01:~# kubectl get po -o wide
NAME    READY   STATUS      ... NODE     ...
sleep   1/1     Running     ... host02   ...
sleep3  0/1     Pending     ... <none>   ...
```

The Pod will wait for the hardware to be available. Let's delete our original Pod to free up room:

```
root@host01:~# kubectl delete pod sleep
pod/sleep deleted
```

Our new Pod will now start running:

```
root@host01:~# kubectl get po -o wide
NAME    READY   STATUS      ... NODE     ...
sleep3  1/1     Running     ... host02   ...
```

As before, the Pod was scheduled onto host02 because of the special hardware requirement.

Device drivers work identically from an allocation standpoint. In both cases, we use the limits field to identify our hardware requirements. The only difference is that we don't need to patch the node manually to record the resource, because kubelet updates the node's status automatically when the device driver registers. Additionally, kubelet invokes the device driver to perform any necessary allocation and configuration of the hardware when a container is created.

Final Thoughts

Unlike ideal applications, in the real world we often must deal with closely coupled application components and the need for specialized hardware. It's critical that we account for those application requirements without losing the flexibility and resiliency that we gain from deploying our application to a Kubernetes cluster. In this chapter, we've seen how affinity and device drivers allow us to provide hints and resource requirements to the scheduler while still allowing it the flexibility to manage the application at scale dynamically.

Scheduling is not the only concern we might have as we consider how to obtain the desired behavior and performance from real-world applications. In the next chapter, we'll see how we can shape the processing and memory allocation for our Pods through the use of quality-of-service classes.

19

TUNING QUALITY OF SERVICE

Ideally, our applications would use minimal or highly predictable processing, memory, storage, and network resources. In the real world, though, applications are "bursty," with changes in load driven by user demand, large amounts of data, or complex processing. In a Kubernetes cluster, where application components are deployed dynamically to various nodes in the cluster, uneven distribution of load across those nodes can cause performance bottlenecks.

From an application architecture standpoint, the more we can make the application components small and scalable, the more we can evenly distribute load across the cluster. Unfortunately, it's not always possible to solve performance issues with horizontal scaling. In this chapter, we'll look at how we can use resource specifications to provide hints to the cluster about how to schedule our Pods, with the goal of making application performance more predictable.

Achieving Predictability

In normal, everyday language, the term *real time* has the sense of something that happens quickly and continuously. But in computer science, we make a distinction between *real time* and *real fast* to such a degree that they are thought of as opposites. This is due to the importance of predictability.

Real-time processing is simply processing that needs to keep up with some activity that is happening in the real world. It could be anything from airplane cockpit software that needs to keep up with sensor data input and maintain up-to-date electronic flight displays, to a video streaming application that needs to receive and decode each frame of video in time to display it. In real-time systems, it is critical that we can guarantee that processing will be "fast enough" to keep up with the real-world requirement.

Fast enough is all we need. It's not necessary for the processing to go any faster than the real world, as there isn't anything else for the application to do. But even a single time interval when the processing is slower than the real world means we fall behind our inputs or outputs, leading to annoyed movie watchers—or even to crashed airplanes.

For this reason, the main goal in real-time systems is predictability. Resources are allocated based on the worst-case scenario the system will encounter, and we're willing to provide significantly more processing than necessary to have plenty of margin on that worst case. Indeed, it's common to require these types of systems to stay under 50 percent utilization of the available processing and memory, even at maximum expected load.

But whereas responsiveness is always important, most applications don't operate in a real-time environment, and this additional resource margin is expensive. For that reason, most systems try to find a balance between predictability and efficiency, which means that we are often willing to tolerate a bit of slower performance from our application components as long as it is temporary.

Quality of Service Classes

To help us balance predictability and efficiency for the containers in a cluster, Kubernetes allocates Pods to one of three different Quality of Service classes: BestEffort, Burstable, and Guaranteed. In a way, we can think of these as descriptive. BestEffort is used when we don't provide Kubernetes with any resource requirements, and it can only do its best to provide enough resources for the Pod. Burstable is used when a Pod might exceed its resource request. Guaranteed is used when we provide consistent resource requirements and our Pod is expected to stay within them. Because these classes are descriptive and are based solely on how the containers in the Pod specify their resource requirements, there is no way to specify the QoS for a Pod manually.

The QoS class is used in two ways. First, Pods in a QoS class are grouped together for Linux control groups (cgroups) configuration. As we saw in Chapter 3, cgroups are used to control resource utilization, especially processing and memory, for a group of processes, so a Pod's cgroup affects its priority in use of processing time when the system load is high. Second, if the node needs to start evicting Pods due to lack of memory resources, the QoS class affects which Pods are evicted first.

BestEffort

The simplest case is one in which we declare a Pod with no limits. In that case, the Pod is assigned to the BestEffort class. Let's create an example Pod to explore what that means.

NOTE *The example repository for this book is at* https://github.com/book-of -kubernetes/examples. *See "Running Examples" on page xx for details on getting set up.*

Here's the Pod definition:

best-effort.yaml
```
---
apiVersion: v1
kind: Pod
metadata:
  name: best-effort
spec:
  containers:
  - name: best-effort
    image: busybox
    command: ["/bin/sleep", "infinity"]
  nodeName: host01
```

This definition includes no resources field at all, but the QoS class would be the same if we included a resources field with requests but no limits.

We use nodeName to force this Pod onto host01 so that we can observe how its resource use is configured. Let's apply it to to the cluster:

```
root@host01:~# kubectl apply -f /opt/best-effort.yaml
pod/best-effort created
```

After the Pod is running, we can look at its details to see that it has been allocated to the BestEffort QoS class:

```
root@host01:~# kubectl get po best-effort -o json | jq .status.qosClass
"BestEffort"
```

We can use the cgroup-info script we saw in Chapter 14 to see how the QoS class affects the cgroup configuration for containers in the Pod:

```
root@host01:~# /opt/cgroup-info best-effort

Container Runtime
-----------------
Pod ID: 205...
```

```
Cgroup path: /kubepods.slice/kubepods-besteffort.slice/kubepods-...

CPU Settings
------------
CPU Shares: 2
CPU Quota (us): -1 per 100000

Memory Settings
---------------
Limit (bytes): 9223372036854771712
```

The Pod is effectively unlimited in CPU and memory usage. However, the Pod's cgroup is under the *kubepods-besteffort.slice* path, reflecting its allocation to the BestEffort QoS class. This allocation has an immediate effect on its CPU priority, as we can see when we compare the cpu.shares allocated to the BestEffort class compared to the Burstable class:

```
root@host01:~# cat /sys/fs/cgroup/cpu/kubepods.slice/kubepods-besteffort.slice/cpu.shares
2
root@host01:~# cat /sys/fs/cgroup/cpu/kubepods.slice/kubepods-burstable.slice/cpu.shares
1157
```

As we saw in Chapter 14, these values are relative, so this configuration means that when our system's processing load is high, containers in Burstable Pods are going to be allocated more than 500 times the processor share that containers in BestEffort Pods receive. This value is based on the number of Pods that are already in the BestEffort and Burstable QoS classes, including the various cluster infrastructure components already running on *host01*, thus you might see a slightly different value.

The *kubepods.slice* cgroup sits at the same level as cgroups for user and system processes, so when the system is loaded it gets an approximately equal share of processing time as those other cgroups. Based on the *cpu .shares* identified within the *kubepods.slice* cgroup, BestEffort Pods are receiving less than 1 percent of the total share of processing compared to Burstable Pods, even without considering any processor time allocated to Guaranteed Pods. This means that BestEffort Pods receive almost no processor time when the system is loaded, so they should be used only for background processing that can run when the cluster is idle. In addition, because Pods are placed in the BestEffort class only if they have no limits specified, they cannot be created in a Namespace with limit quotas. So most of our application Pods will be in one of the other two QoS classes.

Burstable

Pods are placed in the Burstable class if they specify both requests and limits and if those two specifications are different. As we saw in Chapter 14, the requests specification is used for scheduling purposes, whereas the limits specification is used for runtime enforcement. In other words, Pods in this situation can have "bursts" of resource utilization above their requests level, but they cannot exceed their limits.

Let's look at an example:

```
---
apiVersion: v1
kind: Pod
metadata:
  name: burstable
spec:
  containers:
  - name: burstable
    image: busybox
    command: ["/bin/sleep", "infinity"]
    resources:
      requests:
        memory: "64Mi"
        cpu: "50m"
      limits:
        memory: "128Mi"
        cpu: "100m"
    nodeName: host01
```

This Pod definition supplies both requests and limits resource requirements, and they are different, so we should expect this Pod to be placed in the Burstable class.

Let's apply this Pod to the cluster:

```
root@host01:~# kubectl apply -f /opt/burstable.yaml
pod/burstable created
```

Next, let's verify that it was assigned to the Burstable QoS class:

```
root@host01:~# kubectl get po burstable -o json | jq .status.qosClass
"Burstable"
```

Indeed, the cgroup configuration follows the QoS class and the limits we specified:

```
root@host01:~# /opt/cgroup-info burstable

Container Runtime
-----------------
Pod ID: 8d0...
Cgroup path: /kubepods.slice/kubepods-burstable.slice/kubepods-...

CPU Settings
------------
CPU Shares: 51
CPU Quota (us): 10000 per 100000
```

```
Memory Settings
---------------
Limit (bytes): 134217728
```

The limits specified for this Pod were used to set both a CPU limit and a memory limit. Also, as we expect, this Pod's cgroup is placed within *kubepods-burstable.slice*.

Adding another Pod to the Burstable QoS class has caused Kubernetes to rebalance the allocation of processor time:

```
root@host01:~# cat /sys/fs/cgroup/cpu/kubepods.slice/kubepods-besteffort.slice/cpu.shares
2
root@host01:~# cat /sys/fs/cgroup/cpu/kubepods.slice/kubepods-burstable.slice/cpu.shares
1413
```

The result is that Pods in the Burstable QoS class now show a value of 1413 for *cpu.shares*, whereas Pods in the BestEffort class still show 2. This means that the relative processor share under load is now 700 to 1 in favor of Pods in the Burstable class. Again, you may see slightly different values based on how many infrastructure Pods Kubernetes has allocated to host01.

Because Burstable Pods are scheduled based on requests but cgroup runtime enforcement is based on limits, a node's processor and memory resources can be overcommitted. It works fine as long as the Pods on a node balance out one another so that the average utilization matches the requests. It becomes a problem if the average utilization exceeds the requests. In that case, Pods will see their CPU throttled and may even be evicted if memory becomes scarce, as we saw in Chapter 10.

Guaranteed

If we want to increase predictability for the processing and memory available to a Pod, we can place it in the Guaranteed QoS class by giving the requests and limits equal settings. Here's an example:

guaranteed.yaml
```
---
apiVersion: v1
kind: Pod
metadata:
  name: guaranteed
spec:
  containers:
  - name: guaranteed
    image: busybox
    command: ["/bin/sleep", "infinity"]
    resources:
      limits:
        memory: "64Mi"
```

```
      cpu: "50m"
  nodeName: host01
```

In this example, only `limits` is specified given that Kubernetes automatically sets the `requests` to match the `limits` if `requests` is missing.

Let's apply this to the cluster:

```
root@host01:~# kubectl apply -f /opt/guaranteed.yaml
pod/guaranteed created
```

After the Pod is running, verify the QoS class:

```
root@host01:~# kubectl get po guaranteed -o json | jq .status.qosClass
"Guaranteed"
```

The cgroups configuration looks a little different:

```
root@host01:~# /opt/cgroup-info guaranteed

Container Runtime
-----------------
Pod ID: 146...
Cgroup path: /kubepods.slice/kubepods-...

CPU Settings
------------
CPU Shares: 51
CPU Quota (us): 5000 per 100000

Memory Settings
---------------
Limit (bytes): 67108864
```

Rather than place these containers into a separate directory, containers in the Guaranteed QoS class are placed directly in *kubepods.slice*. Putting them in this location has the effect of privileging containers in Guaranteed Pods when the system is loaded because those containers receive their CPU shares individually rather than as a class.

QoS Class Eviction

The privileged treatment of Pods in the Guaranteed QoS class extends to Pod eviction as well. As described in Chapter 3, cgroup enforcement of memory limits is handled by the OOM killer. The OOM killer also runs when a node is completely out of memory. To help the OOM killer choose which containers to terminate, Kubernetes sets the `oom_score_adj` parameter based on the QoS class of the Pod. This parameter can have a value from −1000 to 1000. The higher the number, the more likely the OOM killer will choose a process to be killed.

The oom_score_adj value is recorded in */proc* for each process. The automation has added a script called *oom-info* to retrieve it for a given Pod. Let's check the values for the Pods in each QoS class:

```
root@host01:~# /opt/oom-info best-effort
OOM Score Adjustment: 1000
root@host01:~# /opt/oom-info burstable
OOM Score Adjustment: 968
root@host01:~# /opt/oom-info guaranteed
OOM Score Adjustment: -997
```

Pods in the BestEffort QoS class have the maximum adjustment of 1000, so they would be targeted first by the OOM killer. Pods in the Burstable QoS class have a score calculated based on the amount of memory specified in the requests field, as a percentage of the node's total memory capacity. This value will therefore be different for every Pod but will always be between 2 and 999. Thus, Pods in the Burstable QoS class will always be second in priority for the OOM killer. Meanwhile, Pods in the Guaranteed QoS class are set close to the minimum value, in this case −997, so they are protected from the OOM killer as much as possible.

Of course, as mentioned in Chapter 3, the OOM killer terminates a process immediately, so it is an extreme measure. When memory on a node is low but not yet exhausted, Kubernetes attempts to evict Pods to reclaim memory. This eviction is also prioritized based on the QoS class. Pods in the BestEffort class and Pods in the Burstable class that are using more than their requests value (high-use Burstable) are the first to be evicted, followed by Pods in the Burstable class that are using less than their requests value (low-use Burstable) and Pods in the Guaranteed class.

Before moving on, let's do some cleanup:

```
root@host01:~# kubectl delete po/best-effort po/burstable po/guaranteed
pod "best-effort" deleted
pod "burstable" deleted
pod "guaranteed" deleted
```

Now we can have a fresh start when we look at Pod priorities later in this chapter.

Choosing a QoS Class

Given this prioritization in processing time and eviction priority, it might be tempting to place all Pods in the Guaranteed QoS class. And there are application components for which this is a viable strategy. As described in Chapter 7, we can configure a HorizontalPodAutoscaler to make new Pod instances automatically if the existing instances are consuming a significant percentage of their allocated resources. This means that we can request a reasonable limits value for Pods in a Deployment and allow the cluster to automatically scale the Deployment if we're getting too close to the limit across those Pods. If the cluster is running in a cloud environment, we can even extend autoscaling to the node level, dynamically creating new cluster nodes when load is high and reducing the number of nodes when the cluster is idle.

Using only Guaranteed Pods together with autoscaling sounds great, but it assumes that our application components are easily scalable. It also only works well when our application load consists of many small requests, so that an increase in load primarily means we are handing similar-sized requests from more users. If we have application components that periodically handle large or complex requests, we must set the limits for those components to accommodate the worst-case scenario. Given that Pods in the Guaranteed QoS class have requests equal to limits, our cluster will need enough resources to handle this worst-case scenario, or we won't even be able to schedule our Pods. This results in a cluster that is largely idle unless the system is under its maximum load. Similarly, if we have scalability limitations such as dependency on specialized hardware, we might have a natural limit on the number of Pods we can create for a component, forcing each Pod to have more resources to handle its share of the overall load.

For this reason, it makes sense to balance the use of the Guaranteed and Burstable QoS classes for our Pods. Any Pods that have consistent load, or that can feasibly be scaled horizontally to meet additional demand, should be in the Guaranteed class. Pods that are harder to scale, or need to handle a mix of large and small workloads, should be in the Burstable class. These Pods should specify their requests based on their average utilization, and specify limits based on their worst-case scenario. Specifying resource requirements in this way will ensure that the cluster's expected performance margin can be monitored by simply comparing the allocated resources to the cluster capacity. Finally, if a large request causes multiple application components to run at their worst-case utilization simultaneously, it may be worth running performance tests and exploring anti-affinity, as described in Chapter 18, to avoid overloading a single node.

Pod Priority

In addition to using hints to help the Kubernetes cluster understand how to manage Pods when the system is highly loaded, it is possible to tell the cluster directly to give some Pods a higher priority than others. This higher priority applies during Pod eviction, as Pods will be evicted in priority order within their QoS class. It also applies during scheduling because the Kubernetes scheduler will evict Pods if necessary to be able to schedule a higher-priority Pod.

Pod priority is a simple numeric field; higher numbers are higher priority. Numbers greater than one billion are reserved for critical system Pods. To assign a priority to a Pod, we must create a *PriorityClass* resource first. Here's an example:

essential.yaml ---
```
apiVersion: scheduling.k8s.io/v1
kind: PriorityClass
```

```
metadata:
  name: essential
value: 999999
```

Let's apply this to the cluster:

```
root@host01:~# kubectl apply -f /opt/essential.yaml
priorityclass.scheduling.k8s.io/essential created
```

Now that this PriorityClass has been defined, we can apply it to Pods. However, let's first create a large number of low-priority Pods through which we can see Pods being preempted. We'll use this Deployment:

```
---
kind: Deployment
apiVersion: apps/v1
metadata:
  name: lots
spec:
  replicas: 1000
  selector:
    matchLabels:
      app: lots
  template:
    metadata:
      labels:
        app: lots
    spec:
      containers:
      - name: sleep
        image: busybox
        command: ["/bin/sleep", "infinity"]
        resources:
          limits:
            memory: "64Mi"
            cpu: "250m"
```

This is a basic Deployment that runs sleep and doesn't request very much memory or CPU, but it does set replicas to 1000, so we're asking our Kubernetes cluster to create 1,000 Pods. The example cluster isn't large enough to deploy 1,000 Pods, both because we don't have sufficient resources to meet the specification and because a node is limited to 110 Pods by default. Still, let's apply it to the cluster, as shown in Listing 19-1, and the scheduler will create as many Pods as it can:

```
root@host01:~# kubectl apply -f /opt/lots.yaml
deployment.apps/lots created
```

Listing 19-1: Deploy lots of Pods

Let's describe the Deployment to see how things are going:

```
root@host01:~# kubectl describe deploy lots
Name:                  lots
Namespace:             default
...
Replicas:              1000 desired ... | 7 available | 993 unavailable
...
```

We managed to get only seven Pods in our example cluster, given the number of Pods already running for cluster infrastructure components. Unfortunately, that's all the Pods we'll get:

```
root@host01:~# kubectl describe node host01
Name:               host01
  (Total limits may be over 100 percent, i.e., overcommitted.)
Allocated resources:
...
  Resource           Requests      Limits
  --------           --------      ------
  cpu              ❶ 1898m (94%)   768m (38%)
  memory             292Mi (15%)   192Mi (10%)
  ephemeral-storage  0 (0%)        0 (0%)
  hugepages-2Mi      0 (0%)        0 (0%)
...
```

The data for host01 shows that we've allocated 94 percent of the available CPU ❶. But each of our Pods is requesting 250 millicores, so there isn't enough capacity remaining to schedule another Pod on this node. The other two nodes are in a similar situation, with insufficient CPU room to schedule any more Pods. Still, the cluster is performing just fine. We've theoretically allocated all of the processing power, but those containers are just running sleep, and as such, they aren't actually using much CPU.

Also, it's important to remember that the requests field is used for scheduling, so even though we have a number of infrastructure BestEffort Pods that specify requests but no limits and we have plenty of Limits capacity on this node, we still don't have any room for scheduling new Pods. Only Limits can be overcommitted, not Requests.

Because we have no more CPU to allocate to Pods, the rest of the Pods in our Deployment are stuck in a Pending state:

```
root@host01:~# kubectl get po | grep -c Pending
993
```

All 993 of these Pods have the default pod priority of 0. As a result, when we create a new Pod using the essential PriorityClass, it will jump to the front of the scheduling queue. Not only that, but the cluster will evict Pods as necessary to enable it to be scheduled.

Here's the Pod definition:

needed.yaml
```
---
apiVersion: v1
kind: Pod
metadata:
  name: needed
spec:
  containers:
  - name: needed
    image: busybox
    command: ["/bin/sleep", "infinity"]
    resources:
      limits:
        memory: "64Mi"
        cpu: "250m"
  priorityClassName: essential
```

The key difference here is the specification of the priorityClassName, matching the PriorityClass we created. Let's apply this to the cluster:

```
root@host01:~# kubectl apply -f /opt/needed.yaml
pod/needed created
```

It will take the cluster a little time to evict another Pod so that this one can be scheduled, but after a minute or so it will start running:

```
root@host01:~# kubectl get po needed
NAME     READY   STATUS    RESTARTS   AGE
needed   1/1     Running   0          36s
```

To allow this to happen, one of the Pods from the lots Deployment we created in Listing 19-1 had to be evicted:

```
root@host01:~# kubectl describe deploy lots
Name:                lots
Namespace:           default
CreationTimestamp:   Fri, 01 Apr 2022 19:20:52 +0000      .
Labels:              <none>
Annotations:         deployment.kubernetes.io/revision: 1
Selector:            app=lots
Replicas:            1000 desired ... | ❶ 6 available | 994 unavailable
```

We're now down to only six Pods available in the Deployment ❶, as one Pod was evicted. It's worth noting that being in the Guaranteed QoS class did not prevent this Pod from being evicted. The Guaranteed QoS class gets priority for evictions caused by node resource usage, but not for eviction caused by the scheduler finding room for a higher-priority Pod.

Of course, the ability to specify a higher priority for a Pod, resulting in the eviction of other Pods, is powerful and should be used sparingly. Normal users do not have the ability to create a new PriorityClass, and administrators can apply a quota to limit the use of a PriorityClass in a given Namespace, effectively limiting normal users from creating high-priority Pods.

Final Thoughts

Deploying an application to Kubernetes so that it is performant and reliable requires an understanding of the application architecture and of the normal and worst-case load for each component. Kubernetes QoS classes allow us to shape the way that Pods are deployed to nodes to achieve a balance of predictability and efficiency in the use of resources. Additionally, both QoS classes and Pod priorities allow us to provide hints to the Kubernetes cluster so the deployed applications degrade gracefully as the load on the cluster becomes too high.

In the next chapter, we'll bring together the ideas we've seen on how to best use the features of a Kubernetes cluster to deploy performant, resilient applications. We'll also explore how we can monitor those applications and respond automatically to changes in behavior.

20

APPLICATION RESILIENCY

Over the course of this book, we've seen how containers and Kubernetes enable scalable, resilient applications. Using containers, we can encapsulate application components so that processes are isolated from one another, have separate virtualized network stacks, and a separate filesystem. Each container can then be rapidly deployed without interfering with other containers. When we add Kubernetes as a container orchestration layer on top of the container runtime, we are able to include many separate hosts into a single cluster, dynamically scheduling containers across available cluster nodes with automatic scaling and failover, distributed networking, traffic routing, storage, and configuration.

All of the container and Kubernetes features we've seen in this book work together to provide the necessary infrastructure to deploy scalable, resilient applications, but it's up to us to configure our applications correctly to take advantage of what the infrastructure provides. In this chapter, we'll take another look at the todo application we deployed in Chapter 1. This time, however, we'll deploy it across multiple nodes in a Kubernetes cluster, eliminating single points of failure and taking advantage of the key features that Kubernetes has to offer. We'll also explore how to monitor the performance of our Kubernetes cluster and our deployed application so that we can identify performance issues before they lead to downtime for our users.

Example Application Stack

In Chapter 1, we deployed todo onto a Kubernetes cluster running k3s from Rancher. We already had some amount of scalability and failover available. The web layer was based on a Deployment, so we were able to scale the number of server instances with a single command. Our Kubernetes cluster was monitoring those instances so failed instances could be replaced. However, we still had some single points of failure. We had not yet introduced the idea of a highly available Kubernetes control plane, so we chose to run k3s only in a single-node configuration. Additionally, even though we used a Deployment for our PostgreSQL database, it was lacking in any of the necessary configuration for high availability. In this chapter, we'll see the details necessary to correct those limitations, and we'll also take advantage of the many other Kubernetes features we've learned.

Database

Let's begin by deploying a highly available PostgreSQL database. Chapter 17 demonstrated how the Kubernetes Operator design pattern uses CustomResourceDefinitions to extend the behavior of a cluster, making it easy to package and deploy advanced functionality. We'll use the Postgres Operator we introduced in that chapter to deploy our database.

NOTE *The example repository for this book is at* https://github.com/book-of
-kubernetes/examples. *See "Running Examples" on page xx for details on getting set up. This chapter uses a larger six-node cluster to provide room for the application and all the monitoring components that we'll be deploying. See the README.md file for this chapter for more information.*

The automation for this chapter has already deployed the Postgres Operator together with its configuration. You can inspect the Postgres Operator and its configuration by looking at the files in */etc/kubernetes/components*. The operator is running in the todo Namespace, where the todo application is also deployed. Many operators prefer to run in their own Namespace and operate across the cluster, but the Postgres Operator is designed to be deployed directly into the Namespace where the database will reside.

Because we're using the Postgres Operator, we can create a highly available PostgreSQL database by applying a custom resource to the cluster:

database.yaml
```
---
apiVersion: "acid.zalan.do/v1"
kind: postgresql
```

```
  metadata:
❶ name: todo-db
  spec:
    teamId: todo
    volume:
      size: 1Gi
      storageClass: longhorn
❷ numberOfInstances: 3
    users:
❸   todo:
      - superuser
      - createdb
    databases:
❹   todo: todo
    postgresql:
      version: "14"
```

All of the files shown in this walkthrough have been staged to the */etc/kubernetes/todo* directory so that you can explore them and experiment with changes. The todo application is automatically deployed, but it can take several minutes for all the components to reach a healthy state.

The Postgres Operator has the job of creating the Secrets, StatefulSets, Services, and other core Kubernetes resources needed to deploy PostgreSQL. We're only required to supply the configuration it should use. We start by identifying the name for this database, todo-db ❶, which will be used as the name of the primary Service that we'll use to connect to the primary database instance, so we'll see this name again in the application configuration.

We want a highly available database, so let's specify three instances ❷. We also ask the Postgres Operator to create a todo user ❸ and to create a todo database with the todo user as the owner ❹. This way, our database is already set up and we only need to populate the tables to store the application data.

We can verify that the database is running in the cluster:

```
root@host01:~# kubectl -n todo get sts
NAME       READY   AGE
todo-db    3/3     6m1s
```

The todo-db StatefulSet has three Pods, all of which are ready.

Because the Postgres Operator is using a StatefulSet, as we saw in Chapter 15, a PersistentVolumeClaim is allocated for the database instances as they are created:

```
root@host01:~# kubectl -n todo get pvc
NAME                STATUS   ... CAPACITY   ACCESS MODES   STORAGECLASS   AGE
pgdata-todo-db-0    Bound    ... 1Gi        RWO            longhorn       10m
pgdata-todo-db-1    Bound    ... 1Gi        RWO            longhorn       8m44s
pgdata-todo-db-2    Bound    ... 1Gi        RWO            longhorn       7m23s
```

These PersistentVolumeClaims will be reused if one of the database instance Pods fails and must be re-created, and the Longhorn storage engine is distributing its storage across our entire cluster, so the database will retain the application data even if we have a node failure.

Note that when we requested the Postgres Operator to create a todo user, we didn't specify a password. For security, the Postgres Operator automatically generates a password. This password is placed into a Secret based on the name of the user and the name of the database. We can see the Secret created for the todo user:

```
root@host01:~# kubectl -n todo get secret
NAME                                                   TYPE      DATA   AGE
...
todo.todo-db.credentials.postgresql.acid.zalan.do      Opaque    2      8m30s
```

We'll need to use this information to configure the application so that it can authenticate to the database.

Before we look at the application configuration, let's inspect the Service that the Postgres Operator created:

```
root@host01:~# kubectl -n todo get svc todo-db
NAME      TYPE        CLUSTER-IP       EXTERNAL-IP   PORT(S)     AGE
todo-db   ClusterIP   10.110.227.34    <none>        5432/TCP    59m
```

This is a `ClusterIP` Service, meaning that it is reachable from anywhere inside the cluster but is not externally exposed. That matches perfectly with what we want for our application, as our web service component is the only user-facing component and thus the only one that will be exposed outside the cluster.

Application Deployment

All of our application's data is in the PostgreSQL database, so the web server layer is stateless. For this stateless component, we'll use a Deployment and set up automatic scaling.

The Deployment has a lot of information, so let's look at it step by step. To see the entire Deployment configuration and get a sense of how it all fits together, you can look at the file */etc/kubernetes/todo/application.yaml* on any of the cluster nodes.

The first section tells Kubernetes that we're creating a Deployment:

```
---
kind: Deployment
apiVersion: apps/v1
metadata:
  name: todo
  labels:
    app: todo
```

This part is simple because we're only specifying the metadata for the Deployment. Note that we don't include the `namespace` in the metadata. Instead, we provide it to Kubernetes directly when we apply this Deployment to the cluster. This way, we can reuse the same Deployment YAML for development, test, and production versions of this application, keeping each in a separate Namespace to avoid conflict.

The `label` field is purely informational, though it also provides a way for us to query the cluster for all of the resources associated with this application by matching on the label.

The next part of the Deployment YAML specifies how the cluster should handle updates:

```
spec:
  replicas: 3
  strategy:
    type: RollingUpdate
    rollingUpdate:
      maxUnavailable: 30%
      maxSurge: 50%
```

The `replicas` field tells Kubernetes how many instances to create initially. The autoscaling configuration will automatically adjust this.

The `strategy` field allows us to configure this Deployment for updates without any application downtime. We can choose either `RollingUpdate` or `Recreate` as a strategy. With `Recreate`, when the Deployment changes, all of the existing Pods are terminated, and then the new Pods are created. With `RollingUpdate`, new Pods are immediately created, and old Pods are kept running to ensure that this application component can continue functioning while it is updated.

We can control how the rolling update operates using the `maxUnavailable` and `maxSurge` fields, which we can specify either as integer numbers or as a percentage of the current number of replicas. In this case, we specified 30 percent for `maxUnavailable`, so the Deployment will throttle the rolling update process to prevent us from falling below 70 percent of the current number of replicas. Additionally, because we set `maxSurge` at 50 percent, the Deployment will immediately start new Pods until the number of Pods that are running or in the creation process reaches 150 percent of the current number of replicas.

The `RollingUpdate` strategy is the default, and by default, both `maxSurge` and `maxUnavailable` are 25 percent. Most Deployments should use the `RollingUpdate` strategy unless it is absolutely necessary to use `Recreate`.

The next part of the Deployment YAML links the Deployment to its Pods:

```
  selector:
    matchLabels:
      app: todo
  template:
```

```
metadata:
  labels:
    app: todo
```

The selector and the labels in the Pod metadata must match. As we saw in Chapter 7, the Deployment uses the selector to track its Pods.

With this part, we've now begun defining the template for the Pods this Deployment creates. The rest of the Deployment YAML completes the Pod template, which consists entirely of configuration for the single container this Pod runs:

```
spec:
  containers:
  - name: todo
    image: bookofkubernetes/todo:stable
```

The container name is mostly informational, though it is essential for Pods with multiple containers so that we can choose a container when we need to retrieve logs and use exec to run commands. The image tells Kubernetes what container image to retrieve in order to run this container.

The next section of the Pod template specifies the environment variables for this container:

```
env:
- name: NODE_ENV
  value: production
- name: PREFIX
  value: /
- name: PGHOST
  value: todo-db
- name: PGDATABASE
  value: todo
- name: PGUSER
  valueFrom:
    secretKeyRef:
      name: todo.todo-db.credentials.postgresql.acid.zalan.do
      key: username
      optional: false
- name: PGPASSWORD
  valueFrom:
    secretKeyRef:
      name: todo.todo-db.credentials.postgresql.acid.zalan.do
      key: password
      optional: false
```

Some of the environment variables have static values; they're expected to remain the same for all uses of this Deployment. The PGHOST environment variable matches the name of the PostgreSQL database. The Postgres Operator has created a Service with the name todo-db in the todo Namespace where these Pods will run, so the Pods are able to resolve this hostname to the Service IP address. Traffic destined for the Service IP address is then routed to the primary PostgreSQL instance using the `iptables` configuration we saw in Chapter 9.

The final two variables provide the credentials for the application to authenticate to the database. We're using the ability to fetch configuration from a Secret and provide it as an environment variable to a container, similar to what we saw in Chapter 16. However, in this case, we need the environment variable to have a different name from the key name in the Secret, so we use a slightly different syntax that allows us to specify each variable name separately.

Finally, we declare the resource requirements of this container and the port it exposes:

```
resources:
  requests:
    memory: "128Mi"
    cpu: "50m"
  limits:
    memory: "128Mi"
    cpu: "50m"
ports:
- name: web
  containerPort: 5000
```

The `ports` field in a Pod is purely informational; the actual traffic routing will be configured in the Service.

Within the `resources` field, we set the `requests` and `limits` to be the same for this container. As we saw in Chapter 19, this means that Pod will be placed in the `Guaranteed` Quality of Service class. The web service component is stateless and easy to scale, so it makes sense to use a relatively low CPU limit, in this case, 50 millicores, or 5 percent of a core, and rely on the autoscaling to create new instances if the load becomes high.

Pod Autoscaling

To automatically scale the Deployment to match the current load, we use a HorizontalPodAutoscaler, as we saw in Chapter 7. Here's the configuration for the autoscaler:

scaler.yaml
```
---
apiVersion: autoscaling/v2
kind: HorizontalPodAutoscaler
metadata:
  name: todo
  labels:
    app: todo
spec:
```

```
scaleTargetRef:
  apiVersion: apps/v1
  kind: Deployment
  name: todo
minReplicas: 3
maxReplicas: 10
metrics:
- type: Resource
  resource:
    name: cpu
    target:
      type: Utilization
      averageUtilization: 50
```

As we did in our earlier example, we apply a label to this resource purely for informational purposes. Three key configuration items are necessary for this autoscaler. First, the scaleTargetRef specifies that we want to scale the todo Deployment. Because this autoscaler is deployed to the todo Namespace, it finds the correct Deployment to scale.

Second, we specify a range for minReplicas and maxReplicas. We choose 3 as the minimum number of replicas, as we want to make sure the application is resilient even if we have a Pod failure. For simplicity, we didn't apply the anti-affinity configuration we saw in Chapter 18, but this may also be a good practice to avoid having all of the instances on a single node. We choose a maximum number of replicas based on the size of our cluster; for a production application, we would measure our application load and choose based on the highest load we expect to handle.

Third, we need to specify the metric that the autoscaler will use to decide how many replicas are needed. We base this autoscaler on CPU utilization. If the average utilization across the Pods is greater than 50 percent of the Pod's requests, the Deployment will be scaled up. We set the requests at 50 millicores, so this means that an average utilization greater than 25 millicores will cause the autoscaler to increase the number of replicas.

To retrieve the average CPU utilization, the autoscaler relies on a cluster infrastructure component that retrieves metrics data from the kubelet service running on each node and exposes that metrics data via an API. For this chapter, we have some extra cluster monitoring functionality to demonstrate, so the automation has skipped the regular metrics server component we described in Chapter 6. We'll deploy an alternative later in this chapter.

Application Service

The final cluster resource for our application is the Service. Listing 20-1 presents the definition we're using for this chapter.

service.yaml
```
---
kind: Service
apiVersion: v1
```

```
metadata:
  name: todo
  labels:
    app: todo
spec:
  type: NodePort
  selector:
    app: todo
  ports:
  - name: web
    protocol: TCP
    port: 5000
    nodePort: 5000
```

Listing 20-1: Todo Service

We use the same `selector` that we saw in the Deployment to find the
Pods that will receive traffic sent to this Service. As we saw in Chapter 9, the
`ports` field of a Service is essential because `iptables` traffic routing rules are
configured only for the ports we identify. In this case, we declare the `port` to
be 5000 and don't declare a `targetPort`, so this Service will send to port 5000
on the Pods, which matches the port on which our web server is listening.
We also configure a `name` on this port, which will be important later when we
configure monitoring.

For this chapter, we're exposing our application Service using `NodePort`,
which means that all of our cluster's nodes will be configured to route traffic
to the Service that is sent to the `nodePort` for any host interface. Thus, we can
access port 5000 on any of our cluster's nodes and we'll be routed to our
application:

```
root@host01:~# curl -v http://host01:5000/
...
< HTTP/1.1 200 OK
< X-Powered-By: Express
...
<html lang="en" data-framework="backbonejs">
    <head>
        <meta charset="utf-8">
        <title>Todo-Backend client</title>
        <link rel="stylesheet" href="css/vendor/todomvc-common.css">
        <link rel="stylesheet" href="css/chooser.css">
    </head>
...
</html>
```

This Service traffic routing works on any host interface, so the todo application can be accessed from outside the cluster as well. The URL is different depending on whether you're using the Vagrant or Amazon Web

Services configuration, so the automation for this chapter includes a message with the URL to use.

NODEPORT, NOT INGRESS

When we deployed todo in Chapter 1, we exposed the Service using an Ingress. The Ingress, as we saw in Chapter 9, consolidates multiple Services such that they can all be exposed outside the cluster without requiring each Service to have a separate externally routable IP address. We'll expose a monitoring service later in this chapter, so we have multiple Services to expose outside the cluster. However, because we're working with an example cluster on a private network, we don't have the underlying network infrastructure available to use an Ingress to its full potential. By using a NodePort instead, we're able to expose multiple Services outside the cluster in a way that works well with both the Vagrant and Amazon Web Services configurations.

We've now looked all of the components in the todo application, using what we've learned in this book to eliminate single points of failure and maximize scalability.

You can also explore the source code for the todo application at *https://github.com/book-of-kubernetes/todo*, including the *Dockerfile* that's used to build the application's container image and the GitHub Actions that automatically build it and publish it to Docker Hub whenever the code changes.

However, although our Kubernetes cluster will now do its best to keep this application running and performing well, we can do more to monitor both the todo application and the Kubernetes cluster.

Application and Cluster Monitoring

Proper application and cluster monitoring is essential for applications, for multiple reasons. First, our Kubernetes cluster will try to keep the applications running, but any hardware or cluster failures could leave an application in a non-working or degraded state. Without monitoring, we would be dependent on our users to tell us when the application is down or behaving badly, which is poor user experience. Second, if we do see failures or performance issues with our application, we're going to need data to diagnose them or to try to identify a pattern in order to find a root cause. It's a lot easier to build in monitoring ahead of time than to try to apply it after we're already seeing problems. Finally, we may have problems with our cluster or application that occurs below the level at which users notice, but that indicates potential performance or stability issues. Integrating proper monitoring allows us to detect those kinds of issues before they become a bigger headache. It also allows us to measure an application over time to make sure that added features aren't degrading its performance.

Fortunately, although we do need to think about monitoring at the level of each of our application components, we don't need to build a monitoring framework ourselves. Many mature monitoring tools are already designed to work in a Kubernetes cluster, so we can get up and running quickly. In this chapter, we'll look at kube-prometheus, a complete stack of tools that we can deploy to our cluster and use to monitor both the cluster and the todo application.

Prometheus Monitoring

The core component of kube-prometheus is, as the name implies, the open source Prometheus monitoring software. Prometheus deploys as a server that periodically queries various metrics sources and accumulates the data it receives. It supports a query language that is optimized for "time series" data, which makes it easy to collect individual data points showing a system's performance at a moment in time. It then aggregates those data points to get a picture of the system's load, resource utilization, and responsiveness.

For each component that exposes metrics, Prometheus expects to reach out to a URL and receive data in return in a standard format. It's common to use the path */metrics* to expose metrics to Prometheus. Following this convention, the Kubernetes control plane components already expose metrics in the format that Prometheus is expecting.

To illustrate, we can use curl to visit the */metrics* path on the API server to see the metrics that it provides. To do this, we'll need to authenticate to the API server, so let's use a script that collects a client certificate for authentication:

api-metrics.sh
```
#!/bin/bash
conf=/etc/kubernetes/admin.conf
...
curl --cacert $ca --cert $cert --key $key https://192.168.61.10:6443/metrics
...
```

Running this script returns a wealth of API server metrics:

```
root@host01:~# /opt/api-server-metrics.sh
...
# TYPE rest_client_requests_total counter
rest_client_requests_total{code="200",host="[::1]:6443",method="GET"} 9051
rest_client_requests_total{code="200",host="[::1]:6443",method="PATCH"} 25
rest_client_requests_total{code="200",host="[::1]:6443",method="PUT"} 21
rest_client_requests_total{code="201",host="[::1]:6443",method="POST"} 179
rest_client_requests_total{code="404",host="[::1]:6443",method="GET"} 155
rest_client_requests_total{code="404",host="[::1]:6443",method="PUT"} 1
rest_client_requests_total{code="409",host="[::1]:6443",method="POST"} 5
rest_client_requests_total{code="409",host="[::1]:6443",method="PUT"} 62
rest_client_requests_total{code="500",host="[::1]:6443",method="GET"} 18
rest_client_requests_total{code="500",host="[::1]:6443",method="PUT"} 1
...
```

This example illustrates only a few of the hundreds of metrics that are collected and exposed. Each line of this response provides one data point to Prometheus. We can include additional parameters for the metric in curly braces, allowing for more complex queries. For example, the API server data in the preceding example can be used to determine not only the total number of client requests served by the API server but also the raw number and percentage of requests that resulted in an error. Most systems are resilient to a few HTTP error responses, but a sudden increase in error responses is often a good indication of a more serious issue, so this is valuable in configuring a reporting threshold.

In addition to all of the data that the Kubernetes cluster is already providing to Prometheus, we can also configure our application to expose metrics. Our application is based on Node.js, so we do this using the prom-client library. As demonstrated in Listing 20-2, our todo application is exposing metrics at */metrics*, like the API server.

```
root@host01:~# curl http://host01:5000/metrics/
# HELP api_success Successful responses
# TYPE api_success counter
api_success{app="todo"} 0

# HELP api_failure Failed responses
# TYPE api_failure counter
api_failure{app="todo"} 0
...
# HELP process_cpu_seconds_total Total user and system CPU time ...
# TYPE process_cpu_seconds_total counter
process_cpu_seconds_total{app="todo"} 0.106392
...
```

Listing 20-2: Todo metrics

The response includes some default metrics that are relevant to all applications. It also includes some counters that are specific to the todo application and track API usage and responses over time.

Deploying kube-prometheus

At this point, our Kubernetes cluster and our application are ready to provide these metrics on demand, but we don't yet have a Prometheus server running in the cluster to collect them. To fix this, we'll deploy the complete kube-prometheus stack. This includes not only a Prometheus Operator that makes it easy to deploy and configure Prometheus but also other useful tools, such as Alertmanager, which can trigger notifications in response to cluster and application alerts, and Grafana, a dashboard tool that we'll use to see the metrics we're collecting.

To deploy kube-prometheus, we'll use a script that's been installed in */opt*. This script downloads a current kube-prometheus release from GitHub and applies the manifests.

Run the script as follows:

```
root@host01:~# /opt/install-kube-prometheus.sh
...
```

These manifests also include a Prometheus Adapter. The Prometheus Adapter implements the same Kubernetes metrics API as the `metrics-server` we deployed to the clusters throughout Part II, so it exposes CPU and memory data obtained from `kubelet`, enabling our HorizontalPodAutoscaler to track CPU utilization of our `todo` application. However, it also exposes that utilization data to Prometheus so that we can observe it in Grafana dashboards. For this reason, we use the Prometheus Adapter in this chapter in place of the regular `metrics-server`.

We can see the Prometheus Adapter and the other components by listing Pods in the `monitoring` Namespace:

```
root@host01:~# kubectl -n monitoring get pods
NAME                                     READY   STATUS    RESTARTS   AGE
alertmanager-main-0                      2/2     Running   0          14m
alertmanager-main-1                      2/2     Running   0          14m
alertmanager-main-2                      2/2     Running   0          14m
blackbox-exporter-6b79c4588b-pgp5r       3/3     Running   0          15m
grafana-7fd69887fb-swjpl                 1/1     Running   0          15m
kube-state-metrics-55f67795cd-mkxqv      3/3     Running   0          15m
node-exporter-4bhhp                      2/2     Running   0          15m
node-exporter-8mc5l                      2/2     Running   0          15m
node-exporter-ncfd2                      2/2     Running   0          15m
node-exporter-qp7mg                      2/2     Running   0          15m
node-exporter-rtn2t                      2/2     Running   0          15m
node-exporter-tpg97                      2/2     Running   0          15m
prometheus-adapter-85664b6b74-mglp4      1/1     Running   0          15m
prometheus-adapter-85664b6b74-nj7hp      1/1     Running   0          15m
prometheus-k8s-0                         2/2     Running   0          14m
prometheus-k8s-1                         2/2     Running   0          14m
prometheus-operator-6dc9f66cb7-jtrqd     2/2     Running   0          15m
```

In addition to the Prometheus Adapter, we see Pods for Alertmanager, Grafana, and various exporter Pods, which collect metrics from the cluster infrastructure and expose it to Prometheus. We also see Pods for Prometheus itself and for the Prometheus Operator. The Prometheus Operator automatically updates Prometheus whenever we change the custom resources that the Prometheus Operator is monitoring. The most important of those custom resources is the Prometheus resource shown in Listing 20-3.

```
root@host01:~# kubectl -n monitoring describe prometheus
Name:         k8s
Namespace:    monitoring
...
API Version:  monitoring.coreos.com/v1
```

```
Kind:       Prometheus
...
Spec:
...
  Image:   quay.io/prometheus/prometheus:v2.32.1
...
  Service Account Name:  prometheus-k8s
  Service Monitor Namespace Selector:
  Service Monitor Selector:
...
```

Listing 20-3: Prometheus configuration

The Prometheus custom resource allows us to configure which Namespaces will be watched for Services to monitor. The default configuration presented in Listing 20-3 does not specify a value for the Service Monitor Namespace Selector or the Service Monitor Selector. For this reason, by default the Prometheus Operator will be looking for monitoring configuration in all Namespaces, with any metadata label.

To identify specific Services to monitor, the Prometheus Operator keeps an eye out for another custom resource, *ServiceMonitor*, as demonstrated in Listing 20-4.

```
root@host01:~# kubectl -n monitoring get servicemonitor
NAME                        AGE
alertmanager-main           20m
blackbox-exporter           20m
coredns                     20m
grafana                     20m
kube-apiserver              20m
kube-controller-manager     20m
kube-scheduler              20m
kube-state-metrics          20m
kubelet                     20m
node-exporter               20m
prometheus-adapter          20m
prometheus-k8s              20m
prometheus-operator         20m
```

Listing 20-4: Default ServiceMonitors

When we installed kube-prometheus, it configured multiple ServiceMonitor resources. As a result, our Prometheus instance is already watching the Kubernetes control plane components and the kubelet services running on our cluster nodes. Let's see the targets from which Prometheus is scraping metrics and see how those metrics are used to populate dashboards in Grafana.

Cluster Metrics

The installation script patched the Grafana and Prometheus Services in the `monitoring` Namespace to expose them as `NodePort` Services. The automation scripts print the URL you can use to access Prometheus. The initial page looks like Figure 20-1.

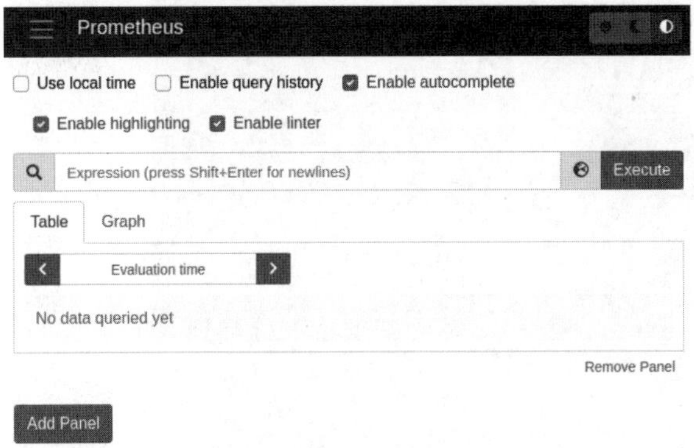

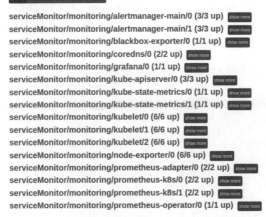

Figure 20-1: Prometheus initial page

Click the **Targets** item underneath the **Status** menu on the top menu bar to see which components in the cluster Prometheus is currently scraping. Click **Collapse All** to get a consolidated list, as shown in Figure 20-2.

Targets

All   Unhealthy   Expand All

serviceMonitor/monitoring/alertmanager-main/0 (3/3 up) show more
serviceMonitor/monitoring/alertmanager-main/1 (3/3 up) show more
serviceMonitor/monitoring/blackbox-exporter/0 (1/1 up) show more
serviceMonitor/monitoring/coredns/0 (2/2 up) show more
serviceMonitor/monitoring/grafana/0 (1/1 up) show more
serviceMonitor/monitoring/kube-apiserver/0 (3/3 up) show more
serviceMonitor/monitoring/kube-state-metrics/0 (1/1 up) show more
serviceMonitor/monitoring/kube-state-metrics/1 (1/1 up) show more
serviceMonitor/monitoring/kubelet/0 (6/6 up) show more
serviceMonitor/monitoring/kubelet/1 (6/6 up) show more
serviceMonitor/monitoring/kubelet/2 (6/6 up) show more
serviceMonitor/monitoring/node-exporter/0 (6/6 up) show more
serviceMonitor/monitoring/prometheus-adapter/0 (2/2 up) show more
serviceMonitor/monitoring/prometheus-k8s/0 (2/2 up) show more
serviceMonitor/monitoring/prometheus-k8s/1 (2/2 up) show more
serviceMonitor/monitoring/prometheus-operator/0 (1/1 up) show more

Figure 20-2: Prometheus targets

This list matches the list of ServiceMonitors we saw in Listing 20-4, showing us that Prometheus is scraping Services as configured by the Prometheus Operator.

We can use the Prometheus web interface to query data directly, but Grafana has already been configured with some useful dashboards, so we can more easily see the data there. The automation scripts print the URL you can use to access Grafana. Log in using the default admin as the username and admin as the password. You will be prompted to change the password; you can just click *Skip*. At this point you should see the Grafana initial page, as shown in Figure 20-3.

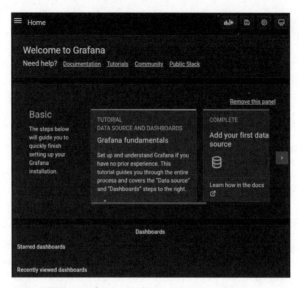

Figure 20-3: Grafana initial page

From this page, choose the **Browse** item under **Dashboards** in the menu. There are many dashboards in the *Default* folder. For example, by selecting **Default** and then selecting **Kubernetes ▶ Compute Resources ▶ Pod**, you can see a dashboard, depicted in Figure 20-4, that shows CPU and memory usage over time for any Pod in the cluster.

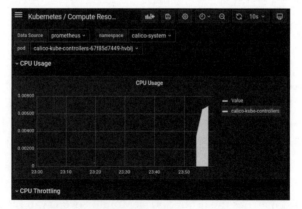

Figure 20-4: Pod compute resources

All of the todo database and application Pods are selectable in this dashboard by first selecting the todo Namespace, so we can already get valuable information about our application by using nothing more than the default monitoring configuration. This is possible because the Prometheus Adapter is pulling data from the `kubelet` services, which includes resource utilization for each of the running Pods. The Prometheus Adapter is then exposing a */metrics* endpoint for Prometheus to scrape and store, and Grafana is querying Prometheus to build the chart showing usage over time.

There are numerous other Grafana dashboards to explore in the default installation of `kube-prometheus`. Choose the *Browse* menu item again to select other dashboards and see what data is available.

Adding Monitoring for Services

Although we are already getting useful metrics for our `todo` application, Prometheus is not yet scraping our application Pods to pull in the Node.js metrics we saw in Listing 20-2. To configure Prometheus to scrape our `todo` metrics, we'll need to provide a new ServiceMonitor resource to the Prometheus Operator, informing it about our `todo` Service.

In a production cluster, the team deploying an application like our `todo` application wouldn't have the permissions to create or update resources in the `monitoring` Namespace. However, the Prometheus Operator looks for ServiceMonitor resources in all Namespaces by default, so we can create a ServiceMonitor in the `todo` Namespace instead.

First, though, we need to give Prometheus permission to see the Pods and Services we've created in the `todo` Namespace. As this access control configuration needs to apply only in a single Namespace, we'll do this by creating a Role and a RoleBinding. Here's the Role configuration we'll use:

rbac.yaml
```
---
apiVersion: rbac.authorization.k8s.io/v1
kind: Role
metadata:
...
  name: prometheus-k8s
rules:
  - apiGroups:
    - ""
    resources:
    - services
    - endpoints
    - pods
    verbs:
    - get
    - list
    - watch
...
```

We need to make sure we allow access to Services, Pods, and Endpoints, so we confirm that these are listed in the resources field. The Endpoint resource records the current Pods that are receiving traffic for a Service, which will be critical for Prometheus to identify all of the Pods it scrapes. Because Prometheus needs only read-only access, we specify only the get, list, and watch verbs.

After we have this Role, we need to bind it to the ServiceAccount that Prometheus is using. We do that with this RoleBinding:

rbac.yaml
```
---
apiVersion: rbac.authorization.k8s.io/v1
kind: RoleBinding
metadata:
...
  name: prometheus-k8s
roleRef:
  apiGroup: rbac.authorization.k8s.io
  kind: Role
  name: prometheus-k8s
subjects:
  - kind: ServiceAccount
    name: prometheus-k8s
    namespace: monitoring
```

The roleRef matches the Role we just declared in the preceding example, whereas the subjects field lists the ServiceAccount Prometheus is using, based on the information we saw in Listing 20-3.

Both of these YAML resources are in the same file, so we can apply them both to the cluster at once. We need to make sure we apply them to the todo Namespace, as that's the Namespace where we want to enable access by Prometheus:

```
root@host01:~# kubectl -n todo apply -f /opt/rbac.yaml
role.rbac.authorization.k8s.io/prometheus-k8s created
rolebinding.rbac.authorization.k8s.io/prometheus-k8s created
```

Now that we've granted permission to Prometheus to see our Pods and Services, we can create the ServiceMonitor. Here's that definition:

svc-mon.yaml
```
---
apiVersion: monitoring.coreos.com/v1
kind: ServiceMonitor
metadata:
  name: todo
spec:
  selector:
    matchLabels:
      app: todo
  endpoints:
    - port: web
```

A ServiceMonitor uses a selector, similar to a Service or a Deployment. We previously applied the app: todo label to the Service, so the matchLabels field will cause Prometheus to pick up the Service. The endpoints field matches the name of the port we declared in the Service in Listing 20-1. Prometheus requires us to name the port in order to match it.

Let's apply this ServiceMonitor to the cluster:

```
root@host01:~# kubectl -n todo apply -f /opt/svc-mon.yaml
servicemonitor.monitoring.coreos.com/todo created
```

As before, we need to make sure we deploy this to the todo Namespace because Prometheus will be configured to look for Services with the appropriate label in the same Namespace as the ServiceMonitor.

Because the Prometheus Operator is watching for new ServiceMonitor resources, using the API we saw in Chapter 17, it picks up this new resource and immediately reconfigures Prometheus to start scraping the Service. Prometheus then takes a few minutes to register the new targets and start scraping them. If we go back to the Prometheus Targets page after this is complete, the new Service shows up, as illustrated in Figure 20-5.

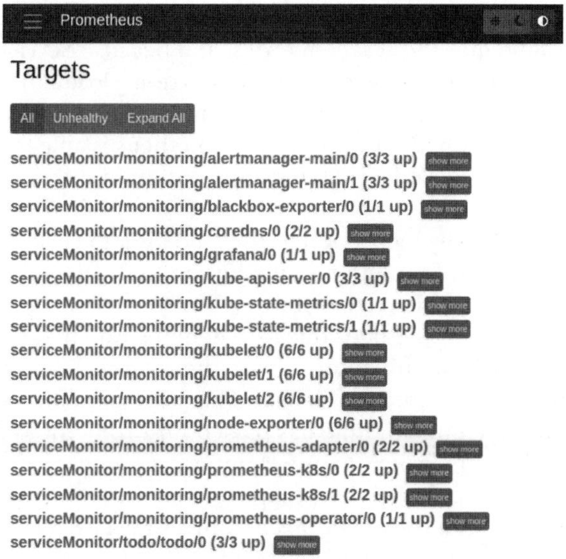

Figure 20-5: Prometheus monitoring todo

If we click the **show more** button next to the todo Service, we see its three Endpoints, shown in Figure 20-6.

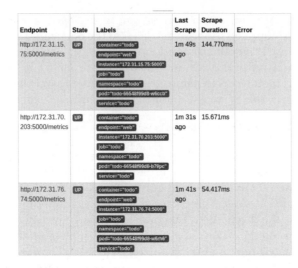

Endpoint	State	Labels	Last Scrape	Scrape Duration	Error
http://172.31.15. 75:5000/metrics	UP	container="todo" endpoint="web" instance="172.31.15.75:5000" job="todo" namespace="todo" pod="todo-66548f99d8-w6ccb" service="todo"	1m 49s ago	144.770ms	
http://172.31.70. 203:5000/metrics	UP	container="todo" endpoint="web" instance="172.31.70.203:5000" job="todo" namespace="todo" pod="todo-66548f99d8-b79pc" service="todo"	1m 31s ago	15.671ms	
http://172.31.76. 74:5000/metrics	UP	container="todo" endpoint="web" instance="172.31.76.74:5000" job="todo" namespace="todo" pod="todo-66548f99d8-w6rh6" service="todo"	1m 41s ago	54.417ms	

Figure 20-6: Todo Endpoints

It may be surprising that we created a ServiceMonitor, specifying the todo Service as the target, and yet Prometheus is scraping Pods. However, it's essential that Prometheus works this way. Because Prometheus is using a regular HTTP request to scrape metrics, and because Service traffic routing chooses a random Pod for every new connection, Prometheus would get metrics from a random Pod each time it did scraping. By reaching behind the Service to identify the Endpoints, Prometheus is able to scrape metrics from all the Service's Pods, enabling aggregation of metrics for the entire application.

We've successfully incorporated the Node.js and custom metrics for the todo application into Prometheus, in addition to the default resource utilization metrics already collected. Before we finish our look at application monitoring, let's run a Prometheus query to demonstrate that the data is being pulled in. First, you should interact with the todo application using the URL printed out by the automation scripts. This will ensure that there are metrics to display and that enough time has passed for Prometheus to scrape that data. Next, open the Prometheus web interface again, or click **Prometheus** at the top of any Prometheus web page to go back to the main page. Then, type **api_success** into the query box and press ENTER. Custom todo metrics should appear, as illustrated in Figure 20-7.

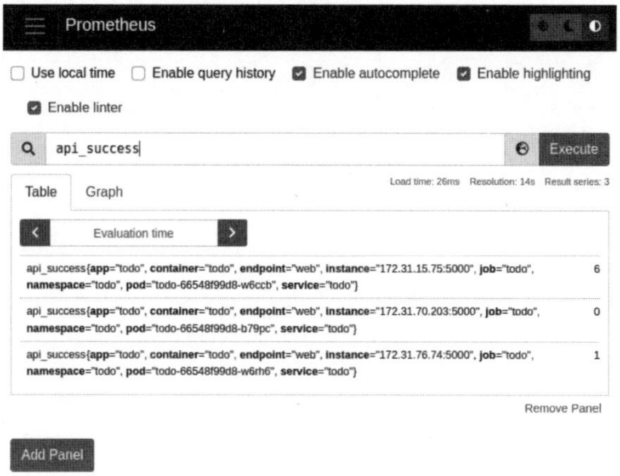

Figure 20-7: Todo metric query

We're now able to monitor both the Kubernetes cluster and the todo application.

Final Thoughts

In this chapter, we've explored how the various features of containers and Kubernetes come together to enable us to deploy a scalable, resilient application. We've used everything we learned about containers—Deployments, Services, networking, persistent storage, Kubernetes Operators, and role-based access control—to not only deploy the todo application but also configure Prometheus monitoring of our cluster and our application.

Kubernetes is a complex platform with many different capabilities, and new capabilities are being added all the time. The purpose of this book is not only to show you the most important features you need to run an application on Kubernetes, but also to give you the tools to explore a Kubernetes cluster for troubleshooting and performance monitoring. As a result, you should be equipped to explore new features as they are added to Kubernetes and to conquer the challenges of deploying complex applications and getting them to perform well.

INDEX

configuration (*continued*)
files, 272, 273, 278, 281
repository, 274–276
containerd, 23, 25–27, 29, 32, 91, 107,
206, 208
container engine, 23, 83, 203
container image, 8, 9, 13, 23, 24, 35,
52, 69–72, 74, 75, 77, 81–83,
98, 101, 112–114, 116, 155,
173, 180, 181, 185, 208, 260,
272, 278, 285, 328
Container Network Interface, 28, 100,
129, 130, 145, 147, 148, 239
container orchestration, 3, 9, 14, 17,
37, 51, 84, 87, 88, 188, 323
container platform, 9, 23
container runtime, 9, 19, 23, 24, 27,
30, 32, 173, 174, 176, 178, 205,
206, 208, 212, 213, 218, 233,
235, 237, 238, 248, 265, 270,
278, 323
Container Runtime Interface, 27, 113,
208
containers, 3, 7, 8, 12, 17, 22, 32, 107,
108, 111, 128, 167, 219, 233,
249, 279, 292, 310, 323, 343
environment variables, 12, 70, 74,
82, 178, 179, 183, 253,
264–266, 268, 269, 272, 273,
278, 328, 329
exit code, 122, 178, 181, 221
filesystems, 11, 21, 22, 32, 53, 67,
70–72, 74, 78, 80, 81, 83, 84,
112, 323
image building, 75, 180
image layers, 73–78, 81
limits, 33, 49, 122, 170, 214,
232–235, 238, 244–246, 248,
310–317, 319, 329
logs, 179, 182
networking, 11, 13, 22, 26, 28, 32,
49, 51, 67, 112, 128, 129, 131,
134, 138, 160, 343
non-root user, xxi
overhead, 8, 14, 46, 67, 77, 78, 84,
209
packaging, 8, 17, 23, 69, 84
port forwarding, 13, 76, 103, 131,
134, 183, 184

private image, 174, 175
registry, 70, 76, 77, 174, 175
storage, 67, 72, 81
versioning, 8, 10, 72, 74–76
volume mount, 12, 26, 30, 112, 125,
251–253, 260, 272–274, 303
Container Storage Interface, 102, 108,
250, 251, 258
Control groups. *See* Linux: cgroups
copy on write, 78
CoreDNS, 156
coupling, 4, 296, 306
CPU instruction sets, 168
CRD. *See* CustomResourceDefinition
CRI (Container Runtime Interface),
27, 113, 208
crictl, 27, 28, 35, 36, 41, 45, 52, 55, 56,
91, 105, 107, 113, 114, 126,
132, 208, 217, 237, 251, 252
CRI-O, 26–29, 32, 36, 39, 41, 43, 45,
52, 55, 57, 58, 60, 62, 63, 65,
66, 206, 208
cron, 124
CronJob, 122–124, 243, 264
cross-cutting concerns, 87–89, 106
CSI. *See* Container Storage Interface
curl, 76, 93, 101, 103, 109, 154, 165,
189, 190, 199, 221–223, 231,
232, 260, 261, 284, 303, 304,
333
customization, 89, 279, 280, 285, 288,
292
CustomResourceDefinition, 145,
280–284, 286, 288, 289, 291,
292, 324
Postgresql, 288–290
Sample, 282, 283, 286–288

D

DaemonSet, 101, 108, 122, 127, 128,
131, 145, 146, 158, 211, 213,
250, 298
data centers, 297
dd, 72
Debian, 70, 71
declarative configuration, 14, 89, 90,
111, 119, 280
denial-of-service, 234

limits (*continued*)

    CPU, 34, 38–45, 47, 173, 235, 237, 314, 329

    memory, 43–45, 47, 235–239, 314

    network, 47, 48, 131, 234, 238, 240–243

Linux, 180

    cgroups, 37–41, 43, 44, 46, 47, 49, 236–238, 310–312, 314, 315

    chroot, 22

    Completely Fair Scheduler, 34

    distribution, 10, 74

    kernel, 10–12, 22, 27, 31, 32, 34, 78, 91, 92, 248

    namespaces, 19, 25, 29–32, 49, 51, 55–65, 76, 129–134, 137, 171, 208

    OOM killer, 46

    permissions, 21, 22, 32

    PID, 25, 30, 31, 36, 39, 56, 112

    scheduler, 34

    signal, 31, 32, 46

    swap, 43

    traffic control, 47–49, 239, 240, 242, 243

    users, xxi, 21, 44

load balancing, 7, 9, 14, 17, 67, 88, 96, 109, 149, 151–154, 159, 160, 164, 165, 192, 228, 232, 254, 267, 309, 314, 317, 321, 330

Longhorn, 102, 103, 106, 108, 194, 211, 213, 250–252, 255, 257, 258, 280, 326

long polling, 284

lsns, 25, 30, 31, 55

M

macvlan, 149

masquerade. *See* Network Address Translation

memory access error, 179

message-driven architecture, 153

metrics server, 104, 105, 121, 157, 158, 194, 207, 236

microservice, 5–7, 17, 51, 87, 89, 109, 228

Microsoft Azure, 96, 250

modularity, 4

monitoring, 8, 9, 14, 16, 17, 116, 119–121, 187, 188, 205, 218, 321, 324, 330–333, 336, 339, 342, 343

mount, 79, 80, 209, 210

multitasking, 20

multitenancy, 37, 38, 88, 106, 233, 268

Multus, 144–147

Mythical Man-Month, The, 5

N

Namespace, 102, 104, 106–108, 114, 127, 156–158, 194–198, 200–202, 243–245, 247, 248, 268, 269, 282, 288, 312, 321, 324, 327, 336, 339–341

    calico-system, 102, 107, 127

    default, 107, 108, 113–115, 156, 158, 165, 197, 199, 202, 287

    kube-system, 107, 156–158, 193, 197, 200, 202

    longhorn-system, 108

    monitoring, 335, 337, 339

    sample, 194, 195, 197, 199, 200, 202, 244, 245

    todo, 324, 328, 330, 338–341

namespaces, Linux. *See* Linux: namespaces

Nano, 182

NAT. *See* Network Address Translation

ndots, 157

network

    bandwidth, 6, 296, 300, 302

    bridge, 25, 51, 60–64, 92, 133

    burst, 243

    egress, 47, 48, 242

    firewall, 26, 61, 91, 92, 133, 135, 139, 158–160, 216

    fragmentation, 143

    ingress, 242

    jumbo frames, 144

    latency, 296

    MAC, 60, 137, 138, 140–143

    maximum transmission unit, 143

    MTU, 143

    namespaces. *See* Linux: namespaces

X

xxd, 277

Y

YAML multiline string, 273
yum, 11

The fonts used in *The Book of Kubernetes* are New Baskerville, Futura, The Sans Mono Condensed, and Dogma. The book was typeset with LaTeX 2_ε package nostarch by Boris Veytsman *(2008/06/06 v1.3 Typesetting books for No Starch Press)*.

More no-nonsense books from  **NO STARCH PRESS**

Never before has the world relied so heavily on the Internet to stay connected and informed. That makes the Electronic Frontier Foundation's mission—to ensure that technology supports freedom, justice, and innovation for all people— more urgent than ever.

For over 30 years, EFF has fought for tech users through activism, in the courts, and by developing software to overcome obstacles to your privacy, security, and free expression. This dedication empowers all of us through darkness. With your help we can navigate toward a brighter digital future.